Preface

Electronic Commerce: A Manager's Guide is a companion to our earlier tome: *Frontiers of Electronic Commerce*. The widespread success of the first book bears witness to the need for more easily understood, independent information about what is happening in the fast-changing world of electronic commerce.

Why Is Electronic Commerce Important?

As we approach the year 2000, we can no longer look to the past as a guide to the future. In the face of strong market forces created by electronic commerce and mounting competition, corporations can no longer plod along historical tracks or seek the preservation of the status quo. Companies are discovering that old solutions do not work with new problems. The business parameters have changed, and so have the risks and payoffs.

However, in order to figure out the answers, we need to understand why, where, and when electronic commerce is important. Electronic commerce is becoming critical in three interrelated dimensions: customer-to-business interactions, intra-business interactions, and business-to-business interactions.

In the customer-to-business dimension, electronic commerce is enabling the customer to have an increasing say in what products are made, how products are made (movement from make-to-stock to a build-to-order model) and how services are delivered (movement from a slow order fulfillment process with little understanding of what is taking place inside the firm, to a faster and more open process with customers having greater control).

Electronic commerce is also a catalyst for dramatic changes in internal organizational functioning, as evidenced by the rapid proliferation of Intranets. It is facilitating an organizational model that is fundamentally different from the past, one that is characterized by the shift from a hierarchical command-and-control organization to the information-based organi-

iii

zation. The emerging forms of techno-organizational structure involve changes in managerial responsibilities, communication and information flows, and work-group structures.

Electronic commerce is also impacting business-to-business interactions. Electronic commerce facilitates the network form of organization where small flexible firms rely on other "partner" companies for component supplies and product distribution to meet changing customer demand more effectively. Hence, an end-to-end relationship management solution (often called *integrated* or *extended supply-chain management*) is a desirable goal that is needed to manage the chain of networks linking customers, workers, suppliers, distributors, and even competitors. The management of "online transactions" in the supply chain assumes a central role.

In the face of market changes, corporations can no longer be insular in nature. In order to be successful, management has to come to grips with the changes taking place in the various market spaces. In the same vein, managers cannot operate effectively without some major regauging of mindset, attitudes, skills, and knowledge.

What Makes This Book Different?

In this book readers will find a well-researched analytical evaluation of the management issues and concerns affecting electronic commerce in the service provider businesses, banking, retail, electronic publishing, and Intranet applications. The analytical approach to understanding management issues presented in this book differs considerably from the anecdotes, testimonials, and case studies so commonly found in the popular press.

Instead of a dry summary of the facts, we tried to state clearly our opinions on all the major issues. We have done this because all organizations, large and small, will be (or already are) making major electronic commerce-related investment decisions to stay in business and be competitive. Making investment decisions is difficult and we believe it is helpful to hear an opinion rather than just a set of dry facts.

To Whom Is This Book Addressed?

This book provides a broad audience with a quick introduction to the major issues and topics in electronic commerce. We assume that the audience has no prior exposure to electronic commerce except an appreciation that it is an important topic in shaping the future of business.

More specifically, the book is targeted at business managers and professionals involved with online applications, as well as information technology professionals and users who want to keep abreast of the latest management trends and issues. This book unravels the management implications of electronic commerce for executives of those organizations that are participating in or looking to participate in designing, building, or managing electronic commerce applications. It is equally useful for board members, investors, attorneys, accountants, consultants, and others who are intimately involved in managing new online ventures.

In a nutshell, this book bridges a knowledge gap that currently exists between the technical experts who are implementing electronic commerce applications and management who have to make operational and strategic decisions about electronic commerce technology and its business applications.

How Is This Book Organized?

Chapter 1 defines electronic commerce, explains the industry framework, and outlines some broad management issues that are of concern. Chapter 2 examines the Internet and the Internet Access Provider industry.

Chapters 3 and 4 introduce the World Wide Web, and discuss the various business applications that are suitable for it, as well as the technology behind it. Chapter 3 offers an explanation of how the Web is being used to develop public Internet and private Intranet applications. Chapter 4 explains the technology behind the Web and the new directions of Web technology.

Chapter 5 discusses the important topic of security by elaborating on firewalls and transaction and data security methods used on the Web. Chapter 6 looks at the emerging electronic payment systems—electronic cash, electronic checks, encrypted credit cards, and smart cards—which enable buying and selling on the Internet. Since many of the new electronic payment mechanisms are based on fool-proof transaction security, readers are urged to read Chapter 5 before reading Chapter 6.

Chapters 7 (online banking), 8 (online retailing), and 9 (online publishing) explain how key industries—banking, retailing, and publishing—are being reshaped by electronic commerce and discuss the crucial management issues in these industries.

Chapters 10 (Intranets and supply-chain management), 11 (Intranets and Customer Asset Management), 12 (Intranets and manufacturing), and 13 (Intranets and corporate finance) focus on applications of electronic commerce that are suitable for implementation on the Intranets.

The epilogue summarizes the main points of the book.

Acknowledgments

There are many people who deserve our thanks for helping with this book. We thank our unknown reviewers and others who helped immensely during the arduous process, in particular: Joseph Bailey, Julie Crawford, Lucien N. Dancanet, David Klur, Edward J. Krall, Susan Kutor, Steve Matthesen, and Marcia Robinson, and of course our editors, Tom Stone and Debbie Lafferty, whose names almost, but not quite, fit into our ordering. Acting on all of the comments we received was painful, but has made this a better book. Of course, we bear the blame for any errors, not these intrepid folks.

Dr. Ravi Kalakota
kalakota@uhura.cc.rochester.edu

Dr. Andrew Whinston
abw@uts.cc.utexas.edu

Contents

Chapter 1

Introduction to Electronic Commerce

Chapter Outline

Wherever they turn, corporate executives and consumers are besieged by futuristic scenarios of business facilitated by electronic commerce. A once obscure concept found only in science fiction, "cyberspace" has become one of the most exciting trends in business. Even television advertisements have begun to guide consumers to company Web sites for additional product/service information. Regular coverage in the media, Wall Street's growing interest in the technology sector, and a steady stream of product announcements have helped to foster public interest in the online phenomenon.

Such hype about the future of online commerce is often reinforced by the media attention that is focused on blockbuster mergers such as Time Warner/Turner Broadcasting, NYNEX/Bell Atlantic, Chase/Chemical Bank, CBS/Westinghouse, and ABC Cap Cities/Disney. These companies are positioning themselves to be competitive in the next decade, and information technology of all types is the force behind corporate reorganization.

However, few managers (and consumers) understand the underlying economic and technological reasons why companies in the banking, entertainment, telecommunications, and manufacturing industries are being forced to reorganize. Most managers, however, perceive a radical paradigm

1

shift in the way technology is viewed in the business world. The traditional view of information technology was of a support or operational tool that was not worthy of management's time. That viewpoint has changed dramatically in the last five years. Today, technology is seen as a major driver of corporate strategy and business re-engineering.

Two turning points in the past decade of business computing help explain the recent impact of electronic commerce: personal computers, circa 1983, and local area networks and client/server computing, circa 1989. In 1983, few individuals and organizations understood the impact that affordable desktop computers would have on corporate and home computing. Likewise, in 1989, few companies foresaw the enormous role that client/server computing would play in corporate downsizing. In 1996, we are going through a similar phase with electronic commerce. Managers are only beginning to comprehend the electronic commerce landscape.

Part of the difficulty in understanding electronic commerce lies in the fact that the growth of electronic commerce is happening so quickly and in so many different directions that even experts are at a loss to find any established business models for comparison. People have compared the rise of electronic commerce to the radio industry in the 1920s, television in the 1950s, video players in the 1970s, and personal computers in the 1980s. While these technologies had a significant impact, they pale in comparison to the impact that electronic commerce may have on business.

Many wonder whether electronic commerce is simply a fad. While the answer is a resounding no, it is necessary to point out that like every new technology and management technique, electronic commerce has been overhyped and oversold in terms of its short-term potential. However, the long-term importance of electronic commerce cannot be underestimated and requires prudent contemplation and planning on the part of investors, strategists, and management. In the short run, electronic commerce will not solve all of the difficulties in the exchange of funds and information, but in the long run it is likely to alter, even replace, nonelectronic business models of customer interaction and service delivery.

In the marketplace the electronic commerce focus is shifting from an emphasis on pure technology to a more technology-supported strategic action. This means that to realize the full potential of electronic commerce, organizations must be willing to change the way they do business. History has shown that large gains in productivity and market share take place when technological change is combined with organizational restructuring. Not only is business conducted more efficiently, but also new business opportunities are often created.

Clearly, management needs to play a larger role in the formulation and implementation of electronic commerce strategies. Developing electronic commerce applications and services raises so many business issues that developing a business strategy should not be left solely to the Information Systems department. "Doing business online" sounds technical, and organizations often delegate the task to the technical departments. A better approach is to develop a cross-functional team composed of technical staff as well as marketing and finance personnel. The team should be seasoned with "techno-illiterates" who may not be able to operate the PC but who understand the core business.

This chapter answers some of the most frequently asked questions about electronic commerce. It defines electronic commerce, and explains both the industry framework and supporting software infrastructure. The chapter also shows how electronic commerce fits with other management ideologies, and it examines some of the managerial issues companies face as electronic commerce becomes a locus of economic activity at the product, process, system, and market levels.

1.1 Defining Electronic Commerce

Depending on whom you ask, electronic commerce has different definitions.

From a *communications* perspective, electronic commerce is the delivery of information, products/services, or payments via telephone lines, computer networks, or any other means.

From a *business process* perspective, electronic commerce is the application of technology toward the automation of business transactions and workflows.

From a *service* perspective, electronic commerce is a tool that addresses the desire of firms, consumers, and management to cut service costs while improving the quality of goods and increasing the speed of service delivery.

From an *online* perspective, electronic commerce provides the capability of buying and selling products and information on the Internet and other online services.

All of the above definitions are valid. It is just a matter of which lens is used to view the electronic commerce landscape. Broadly speaking, electronic commerce emphasizes the generation and exploitation of new business opportunities and, to use popular phrases: "generate business value" or "do more with less."

Electronic commerce endeavors to improve the execution of business transactions over various networks. These improvements may result in more effective performance (better quality, greater customer satisfaction, and better corporate decision making), greater economic efficiency (lower costs), and more rapid exchange (high speed, accelerated, or real-time interaction). More specifically, electronic commerce enables the execution of information-laden transactions between two or more parties using interconnected networks. These networks can be a combination of POTS (plain old telephone system), cable TV, leased lines, and wireless. Information-based transactions are creating new ways of doing business and even new types of business.

What exactly is a transaction? Transactions are exchanges that occur when one economic entity sells a product or service to another entity. A transaction takes place when a product or service is transferred across a technologically separable interface that links a consumer (client) with a producer (server). When buyer/seller transactions occur in the electronic marketplace, information is accessed, absorbed, arranged, and sold in different ways (see Fig. 1.1). To manage these transactions, electronic commerce also incorporates transaction management, which organizes, routes, processes, and tracks transactions. Electronic commerce also includes consumers making electronic payments and funds transfers.

Another way of looking at electronic commerce is to view it as a production process that converts digital inputs into value-added outputs through a set of intermediaries (see Fig. 1.2). For example, in the case of online trading, production processes can add value by including more value-added processing (such as trend analysis) on the raw information (stock quotes) supplied to customers. Other value-added processing might include the charting of thirty-day moving averages, industry sector performance analysis, and other processing that results in more refined information leading to better decision making.

The business rationale for the use of electronic commerce can be explained by the simple equation: Profit = Revenue – Costs. Firms use technology to either lower operating costs or increase revenue. Depending on

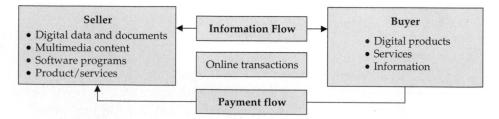

Figure 1.1   Buyer/Seller Transactions

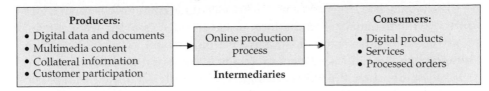

Figure 1.2   Production Type Transactions

how it is applied, electronic commerce has the potential to increase revenue by creating new markets for old products, creating new information-based products, and establishing new service delivery channels to better serve and interact with customers. The transaction management aspect of electronic commerce can also enable firms to reduce operating costs by enabling better coordination in the sales, production, and distribution processes (or better supply-chain management), and to consolidate operations and reduce overhead.

Currently, the goal of most electronic commerce research and its associated implementations is to reduce the "friction" in online transactions. Friction is often described in economics as transaction cost. Friction can arise from inefficient market structures linking buyers, sellers, and intermediaries; inefficient organizational structures (operating units, business processes, and workflows); and inefficient combinations of the technological activities required to make a transaction. Ultimately, the reduction of friction in online commerce will enable smoother transactions between buyers, intermediaries, and sellers.

Brief History of Electronic Commerce

The need for electronic commerce stems from the demand within business and government to make better use of computing and to better apply computer technology to improve customer interaction, business processes, and information exchange both within an enterprise and across enterprises.

During the 1970s, the introduction of electronic funds transfer (EFT) between banks over secure private networks changed financial markets. Electronic funds transfer optimizes electronic payments with electronically provided remittance information. Today there are many EFT variants, including the debit card whose use is becoming ubiquitous at points of sales (POS) in grocery stores and retail outlets, and direct deposits to employee bank accounts. Each day, over $4 trillion change hands via EFT over the computer networks linking banks, automated clearinghouses, and companies. The U.S. Treasury Department estimates that 55 percent of all payments by the federal government in 1995 were made by EFT.

⟩ During the late 1970s and early 1980s, electronic commerce became widespread within companies in the form of electronic messaging technologies: electronic data interchange (EDI) and electronic mail. Electronic messaging technologies streamline business processes by reducing paperwork and increasing automation. Business exchanges traditionally conducted with paper, such as checks, purchase orders, and shipping documents, are conducted electronically. Electronic data interchange allows companies to send/receive business documents (such as purchase orders) in a standardized electronic form to/from their suppliers. For example, combined with just-in-time (JIT) manufacturing, EDI enables suppliers to deliver parts directly to the factory floor, resulting in savings in inventory, warehousing, and handling costs. Electronic mail does much the same for unstructured organizational communications both inside and across the organizational boundaries.

Over the years, EDI has evolved into several different technologies (see Fig. 1.3). Electronic data interchange has been particularly successful for retail category management. Category management seeks to meet customer needs by putting the right product, at the right price, in the right amount, in the right place on the store shelf. All products are divided into distinctly manageable groups, such as ready-to-eat cereal, and category managers make decisions on all similar items in a category instead of focusing on a single product. Instead of just buying the lowest priced items, buyers utilize information about buying patterns and employ EDI technology to seek the largest savings for "hot" items in a category. This technology has improved buying practices and reduced costs for both manufacturers and retailers.

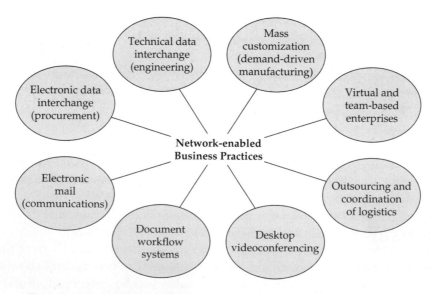

Figure 1.3   Network-enabled Business Practices

● In the late 1980s and early 1990s electronic messaging technologies became an integral part of workflow or collaborative computing systems (also called *groupware*). A prominent example of such systems is Lotus Notes. Groupware focused primarily on taking existing nonelectronic methods and grafting them onto an electronic platform for improved business process efficiency. Although hyped as the "killer app" in the early 1990s, groupware efforts resulted in small gains in productivity and efficiency.

• In the mid-1980s, a completely different type of electronic commerce technology spread among consumers in the form of online services that provided a new form of social interaction (such as chat rooms and inter-relay chat [IRC]) and knowledge sharing (such as news groups and File Transfer Programs). Social interaction created a sense of virtual community among the cyberspace inhabitants and helped give rise to the concept of a "global village." At the same time, information access and exchange have become more affordable. By using the global Internet, people can communicate with others around the world at ever-decreasing costs. Despite the presence of these networks, the one key ingredient missing until recently was utility and ease of use.

• In the 1990s, the advent of the World Wide Web on the Internet (see Chapter 3) represents a turning point in electronic commerce by providing an easy-to-use technology solution to the problem of information publishing and dissemination. The Web made electronic commerce a cheaper way of doing business (economies of scale) and enabled more diverse business activities (economies of scope). The Web also enabled small businesses to compete on a more equal technological footing with resource-rich multinational companies. For example, in Web-based electronic publishing, giant companies like Time Warner, Disney, and others are working overtime to keep up with upstarts who can enter the new marketplace of several million customers with a minimal infrastructure investment: a PC, a modem, and an Internet account. These new economies are forcing traditional companies to reconceptualize cost structures in order to remain competitive.

1.2 Forces Fueling Electronic Commerce

Interest in electronic commerce is being fueled by economic forces, customer interaction forces, and technology-driven digital convergence.

Economic Forces

Under relentless pressure to reduce costs and stay competitive, firms are attracted to the economic efficiencies offered by electronic commerce. These economic efficiencies include low-cost technological infrastructures that reduce the cost burden of technology upgrades and obsolescence, low-cost and accurate electronic transactions with suppliers, the low cost of global information sharing and advertising, and the ability for firms to provide low-cost customer service alternatives to expensive retail bank branches and telephone call centers.

The economic forces motivating the shift to electronic commerce are internal as well as external. The immediate application of electronic commerce is in the internal integration of firms' operations. External integration molds the vast network of suppliers, government agencies, large corporations, and independent contractors into a single community with the ability to communicate across any computer platform. The automobile industry, where just-in-time (JIT) manufacturing methods forced Ford and General Motors to rely on EDI to interact with their suppliers, is a classic example of external integration.

Internal integration is perhaps even more vital than linking with the outside. In an internally integrated organization, incoming orders are received electronically and the information is automatically sent not only to production, but to shipping, billing, and inventory systems as well. Internal integration also ensures that critical data is stored digitally in formats and on media that permit instantaneous retrieval and electronic transmission.

The ability to coordinate the movement of information is key to both external and internal integration, and firms need to find ways to design business processes that change the way data is created, manipulated, and distributed. While technology is important to information integration, coordination of that information is indispensable. Coordination requires that employees, customers, and suppliers work together to solve problems, improve services, and create new products.

Marketing and Customer Interaction Forces

Companies also employ electronic commerce to provide marketing channels, to target microsegments or small audiences, and to improve post-sales customer satisfaction by creating new channels of customer service and support. Companies want to supply target consumers with product and service information in greater detail than that provided in a television or full-page advertisement. As more companies flood the marketplace with new products, target marketing is becoming an increasingly important tool of differentiation. Not only are new types of products emerging, but so are new players in old product categories, new spins on traditional plans, new pricing strategies, new target markets, new market research methods, and more.

The message for marketers is clear: the purchasing climate and the products change quickly. In order to be competitive, marketing executives must employ technology to develop low-cost customer-prospecting methods, establish close relationships with customers, and develop customer loyalty. Marketers must adapt to a business world in which traditional concepts of differentiation no longer hold; in this world "quality" has a new meaning, "content" may not be equated with "product," and "distribution" may not automatically mean "physical location."

In this new environment, brand equity (or the premium attached to an established brand name) can rapidly evaporate, and marketers need to understand how customers allocate their loyalty. Given the proliferation of choices, consumers view brand names with growing indifference. For the manufacturer, establishing a new brand is a formidable task, and with increased competition it is taking longer to break through and develop the customer base. Maintaining an existing brand is not much easier. In light of this, marketers in all industries are seeking new ways of interacting with customers and delivering services.

Technology and Digital Convergence

Digital technology has made it possible to convert characters, sounds, pictures, and motion video into a bit stream that can be combined, stored, manipulated, and transmitted quickly, efficiently, and in large volumes without loss of quality. As a result, electronic commerce and the multimedia revolution are driving the previously disparate industries such as communications, entertainment, publishing, and computing worlds into ever-closer contact, forcing industries with traditionally different histories and cultures to compete and cooperate.

The relentless advance of technology, the emergence of multimedia standards, and the shift to distributed computing and internetworking are providing the raw power for the "digital convergence." Convergence has two dimensions: convergence of content, and convergence of transmission technology.

Convergence of Content   Regardless of its original form, convergence of content ensures that digitized information (expressed as computer-based ones and zeros) can be processed, searched, sorted, enhanced, converted, compressed, encrypted, replicated, and transmitted at low cost; this tool has profound implications for content-based industries like newspapers, magazines, and books.

Convergence of content enables sophisticated information publishing and browsing tools. For instance, content convergence is the fundamental idea behind the browser industry exemplified by the meteoric rise of Netscape Communications, a browser-provider which, in the space of a year, developed from nothing into a company worth approximately $6 billion.

Content convergence also enables companies to use networked databases and electronic publishing to improve corporate and individual decision making and information processing. Except for production, distribution, and delivery of physical goods, commerce consists of forms of information gathering, processing, manipulation, and distribution. Content convergence facilitates the creation of a computer and network infrastructure that enables the coordination and integration of business processes or workflows.

Convergence of Transmission   Convergence of transmission compresses and stores digitized information so that it can travel through existing phone, wireless, and cable wiring systems. Convergence of transmission is a convergence of communication equipment that provides the "pipelines" to transmit voice, data, image, and video over the same line. Transmission convergence over a single line makes it easier to connect computers, high-speed peripherals, and consumer electronic devices, and to enhance a wide range of image-intensive or multimedia applications. From a business angle, convergence of transmission results in easier access to networks and in the creation of new, low-cost delivery channels for new and old products aimed at either existing customers or new customer segments.

Until recently, the convergence of voice and data networks has been an elusive goal because of irreconcilable differences between local area network (LAN) and private branch exchange (PBX) technologies. However, the emergence of a new network technology called asynchronous transfer mode (ATM) changes this picture. Today, we can see a path that leads to total integration of voice with video and data networking, from the wide area network (WAN) all the way to the desktop. Installing a single, integrated network reduces on-site cabling requirements and eliminates redundant wiring to work groups.

Transmission convergence is also facilitated in part by the convergence of information-access devices—essentially the blurring of lines among telephones, computers, and televisions. Other technologies such as cable modems, hybrid fiber/coaxial systems, and asymmetrical digital subscriber line (ADSL), which uses traditional twisted-pair telephone wires, offer the prospect of almost unlimited bandwidth to the home. These access technologies are becoming increasingly multifaceted and have the sophistication to switch between various functions.

Implications of Various Forces

Economic and marketing forces and digital convergence have influenced how industries are repositioning themselves to take advantage of new opportunities, including the creation of entirely new service delivery channels, the development of new markets for existing products, and the development of new information-based products for the online environment. For instance, digital convergence is reshaping the competitive environment for telecommunications services around the globe. In response to the intensified competition and reduced margins on basic telephone services in telecom markets, network operators are building new computer-driven intelligent networks in order to offer a wide range of value-added services. These services foreshadow a looming battle between rival cable TV and telephone network operators over which systems will deliver video-on-demand, video games, home shopping and banking, and other interactive consumer services to the home.

But before companies can exploit the capabilities of electronic commerce and make it an industrial-strength tool for business, they need to understand the technological framework better.

1.3 Electronic Commerce Industry Framework

Electronic commerce not only affects transactions between parties, it also influences the way markets will be structured. Traditionally, market ties were created through the exchange of goods, services, and money. Electronic commerce adds a new element: information. Market ties, such as those forming around online payments, are now based on information goods, information services, and electronic money. Although banks have traditionally dominated payment processing, new organizations, such as Intuit and Microsoft, have begun to process payment transactions online. Technology has enabled the creation of new market opportunity that enables new players to step in, creating a whole new set of market dynamics.

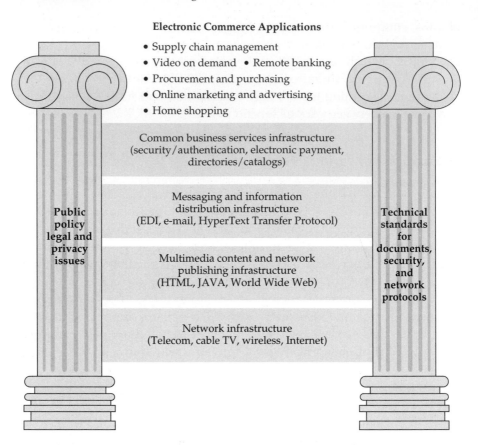

Figure 1.4   Generic Framework for Electronic Commerce

To better understand the market structure that is developing around electronic commerce, we have developed a simple framework (see Fig. 1.4) that succinctly captures the developments in this area [KALA96]. Even those aware of the importance of electronic commerce have little understanding of online jargon, or how the industry is structured. Such confusion is further entrenched by the media's use of different names to refer to the same phenomenon or its various elements: the Information Superhighway, the Internet, Cyberspace, Interactive Multimedia, and so on. It is important for businesses to understand the overall industry in order to develop business strategies that employ electronic commerce.

The next section will explain each aspect of the electronic commerce infrastructure in detail, beginning with the most broadly based term: the Information Superhighway Infrastructure.

The Information Superhighway

The Information Superhighway has many different types of transport systems and does not function as a monolithic entity; there is no single interstate highway that connects the digital equivalent of Los Angeles to Miami. Instead, the architecture is a mixture of many forms of high-speed network transport, whether it be land-based telephone, air-based wireless, modem-based PC, or satellite-based. For instance, mail sent from a portable PC in the French Riviera to a computer in Los Angeles might travel across several different types of transport networks interconnected with each other before it reaches its destination.

The players in this industry segment can be called *information transport providers*. They include: telecommunication companies that provide phone lines; cable TV systems that provide coaxial cables and direct broadcast satellite (DBS) networks; wireless companies that provide mobile radio and satellite networks; and computer networks, including private networks like CompuServe or America Online, and public data networks like the Internet.

This industry segment also includes hardware and software tools that provide an interface with the various network options, and to the customer premises equipment (CPE), or terminal equipment, which is a generic term for privately owned communications equipment that is attached to the network. This category of subscriber terminal equipment can be divided into three parts: cable TV set-top boxes, computer-based telephony, and networking hardware (hubs, wiring closets, and routers or digital switches). The terminal equipment is in fact the gateway to information services, commercial transactions, and 500 digitally compressed channels.

The biggest area of growth over the last five years has been in the router business. Routers and digital switches help to connect large networks (or internetworks). Routers are devices that can connect the local area networks (LANs) inside various organizations with the wide area networks (WANs) of various network providers. This interconnection enables easy communication between separate networks across geographical distances and provides access to distributed computing resources. The router industry is a multibillion dollar industry that is dominated by players such as Cisco, Bay Networks, and 3COM, all three of which supply equipment that links data communications networks through the Internet. In a recent valuation by *BusinessWeek*, Cisco was rated as the fortieth largest company in America, with a market value of $26 billion. Not bad for a company with an extremely specialized product.

Multimedia Content and Network Publishing

The Information Superhighway is the transportation foundation that enables the transmission of content. The electronic system through which content is transmitted is analogous to the nonelectronic world in which different types of products (content) are stored in distribution centers (network publishing servers) before they are loaded onto various vehicles for transport.

Currently, the most prevalent architecture that enables network publishing is the World Wide Web. The Web allows small businesses and individuals to develop content in the form of HyperText Markup Language (HTML) and publish it on a Web server. In short, the Web provides a means to create product information (content) and a means to publish it in a distribution center (network server).

Messaging and Information Distribution

The information content transferred over the network consists of text, numbers, pictures, audio, and video. However, the network does not differentiate among content as everything is digital, that is, combinations of ones and zeros. Once content has been created and stored on a server, vehicles, or messaging and information distribution methods, carry that content across the network. The messaging vehicle is called *middleware software* that sits between the Web servers and the end-user applications and masks the peculiarities of the environment. Messaging and information distribution also includes translators that interpret and transform data formats.

Messaging vehicles provide ways for communicating nonformatted (unstructured) as well as formatted (structured) data. Unstructured messaging vehicles are fax, electronic mail (e-mail), and form-based systems like Lotus Notes. Structured documents messaging consists of the automated interchange of standardized and approved messages between computer applications via telecommunications lines. Purchase orders, shipping notices, and invoices are examples of structured document messaging.

For the purposes of electronic commerce, existing messaging mechanisms must be extended to incorporate reliable, unalterable message delivery that is not subject to repudiation, to be able to acknowledge and give proof of delivery when required. The challenge in the development of messaging software is to make it work across a variety of communications devices (PCs, workstations, set-top boxes, and wireless communicators), interfaces (characters, graphics, and virtual reality), and networks (satellites, cable, twisted pair, fiber optics, and wireless).

Common Business Services Infrastructure

Doing business online has received attention for its potential, as well as for such shortcomings as inadequate directories, inadequate online payment instruments, and inadequate information security. The common business services infrastructure attempts to address these shortcomings.

This infrastructure includes the different methods for facilitating online buying and selling processes. In online commerce, the buyer sends an electronic payment (a form of electronic check or digital cash) as well as some remittance information to the seller. Settlement occurs when the payment and remittance information are authenticated by the seller and accepted as valid.

In order to enable online payment for information and ensure its safe delivery, the payment services infrastructure needs to develop encryption (making contents indecipherable except for the intended recipient) and authentication (making sure that customers are who they say they are) methods that ensure security of contents traveling on the network. In addition to generic payment services, electronic commerce will need to accommodate other desirable payment-related services such as currency exchange, cash management, escrow, investment and brokerage, financial information and reporting, and billing and payment. The development of secure transactions and secure online payment instruments (such as digital cash and electronic checks) is currently one of the most active areas of electronic commerce research/development.

Other Key Support Layers

Public policy and technical standards are the two support pillars for all electronic commerce applications and infrastructure.

Public Policy   Public policy related to electronic commerce encompasses such issues as universal access, privacy, and information pricing. Unlike business activities, which are governed by the Commercial Code and detailed case histories, electronic commerce currently poses basic policy and legal questions. Information traffic policy issues deal with the cost of accessing information, regulation to protect consumers from fraud and to protect their right to privacy, and the policing of global information traffic to detect information piracy or pornography. Again, the issues themselves, let alone solutions, are just now evolving and will become increasingly important as more people enter the electronic marketplace.

Technical Standards   Technical standards dictate the specifics of information publishing tools, user interfaces, and transport. Standards are essential to ensure compatibility across the entire network. Just as traditional transportation networks such as railroads face difficulties with different track standards in different countries, differing standards in electricity distribution (110 versus 200 volts) and video distribution (Sony BETA versus VHS), limit worldwide use of many products.

Final Word on the Framework   While fundamental computing issues are just now being raised and solved, a variety of industries are developing new applications that target both consumers and businesses. Experiments are necessary in order to predict which applications will be successful, but these experiments require an infrastructure. And in order to plan the infrastructure, hard choices have to be made about which applications might be successful. This is a classic chicken-and-egg dilemma that Microsoft, for one, negotiates quite well.

Putting the Framework into Action: Microsoft Corporation

Microsoft is an excellent case study of a company that understands the importance of the various aspects of the electronic commerce framework discussed so far. The logic behind the acquisitions and strategic partnerships Microsoft has undertaken in the field of electronic commerce is simple: once users install Windows 95 on their desktop, with the click of a mouse, these users can sign up for Microsoft Network (MSN). This system allowed Microsoft to cut into the market share of online service providers like America Online and software providers like Netscape, and it provided Microsoft with a competitive edge so big that rivals complained to the Justice Department. Complainants reasoned that Microsoft not only essentially controlled the user interface, but also controlled the "plumbing" that allows users access to the Internet. Microsoft could thus easily deny access to other competing applications.

   In terms of the aspects of the electronic commerce infrastructure already discussed, Microsoft began its efforts by establishing a key link to the Internet. When Microsoft decided to build the Microsoft Network (MSN), it bought a 20 percent stake in UUNET Technologies, a company that provides consumers with access to the Internet (see Chapter 2). UUNET gave Microsoft access to a telecommunications infrastructure that reaches several hundred cities in the United States. It also made Microsoft independent of any access provider.

Microsoft then launched an intensive effort to build an attractive content base. Instead of spending money developing its own content, Microsoft decided to attract content away from other providers such as America Online and CompuServe. Although content is key, its providers have little leverage in the online marketplace. In general, content providers (such as magazines, newspapers, and TV networks) receive meager royalties (usually 10 to 30 percent) based on online usage fees, and a small bounty for drawing new subscribers to a service.

Microsoft developed a business model that allows each content provider to set fees and to retain the majority of revenues (around 70 percent) generated by their content. Microsoft receives 20 percent of advertising revenues and a 5 percent commission on goods sold on MSN but delivered by other methods. With this business model, it was able to garner support from content providers seeking more lucrative contracts.

In terms of network servers, Microsoft has developed a Web server called Internet Information System that it is bundling with Windows NT 4.0 operating systems. Microsoft is also active in messaging and information distribution, and is involved with various consortia and standards organizations that are developing standards for such distribution.

In the area of common business services, Microsoft launched a preemptive strike by making a $1.5 billion bid for Intuit, the maker of the popular personal finance software, Quicken. This merger would have given Microsoft the capability to perform transaction processing, an important component of the electronic commerce framework. The merger was shelved when the U.S. Justice Department launched an antitrust investigation against Microsoft. In order to provide the transaction processing capability Microsoft sought through Intuit, Microsoft has redoubled efforts to improve Microsoft Money to match the functionality of Intuit's Quicken product (see Chapter 7).

Finally, Microsoft is working with various applications vendors. With the other elements of electronic commerce infrastructure in place, applications will proliferate. For instance, Wal-Mart and Microsoft recently made a deal to provide online shopping services. Wal-Mart, in the summer of 1996, introduced an Internet site through Microsoft's Merchant Server. Customers will browse and pay for merchandise through PCs. The products will be delivered by regular mail (see Chapter 8).

Microsoft is betting heavily that the use of electronic commerce will increase dramatically as technology improves, and that consumer-oriented electronic commerce will increase accordingly. Microsoft also realizes that there is already enough technology available to provide exciting online services; the challenge lies in selling these ideas and services to the consumer. Microsoft is making technological improvements that will increase the appeal of electronic commerce to consumers: improvements in the user interface, better and easier payments, and the development of intelligent agents (or digital butlers) that will take care of mundane tasks like meeting scheduling.

1.4 Types of Electronic Commerce

There are three distinct general classes of electronic commerce applications: inter-organizational (business-to-business), intra-organizational (within business), and customer-to-business.

Inter-organizational Electronic Commerce

From the inter-organizational perspective, electronic commerce facilitates the following business applications:

- **Supplier management.** Electronic applications help companies reduce the number of suppliers and facilitate business partnerships by reducing purchase order (PO) processing costs and cycle times, and by increasing the number of POs processed with fewer people.

- **Inventory management.** Electronic applications shorten the order-ship-bill cycle. If the majority of a business's partners are electronically linked, information once sent by fax or mail can now be instantly transmitted. Businesses can also track their documents to ensure that they were received, thereby improving auditing capabilities. This also helps to reduce inventory levels, improve inventory turns, and eliminate out-of-stock occurrences.

- **Distribution management.** Electronic applications facilitate the transmission of shipping documents such as bills of lading, purchase orders, advanced ship notices, and manifest claims, and enable better resource management by ensuring that the documents themselves contain more accurate data.

- **Channel management.** Electronic applications quickly disseminate information about changing operational conditions to trading partners. Technical, product, and pricing information that once required repeated telephone calls and countless labor hours can now be posted to electronic bulletin boards. By electronically linking production-related information with international distributor and reseller networks, companies can eliminate thousands of labor hours and ensure accurate information sharing.

- **Payment management.** Electronic applications link companies with suppliers and distributors so that payments can be sent and received electronically. Electronic payment reduces clerical error, increases the speed at which companies compute invoices, and lowers transaction fees and costs.

In the 1980s, Wal-Mart stores implemented a famous system of inter-organizational electronic commerce. Wal-Mart invested half a billion dollars in computer and satellite communications networks, bar code systems, scanners, and other equipment linking each point-of-sale terminal to distribution centers and headquarters in Bentonville, Arkansas. Many believe that this system enabled Wal-Mart to manage the explosive retail sales growth that catapulted the company to the number one position in the U.S. retail business. The system enabled the company to maintain high service levels and increase sales, while reducing inventory costs by three-fourths. Further, Wal-Mart empowered individual stores to order directly from even overseas suppliers, reducing inventory restocking time from an industry average of six weeks to thirty-six hours. Moreover, by tracking every sale through point-of-sales devices, Wal-Mart stores were better able to keep their stores well-stocked, while maintaining tight inventories and low prices [DM92].

Small companies are also beginning to see the benefits of adopting electronic commerce to cut sales, production, and delivery costs. Most of the paper documents exchanged between trading partners (invoices, checks, purchase orders, financial reports) are in electronic form at their point of origin but are printed and re-entered at the point of receipt. Electronic data interchange is an increasingly attractive alternative to the current process of printing, mailing, and rekeying, which is costly, time-consuming, and error-prone.

Intra-organizational Electronic Commerce

The purpose of intra-organizational applications is to help a company maintain the relationships that are critical to delivering superior customer value. How is this accomplished? By paying close attention to integrating various functions in the organization. From this perspective intra-organizational electronic commerce facilitates the following business applications:

- **Workgroup communications.** These applications enable managers to communicate with employees using electronic mail, videoconferencing, and bulletin boards. The goal is to use technology to increase the dissemination of information, resulting in better informed employees.

- **Electronic publishing.** These applications enable companies to organize, publish, and disseminate human resources manuals, product specifications, and meeting minutes using tools such as the World Wide Web. The goal is to provide the information to enable better strategic and tactical decision making throughout the firm. Also, online publishing shows immediate and clear benefits: reduced costs for printing and distributing documentation, faster delivery of information, and reduction of outdated information.

- **Sales force productivity.** These applications improve the flow of information between the production and sales forces, and between the firms and customers. By better integrating the sales forces with other parts of the organization, companies can have greater access to market intelligence and competitor information, which can be funneled into better strategy. The goal is to allow firms to collect market intelligence quickly and to analyze it more thoroughly.

Within intra-organizational electronic commerce, the largest area of growth can be seen in the development of "Corporate Intranets." Today, Intranets are primarily set up to publish and access vital corporate information. Some of the most common types of information are: Human Resources information, employee communications, product development and project management data, internal catalogs, sales support data, equipment and shipment tracking, and accessing corporate databases (see Chapter 3).

Consumer-to-Business Electronic Commerce

In electronically facilitated consumer-to-business transactions, customers learn about products through electronic publishing, buy products with electronic cash and other secure payment systems, and even have information goods delivered over the network.

From the consumer's perspective, electronic commerce facilitates the following economic transactions:

- **Social interaction.** Electronic applications enable consumers to communicate with each other through electronic mail, videoconferencing, and news groups.

- **Personal finance management.** Electronic applications like Quicken enable consumers to manage investments and personal finances using online banking tools.

• **Purchasing products and information.** Electronic applications enable consumers to find online information about existing and new products/services.

Consumers consistently demand greater convenience and lower prices. Electronic commerce provides consumers with convenient shopping methods, from online catalog ordering to phone banking, both of which eliminate the costs of expensive retail branches (or Bricks and Mortar). Electronic commerce facilitates factory orders by eliminating many intermediary steps, thereby lowering manufacturers' inventory and distribution costs, and indirectly providing consumers with lower prices.

Within the customer-to-business segment, the notion of online intermediation is gaining ground and merits discussion.

Intermediaries and Electronic Commerce

Intermediaries (or electronic brokers) are economic agents that stand between the parties of a contract (or transaction), namely buyers and sellers, and perform functions necessary to the fulfillment of a contract. Most firms in the financial service sector, including banks, insurance companies, mutual funds, and venture capital firms, are intermediaries. Other well-known forms of intermediaries are brokers, agents, traders, and mediators. A given intermediary implementation can serve concurrently in more than one of these forms, or roles. Table 1.1 lists a variety of online intermediaries in electronic commerce.

Consider online retailing. Online intermediaries change the traditional retail distribution pipeline. Traditionally, nearly every stage of a product's life cycle, including design, manufacturing, warehousing, marketing, packing, and shipping, would be handled by the same firm. Online products are handled differently. A company sends out a description of a product via public information, a consumer responds with an order, the vendor modifies the product to suit individual tastes, and the product is shipped directly to the buyer's home or business. The result is more efficient production and distribution and, at least in theory, lower prices.

Clearly, many opportunities exist for intermediaries who process and add value to information along the transactional chain. Information-based products range from the technologically simple (such as order taking) to highly sophisticated (such as customized manufacturing). In a simple case, customers can order flowers through online intermediaries that divert the order to regular stores for delivery. In more complex cases, intermediaries create software that allows customers to view and choose cars by computer,

Table 1.1   Different Types of Online Intermediaries

Type of Intermediary	*Definition and Examples*
Equipment providers	Servers (Sun Microsystems), Clients (Compaq), Routers (Cisco), and Network Cards (3COM)
Network access providers	America Online, CompuServe, Prodigy, NetCom, UUNET, and PSI
Information access providers	Netscape (Navigator browser and Commerce server), Adobe (Acrobat viewer), and Microsoft (Explorer)
Payment/transaction processors	First Virtual, DigiCash, VISA, and MasterCard
Financial intermediaries	Quicken, Microsoft Money, Meca Software
Web server providers and designers	Consultants and providers who help users design and set up World Wide Web pages for a substantial fee
Information directory providers	Yahoo, Alta Vista, Excite, Lycos, and InfoSeek
Information rating services	Consumer Reports, Edmunds Car Guide

eliminating time-consuming trips to the car lot. These programs then provide valuable data to the car companies' manufacturing and inventory systems that actually control the production and distribution of the car.

In online retailing, intermediaries are doing extremely well by packaging and selling information via computer networks. The online catalog business is one of the most efficient and successful intermediation-based industries. A successful example is CUC International Inc. in Greenwich, Connecticut. CUC's customers browse through a vast computer database that lists more than two hundred fifty brand-name products, including appliances, luggage, and jewelry. CUC electronically forwards customer orders to the products' manufacturers, who then ship the merchandise directly to the customer. Because CUC does not need bricks, mortar, labor, or physical transportation to store and ship products, it is able to offer customers lower prices than those provided by traditional retailers (see Chapter 8).

In the online marketplace a new type of intermediary called *electronic brokerages* has emerged as a key element. Technically speaking, a brokerage is a service that provides functions by which to interconnect, adapt, and facilitate services offered by other parties. For example, it is often desirable for information to be combined to allow construction of more value-added information products. The brokerage can bring together the various pieces. In the evolution of information products, it is often the case that when a proprietary information product becomes widely available, its interface is not compatible to all potential customers. In such a scenario, a brokerage serves to provide a common interface to the service without modifying either the product's original interface or the applications that seek to use the service. Consequently, brokers ameliorate some aspects of interoperability that might otherwise require an unattainable consensus to realize a formal standard.

At the electronic commerce software level, the intermediation function is increasingly being implemented via software agents that have "intelligence"; that is, they follow guidelines and have autonomy to react proactively to conditions they sense from the environment.

In short, whether a strict, general, or electronic interpretation is adopted, it is clear that intermediaries comprise a significant portion of the online economy. Therefore, understanding the forces that give rise to the demand for intermediaries, as well as the characteristics and structure of intermediated online markets, is crucial to understanding the operations of electronic markets.

1.5 Key Questions for Management

Electronic commerce has opened a new universe for consumers and organizations, and it demands new management approaches. If exploited cleverly, electronic commerce has the potential to increase corporate profits through better customer acquisition and retention, new information-based products and services, and more efficient operations.

However, companies must rethink their strategy, products, and business processes in order to develop a cohesive management approach. During this effort, many difficult questions need to addressed such as:

What should be the long-term and short-term corporate strategy?

What is the new business model in the electronic commerce world?

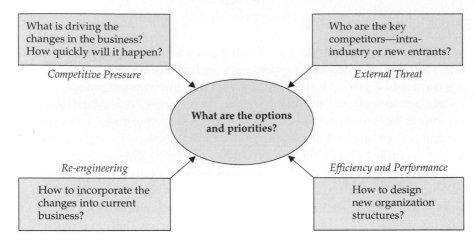

Figure 1.5   Key Questions For Management

How should the corporation invest in electronic commerce technology?

What new products and services should be offered or developed?

What organizational structures will best reach, interact with, and serve customers?

These questions have no easy answers. To respond to the new opportunities and competitive threats, management must anticipate technological and consumer behavioral changes. Figure 1.5 illustrates the key concerns and broad questions that management will need to address in the context of electronic commerce. While these questions are generic, executives can use them to analyze their business environment and corporate situation.

Competitive Pressure

Today's business environment is characterized by several dynamic forces. These dynamic forces are familiar to most managers, but they bear repeating as they form the basis for the new competitive framework of electronic commerce. These forces include: increased customer service and product expectations, shorter product life cycles, increased product/feature/option proliferation, the erosion of product and geographic boundaries, consumer demand fluctuations, and increased pressure on margins.

But this now familiar list of forces provides neither a framework for understanding the changes brought about by electronic commerce nor a way to think about how the future might evolve. What does provide such a framework, we believe, is a functional view of electronic commerce.

All companies, whether online or off-line, require that certain basic functions be performed. For example, all companies that want to do business online require methods for collecting payments. In contrast, the institutional arrangements used to carry out the payment function may change over time and differ across platforms.

Fundamentally, the underlying business functions that electronic commerce affects differ very little from what exists today. Specifically, electronic commerce must provide the following functionality:

Methods of making payments in order to facilitate the exchange of goods and services.

Ways to transfer different types of content over time and across distances.

Mechanisms for pooling resources to manufacture products more efficiently.

Methods of managing and coordinating decentralized decision making in various sectors of the firm.

Although the set of functions does not change, the way each is performed varies depending on the level of technology, sophistication of business processes, and other factors. Furthermore, the performance of each function changes over time as product innovation, improved technology, and competitive forces make increased efficiency of the function possible.

Competition and technological improvements are sparking innovators to discover new, more efficient ways to fulfill such basic functions as reading news and managing stock portfolios. Finally, functions are performed more efficiently, and institutions adapt to the changes. For instance, stockbrokers such as E-trade provide online trading privileges, thereby allowing customers to bypass traditional brokers and undertake that function themselves. This has greatly reduced the cost of transactions and results in a change in the institutional form itself.

External Threat

Companies need to be careful when evaluating and identifying inter- and intra-industry competitors in the electronic commerce landscape. Management has the unenviable task of factoring technology trends, competitor motives, and customer behavior issues into coherent long-term strategies. The scale and scope of available choices makes strategic decision making extremely complex.

Take for instance, financial services. Digital cash, online banking, stored value cards, and smart cards (see Chapter 6) currently play a small role in financial services. Nevertheless, it has become increasingly clear that both depository institutions and their nondepository competitors are planning for a future in which these new means of engaging in banking and commerce will play a major and perhaps dominant role. However, identifying competitors and threats is not easy given the interdependencies in the various financial products and services.

With many competitors to worry about, management needs to determine what corporate goals they hope to accomplish through electronic commerce in an information-driven economy. While this seems like common sense, it is often the step where corporations falter. To succeed, an organization must go through the following steps: (a) develop a robust electronic commerce strategy, driven by the business problem at hand, the corporate objectives, and the core competencies (things that the company is good at); and (b) integrate the technology into high value-added areas such as distribution, sales and marketing, and customer management.

In the case of developing corporate strategy, it is often difficult to determine which approaches are suitable for electronic commerce. It is also difficult to determine which approaches are risky, and, if the degree of risk can be quantified, how to minimize that risk. Whatever the approach, management should build a strong, quantifiable business case to ensure that they pursue only projects that have a high return on investment and that deliver a high value to the customer. It has been proven time and time again that consumers are not highly motivated by sophisticated technology or gadgets; technology-based products and services that offer real value must be communicated in a customer-specific context.

Embedding the technology into the business functions requires firms to evaluate business processes and plan for, acquire, and implement the necessary architecture. The business strategy must take the lead in defining the role of electronic commerce. Also, electronic commerce should be seen as an enabler, not as a means to itself. We take the stand that the power of electronic commerce lies not so much in technology alone, as in the integration and application of technology to achieve a better product or service for the customer, resulting in a better market position for the corporation.

Incorporating Changes

The prospect of building a completely new set of business applications can be daunting. In an endeavor to find the right approach, management has attempted many so-called business revolutions (see Table 1.2) such as busi-

Table 1.2 Management Ideologies of the 1980s and 1990s

Terms	Definition of Concept
Total Quality	A management approach which focuses on creating an organization that can consistently meet internal and external customer requirements and expectations in every transaction. TQM requires systematic long-term development of processes that are flexible, responsive, and constantly improving in quality.
Time Compression	A management approach that focuses on compacting the time taken to design, produce, deliver, and service new products. Time compression endeavors to improve cycle times and move toward more flexible production called "mass customization."
Customer Service	A management approach that focuses on customer service as the main business priority. The move toward a service economy is placing a greater emphasis on service as a competitive differentiator.
Business Process Reengineering	A management approach that focuses on the analysis and redesign of organization structures and business processes in order to achieve improvements in cost, quality, and speed.

ness reengineering, process innovation, time compression, and total quality management. These management ideologies endeavor to integrate business processes so that they react to market-induced requirements for flexibility and product/service quality while slashing both turnaround times and costs.

These ideologies emphasized cost reduction through downsizing and improved operational efficiencies. Yet in nearly every industry this is only part of the equation for creating value. Success today lies in being smarter and faster than the competition, not just smaller and more cost-efficient. While recognizing the need for agility and capturing market share are important, the actual challenge lies in implementing the vision. This new vision requires a fundamentally different implementation approach.

Interestingly, if one looks closely, the goals of the earlier so-called revolutions and electronic commerce are remarkably similar: reduce costs, shorten product cycle times, expedite customer response, and improve service quality. The basic difference is that while most earlier management ideologies fell short in practical application of good ideas, electronic commerce remedies this by providing the technological tools to facilitate the reengineering of most business processes.

Electronic commerce implementations require a fresh perspective on the function of an application, the role of the user, and the use of development tools themselves. On the other hand, building a new class of applications affords companies with the rare opportunity of beginning with the right set of tools and a robust framework rather than a hodgepodge of technologies.

But make no mistake, electronic commerce projects are often complex, as they combine leading-edge technologies with process change. From an application perspective, speed compliance, modularity and completeness, and extensibility are important, as is careful attention to business processes and organizational factors.

Designing New Organizational Structures

Electronic commerce can and will impact organizational structures. Why? Because, the organizational structure must grant companies the flexibility needed to do business in response to market requirements. Firms need to ask themselves how best to design and implement new organizational structures, how to measure the performance of these new organizational structures, and how to incorporate new innovations like mobile computing and software agents into business process design.

One of the immediate effects of technology on organization structure can be seen in advertising and marketing communications departments that are being revolutionized by Web-based publishing. For instance, Xerox Corp. has over three hundred employees from several departments involved in maintaining the quality and consistency of Xerox Web pages.

Clearly, these large companies need to determine the right organization structure for managing large-scale Web efforts and to discern whether such management is a business operations issue where efficiency is key, or a software development issue where creativity is crucial. These and other questions become pertinent and crucial as companies move into the uncharted waters of electronic commerce.

Managerial Options and Priorities

In the process of developing new business theories and strategies, managers must consider what kind of tactics and strategy to adopt. Managers also need to consider the immediate impact of electronic commerce on key business areas such as management of sales and distribution channels, pricing policy, convergence of products and services, entrepreneurship, and managing new consumer interfaces.

For most organizations, conducting a cost-benefit analysis is an important prerequisite for making a large investment. Unfortunately, few organizations have effective methods for evaluating the payback of new applications, especially early on. Often, payoffs are not predictable and applications must be in place and used for some time before benefits are realized. Even then, the benefits may vary widely, depending on the degree to which organizations change the way they work. Finally, the pressure for short-term payoffs can curtail or derail implementation. Organizations often overlook longer term, less tangible benefits such as improved customer service, the ability to gather more reliable information more quickly for more people, and improved efficiencies.

Along with specifying long-term and short-term strategy, firms need to examine how electronic commerce will change fundamental business processes. For instance, banking professionals need to determine how widespread home banking, as well as the use of new forms of financial instruments (such as digital cash), will change existing banking processes. The banking industry may also experience employment shifts, such as a reduction in clerks and tellers, and an increase in information-processing specialists who monitor transaction trends, security threats, and so on.

And finally, a portion of the dilemma in planning for electronic commerce is due to the fact that many organizations and managers assume a future in which electronic commerce on the Internet (or its progeny) will be a given. In this vision, high bandwidth internetworks are everywhere. Consumers surf in and out of multimedia databases all over the world and make payments using digital currency. Software agents help users at every turn. All security problems are solved; all consumer privacy fears assuaged. This future is free of complications. The hard part for most companies is managing the evolution of online commerce and charting a path that ensures future survival.

1.6 Summary

This chapter defined the notion of electronic commerce and presented the history behind its evolution. Once the source of science fiction, electronic commerce—conducted in and around the global marketplace—is now a reality with enormous potential. We discussed the various forces that fuel the growth of electronic commerce, namely economic, marketing, and customer interaction and digital convergence. A framework for thinking about electronic commerce was also presented. The framework is illustrated with a case study of how Microsoft is approaching the electronic commerce landscape.

We also discussed the different types of electronic commerce applications, namely, inter-organizational (business-to-business), intra-organization (within business), and customer-to-business. However, exploiting electronic commerce requires a number of management decisions for companies—about the industry, competition, operationalization, and organization structure. Making these decisions in an integrated way is quite a challenge.

Chapter 2

The Internet and the Access Provider Industry

Chapter Outline

The Internet is not a new phenomenon. Its roots lie in a collection of computers that were linked together in the 1960s as a project of the Advanced Research Projects Agency (ARPA) of the U.S. Department of Defense. Initially, ARPA linked together the four mainframe computers at Stanford Research Institute, the University of California at Los Angeles, the University of California at Santa Barbara, and the University of Utah.

The initial goal was to create a network that enables the safe transmittal of data between military computers at different sites through redundant communication routes. The redundancy in communication lines was to ensure uninterrupted data transfer in case of a war. In addition, computer functions were decentralized so that no single site would become the potentially vulnerable site. In the ensuing years, other government networks were hooked up to the ARPANET and the whole become the Internet [KALA96].

Since the mid-1980s, the National Science Foundation (NSF), an agency of the U.S. government, and other government entities controlled access to the Internet. Internet use by individuals or businesses not affiliated with one of these organizations was virtually nonexistent. In its early days, the Internet had no commercial purpose and was not designed to provide any.

31

Largely because it was funded through research grants from the NSF and other government agencies, during the 1980s the Internet was used primarily for technical, academic, and scientific research.

In 1991, the NSF eased restrictions and allowed commercial traffic onto the Internet. This action was tantamount to opening the floodgates of the Amazon River. In April 1995, the U.S. government further relinquished control of the Internet to independent governing bodies, which relaxed the restrictions for Internet access. Companies were allowed to provide unfettered for-profit Internet access.

Ever since commercial use of the Internet was allowed, the growth in subscribers and traffic has been phenomenal. According to Internet Society estimates, the Internet now has 30 million users on 10 million computers connected to over 240,000 networks in over 100 countries. Further, it is estimated that one million more people become Internet users each month.

It is a matter for raging debates as to how many consumers are active Internet users; estimates vary from 6 to 24 million. However, by comparison, the decade-old cellular industry has only recently crossed the 25 million subscriber level in the United States. It is often said that there has been no other technology or innovation in modern history that comes close to the Internet in terms of speed of adoption, significance, and impact.

Table 2.1 shows the exponential growth in host computers (computers that deliver information and services to users) connected to the Internet. Table 2.2 shows the exponential increase in network bandwidth, a term used to describe the size of the "pipe" that pumps information across the network.

2.1 Internet Service Providers

To support the rapidly growing commercial Internet landscape, an entirely new industry called Internet Service Providers (ISPs) has emerged in the last five years. The allure of the Internet has been fanned to some extent by the very high profile initial public offerings (IPOs) of some service providers.

Until 1995, there were no publicly traded companies whose principal business was Internet-related, or whose primary revenue source came from Internet-related services. In a span of six months, many such publicly traded companies appeared, and the volatility and hype surrounding the Internet stocks have been the talk of the financial circles. Interest in the Internet and the enormous amount of investment pumped into both public and private Internet-related companies have reached a large enough level to warrant serious attention by Wall Street.

Table 2.1   Host Computer Growth

Date	Host Computers
1969	4
08/81	213
08/83	562
10/85	1,961
12/87	28,174
10/89	159,000
10/90	313,000
10/91	617,000
10/92	1,136,000
10/93	2,056,000
07/94	3,212,000
07/95	6,642,000
01/96	9,472,000

Table 2.2   Internet Bandwidth Growth

Year	Bandwidth
1969	9.6 Kbps
1985	56 Kbps
1987	1.544 Mbps (T1 Speed)
1989	45 Mbps (T3 Speed)
1995	155 Mbps
1997	622 Mbps
1998	1,024 Mbps
2000	2,048 Mbps

The Internet Service Provider industry offers a wide variety of enabling technologies and services that are not often apparent to the average consumer. These service providers offer a variety of technologies and services, including:

Internet access for consumers and organizations (such as America Online, Prodigy, CompuServe, and Microsoft Network).

Network management, systems integration, and backbone access services for other service providers (such as UUNET, PSI, BBN).

Client and server software for navigating and publishing content on the Internet (such as Netscape, Microsoft, NetManage, and QuarterDeck).

Payment systems for online purchases (such as First Virtual, CyberCash, OpenMarket).

All of these technologies and services are experiencing rapid growth. In particular, the Internet access market has the enviable position of being the means through which other service providers reach end users. The down side to this profitable position is that access providers like America Online are experiencing classic growing pains; they need to maintain profitability, satisfy customers, and yet not fall behind competition in keeping up with the innovation that characterizes the Internet industry.

Clearly, rapid growth and commercialization require professional management, and managers need to find a balance between creativity and control, and between spectacular growth and a stable infrastructure. Managers also need to consider issues such as quality service, customer loyalty, and cost of additional capacity. Finally, they also need to ensure network reliability and security. With a user base that has increased over 1,000 percent in six years, the motivation for better management practices is obvious.

In order to explain the workings of the Internet and the access provider industry, this chapter will outline the business drivers behind the Internet, and provide a succinct explanation of Internet-related terminology. It will then focus on the access provider marketplace and examine the various strengths and weaknesses of market competitors. The chapter concludes with an examination of some of the management challenges that need to be addressed in the immediate future.

Key Market Drivers for the Internet

Since the Internet was opened to commercial usage, it has grown dramatically as it demonstrated potential for businesses to reach consumers. Retailers, publishers, and entertainment providers are flocking to the

Internet and experimenting with ways to create applications that will capture the imagination—and money—of millions of users worldwide. Although consumers will probably never use the Internet to watch television due to bandwidth limitations, individuals are using the Internet to retrieve news information, handle many forms of shopping, and engage in a wide variety of virtual experiences such as museum tours and concerts.

Another driver is business-to-business commerce. For instance, many businesses use the Internet to quickly find product information. One of the innovative companies catering to this marketplace is Industry.Net (http://www.industry.net), a developer of the world's largest online database for business and industry. Over 4,000 companies currently maintain electronic Business Centers in the company's Marketplace. The database contains over 500,000 files, including product descriptions, manufacturer and supplier information, and catalogs and brochures. The service also allows buyers and sellers within specific industry segments to exchange purchasing information about products and services important to their segment and, soon, to conduct actual transactions online.

Another driver is software innovation. Many business applications that are taken for granted today first appeared on the Internet in the mid- to late 1980s. These include electronic mail, news groups (or bulletin boards), and more recently the World Wide Web (WWW). The success of many of these applications resulted in products that are widely used in the corporate world.

However, the engineering, military, and computing uses that were responsible for the Internet's early growth are not the applications that are fueling interest today. For example, pressure on the average consumer's free time is creating an interest in applications such as online banking, online retailing, and fast access to real-time information from a variety of sources. Although some applications may never achieve commercial success, others could easily become the standard for how we live, work, learn, and entertain ourselves in the coming millennium.

Not surprisingly, the Internet's vibrancy is attracting legions of businesses and investors who see new markets for products and services for a changing user base. The early users of the Internet were technical experts. They had to be able to deal with the "unfriendly" UNIX interface. Today the Internet is attracting a new type of user: one who is not interested in the technology, but in ways the Internet can make life easier.

Who Is Making Money on the Internet?

A frequently asked question is: Who is making money on the Internet? We believe that Internet contributes profitability in five phases.

The first phase began in 1991–1993 when hardware providers increased sales as both companies and consumers purchased increasing numbers of PCs, routers, and modems. Because the infrastructure is currently undergoing rapid construction, companies that provide modems and internetworking equipment have experienced strong demand. Even today there is continued strength in this sector because of increasing demand and improving price/performance characteristics.

The second phase (1993–1996) saw increased revenues (and profits) for Internet access providers and various online services, such as America Online. Internet access providers provide connection to the Internet for both the consumer and the commercial markets. Recently there has been increased speculation about the future of online services. We believe that the Internet does not invalidate the business model of companies such as America Online. There will always be a segment of the population that wants the ease of use that America Online provides, along with the attractively repackaged content. We do believe, however, that the more sophisticated user will eventually gravitate toward the lower-cost, direct-access providers.

The third phase (1994–present) saw a rise in demand for high bandwidth transmission lines that are run by telecommunications companies—regional bell operating companies (RBOCs) for the local loop, cable providers with cable modems, and long-distance providers such as AT&T for the backbone. Clearly, this is one segment that should experience strong and sustained demand growth as more users log on to the Internet and require increasing bandwidth to transmit graphics-laden and multimedia content.

The fourth phase (1995–present) will see an emphasis on information organization and structuring as content expands and becomes chaotic. For instance, the fact that with few entry barriers anyone can establish a presence on the Internet and the Web so easily is driving growth, causing clutter and a proliferation of material of dubious value. Internet software professionals—the consultants and electronic publishing/programming specialists—and intermediaries who specialize in information brokering and content organization are becoming key players.

Finally, once both the structure and customer base are in place, content will provide the focus for profits and revenue growth. Many traditional media companies are attempting to take advantage of this growing new medium. In this phase, the battle for market share will depend on copyrights. When this occurs, copyright ownership will become important and valuable. Also, the emphasis on content will fuel the evolution of the personal computer from a stand-alone tool to a network front-end capable of distributed computing. This trend is evident in the development of Internet appliances and the recent release of Microsoft Windows NT operating system. However, realizing this nascent potential is contingent on the availability of high-speed network links.

Clarifying Internet Terminology

The Internet is a network of networks, or an "internetwork," linking computers worldwide. In its physical form, the Internet is composed of wires, routers, and communication links. It is similar in many respects to today's telephone system. The "transport" lines that convey information on the Internet are mainly leased from telephone companies such as MCI and connected to computers called routers, which guide coded data toward their destinations. The main difference is that the Internet as a whole does not "belong" to any one telephone company, and it has no central control. No one "owns" the Internet, and for lack of a better term it can be regarded as a "socialist collective."

One can also view the Internet as a collection of computer networks composed of computers that use dissimilar operating systems and contain a variety of content. The information content on the Internet is located in independently owned, high-capacity computers called "servers." These servers are linked to regional networks which in turn connect to the "backbone" of the Internet. There are seven network access points (NAPs) or primary access points on the backbone. Think of the backbone as the interstate highway; the NAPs are the entry and exit points on that highway.

Another way of understanding the Internet is based on the language spoken (protocol) by inhabitants (computers). Two types of language classifications exist:

Academic (also known as the Core Internet). In the Academic Internet all the computers speak the nonproprietary language Transport Control Protocol/Internet Protocol (TCP/IP), a language protocol that allows communication between heterogeneous machines such as Apple PowerPCs, desktop Windows PCs, and UNIX-based computers. Over the years, the TCP/IP protocol has proven itself as an elegant solution to a complex interconnection problem and has become a de facto industry standard. The adoption of TCP/IP as a universally accepted protocol has been a driving force behind the growth of the Internet.

Business (also called Consumer Internet). In the Business Internet the host computers can speak a variety of languages other than TCP/IP, including X.25 (popular in Europe and with telcos) and Novell Netware, a widely used local area networking standard that speaks a language called IPX. The Business Internet consists of commercial online services (such as CompuServe), value-added networks (such as IBM Advantis), and other electronic mail-only services (such as MCIMail). During the early phase, these organizations connected to the Internet using gateways and software proprietary to a certain manufacturer.

The Academic and Business networks usually talk to each other via gateways stationed at the network border. These gateways serve as language (protocol) translators. In the past, because only mail gateways were common, the most widely used application (or the least common denominator) for the entire Internet was electronic mail. In this capacity, the Internet rapidly developed as a universal electronic messaging infrastructure spanning more than one hundred countries.

In 1993–1994, with the enormous popularity of the World Wide Web, many Business service providers realized that implementing gateways for every popular application that runs on the Academic Internet would be too expensive and time-consuming. As customers were threatening to move to services that offered those capabilities, access providers were forced to provide gateways to the Academic Internet's Web. It took most providers two years to develop these services to respond to customer demand. During this period many experienced users simply switched to access providers who were providing TCP/IP services.

Business Internet service providers have realized that it is futile to fight the trend. The Academic Internet's constant innovation, open connectivity, valuable information, and varied set of applications have proven to be a magnet to the customers of nearly every other kind of computer network. Bowing to customer demand, almost all business networks have attached themselves to the Internet. More recently, Business Internet providers have begun to adopt the TCP/IP as the standard language on their own networks, thus allowing smooth linkage with the Academic Internet.

Another reason for moving toward a common infrastructure is the cost. Unlike telephony, where charges are based on variable cost, Internet access for Business Internet users (such as the corporate customer) using a leased line connection is geared to a fixed cost structure. Customers pay a fixed monthly fee based on the capacity of their connection. Once the connection to the Internet is established, there is no charge for usage. There are no variable costs associated with an Internet connection, making it an attractive solution for multisite business communications.

2.2 Companies Providing Internet Access

So far, the most successful Internet business is selling access. Internet access providers (IAPs) provide companies and individuals with for-pay access to the various Internet applications and resources. These service providers do not offer their own content (such as files to download, online stock reports, and shopping malls), but provide a door through which users travel to reach content. These providers are mostly entrepreneurs who view themselves as online "real-estate property developers."

The different types of IAPs are: telco or cable companies, online services, national independents, regionals, and local providers.

Telco companies.   Long-distance telephone companies (AT&T, MCI, and Sprint) and regional telephone companies (Ameritech, Pacific Bell, and Bell Atlantic) have traditionally focused on bringing larger business users "on-network," leaving the consumer market to smaller Internet access providers who directly serve at-home users. Now telephone companies are aggressively moving into the consumer access market. Sprint was first to enter in 1991, MCI and Ameritech in 1994, AT&T in 1996, and others announce their entrance each month. Telcos are usually large in size and have balance sheets of billions of dollars.

Cable companies.   With the advent of cable modems, cable companies (Time Warner, TCI) are reinventing themselves as access providers for home users. Motorola, General Instrument, and other suppliers of equipment to the cable industry are developing modems that can connect personal computers with the Internet via coaxial cable at speeds much higher than conventional telephone modems. Cable companies are developing plans to bundle Internet access with other services and may well be the contenders to the telcos.

Online companies.   Companies such as America Online, CompuServe, Prodigy, and Microsoft Network package a range of information and Internet access for a monthly fee. These services can be accessed through a modem via a local telephone number. Monthly fees begin below ten dollars, but charges for additional hours of usage or extra services (including Internet access) vary and can be substantial. The old model of providing proprietary and limited user connectivity is changing to a more Internet-friendly strategy that allows users to take advantage of the growth in the Internet applications.

National independents.   Companies such as PSI, UUNET, and Newton are commercial, for-profit entities that offer connectivity services nationwide or in some cases internationally. This group of access providers target business users and other smaller service providers who do not have the resources to provide widespread coverage. For example, UUNET provides monthly service to business customers at rates beginning at four hundred dollars. Other companies lease telecommunications links from UUNET and provide a package of services (graphical interfaces, navigational tools, and customer support) for the end user. For instance, UUNET is the provider of network services for Microsoft Network.

Regionals. In the past, regional nonprofit university-affiliated enterprises (such as SURAnet, NEARnet, NYSERnet, and BARRnet) offered services to the academic/research communities within one state or within regional interstate areas. With the elimination of NSF subsidies, these enterprises are aggressively entering the commercial marketplace. Today, many of these regional providers are forming strategic alliances with larger players in order to develop the critical mass necessary to compete against larger online companies.

Local service providers. Commonly called "mom and pop shops," these small businesses support anywhere from one to ten thousand customers. They operate in one physical location and offer services within a single metropolitan area. Basic rates currently start at less than $20 per month. Since local service providers target the more experienced users, they tend to provide less customer support than other types of IAPs.

Internet Topology

Although the Internet is a "network of networks" and a virtual maze of interconnections, Internet topology is relatively simple. Home users dial into a local access provider through PC modems that use the twisted-pair telephone lines already in their homes. Internet communications over twisted-pair can be relatively slow, and businesses, which typically require a higher-speed connection than that afforded by twisted pair, can opt for higher-speed connections such as Integrated Digital Systems Network (ISDN), 1.544 Mbps (T-1 lines), or 45 Mbps (T-3 lines).

All lines, regardless of speed, are routed to a local access provider (on-ramp), which switches the user through the user's Internet access provider's direct connection into the closest network access point (NAP). Early on, the Internet's communication backbone was direct, physical telephone line connections between the original governmental and educational organizations that made up the Internet. Additional organizations joining the Internet were physically connected to the network. As demand for

Internet access increased, direct access became infeasible. Instead, independent companies were empowered by the NSF to provide "for-profit" Internet access. Almost overnight a multimillion-dollar network access business arose.

In order to provide cost-effective commercial Internet access to a rapidly growing national customer base, access providers built proprietary, high-speed nationwide communication networks. These networks, which are still being constructed, include local access points (named points of presence, or POPs), allowing users access to the Internet via a local phone call. These POPs are in turn connected by high-speed telephone circuits to central hubs. The hubs, in turn, are connected to a high-capacity network backbone, which is physically connected to the Internet at geographically dispersed access points.

Figure 2.1 details an "on-ramp" to the Internet. Some larger firms serve a diversity of customers ranging from individual users to large organizations to other access providers. For instance, MCI provides backbone services as well as Internet access to individuals and other local access providers. Although many companies offer Internet access, not all IAPs provide unrestricted access. While commercial access is almost always direct, dial-up access may or may not be. Direct Internet access essentially

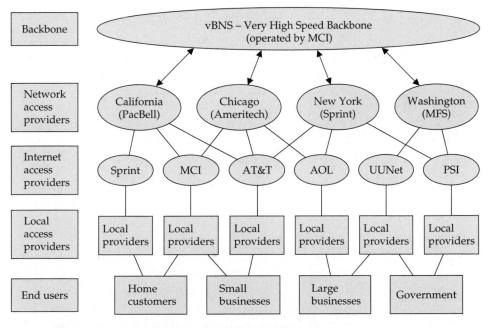

Figure 2.1   Current Internet Network Architecture

means that the user becomes an equal, or "peer," on the network, receiving unlimited access to all services and features of the Internet. The IAPs AT&T WorldNet, Netcom, and the Microsoft Network (MSN) all offer direct Internet access for the dial-up user.

Most proprietary online services (such as America Online) offer indirect access. Indirect Internet access through an online service company entails an extra step. Users must first connect to the online service company's network, and then are routed through the online provider's Internet gateway. Because the user must go through the online service provider, that provider can restrict the user's access to certain Internet areas or features. Further, since the user must navigate the online service provider's dedicated network, which often is usage-fee based, indirect access can be slower and more costly than direct access. Indirect Internet connection is losing ground as a business model. However, for online subscribers who use the Internet infrequently, this limited access is acceptable.

Internet access is structured differently outside the United States. There are now a large number of backbone and mid-level networks in other countries. For example, most western European countries have national networks attached to EBone, the European backbone. Many of the local access lines and backbones are owned and administered by the national telephone companies (called PTTs). This can lead to a conflict of interests, with some Asian and European telephone companies holding back the development of the Internet as they fear it will adversely affect their revenues. The Internet infrastructure outside the United States is still immature and quite inefficient in some places. For example, the connections between European countries are often slow or of low quality, so it is common to see traffic between two European countries routed through the U.S. backbone.

Differentiating Market Segments: Commercial versus Consumer

Finding a good Internet service provider is a topic of inquiry in cyberspace. After discussing the different types of providers, it makes sense to identify the different market segments that they target. The two broad categories of Internet service markets are consumer and commercial/government.

Consumers are ordinary folk sitting at home (mostly in the evenings) in front of their modem-equipped PCs, roaming cyberspace in search of a wide variety of information, entertainment, and companionship. Today this market is relatively small (over $2 billion), but subscriber growth, fueled by increasing awareness of the plethora of information available online, the cost-effectiveness of global electronic mail, and the intrigue of chat groups or forums, is high, increasing by approximately 35 percent a year.

Commercial/government users represent a bigger potential market than the consumer market. These users are both consumers of Internet services as well as producers of content. Commercial users have two uses for the Internet:

1. *Providing Internet access for employees.* There are many reasons businesses provide Internet access for employees. For example, the e-mail component of the Internet provides an alternative to voice-based communication with customers, fellow employees, and partners. Other uses include accessing human resources data and sales information, and obtaining marketing and competitive information.

2. *Using the World Wide Web to make information about the company available to the public.* Publishing on the Web enables companies to promote their products and services online to a huge audience of prospective customers. Customers can access information on demand without any sales pressure. Maintaining a Web site is less costly than mailing bulky product catalogs, and customers waste less time manually sifting through volumes of directories.

Rough estimates place the market value of commercial and government users at 12–15 million users with a growth rate of 10 percent per year. Electronic mail is the main application used by the commercial market segment. However, applications providing "content" such as electronic publishing, which allows dissemination of corporate/government information on products/services (marketing, technical support, training, and so on), are growing in popularity. Regardless of what they are being used for, online service providers obtain a fee for providing access, packaging the information attractively, and hosting the servers that store the information.

Consumer and commercial Internet user demands are quite different (see Table 2.3). Commercial customers require reliable and secure higher-speed network connections with fast response times, and twenty-four hours a day, seven days a week (24×7 service) support. Understandably, corporate users are willing to pay higher fees for the industrial-strength features such as reliability associated with the online service.

Home consumers are less worried about reliability, but are more price conscious. To deal with price-sensitive consumers, access providers have developed a business model that relies on subscriber volume and low usage rates. However, this model does not account for "churn," the number of customers canceling the service, which can run 4 to 5 percent per month. Churn is a big problem in the consumer segment.

Internet access providers must plan their investments in technology and networks in accordance with the markets they serve. For example, if access

Table 2.3 The Commercial versus the Consumer Model of Internet Access

	Commercial Model	*Consumer Model*
Access fee	Typical access fee >$500/month	Typical access fee of $10–$20/month
Industrial-strength features	Required	Welcome, but not as important as affordability
Type of connection	High-speed leased lines	Relatively slow dial-up
Internet services opportunity	Both producers and consumers of content	Consumers of content
Service required	Less often, but of high quality	More often, but quality-tolerant
Customer loyalty	High	Low

providers target consumers rather than corporate users, they will need a larger number of POPs (sites that permit users to make only a local rather than a long distance phone call). Corporations tend to be clustered in key metropolitan areas, whereas consumers are spread out over wider areas.

2.3 Internet versus Online Services

It is not surprising that people are often confused about the difference between the Internet and online services. While Internet usage has largely remained in the educational and, more recently, commercial environments, an entire online services industry targeted toward the consumer has been operating in relative obscurity for years (CompuServe began in 1969), chalking up an impressive subscribership that ranges from 5 to 15 million depending on whom you ask.

Most online service providers offer a proprietary service targeted primarily at individuals/consumers. A user dials up a service, which acts as a database of information received from other sources. Online services traditionally have been "closed systems," consisting of their own network of servers. Apart from the transmission of electronic mail, online service providers typically did not interface with the Internet. For instance,

America Online provides access to a flight reservation system called Easy-Sabre, which is not available on the Internet.

However, the "closed" model is rapidly giving way to a more "open" model in which online services are becoming "gateways" to the Internet. In this case, the user calls the access provider who, in turn, is connected to the Internet backbone. The speed and efficiency of the data transmission depend on the type of user modem and the connection that the access provider has with the backbone of the Internet.

Table 2.4 lists the key differences between online services and the Internet.

Table 2.4 Comparison of Internet and Online Services

	Internet	*Online Services*
Key characteristic	Content and user interface independent of service.	Content and user interface inextricably linked to the service.
Source(s) of revenue	Primarily subscribers based on fixed access charges.	Subscribers based on fixed and variable access charges and content providers.
User characteristics	More technical users who can survive on their own.	Fewer technical consumer and corporate users.
Pricing	Relatively flat: $20/month for consumers, $500–$1000/month for corporations.	Low (around $10) for first few (usually 5) hours, then $2–$3/hour thereafter; extra for specific content.
Advantages	Opportunity for innovation; ease of use.	Richer content; open to Internet access.

A number of key features distinguish an Internet Access Provider, such as Netcom, from a full service provider, such as America Online (AOL). These differences include: open versus closed architecture, controlled versus uncontrolled content, metered versus flat pricing schemes, and innovation versus control.

Open versus Closed Architecture

America Online was started in 1985 before direct Internet access existed. It was based on a "closed" model in which a host computer stores the information and users dial in to access that information for a fee. On the other hand, the Internet is an "open" model, with thousands of computer networks and free information on a variety of subjects.

The offerings of online companies are limited by their host computers. In contrast, an Internet access provider like Netcom, which is based on a TCP/IP "open" model, provides access to a broad array of Internet applications and information sources. Netcom users can literally navigate from server to server to access information. Netcom's "open" architecture allows it to take advantage of several good public domain programs available on the Internet without having to invest in a significant research and development effort.

Controlled Content versus Uncontrolled Content

America Online is like a small library; the Internet is more like a consortium of libraries linking literally millions of volumes of information, as well as graphics and sound files. The big challenge for online companies in the past was to build content in much the same way as libraries buy books; they endeavored to create a small but well-endowed library for their patrons to visit. For instance, the *New York Times* is available through America Online. In contrast, Internet access providers do not provide any content; they provide access to content on the Internet. For instance, the *San Jose Mercury News* publishes information on its Web server and any Internet user can access it for a fee. The Internet has an abundance of both free and for-pay content.

The small library/global library analogy gives an impression of the differences in content and use of online services and the Internet. For instance, AOL has a few hundred so-called "chat groups" centering around certain communities of interest. In contrast, the Internet has literally thousands of uncensored news groups about virtually every topic under the sun.

Metered Pricing versus Flat Pricing

Full service online providers follow a metered pricing model that charges users on the basis of hours of usage and the type of content accessed. The AOL pricing model, for example, charges $10 a month for the first five hours of service, and $2–$3 an hour thereafter. Internet access providers charge a flat rate ($25 a month) for unlimited access.

Consumers are very price-sensitive, and AOL is attempting to differentiate itself by providing different consumer segments with a variety of content-plus-service options and pricing models. Traditional online services can act as Internet access providers, but because of the overhead associated with value-added services, simply providing access to the Internet can be expensive. To circumvent this problem, AOL launched a separate service called Global Network Navigator that provides access to the Internet, but no access to the traditional online services.

Innovation versus Control

Through a more user-friendly and better-integrated environment, AOL currently delivers a richer consumer experience than Netcom. However, through the innovation of multiple technology and service providers, the open architecture of the Internet will become more user-friendly, and offer a much greater diversity of content for business users and consumers.

The Internet's informal nature encourages innovation. Ultimately, the real creators of value for the Internet will be content providers. Since the Internet through the World Wide Web (see Chapter 3) makes everyone a publisher, there will likely be millions of organizations and individuals who will provide information, entertainment, education, and software programs online. This in turn will spark innovation as users will need to rely on aggregators, search engines, and smart agent software that will help them find what it is they are looking for.

The Internet is also innovative in terms of performance and speed. Online service providers cannot match the Internet's improvements in bandwidths. By the year 2000, it is expected that the Internet backbone will a have a transmission capacity of approximately 2048 Mbps, almost fifteen times today's speed of 155 Mbps.

2.4 Predicting the Future of the IAP Market

In the future, four organizational and technology trends will drive the growth and consolidation of the IAP industry: the trend toward virtual organizations where mobile users, third party contractors, and telecommuters all enjoy the same network access available at corporate headquarters; the trend toward higher performance networking that combines data, voice, and video; the trend toward integration of local- and wide-area networks; and the trend toward universal online access.

Clearly the Internet access provider industry is as complex and varied as the disparate market segments it serves. Service providers range from large telephone companies with sophisticated networks to small organizations with a single server. Fast-growing industries are often composed of companies that are nimble enough to meet the demands of the marketplace. Likewise, the service provider industry of the future will feature a few strong players who can best address the following needs:

Convergence of voice and data networks.

Speed and capacity management problems because of tremendous user growth.

Improved customer service to guide users through the technology maze.

Marketing to new audiences.

Deployment of new access technology such as ISDN and cable modems.

Convergence Leading to Competition

Leading communications carriers such as MCI, AT&T, and Regional Bell Operating Companies (RBOCs) have noticed the increasing numbers of Internet users. Despite the lower profiles of these larger companies in providing consumer Internet access, the market is too big for them to ignore. Their current Internet strategy is to provide a gateway to the Internet with a single integrated bill for Internet usage and telephone or cable TV usage.

Let us examine one offering: AT&T WorldNet. On February 27, 1996, AT&T announced it would begin offering dial-up Internet access on March 14. The breadth and features of its service were impressive, and they propelled AT&T into the position of being taken as a serious competitor. The announcement sent the stock prices of publicly traded access providers plunging as investors speculated that AT&T's entrance would affect the growth rates and profitability of other publicly traded ISPs—NETCOM, PSINet, and UUNET. Table 2.5 summarizes the key points of the AT&T WorldNet service.

AT&T's success in the Internet access business will ultimately depend on the quality of customer service it provides. Other Internet access providers have learned that the Internet access business is service-intensive. The consumer market needs more hand-holding than the professional user or corporate market. AT&T's marketing effort seems to be targeting the average telephone user, suggesting it is going after the techno-illiterate segment of the market. This appears to be the segment that will require the greatest amount of customer service and support.

Table 2.5 Summarizing AT&T WorldNet Internet Access Service

Pricing	If an AT&T long distance customer: $0/month for the first five hours of usage per month, $2.50/hour thereafter, or $19.95/month for unlimited usage.
	If not an AT&T long distance customer: $4.95/month for the first three hours of usage per month, $2.50/hour thereafter, or $24.95/month for unlimited usage.
Customer Service	Provides support 24 hours/day, seven days/week via a toll-free number.
Software	Netscape Navigator and Microsoft Explorer browsers co-branded with AT&T.
Internet Access	200 local access points of presence with 28.8 Kbps modems (approximately 80 percent of U.S. population covered).
Pros	Brand recognition—Everyone knows the AT&T brand name.
	Competitive pricing—The five free hours/month "teaser" is very attractive.
	Toll-free customer service.
Cons	Quality of customer service tends to vary.
	Quality of connectivity—AT&T initially was having problems with capacity management as too many customers came on-board too quickly.

Although the telcos and cable companies could emerge as a dominant force in the access business, there will still be room for others. In a competitive environment with network architectures that are more open than proprietary, telcos, once telecommunications monopolies, have been slow to understand how to be gateways to Internet products and services. One thing is evident, however: Internet is a world where players are not rewarded purely on the amount of financial capital, but on the basis of innovation and ability to establish a dominant market position.

Service and Capacity Management

Capacity management is an issue that warrants the immediate attention of access providers. Corporate customers, whom various access providers are attempting to attract, will not put up with unreliability as individual consumers. Service outages have plagued online and Internet services. On June 19, 1996, the Netcom experienced a 13-hour unplanned outage. Three days later, Microsoft shut down its network intermittently for 10 hours. The online service had been scheduled for a major power-supply upgrade, but US West was unable to perform the work. America Online's ANS unit, which offers Internet and other network connections to corporate customers, reported that their "backbone" was out of service for about half an hour, affecting about 25 corporate customers.

The increase in online users, combined with the expanded delivery of Web and multimedia capabilities, put enormous strain on America Online in 1995–1996. In order to respond to the demand and reduce the strain on Sprint, their primary carrier, AOL bought out ANS, one of the pioneers in building the original Internet, and built "AOLnet," a network that serves approximately thirty thousand modems in over one hundred and twenty cities.

However, this did not prevent a major service outage on August 7, 1996, that left more than six million AOL subscribers without access to the online service for most of the day. When users of the online service tried to log in, they were greeted by a message saying "Good-bye from America Online. The system is temporarily unavailable. Please try again in 1 hour and 30 minutes. Thank you for calling."

Clearly, online service providers need to strengthen network access for a rapidly growing member base. Large and established online players have the ability to support the voracious consumer appetite for bandwidth. The increasing demand for high bandwidth network infrastructure is driven by: user growth; a rapid proliferation of bandwidth-greedy graphics-intensive Web applications; the growth of audio and video, which also consume large amounts of bandwidth; and the increased traffic generated by the adoption of the Internet as a mainstream conduit of electronic commerce.

Capacity management is not a problem limited to the Internet or online services; it can also be seen in Intranets (or internal corporate TCP/IP networks). Corporate Intranets are slowing down because traffic patterns are changing. There are more users on the networks, and these users are more dispersed. Data is increasingly exchanged across departmental boundaries, and as enterprises move to decentralized computing, data that used to be confined within local work groups is now shuttling between the users' desktops (the clients) and clusters of servers that contain shared information databases, network applications, and other software resources. These changes create bottlenecks at the pressure points where network traffic is thickest: the backbones that link LANs together and the data pipes that converge on centralized servers.

Further, desktop computers have become far more powerful. PC processing power doubles every eighteen months, and PC operating systems that can perform several tasks at once will soon be the norm. These higher performing devices are capable of rapid-fire data rates that can swamp a network, particularly when coupled with bandwidth-devouring applications such as multimedia (graphics, sound, and video), computer-aided design, and Web-based collaborative software (also called *groupware*).

Clearly, some access providers are better positioned than others to provide the necessary bandwidth and capture greater market shares. The telecommunications and cable carriers control the underlying network facilities that national, regional, and local companies must purchase. Further, current online service providers have established customer bases and marketing experience not presently available to new competitors. In the future, we expect to see a flurry of competitive announcements and consolidation among independent Internet access providers.

Customer Service, Loyalty, and Retention

Many Internet access providers pay too little attention to customer service. Initial experience has indicated that while subscriber growth is increasing among various IAPs, customer retention is poor. In other words, a large number of customers "churn," or suspend their service after a short time. The reasons for this churn are: the difficulty in finding information on the Internet, the lack of useful information, and system problems (poorly developed Web sites, inability to access Web sites, and poor service).

Management needs to focus on achieving customer loyalty. While access providers have control over system issues, they have little control over consumer behavior, especially loyalty. In order to ensure consumer loyalty, providers will have to make substantial improvements on the supply side (content/applications), and provide better network service. Also, IAPs need to make significant investments and expand operations in order to improve the level, quality, and timeliness of customer support. In addition, IAPs need to provide unified billing, sales, and technical service to ensure that they are providing their members with a single point of contact.

Marketing

Given the media focus on the Internet, it is not surprising that existing Internet access providers are using this attention to entice curious consumers. However, this is a short term phenomenon, and rather than touting the generic benefits of surfing the Internet, access providers must specifically address how the Internet can solve existing business problems and respond to consumer needs.

As it is not clear how fast the consumer market for Internet services will grow, access providers need to focus on creating consumer demand. Although a sizable market may eventually exist for Internet access, there are no assurances about how the market will materialize nor for the adoption level among individual consumers. For instance, much of what is available on the Internet is quasi-free now, and as companies begin to charge for services, subscriber growth could slow down.

Marketing also needs to focus on issues related to service quality. Subscriber growth is creating problems in the realm of service quality as capacity growth is not able to keep up with demand. Downloading large files, particularly ones containing video, is extremely slow except with a very high-speed connection. Growth is also related to access costs. Increases in access costs could dampen consumer and business enthusiasm. Internet access providers should focus on devising means to influence these trends.

Finally, marketing needs to focus on new avenues. With the tremendous potential for growth, access providers need to focus less on intra-industry competition, and more on shifting consumer attention from TV and movies to online services. Estimates indicate that if the average subscriber increased time spent online from six to ten hours a week, it would generate another $1 billion in industry revenue [MCN95].

Customer Education

The principal methods of competition in the online industry are price, content, ease of use, and customer service. In addition to these, IAPs need to address consumer/corporate concerns in the following areas:

- **Learning curve.** Consumers coming online face an information overload and become scared about the amount of time required to overcome the learning curve. They are also worried about the knowledge obsolescence that frequently accompanies technology.

- **Complexity.** While it may seem easy enough for anyone with a PC and a modem to access the Internet, the task of gaining Internet access involves an understanding of multiple access options and integration with TCP/IP protocol software and corporate networks. This complexity needs to be mitigated by better user interfaces.

- **Security.** Secure conduct of commerce over the Internet is an important issue for risk-averse consumers. Security measures include firewalls (preventing corporate data from external invasions), authentication, data encryption, and transaction validation (see Chapter 5).

- **Speed and reliability.** Customers require stable network operation with maximum uptime and support for a variety of applications. Consumers are often worried about speed and reliability as it directly affects their work. For instance, customers who place a stock order on the Internet do not want to have to wait for more than twenty seconds for a confirmation. Access providers must guarantee customers that transactions are secure and will be carried out as fast as possible.

Corporate users and consumers will migrate toward access providers who minimize the complexity of the Internet. While the open Internet model has tremendous appeal for broad participation by vendors and users alike, it is somewhat like the Wild West in terms of its current lack of hospitality toward new users. Corporate users are also concerned with security and reliability. Consumer usage will accelerate only if technologies and services become easier to use.

In order for the potential of the Internet to be realized, marketing programs must be used to generate customer demand, and content providers must develop interesting and compelling applications for consumers to use. Consumers need to be encouraged and guided in their use of this new communications/information delivery medium.

Changing Technology behind Internet Access

In order to access the Internet via a dial-up connection, the user requires a modem attached to his or her computer. A phone call (usually a local phone call) is made via the modem to the nearest Point of Presence (POP) provided by the selected access provider. Once connection is made between the user's modem and one of the modems at the POP, the user's Internet software initiates a "log-on," a process that combines validation of passwords and account status, which is followed by the choice of Internet protocol which allows a full connection between the user's PC and the service provider's links to the Internet.

Internet access products and services can be categorized as follows:

- **Basic terminal emulation or shell account.** These applications enable PCs to connect to host or mainframe systems as if the users were sitting in front of the appropriate terminal for that particular host computer. Terminal emulation allows user access to all the applications available at the host system (such as IBM mainframes and DEC VAX systems).

- **Dial-up access with SLIP and PPP**. Serial Line IP (SLIP) and Point to Point IP (PPP) are communication protocols that provide a compact way of packaging TCP/IP information packets from the PC for easy movement between many different kinds of computers. They also enable PC users to become part of the Internet and obtain an IP (Internet Protocol) address that allows users to publish information by running their own Web servers on their PCs.

- **Integrated services digital network (ISDN).** POTS (plain old telephone system) is too slow to handle the high-speed data connections required to quickly download the large amounts of information needed for file transfer, graphics, and full motion video. Many users are frustrated by the long response times. Alternative technologies like ISDN are being used for data-intensive Internet applications. Internet access providers such as Netcom are beginning to use ISDN to accommodate faster transmission rates up to 128 Kbps.

- **High-speed (or leased line) access.** Leased circuits at speeds of 56 Kbps, 1.5 Mbps (T1), 10 Mbps, and 45 Mbps (T3) are ideal for those who want to make extensive use of the Internet and require a dedicated line to operate at high bandwidth. Leased lines are useful for companies who can afford the start-up fees (from $500 to $13,000) and monthly fees (from $600 to $42,000).

Table 2.6 summarizes the various access methods.

Network Bandwidth and Internet Access   Speed, simplicity, and economy are key to the evolution and adoption of the Internet. Online users are increasingly impatient with delays and roadblocks to access, especially since they are accustomed to quick response times on their business networks and cable TV networks.

The network response time depends on bandwidth, which is the speed at which information can be sent or received. Response time is usually limited by the speed of the connection to the Internet, since the Internet itself

Table 2.6 Common Internet Access Methods

Type of Internet Access	Protocol	Speed	Cost
Dial-up (shell account): Easy and inexpensive, but cannot use Netscape.	Terminal emulation	9.6, 14.4 Kbps	$6–$20/month, unlimited usage
Dial-up IP: Full access to Internet, but more complex to configure and set up.	SLIP, PPP	14.4 Kbps 28.8 Kbps	$20/month for 20 hours, $1–$2/hour thereafter
Digital dial-up (ISDN): Not widely available, and has problems with procurement and installation.	PPP	64, 128 Kbps	$30–$300/month + installation 1 cent/minute
Leased line: High-speed dedicated link, but can be expensive if not used frequently.	IP	56 Kbps 1.544 Mbps (T1)	$2500 $10K+$1500/month

consists of ultra high-speed "backbone" links (see Fig. 2.1). It is irrelevant that the Internet is capable of transmitting billions of information packets per second when users are hooked up to it with a 28.8 Kbps modem. In the past, most of the applications used on the Internet were character-based, not graphics intensive, and bandwidth was less of an issue. The connections were invariably faster than the information flowing over those connections, and thus the raw speed of transmission was not critical. With the wider selection of content, people are using the Internet more, and slowdowns are occurring. The Internet is taking care of its bandwidth concerns; new high-speed backbones called vBNS (see Fig. 2.1) are being added and upgraded.

While "backbone" bandwidth will eventually evolve to meet demands, the local link from the subscriber's home to the online service provider still runs at a very slow speed. It is becoming apparent that 14.4 Kbps or even 28.8 Kbps will not be sufficient for very long, especially for users who want to publish content. Providers must be hooked up at much higher speeds (from 56 Kbps for low-volume sites to 45 Mbps for the really popular providers) in order to satisfy the information needs of thousands of surfers.

Consequently, the subscriber–service provider link needs to evolve more and more toward high-speed digital connections. There are two competing high-speed technologies available that customers need to choose between: telco's ISDN services and cable modems.

On-Ramp Technology: Is ISDN the Future?   The major attraction of ISDN (Integrated Services Digital Network) technology—and the reason it is being deployed by telcos—is that it provides high-speed access to the Internet over existing telephone wires. ISDN links bypass the digital-to-analog conversion (the modem function) that is usually needed to translate a digital signal from a PC to an analog one that can be sent down the telephone lines. ISDN connections link the user's computer directly to the POP using data rates that are generally either 64 Kbps or 128 Kbps (higher with compression).

ISDN is a multi-purpose system integrating a large variety of voice, data, and image services via a single network. ISDN is what is known as a second generation telecommunication service. The digital computer-related techniques of ISDN urge the development and more efficient use of the telephone network by allowing efficient data communications and telematic services.

ISDN was conceived as a natural evolution of the telephone network based on its existing structure. Because of its ability to transport a wide range of voice and data services simultaneously, ISDN was seen as a prime vehicle to satisfy the telecommunications needs of multimedia services. The introduction of ISDN was expected to allow single service networks to be changed into broadband communications networks capable of carrying a wide range of services.

In order to access ISDN, users need an ISDN adapter to connect their computers to the digital network. A home ISDN connection is called a Basic Rate Interface (BRI) and consists of three data channels, called 2B+D. Users employ the two "B" channels, each of which can send and receive 64 Kbps of data. The "D" channel is for control purposes and is never used by consumers. Users also can bind the two "B" channels together to create a 128 Kbps line. It is expected that telcos will soon begin offering home users installation of ISDN Primary Rate Interface (PRI) lines instead of BRI. PRI circuits are also called 24B+D, which means that up to twenty-four times 64 Kbps channels can be bound together to create a 1.5 Mbps line.

However, consumers cannot currently call up the local phone company, ask for ISDN, and have it installed. Although the telcos promise a lot, they are quite poor at delivery. Furthermore, the consumer is not well informed to know what ISDN specifications to order. In short, while ISDN offers a lot of promise, telcos make it overly difficult for the individual to order the service. Given these problems, it remains to be seen what history has in place for ISDN technology.

On-Ramp Technology: Are Cable Modems the Future?   Today, running a Netscape browser over a 28.8 Kbps dial-up line is like owning a Maserati and being forced to drive it under twenty miles per hour because of the road conditions (limited bandwidth). Cable companies have proposed cable modems as the solution to these bandwidth limitations. Cable wires can carry digital data as much as 1,000 times faster than telephone lines. In other words, a 2 megabit file (about the size of a simple image) that would take 2.3 minutes to download over a telephone line with a 14.4 baud modem would only take 0.5 second to download over a cable wire with a cable modem.

The entire cable industry knows that if it can get Internet users to sample what network access is like at 10 Mbps, they will have a winning product. The cable industry is the major owner of most of the competitive-access-providers market (running fiber access around cities), but is not a force in the consumer market. Consumers have come to resent cable providers for what they feel is price gouging, and may be reluctant to buy their Internet service from the cable industry.

To attract customers, cable companies need to convince consumers of the value of their product. They need to build links to neighborhoods by offering a service, via cable modem, that is so demonstrably better than conventional low-speed dial-up models that the consumer would be willing to pay $25 a month for the cable modem, and an additional $25 a month or more for certain value-added services. Several companies are already providing cable modem access to the Internet at speeds of 10 Mbps for an access charge of $35 to $50 a month. The cable modems used by these companies, estimated to cost between $2000 and $2500, are made by Motorola, LANcity, and Hybrid Networks. A cheap commercially viable cable modem is not yet available. The current challenge for the modem manufacturers is to adopt some form of industry-wide technical standards.

Vendors and users alike are watching CATV-based Internet access very closely. Although CATV technology promises superior performance, the underlying infrastructure will require substantial upgrades, to meet the online service requirements. Specifically, bandwidth capability must be upgraded to handle the interactive aspects of online traffic. Transmissions from home on cable's "upstream path" are less than ideal currently and must be substantially improved. Most multiple system operators (MSOs) are already making these upgrades as part of their push to prepare for video and telephony competition from the Regional Bell Operating Companies (RBOCs) and wireless cable operators.

Changing Technology behind the Access Provider

The previous section examined Internet access technology from the consumer's perspective. Access providers face a different set of technological issues. The requirements placed on an Internet access provider's network are twofold. First, providers must be able to aggregate local user traffic and deliver it (without a toll charge to the individual user) to an Internet gateway. As there are several gateways (or Network Access Points), a high-speed backbone network is essential to bundle the traffic and cost-effectively transport it to and from the Internet.

Access points to the Internet are called points of presence. Small businesses or individual users, who do not have a dedicated link to the Internet, can establish a dial-up connection to a point of presence (POP) using a modem and a telephone line.

Points of presence are necessary to reduce toll charges. Most IAPs establish POPs in major cities to create local Internet gateways that a user can access via a local call. These local gateways, or POPs, include modem pools and network interfaces that convert analog dial-up signals from the user into digital bit streams that can be multiplexed and efficiently transported to a backbone network. At the backbone network, a hub location acts as a server to connect the incoming bit stream to the Internet gateway.

Figure 2.2 illustrates the structure of a POP. The hardware in a POP consists of four main items:

- **Server platform system.** Typically the IAP will be running a powerful UNIX-based server system such as a Sun Sparcstation to serve a multitude of customers.

- **Networking infrastructure.** The networking infrastructure (routers, terminal servers, and switches) provides a point-of-access to the Internet for consumers (typically using modems for dial-up access) and corporate users (using dial-up or leased line access from LANs). Most service providers have installed ATM (Asynchronous Transfer Mode) into their network backbone. This technology provides more room for data traveling over a network.

- **Leased telecommunications lines.** A leased line from a local telephone company.

- **Modems.** In order to allow dial-up users to access the IAP, a batch of modems is required. These can range from racks of single modems to racks of 48 digital modems. The largest player in the analog modem market is US Robotics, while Ascend Communications is leading the way in the ISDN market.

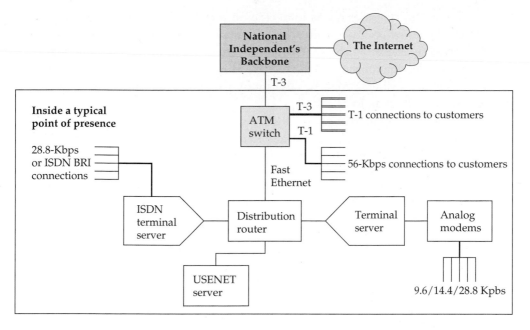

Figure 2.2   Structure of a Point of Presence (POP)

The local loop and backbone elements comprising the POP's access system must have sufficient capacity to offer customers acceptable transmission speeds and grades of service. Given high traffic volumes and contention (or potential blockage rates), each network element must be configured to provide on-demand access for the users. In addition to providing capacity to handle traffic volumes, the IAP must insure that there is route diversity in the network to avoid outages.

In the future, POPs must be engineered to provide more advanced transmission techniques. These include providing ISDN access, allowing users to send and receive information at up to 128 Kbps in contrast to the effective limit of 28.8 Kbps on local dial-up. On the backbone, either Switched Megabit Digital Service (SMDS) or Asynchronous Transmission Mode (ATM) will be required to increase the simultaneous transport of data messages, voice, file transfer, or video images.

Management Problems Facing Access Providers   The requirements for becoming an Internet access provider can be formidable. These include setting up a point of presence (local access ramp) to provide Internet access for a large number of users, providing software services (managing information routing), and setting up distribution backbone systems (getting the message out).

The access provider needs to decide on the right level of service, which affects the users' ability to gain access to the Internet at busy times. This can be varied by adjusting the POP's user/modem ratio. In the past many access providers have been criticized for not having enough modems to service their subscribers properly, with many providers offering a ratio of 40:1 and some as high as 150:1.

As the dial-up market grows and matures, access providers will have to find the optimum ratios required to balance quality of service against additional hardware costs. The subject is important as the ratio dictates how likely consumers are to gain access to the service at any given time. Most ISPs tend to either have an optimum user:modem ratio or say they will add as much hardware as is required to maintain their quality of service. However, this is easier said than done. Upgrading hardware is easy when the provider has only a few hundred users but it becomes increasingly expensive as the number of users grows.

The growth in Internet access is creating interesting problems for service providers with respect to computer addressing (an identification system analogous to telephone numbers). Within the next five years, each person who uses the Internet is going to have to change one or more of the computer programs he or she uses to access and retrieve information from the Internet. Every computer that is attached to the Internet must have a unique Internet Protocol (IP) address, and they are running out.

The current generation of IP addresses look like this: 255.255.255.255. Each part of the IP address is a number between zero and 255, and each has four parts. There are many combinations of numbers that are unusable, and the usable combinations are almost exhausted. The solution is to create a new addressing scheme large enough to satisfy future growth. This new addressing system, Ipv6, is expected replace the current version, called Ipv4, in the near future. Many of the problems associated with this type of address space migration are unknown and could result in some interesting and unanticipated side-effects.

Table 2.7 summarizes the key features of today's Internet, and suggests what users can expect in the future.

2.5 Summary

This chapter introduced the Internet, its commercialization, and the service providers industry and discussed the key factors responsible for the explosive growth in Internet connections. The chapter also discussed the economic and social trends driving the need for data access and exchange that

Table 2.7 Summary of Internet Features

Internet Present	*Internet Future*
Small-volume exchange and transmission of information.	Large-volume, high-speed exchange of data and multimedia.
Single function optimized for asynchronous data transfer.	Multiple functions optimized for digital convergence combining voice, images, and data.
Uniform service grades with absolutely no discrimination.	Varied service grades and multiple service levels based on reliability, priority, and price.
Charges based on usage.	Varied charging system based on traffic patterns and content.

are gaining momentum daily, opening up exciting new opportunities for access providers worldwide.

However, a great deal of uncertainty spans a variety of management issues, including marketing and pricing, consumer behavior, and technology. This is good news for many entrepreneurs: history provides numerous examples where market uncertainty creates the potential for shaping new products and markets, and building a loyal customer base. The ways in which access providers will exploit and shape this immature market remain to be seen.

Chapter 3

World Wide Web— Applications

Chapter Outline

The Internet supports a variety of important tools, such as file transfer, electronic mail, and news groups. However, no single Internet application has grabbed the attention of the marketplace so dramatically as the World Wide Web (WWW), perhaps one of the most popular and fastest growing phenomena in the history of computing. Seemingly overnight, the Web has transformed a bleak, text-based Internet landscape into a colorful cyberworld brimming with social, artistic, and commercial opportunities. Experts anticipate that Web use soon is going to be as prevalent and widespread as telephone use. Instead of asking for a telephone number or e-mail address, people soon will begin to ask for a home page or Web address.

The Web is a global information-sharing architecture that integrates manifold online content and information servers in a fast, cost-effective, and easy-to-use manner. The Web is the software foundation on which many emerging electronic commerce applications are based. Visually, the Web is a point-and-click user interface on the Internet. In terms of content, the Web can be thought of as a gigantic Internet library. It enables the creation, manipulation, organization, and retrieval of documents that contain audio and video clips, graphical images, and formatted text. Web servers, also called Web sites, are the equivalent of library books, and Web "pages" are the specific pages in these books. A Web server is essentially a collection of multimedia pages. Users typically start their exploration of a Web site at the "home page," which often serves as a table of contents. A home page is accessed by entering the domain name of a site. For example, the home page for Ford has the domain name "ford.com," and from there, users can look at other parts of the site.

The growth of Web servers has been astounding. According to the *New Scientist* [NS94], the WWW was growing at roughly one percent a day, a doubling period of less than ten weeks. Matthew Gray's *WebCrawler Report* estimates that the number of Web servers that deliver content to desktop browsers have exploded from an estimated 130 in June 1993 to over 15,700 Web servers in April 1995. Since then, more than 100,000 Web sites have been set up. The growth of Web servers within organizations has also been phenomenal. Rough estimates indicate that for every eight Web servers sold, seven of them are for internal corporate use. Although still in the experimental stage, a relatively high proportion of companies are attempting to incorporate the Internet into their business models. It is estimated that 25 percent of U.S. companies have Internet-related pilot projects underway, while almost 50 percent of U.S. companies have invested in some form of Internet-related infrastructure.

Despite its relative youth, the Web has enabled important advances in the areas of publishing, communications, commerce, and corporate computing. This chapter provides an overview of the Web infrastructure and its role in electronic commerce. Rather than discussing the nitty-gritty details of the Web, this chapter presents a macro-view of the various Web applications. More importantly, the chapter discusses how the initial Web architecture is rapidly evolving in different directions and enabling previously unthinkable applications.

3.1 Brief History of the Web

Ironically, for all its commercial success, the Web initially was developed to enable a fairly prosaic application: document sharing between distant scientists. In 1989, Tim Berners-Lee at CERN (Conseil Européen pour la Recherche Nucléaire, now called European Laboratory for Particle Physics) began the Web project. The goal of the project was two-fold: (a) to develop ways of linking distant documents (hyperlink); and (b) to find ways of enabling users to work together (collaborative authoring). While the second goal has been elusive, the first has had tremendous impact on the computing industry.

As soon as the basic outline of the Web was complete, CERN made all the software source code publicly available. This sharing of source code created a tremendous following among programmers, who, like auto mechanics, like to look at the internals of the engine. The other added advantage was that programmers contributed their efforts to debugging the software and extending its functionality in ways never even envisioned initially. The legitimization of the "freeware" software distribution model is perhaps the reason behind the success of the Web.

The freeware objective was to encourage collaboration among programmers, and several hundred software developers from the United States, particularly from the National Center for Supercomputing Applications (NCSA) at the University of Illinois, were involved in the initial software development of the Web. By using the source code developed at CERN, NCSA programmers developed Mosaic in 1993, the first browser with a graphical user interface.

The key members of the engineering teams that developed the original Mosaic and original Web server software at CERN went on to form Netscape Communications and develop the Netscape Navigator in December 1994. This was the first commercially available browser for the Web to include built-in security capabilities, which facilitate commercial transactions over the Internet.

In 1995, the market for networked computing software was rocked by the Web's movement from "networking technology" to "social phenomenon" in the last half of the year. And the year was marked by a tidal wave of unprecedented events that bordered, occasionally, on hysteria. Netscape, a two-year-old company with essentially no revenue, went public in August, 1995, valued at $1.1 billion, and was valued at more than $5 billion by year end.

To enable its continued development without proprietary influences, the Web project moved from CERN to the Massachusetts Institute of Technology (MIT) in 1995, and is now called the W3 Consortium (www.w3.org). This Consortium coordinates the development of WWW standards to ensure certain uniformity and minimize repetition of effort.

3.2 What Exactly Is the Web?

The Web has rapidly become the *de facto* standard for navigating, publishing information, and executing transactions on the Internet and Intranets. What began as a set of simple protocols and formats has proven to be superb testbed for various sophisticated multimedia, publishing, and retrieval concepts.

Simply stated, the Web is a collection of distributed documents referred to as "pages" located on computers (or servers) all over the world. Servers store hypertext markup language (HTML) files and respond to requests. Through the use of a browser, PC users can find and view server-based documents. Browsers like Netscape ensure easy access to server-based documents, and display multimedia data. Future browsers will include editor-like abilities, application linking, audio and video integration, database front ends, and ways to combine information with transactions.

Components of the Web Architecture   To use the Web, in addition to an Internet connection, a user needs a special piece of software called a Web browser (such as Netscape Navigator). The browser acts as a graphical interface between the user and the Internet—it sends the necessary commands to request data from other computers and then formats them for the user's screen. Documents that are formatted using hypertext markup language (HTML) contain taglines that inform the browser how to format them.

The Web is based on a three-part architecture:

- **HTML**—Hypertext markup language, the format for Web pages, provides both formatting and hyperlinking.

- **HTTP**—Hypertext transfer protocol, the protocol for communications between Web servers and browsers.

- **CGI**—The common gateway interface, the interface for invoking programs from Web servers.

Figure 3.1 shows the components of Web architecture, including Web clients, Web servers, HTTP protocol language for Web client/server com-

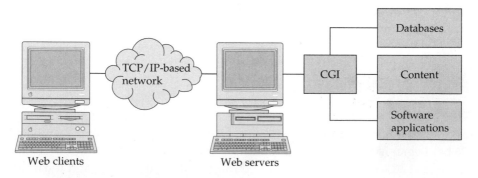

Figure 3.1   The Web Architecture

munication, and applications. These components are explained further in Chapter 4. Within the confines of this architecture, hundreds of entrepreneurs have produced a tidal wave of software programs and tools.

The Web architecture forms the basis for electronic commerce applications that involve building software in which the functions are distributed among application servers (where applications reside), data servers (where most of the data resides), and a group of client computers that are usually networked PCs (where the information users work).

The power and influence of the Web architecture becomes obvious when one considers its profound impact on online services. For instance, CompuServe plans to move its content on to Web servers. Once it does so, subscribers will be able to access CompuServe forums, content, and information services through Microsoft's Internet Explorer, a Web browser, instead of CompuServe's proprietary technology WinCim 3.0. CompuServe's "guided surfing" model attempts to provide a context-based guide to the Internet, with the content personalized to each customer's requirements. The move to the Web will mean that they no longer need to produce their information in two forms.

The Web and Electronic Commerce   Figure 3.2 shows a block diagram depicting the key elements that constitute a Web-based electronic commerce architecture: client browser, Web server, and third-party services. The client browser interacts with the Web server, which then intermediates the inter-

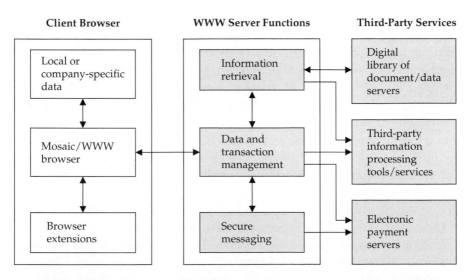

Figure 3.2   Block Diagram Depicting an Electronic Commerce Architecture

action with third-party services. The Web server functions can be categorized into information retrieval, data and transaction management, and security. The third-party services could be other Web servers that provide content, information processing tools, and electronic payment systems. These functions will be elaborated on in subsequent chapters.

The client browser resides on the user's PC and provides an interface to the various types of content. For instance, if the user retrieves a graphics file from a Web server, the browser automatically starts up the browser extension to display the graphics file. Remember that there are many types of graphics formats available—JPEG, GIF, TIFF, BMP, and several others. The browser has to be smart enough to understand what file it is downloading and what browser extension it needs to activate to display the file. Browsers are also capable of manipulating local files.

The client browser/Web server that forms the heart and soul of the Web architecture is considerably more flexible than the traditional mainframe or host-based model it replaces. In host-based computing a mainframe does the processing while users interact with the system through dumb terminals. Compared to the distributed processing seen in the Web architecture, host-based computing is a monolithic system. The Web architecture allows PC users to connect to a network and enhance PC capabilities by providing access to distributed databases and other computing resources. The Web can mask the complexity and incompatibilities of operating systems and allow users to move from application to application and from one release to the next without spending hundreds of dollars on software.

The Web and Intranets   The Web can be used on any TCP/IP network—not just the public Internet, but also private corporate networks. Increasingly, companies are using the Web architecture on internal networks that are not intended for public use. While many organizations are still trying to figure out how to make money using the Web, an increasing number of companies are saving money through the implementation of Intranets. Netscape has stated that approximately half of its server sales are to companies implementing Intranets.

Some of the factors driving the growth in the Intranet marketplace include:

- **Open standards lead to interoperability.** Because Web technology is typically nonproprietary, it is inexpensive. The use of this inexpensive technology allows any kind of a terminal access to information within an organization. Thus, PCs can easily communicate with Macs and UNIX workstations.

- **Ease of use.** Not only are browsers very easy to use for the average employee, but authoring pages in HTML is as simple as adding tag lines to text for administrators. This is particularly important for those kinds of pages or data that change frequently, such as product catalogs, technical manuals, and corporate procedures.

- **Effective middleware.** The Web is increasingly being used as "middleware." Middleware is software that insulates applications from the complexity of the heterogeneous hardware and software. As middleware, the Web isolates applications from system interfaces; enables comprehensive data access and provides data management services; interacts with other applications and provides open communication interfaces for distributed applications; enables workflow integration, software distribution, and upgrade management; and provides security for transaction-based applications.

Although many corporations have Web pages or are in the process of adding them, not much commerce is being transacted on the Web. Most corporate Web sites are being used to provide a presence—marketing in a new medium—for the organization because for now, the Web has mostly information that organizations and individuals do not mind giving away. This is expected to change over time.

3.3 Why Is the Web Such a Hit?

Reasons for the amazing success of the Web include:

> Ease of navigation and use.
>
> Ease of publishing content.
>
> New distribution models.
>
> Enabling a network-centric computing paradigm.
>
> Enabling new intra-business applications.

The Web and Ease of Use

The ease of use is a major driver of Web growth. Using a simple graphical interface, the Web browser (software that resides on the client) issues the commands, makes the connections, and transmits the data with point-and-click simplicity. It allows users to send e-mail and access gopher sites as well as use telnet, FTP, and other functions without having to master arcane commands.

In the Web, sites are interconnected to each other through highlighted (hyperlinked) words. By clicking on the highlighted word, a user can be transported into another Web site that contains a related document without even knowing where that other Web site is! This process can keep continuing because this new site may contain additional hyperlinks to other sites, thus creating a Web of connections.

The combination of hypertext and multimedia is powerful for nontechnical users. For example, a search for semiconductors on Yahoo! (an Internet directory) could lead to Intel's Web site where a user can get financial data, product listings, and other company-specific information. This hyperlinking can continue for some time and is indeed one of the reasons for the Web's huge popularity.

In a sense, the Web makes the Internet dummy-proof. Before the advent of the Web, navigating the Internet was difficult, requiring technical skill and patience. Because of the intuitive nature of hypertext, many nontechnical users are able to navigate the various Internet databases without having to learn complicated commands. Also, the use of graphics and multimedia contributed to a user-friendly environment. Recent advances in multimedia are attracting users who were intimidated or repelled by the text-intensive interfaces of DOS and UNIX.

The Web and Ease of Publishing

Another major reason for the success of the Web is the ease of server setup, administration, and publishing of content. Web Server programs (called HTTPD or HTTP deamons) were placed in the public domain by various companies and could be downloaded for free. The system requirements for running a Web server are minimal. Even individuals with low-end PCs could become information providers on a global scale and compete with large organizations.

The concept of Internet users becoming publishers was unthinkable prior to the Web, as the complex nature of servers made publishing content on networks extremely difficult. The simplicity of HTML allows individual users to become publishers themselves and contribute to the expanding database of documents on the Web. For instance, America Online has a service called "My Home Page," which allows members to quickly and easily create their own personal home page with text, photographs, and graphics.

Web publishing also enables personalized publishing. No longer will subscribers be forced to buy an entire newspaper just to read an article or area of interest to them. Readers can already create their own "newspaper" through services such as PointCast that lets them request certain categories of information. Want the stock market section to be the first page? No problem, stocks can be the first page and the only page. The Web enables the reader to go from being a passive recipient of information to a proactive creator of specialized information available anytime and hyperlinked. In other words, the reader becomes a quasi-publisher.

The Web as a New Distribution Channel

We are reaching a state where virtually any good or service that can be bought, either by businesses or consumers, can be purchased online. Although that is the long-term implication, in the shorter run, companies are excited by the Web's ability to deliver digital goods faster and cheaper than any traditional means and its ability to make certain transactions, such as banking, convenient.

Take for instance, software distribution. Consumers can download it right now (as opposed to mail order, which still would make you wait a day or longer) from sites such as software.net (http://software.net), a site run by CyberSource Corporation, without having to run to the nearest software store. As bandwidth increases, downloading (buying) the latest music CD or video or book or anything that can be digitized becomes instantaneous and far less costly than the traditional model of distribution that includes packaging, physical transport, and middlemen.

The Web and Network-Centric Computing

The success of the Web has opened management's eyes to the power of network computing, and network computing could determine the future of Microsoft, IBM, Oracle, and Sun. When the computing industry last experienced a major shift in computing power—from mainframes and terminals to desktop PCs—many established firms simply failed. Others, like IBM, responded only after seceding control of the PC marketplace to upstarts like Microsoft. To those who missed the early signs of change, these new leaders seemed to come out of nowhere. A similar scenario is occurring today, and this time it is centered around the Web.

The Web epitomizes network-centric computing. With network-centric computing, concerns about the power, speed, memory size, or applications software of PCs are lessened; it is what the computers connect to that matters. For over a decade, Sun Microsystems tried to make this telling point with the slogan, "the network is the computer," but few understood its meaning. Today Sun advertisements feature a dog called "Network" and the promise that whatever you need, Network can get it for you.

Thinking of the network as central, and the computer and its software as peripheral, requires a major shift in business strategy. Evidence of the Web forcing shifts in business strategy are reported quite frequently in popular press. The most famous one is Microsoft, which has revamped its product lines to facilitate the notion of network-centric computing.

The movement toward network-centric computing is expected to fuel the growth of the software industry, even in such mundane areas as word processing. Today, almost all word processing tools can act as authoring tools capable of creating Web content. The proliferation of content-authoring tools has made it relatively easy for individuals to share information containing text, audio, and video clips with a global community. Further, most database proprietary front-ends are slowly being dumped in favor of browser navigation software that provides access to content. More recently, the market has seen a proliferation of plug-ins (such as Progressive Network's RealAudio players and Macromedia's Shockwave), which extend the capabilities of Web browsers. In short, many activities centered around the notion of network-centric computing are under way, and the potential ramifications of such a computing direction remain to be seen.

The Web and New Intra-Business Applications

Over the last decade, business customers have asked the computer industry to provide them with the following:

An open environment that includes products and services from different vendors. This enables customers to buy what they need from whomever they choose.

The ability to network and integrate new technology with existing systems.

The ability to manage computer resources and support users in a way that will reduce costs while implementing business strategies.

The computer industry has been slow in delivering on these requests. With the advent of the Web, which enables the above capabilities, business customers are flocking toward Web-based Intranets. The goal is to to utilize the benefits of the "open" architecture to link users and resources throughout the organization. Preliminary market research indicates that over the next several years, revenues generated in the Intranet segment will dwarf those in the Internet segment.

Firms are beginning to recognize the central role of the Web in planning future systems architecture. However, if the past is any indicator, network-centric or Internet-based computing will no more displace mainframe technology than credit cards replaced checks and paper currency. The reason is that there are certain classes of applications that are not appropriate for the Web, such as applications that handle large-volume transactions in mission-critical areas like transaction processing.

3.4 The Web and Electronic Commerce

Companies use the Web to communicate with customers and suppliers by publishing content on their Web server for widespread distribution. Motivated by the potential for business-to-business as well as business-to-consumer commerce, many firms are taking steps toward selling their products on the Web.

The Web is also changing and reshaping industries whose core business is information transfer between the firm and the consumer. Examples of such business functions include advertising, marketing, sales, and customer service. Industries that engage in information transfer with customers include banking and financial services (see Chapter 7), retailing (see Chapter 8), and electronic publishing and edutainment (see Chapter 9).

Within these industries, the Web is used for four major tasks:

Attracting new customers via marketing and advertising.

Serving existing customers via customer service and support function.

Developing new markets and distribution channels for existing products.

Developing new information-based products.

Marketing and Advertising   Marketing-related uses of the Web include brand-name management, disseminating product catalogs and sales information, and product announcements.

In the physical world, "location, location, location" is the marketing mantra; in the Web world, it is "content, content, content." The significance of the Web's ease of use has not been lost on marketing departments, many of whom believe that the Web provides the friendly interface that will open new channels for interacting with and selling directly to customers. While companies have yet to realize revenues directly from Web sales, the majority of Web usage by business still revolves around activities that do not involve the direct transfer of money.

Advertisers are discovering that innovative, high-quality content attracts consumer attention. Advertisers have to resist the temptation to simply dust off old brochures and put them online. They need to create new offerings to exploit the Internet's unique properties: access to all of a wide range of users; ability to provide unlimited information for a low cost; detailed interaction with customers, particularly critical ones; the ability to create distinct market segments; and the ability to personalize services for individual users.

The Internet technology that makes marketing and advertising feasible is the ability to broadcast information using Web bulletin boards, Web billboards, PointCasting, and Intercasting (see Chapter 9).

Customer Service and Support   The Web is particularly useful in handling information queries that otherwise would be handled by a customer service representative. The Web can perform a variety of customer-oriented tasks including:

- **A new distribution channel for software, software patches, and support information.** Electronic distribution of software isn't a new concept. Years ago, IBM began experimenting with software distribution via satellite. More recently, Seattle-based Online Interactive (OLI) made a pact with Microsoft to distribute the software maker's products via the Internet. However, technological restrictions still affect delivery. Where bandwidth allows, software can be delivered directly to the user's desktop. Where bandwidth is prohibitive, distributors ship the software through delivery services.

- **Customer interaction and query capability.** For example, using the Web, customers of Federal Express (see Fig. 3.3) and United Parcel Service (UPS) can check the location and status of specific overnight packages. Customers can log on to the Federal Express Web page and track the status of their own package. Customer service interaction is made feasible by Web forms and the ability to link the Web server to back-end databases containing copious amounts of information.

- **New avenues for customer relationships.** Customer relationships are very important in high-contact industries like banking, and the Web is helping banks form more direct relationships with their customers. For example, Wells Fargo Bank provides a service that enables customers to check personal bank account balances and recent transactions. Such services provide customers with the information they need to make good financial decisions, and allow banks to better communicate with their customers.

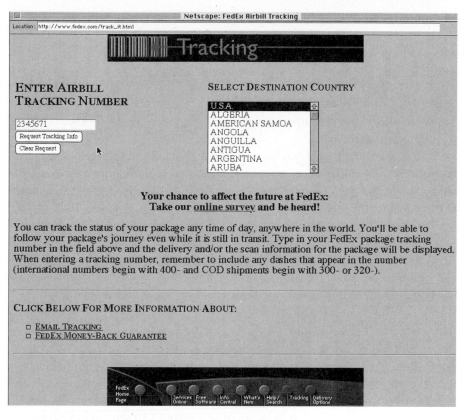

Figure 3.3   FedEx's Online Tracing System.

- **Access to government information.** The Web is also changing the way government agencies interact with and provide information to the public. For example, the Securities and Exchange Commission (SEC) publishes the filings of public companies, information that is invaluable in making investment decisions, on their Web server. Similarly, the Internal Revenue Service (IRS) provides tax information on its server. The Web can also be used to find employment opportunities with government agencies such as the Forest Service.

Developing New Markets and Distribution Channels   The Web will enable firms to build on the assets that they already possess, like brand name recognition, operational infrastructure, information, and customer relationships in order to develop new markets and distribution channels.

The publishing industry provides a number of examples of how the Web has helped to create new markets. For example, Time Warner has created a popular Web site called *Pathfinder* on which they publish segments of their popular magazines like *Time, Money*, and *Sports Illustrated*.

Pathfinder generates revenue by selling advertising and by charging customers for access to online content. Publishers using the Web need to determine how to: convert proprietary online information services into open, pay-per-page services targeted to specific customer segments; translate print-based publication and market expertise into online services focused on defined interest areas; and implement services that enable publishers to receive payment for corporate, professional, and individual copies of copyrighted publications.

The software industry has been a pioneer in using the Internet for product distribution. Computer software companies like Netscape take advantage of the new Web distribution channels to sell and distribute software electronically.

The beauty of the Web marketplace is that it does not differentiate between large and small players. For example, ID software, the maker of *Doom* (a gory game in which a player makes a journey through various levels of rooms and mazes in order to save humanity from homicidal mutants), has used the Web to achieve enormous success. *Doom* was released as shareware on the Internet in December 1993, and is by some estimates the most installed software of all time. According to *Doom* lore, *Doom* was banned from some work sites when companies reported that productivity went down because workers were playing *Doom*. ID software is hoping repeat the success of *Doom* with its new product, *Quake*, which is also being distributed over the Internet.

ID's success illustrates how a small software publisher with almost no marketing budget can take advantage of the Internet to create and distribute new products. The Web broadens the variety of content available to the consumer and offers the creator of content a large market with minimal distribution costs.

Developing New Online Products/Services   An example of the new and innovative Web-based products is Switchboard (Fig. 3.4), an address lookup system that has the ability to search through more than ninety million names nationwide. Using Switchboard, a user can locate individuals or businesses simply by typing the name into the Web page. In just a few seconds, the name or names appear on the computer screen with an address and telephone number. The information on Switchboard is provided by Database America, a demographical gathering company that compiles such data from telephone books and other public documents.

Much like a telephone directory service, Switchboard provides directory assistance for the entire country. Similar in structure to CD-ROM programs that sell for between $50 and $170, the Web version of Switchboard is free.

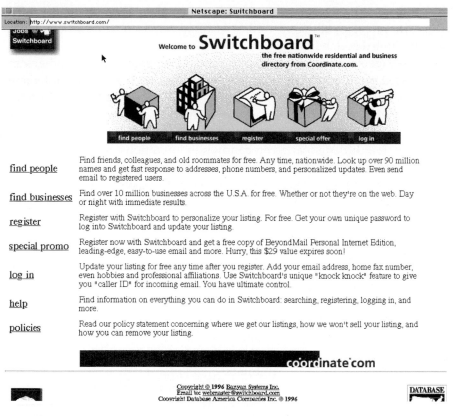

Figure 3.4   The Next Generation of White Pages: switchboard.com.

The service has some shortcomings, but it is cheap, easy-to-use, and, importantly, it allows for the addition of new features. For instance, Switchboard has a "knock-knock" function that controls who can gain access to an individual's e-mail address. Using this feature, an individual who wants to make contact must first send a message through the intermediary system without having access to the actual online address. When the target user reads the note, he or she can decide whether to respond to the sender.

Education and entertainment are two areas where new online products have the potential to do well because of the interactivity enabled by the Web. In the case of education, students can do research and receive instructional material from anywhere without having to physically go to a particular city or academic institution. The longer term potential of education on the Web lies in the creation of new products that enhance the transfer of knowledge from not only companies that are currently in the business of long-distance learning but also from major academic and research institutions. From a user's perspective, the benefits are compelling: the ability to receive education or training whenever and wherever convenient without being tied to the instructor's schedule or location. The economics for the provider are compelling as well: no capital required to build classrooms and unlimited scalability.

In the case of entertainment, players can play games against other game players scattered all over the world. Companies such as Mpath Interactive are already exploring game play on the Web. Users will be able to download software and play others online without regard to the actual whereabouts of each player. Although downloading graphics-intensive games currently is a difficult feat given bandwidth limitations, it is just a matter of time before such downloads are feasible. These opportunities are major revenue opportunities for the game providers, both existing and new entrants, and a new form of entertainment for consumers.

Managing the External Web Interface   Organizations need to realize that customers come to a site because it is there, but they will come back if there is value. Far too many vendors and organizations are focusing on sizzle over substance in the content they are providing online. They are unable to understand that attractive content is not about having flashy graphics, digital video, or sophisticated 3-D graphics.

Why is this the case? In many organizations the external Web site began as a hobby for software programmers. Although many of these sites enjoy higher visibility today, most are managed in an *ad hoc* manner and kept separate from the mainstream business. Much of the material on corporate home pages consists of traditional brochures translated to Web format.

Attractive content is about value and the ability to deliver value at a reasonable price. Today's value-oriented consumers will unflinchingly abandon established brands and migrate toward new ones, even start-ups that offer greater value. Anticipating consumer value migration and profiting from it is the way to go.

Simply stated, capabilities of the Web technology have not been adequately integrated into business infrastructure and day-to-day operations. To incorporate the Web into daily operations, firms need to get to know customers through registration, give them the ability to talk to other customers, supply customers with directories to help them get the information they need, offer transaction capabilities, and improve content and layout based on customer demand. Firms need to invest in the expertise that will make such capabilities easy to establish and manage.

Once Web technology is effectively integrated into the firm's internal operations, its effective use for external interactions becomes a natural and easy extension. Without an adequate internal infrastructure, external interactions will always be strained and limited.

3.5 The Web and Intra-Business Commerce

Although external Web applications garner the media coverage, Intranets are revolutionizing internal, corporate-wide networks. Intranets enable organizations to use the Web as an convenient, low-cost channel for intra-organizational information sharing and distribution, and are the fastest growing segment of the Web. The pharmaceutical giant Eli Lilly & Co. is in the process of linking 16,000 of its 26,000 employees on an Intranet in order to provide ready access to constantly fluctuating corporate information. The 3,000 browsers installed by Eli Lilly to date are estimated to have cost just $80,000, a testament to one of the key attractions of Intranet technology: low cost [IJ96].

Some companies such as AT&T are already deploying Intranets by using Web browsers as the front-ends to their corporate applications. According to published reports [ATT96], AT&T has over sixty internal Web servers supporting the following applications: a system that integrates disparate billing systems from various AT&T business units; an interface to library services, internal research, and external news feeds; a system for ordering office supplies; and an interface to a 30,000-employee contacts database [ATT96]. The Web is allowing many AT&T users to publish and transmit special-interest information that was not previously captured in central data and information repositories.

Intranets are currently being used for the following purposes:

Facilitate faster internal corporate communications.

Facilitate more coordinated work activities.

Facilitate easier management of complex operations with online transaction processing (OLTP).

Facilitate better managerial decision support with online analytical processing (OLAP).

Facilitate better systems management by enabling maintenance and distribution of applications.

Internal Corporate Communications Modern work processes require that people in the workplace have immediate access to information from a variety of sources, and that they can share that information within their group, across the enterprise, and with outside business partners. Ironically, it is sometimes easier to discover certain facts about competitors using the Web than it is to find a document created by a coworker on the local-area network in the next building.

The Intranet approach to publishing corporate information solves this dilemma by linking documents on scattered internal networks together. For example, the 11,000-person McDonnell Douglas company builds planes for over 200 airlines around the world. In addition to delivering airplanes, it delivers a staggering volume of aircraft service bulletins—documents that provide crucial information on how to modify and service the company's airplanes. That amounted to four million pages of documentation every year. So McDonnell Douglas decided to use the Web to disseminate this information, which they can update when necessary.

Internal Web sites are extremely useful. For instance, every company has fundamental business processes: meetings, product planning, budgeting, proposals, sales analysis, and customer tracking. These activities span multiple departments, and often the information generated is either formally recorded or casually organized. Different people need to find and use this information.

There are two types of corporate communications that Intranet Webs can facilitate:

One-to-many applications that enable teams, departments, or entire corporations to set up information pages, reducing bulky, easily outdated, paper-based information. Such applications reduce the costs of producing, printing, shipping, and updating corporate information.

Many-to-many applications include bulletin boards (or news groups) that facilitate exchanges of information between members of a group.

The ability to publish office documents, link them together, and easily navigate among them is essential for work group productivity. For example, the Human Resources (HR) department in every large organization publishes employee handbooks containing information about employment policies, benefit programs, and different types of forms and contacts for various programs and services. Compiling and updating this information is difficult, and at any given time a large percentage of the employees will have incorrect or outdated information. Maintaining handbook information on a Web site not only provides employees with access to the latest information, but also it is cheaper for HR to keep content updated. Electronic publishing is cheaper than the printing cost of $10–$15 per hard copy.

Intranets also solve information access problems. Employees can retrieve information when they need it. Many firms provide kiosks in public areas such as cafeterias and lobbies where employees who do not have PCs at their desks can access and print the information they require. Businesses are aware that the methods of conveying information by paper, fax, and disk are inefficient and costly, and are beginning to use Intranet applications to meet departmental, interdepartmental, and company-wide communication needs.

Groupware, Collaborative Work, and Coordination   Intranet applications can be used for collaborative and workflow support and for spawning and coordinating electronic transactions within and across firms. Since 1990, groupware products have become the established way for companies to create collaborative working environments in which users can communicate, share information, and route documents. The dominant product in the groupware marketplace is Lotus Notes.

It is increasingly evident that groupware and Intranet applications are converging from opposite ends of the technology spectrum—one proprietary and closed and the other nonproprietary and open—to provide similar functionality. For example, conferencing (or electronic discussion) has proven to be one of the most popular groupware applications. Conferencing enables employees to brainstorm, answer questions, and have meetings with video and data; enhances team communications by encouraging group involvement in decision making; builds a valuable corporate knowledge base by archiving ongoing discussions of ideas and issues, as well as formal documents; and allows dispersed teams to work together by enabling discussion without regard to time or location.

Many organizations, especially small- and medium-sized businesses, are now questioning the need for specialized groupware products, and asking if Intranet solutions can offer a less expensive, equally effective alternative. Lotus Notes may be the Rolls-Royce of groupware, but it is overkill for many organizations.

Cost may be the most powerful argument for adopting Intranet-based business approaches. Despite recent price cuts, the entry-level Lotus Notes Client costs approximately $69 per user, whereas commercial Web browsers cost approximately $29 per user. Using a Web server from the public domain, the Intranet start-up costs can be negligible, whereas a single Lotus Notes server costs several thousands of dollars.

In terms of ongoing costs, it is easier to add more clients to an Intranet than to a Notes-based system. Lotus Notes also requires a skilled and often expensive MIS department to set up, maintain, and develop the Notes infrastructure, and the tools that are required for this development are often expensive. On the other hand, Intranet management solutions are relatively inexpensive. Further, the Intranet makes it easy to incorporate new technology from the Web, such as multimedia, thereby considerably reducing upgrade costs.

Online Transaction Processing (OLTP)   Improving operational efficiency requires timely communication across the extended business enterprise, from customers to warehouses, distribution centers, manufacturing factories, and suppliers. The Web provides methods to integrate and access information stored in transaction databases. Figure 3.5 shows the business transactions that are supported by underlying transaction processing systems. For efficiency these systems have to be integrated for smooth information flow.

One of the important applications for online transaction processing is in procurement and inventory management with electronic data interchange (EDI) (see Chapter 12). Electronic data interchange-based procurement simplifies routine transactions, reduces paper handling, and provides an electronic communications framework for daily procurement activities. Using online catalogs and approved supplier lists, firms can easily create requisitions and purchasing documents. Buyers can work from prioritized, to-do lists for paperless document approvals and notification of pending contract expirations. The purchasing department can electronically communicate purchase orders and delivery schedules to the internal and external suppliers. The challenge is to integrate order processes with the follow-up tasks of receiving against advanced shipment notices and associated invoiceless payments.

Companies are reluctant to implement a network-centric computing solution for their OLTP (high-end, mission-critical) applications for several reasons. Given the relative immaturity of the Web, there is very little understanding of how a Web server will function if a firm tries to serve tens of millions of users doing a variety of financial transactions. Firms have solved this problem through the use of mainframes (such as IBM System/390 platforms) capable of handling substantial transaction volumes

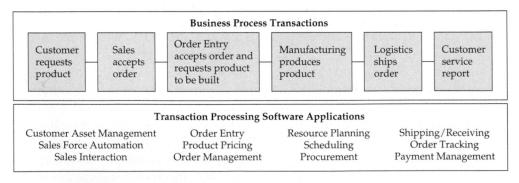

Figure 3.5   Business Processes and Applications in Transaction Processing

(called "robust serving") in banking or service institutions like Federal Express.

Yet transaction volume is not the only major issue. Network-centric computing needs to address issues of failure recovery, audit control, access control, and security. Customers want to have a certain guaranteed level of service, and thus concerns about server availability, configuration, and capacity planning are important. Do the servers log and recover transactions? What happens if the server goes down? Do they lose some operation? These are among the bigger concerns that companies, and customers, are grappling with as they look into the possibility of Intranet-based information architectures.

Web-based Decision Support Applications   Modern business systems no longer simply capture transactions and generate periodic reporting. In the past, it was once enough to have information on sales volume, revenues, and profits; it is now necessary to answer more "what-if" questions involving a number of variables. The answers to these complex questions cannot be found in the transaction-based systems—systems that were never designed to be queried by analysts, and especially not by business users.

To unlock these answers, organizations are building on-line analytical processing (OLAP) applications that help managers make critical decisions based on the comprehensive facts of their business. For instance, using OLAP, manufacturers compare the costs of distribution to decide how best to deliver products worldwide. Financial officers consolidate data from subsidiaries, project expenses and profits, and decide on budgets. Marketing managers analyze order flows and decide how to speed product to market. And advertising brand managers contrast the results of different advertising campaigns to decide which promotions work.

Well-known examples of OLAP include: *Readers' Digest*, which mines its database containing over 100 million records of past customer purchases. Using this database, it can send targeted promotions based on the reader's purchase history. Blockbuster Entertainment uses the video rental history of millions of households to recommend rentals to individual customers. American Express can analyze recent credit card charges and print suggested expenditures on card holders' monthly statements. MCI can analyze phone activity to detect toll fraud.

OLAP products are different from transaction systems. OLTP systems designed for day-to-day business transactions have been gathering detailed financial, operational, and sales transaction data for decades. The problem for decision makers lies in accessing and navigating these data stores in order to find answers to tricky real-world questions. OLAP technology allows users to access, analyze, model, and share data stored in data warehouses, relational databases, and legacy systems. For instance, analysis with an OLAP product might include rotating and drilling data, performing what-if analysis, and forecasting.

In the past, IS departments have made several futile attempts to deliver OLAP-type tools. One approach was to connect managers directly to mainframe operational systems. This approach failed because mainframes are not very user friendly and are designed to excel at the accumulation rather than the dissemination of information. A second IS approach was to create and deploy executive information systems based on specialized hardware and software. The cost of this technology—as much as $10 million to support one hundred users—far exceeded the means of most companies. Today, companies are beginning to use Intranets as the platform for OLAP applications in areas such as inventory management, target marketing, and service operations. The goal is to facilitate the speed with which decision support information can be gathered from the wealth of operational data.

Figure 3.6 shows the architecture of an Intranet-based data warehouse. A data warehouse is a physically separate, dedicated database, often residing on powerful hardware. A snapshot (or copy) of historical and current operational data is loaded into this "warehouse," where "knowledge workers" then sort and analyze it for marketing, manufacturing, and distribution decision support. Data warehousing sifts quickly through terabytes (one terabyte equals one million megabytes) of economic, demographic data, enabling support for strategic decision making.

Web-based Intranets break the access barrier by giving corporations access to all their information in the data warehouse. The number of users interacting with the data can be large. Several data warehouse applications provide the tools to meet information retrieval and business decision-making

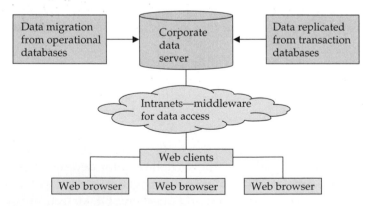

Figure 3.6   Intranet-based Decision Support

demands such as relationship analysis (percent analysis) and preplanned queries that summarize and compare results with history and industry averages. Relationship analysis of operational data provides useful insight. However, to more effectively analyze data relationships, determine trends, and create "what-if" scenarios, decision makers need more sophisticated tools to transform the data into information.

Clearly the effectiveness of data warehousing lies in the ability to separate the decision support database from the transactional database. This allows companies to avoid the performance issues created when decision support queries and transactional updates contend for similar data.

In sum, the question of how to tap the vast amounts of operational and market data in a cost-effective manner remains complex, and the emerging solution is Intranet-based analytic processing. A sizable industry is developing around Intranet data warehousing. This industry is creating tools for both packing data into and extracting results from data warehouses (see Chapter 13).

Other Intranet Applications

While electronic commerce technology and Intranet applications will undoubtedly permeate all corporate information systems, financial, logistics and workflow, and human resources management applications will be the first to be affected. Why? Today, thousands of companies have outdated business systems that will need to be replaced with improved technology capable of supporting greater functionality at a lower cost. This results in huge growth opportunities for electronic commerce within the organization.

Companies will employ Intranet applications for the following:

- **Technology-driven marketing:** database and direct marketing, customer prospecting, and new modes of customer interaction (see Chapter 11).

- **Logistics and supply chain management:** production planning and control, materials management, and product distribution (see Chapter 12).

- **Finance and accounting:** external (financial reporting), cash and treasury management, and internal accounting (such as bookkeeping, cost accounting, controlling, and transaction auditing) (see Chapter 13).

- **Human resources:** personal-data management, payroll accounting, benefits management and planning (see Chapter 13).

- **Decision support/workflow management:** moving, storing, and retrieving documents across business units for better decision making (see Chapter 13).

Within these categories, Intranet applications software can be divided into horizontal and vertical categories. Horizontal or "cross-industry" applications include financial, manufacturing, and human resource software, all of which use generic functionality across all industries (accounting and human resources are common to most market segments).

In contrast, vertical applications automate tasks that are specific to individual market segments and may cross organizational boundaries. For example, a vertical application would track a customer order from sales, production, suppliers, and ultimately to delivery. Another example is a process employed by a drug manufacturer for FDA testing, maintaining proper paperwork procedures throughout the convoluted regulatory process involving various government agencies. Major vertical applications markets include financial services/insurance, retailing, health care, government, and education.

The primary driver for the Intranet market will continue to be business process reengineering, where a competitive environment for information technology is forcing large companies to look at all aspects of their application deployment to gain competitive advantage. This, in turn, is forcing data and applications to become more accessible to decision makers throughout the enterprise.

3.6 Understanding the Intranet Architecture

Intranets are protected by software "firewalls" designed to prevent the more than thirty million Internet users from gaining access to proprietary company data (see Fig. 3.7).

In order to better understand Intranet issues, it helps to look at the evolution of corporate computing, which has been characterized by several distinct stages. During the 1960s, the mainframe was the only option for corporate computing. Computing resources were allocated on a central computer. In the 1970s, mainframe and minicomputer systems with character-oriented user terminals emerged as the principal structure for enterprise computing.

The arrival of the DEC's PDP 11 minicomputer in the 1970s reduced the mainframe's monopoly of the computer market. Minicomputers offered more localized computing at a fraction of the cost of a mainframe. In addition, departmental applications were off-loaded to the minicomputer, taking the strain off the mainframe and resulting in lower costs. Each department and end user participated in a system called *internal time sharing*.

Even with the advent of the minicomputer, users still had difficulty getting the information they needed. The minicomputer suffered from many of

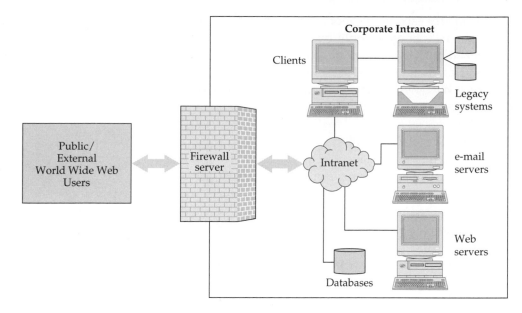

Figure 3.7   Intranet Architecture

the same problems that plague the mainframe. Screen response times were slow. Obtaining centralized information, sorted into various formats and analyses, was daunting. If users required information, they had to go to the MIS group, which then had to figure out how to access the information. Even if the request was not time-consuming or difficult, it often got delayed because of low priority. Given the fact that MIS resources were limited, it sometimes took months for reports to be generated.

In the 1980s, the introduction of PCs made computing more affordable and user friendly. The introduction of IBM's PC in 1981 moved the PC from the hobbyist marketplace into the corporate marketplace. PCs offered something that was previously not available: truly personal computing. Instead of having a desktop terminal connected to a mainframe and sharing the large computer's resources, a PC offered individual users control over computing resources and data. In addition, the PC spawned inexpensive personal productivity applications such as word processing and spreadsheets. These applications allowed PC users better access to, and analysis of, information on a more timely basis.

PC-based computing truly took off with the widespread adoption of Microsoft's Windows operating system. In a few short years, forty million units have been installed and Windows has become the standard interface for corporate desktops. Through Windows, users interact with the computer through icons and menus instead of having to memorize arcane commands for each application. Before the advent of Windows, PC users mastered an average of only two applications because each new application looked different and operated in a unique manner. Each application written for the Windows interface shares a similar look and feel, and today the average Windows PC user is competent with five to six applications.

Client/Server Computing When PCs started to populate corporate desktops, each system resided on an individual's desk and was not linked with others. Companies recognized the benefits of networking or tying systems together to share resources such as file servers and printers and information. Toward the end of the decade, local and enterprise-wide networks connecting these desktop systems became increasingly prevalent, initially for accessing file storage archives (file servers) and electronic mail communications. But few new path-breaking applications have been developed to run on these networks. Many applications still accessed corporate data by emulating a mainframe terminal. In order to obtain real paybacks from networking investments, companies turned toward client/server computing.

Client/server computing emerged as an important new architecture for corporate computing in the early 1990s. In the client/server computing model, application software is divided into two components: a "client" handling functions such as the user interface, local data storage, manipulation and presentation, and a "server" handling tasks such as data management and access, storage, and retrieval for multiple clients. Typically, the client software runs in a single-user desktop system, while the server operates utilizing a mainframe or workstation, and messages between client and server are passed through connecting networks.

With the advent of the Web, client/server computing has evolved into Intranet computing. The focus of the user interface has moved from windows to browsers. Networking has standardized on the already popular TCP/IP protocol. Distributed computing has expanded from simple two-tier (client and server interaction) to three-tier (client, server, and distributed databases and application servers), and is continuing this expansion to N-tier (N = any number) with the addition of Web browsers and servers.

Intranet Advantages and Disadvantages

While Intranets have certain obvious advantages, they also have weaknesses. Deciding to adopt an Intranet should not be an all-or-nothing proposition. Managers can use Intranet tools to complement their existing information infrastructure.

Benefits of Intranet   The business benefits of Intranets include:

- **Publishing ease.** An Intranet is an excellent platform for publishing information internally. It is easily deployable, as the ubiquitous Web browser is available for virtually every operating system. Even novices can learn to do HTML programming and to create Web pages.

- **Cost.** Most organizations have already established TCP/IP networks, and the incremental infrastructure cost of adding Web servers to the network is well within even departmental-level budgets. Further, Web servers do not need as much investment in comparison to software packages such as Lotus Notes.

- **Ease of use.** Corporate users already have Web browsers and can instantly access the information on internal Web sites. New authoring tools in desktop application suites make it easy for novices to create Intranet content.

- **Low maintenance.** With information residing in only one place—the Web server—it is relatively easy and affordable to add new information or to update existing information and make it instantly available. Over time, corporations will build libraries of Web programs that will enable them to build new applications and maintain existing ones with greater speed and lower cost.

- **Scalability.** Corporations will be able to deliver information systems on the least expensive computing platforms available and to scale their computing resources upward or downward as conditions shift. Performance constraints of mainframe computing often necessitate an upgrade to a larger mainframe; on the Web, firms can add more processing power or storage capacity, or reduce the number of desktop PCs in the event of staff reductions.

- **Easy software distribution.** Once PC users are equipped with Web browsers, new Web sites or pages with new information (or new applications) can be added without incurring the expense of locating users, sending them updated client software, and supporting them through the upgrade process.

Drawbacks of Intranet   The possible disadvantages of Intranets are:

- **Collaborative applications for Intranets are not as powerful as those offered by traditional groupware.** For instance, Intranets include no built-in data replication or directory services for remote users, while groupware packages such as Lotus Notes do.

- **Short-term risk.** There are limited tools for linking an Intranet server to databases or other back-end mainframe-based applications. Programming standards for the Web, such as common gateway interface (CGI) and Java, are fairly new and just maturing.

- **Less back-end integration.** With Intranets, firms have to set up and maintain separate applications such as e-mail and Web servers, instead of using one unified system as with groupware.

The benefits of Intranet use outweigh the disadvantages and make it a compelling alternative for many types of applications. The functional areas that can immediately benefit from Intranet technology include human resources, training, sales and marketing, accounting and finance, corporate communications, customer service and support, research and development, and technical documentation.

Management of Intranets

Although Intranets have many advantages, they also create new challenges. The first challenge is meeting coordination and efficiency needs without destroying the independence of decision making and action that makes enterprises flexible. In this context, one of the first questions asked in companies is: What applications should be developed based on Internet or Web technologies? Also, which ones should be ported and which should be developed from the ground up?

By allowing data to be exchanged freely among everyone linked to the corporate Web, regardless of whether employees use PCs, Macs, or workstations, Intranets solve a basic problem for information systems managers. Prior to the Web, almost every time a software application on a corporate network was added or changed, firms had to go through a lengthy deployment process of reconfiguring the network hardware and software. Today, an application designed around the Intranet enables great flexibility in application deployment as the user interface (the Web browser) does not change, the end-user training is minimal (the tools are familiar), and management is easier (system managers do not have to worry about content or network incompatibilities).

Companies that want to develop and deploy Intranet applications should consider the phased approach. The idea is to continue existing migrations to client/server applications and then move on to client/server applications based on distributed objects, the emerging technology for developing network-based applications. Meanwhile, traditional environments, as well as familiar database and decision support solutions, are being "Web-enabled," meaning that users can incorporate familiar tools into Web browsers and servers.

Once an organization has mastered the development of Intranet applications, it is time to deploy and manage them. The second challenge of managing Intranet systems lies in defining quality of service criteria and end-user support. In order to avoid user dissatisfaction and ensure quality of service, managers need to monitor the volume of Intranet traffic and add capacity accordingly. End-user support is also a key management issue, because without adequate support, employees become involved in low-level maintenance at the expense of the functions that most benefit the enterprise. Because Web sites are easy to build and can grow quickly, information system (IS) departments need to put into place policies to incorporate them into the corporate information infrastructure, much as they had to do to manage the PCs and local area networks (LANs) that sprouted in organizations a decade or so ago.

The third challenge of managing Intranet systems is organizing information. Identifying and maintaining information is very important, because over the long term, organizations will need scalable solutions that keep pace with the inevitable increases in Web sites, to hundreds or even thousands, throughout the enterprise.

Why is this critical? Today, some companies have more than half a million documents on their internal Web. Web technology facilitates the creation, publishing, retrieval, and viewing of information. What is not easy or efficient is finding the relevant information within the organization. In the Intranet environment, the role of IS management is changing from controlling gatekeeper to enabling gateway, and some form of data and document organization standards is needed to facilitate this transformation.

In addition to organizing tools such as search engines, administrative tools are required that will help the system managers of the internal Web site manage links and document expiration dates and ownership. Improved security tools will ensure that users are authorized to access the information they seek. Increasingly powerful management tools will also enable an enterprise to support far-reaching and innovative systems without sacrificing control. These tools will become increasingly critical as Web sites grow internally.

The final challenge of managing Intranet systems is recognizing that Intranets are not a technical issue but a management issue. Many companies are grappling with budgets, security methods, business value measurement, and user productivity issues. In addition, organizations are debating how to create advertising content, how to attract customers, and how to charge for transactions. In the short term many companies have three goals: going up the learning curve and understanding what Intranets are capable of; identifying how the Web affects their own particular situation or business; and learning how to use this new technology in their specific business processes. These goals will then have to translate into what management is always concerned about: profitability, productivity, and costs.

3.7 Summary

The key points in the chapter are summarized below:

The Web is an evolving new media paradigm. The Web is currently based on existing or maturing network technologies.

The Web represents a new way for companies to present information and products to their markets. As such it is the fastest growing area of the Internet, with new sites coming on line at the rate of one hundred per day.

The Web enables network-centric computing for running applications. As a new model, it is reminiscent of the emergence of LANs in the 1980s and client/server architectures in the early 1990s. Like these earlier technology waves, the Web is also spurring the development of new and revised tools and approaches to making database information available to users and customers.

As Web technology and practices mature, integration of corporate databases and applications is sure to play an expanding role. A couple of years from now, the Web will be taken for granted as part of the corporate infrastructure.

In summary, the Web-based application industry is young and has few proven products. The market for Web software and services has only recently begun to develop, is rapidly evolving, and is characterized by an increasing number of market entrants. As is typical in the case of a new and rapidly evolving industry, demand and market acceptance for recently introduced products and services are subject to a high level of uncertainty. Clearly, the opportunity for companies developing Web software is great, and the challenges are also quite difficult.

Chapter 4

World Wide Web— Concepts and Technology

Chapter Outline

The Internet and the World Wide Web provide intra-enterprise and inter-enterprise connectivity and application access on a scale unimaginable just a few years ago. By exploiting the broadly available and deployed standards of the Internet and the Web, companies are able to build client/server applications for internal use (Intranets) or for external use (public Internets) to reach and interact with customers, business partners, and suppliers in numerous ways.

Although the Web has existed for only a few years, it is constantly evolving as users and developers learn to use it effectively in both public and private environments. The Web is already forcing Microsoft to adapt its popular Windows operating system. The Web is poised to challenge the Wintel (Windows+Intel) platform dominance for three reasons:

> Virtually all Web applications and technologies are standards-based, thereby eliminating the need for software developers to port to multiple platforms to reach new markets.

> Web technologies are by definition true client/middleware/server applications, enabling users to readily utilize distributed computing and database resources and minimizing the need for end users to frequently upgrade existing hardware, operating systems, or network infrastructures.

> The speed at which new applications can be developed and distributed on the Web will enable Web technology to replace the functionality of many current desktop and platform-centric applications today.

This chapter discusses the technical details of the underlying strata of Web architecture from the perspective of content providers, application developers, managers, and end users. It examines the current status and future trends of the computing tools that are becoming available for building Web applications. In particular, this chapter focuses on the database integration with the Web, Java programming language, and multimedia Web extensions like Virtual Reality Modeling Language (VRML) and RealAudio, all of which will have enormous influence on the evolution of the Web usage.

4.1 Key Concepts behind the Web

The Web is successful because it encompasses a wide range of concepts and technologies that differ markedly in purpose and scope. The key Web concepts include: global hypertext publishing, the universal readership of content, and the client/server interaction.

Global hypertext publishing promotes the idea of a seamless world in which all online information can be accessed and retrieved in a consistent and simple way. Hypertext has resulted in the viability of low-cost publishing. This implies that anyone can publish information anywhere (as long as he or she is connected to the Internet), and anyone (as long as he or she is authorized) can read and download it. Publishing information requires a server program, and reading data requires a client browser. All the clients and servers are connected via the Internet. Standard protocols allow clients to communicate with servers.

Universal readership promotes the idea that, unlike the segmented applications of the past, one application—a universal (or common) user interface—can be used to read a variety of documents. This implies that once information is published it is accessible from any type of computer, in any country, and that any (authorized) person needs to use one simple program to access it. This is accomplished by using a core browser or application that is augmented by supporting applications. The core browser implements only minimal functionality and attempts to offload more specialized work onto the supporting applications.

Client/server interaction allows the Web to grow without any centralized control. In the client/server model, Web browsers (clients) are linked to Web servers that have applications and databases. The advantages of client/server computing are internetworking, multi-platform applications, and the increasing need for open standards. These are the very things the Web accomplishes easily.

Using the above concepts, the Web provides a way to interconnect computers running different operating systems, and display information created in a variety of existing media formats.

4.2 Overview of the Web's Technical Architecture

The popular press often does not differentiate between the multiple uses of the Web. The Web can serve three functions: as part of the operating system (evident in the movement of Microsoft to include access to the Web as part of Windows 95); as a distribution channel for applications (enabling word processing programs or spreadsheet programs to be downloaded so that they run on the operating platform); or as a middleman, called middleware, between database servers and clients. In actual fact, the Web is a combination of all three, and that is what makes it so useful for electronic commerce.

A basic client/server architecture underlies all Web activities. Information is stored on Web servers. Servers store files and respond to requests. Web browsers request information from servers by specifying the "name" of the information. The server simply transfers the requested file back to the client. The client formats the information and displays it on the user's screen.

Information is organized into distributed "pages." These pages are stored as information encoded in hypertext markup language (HTML). Using HTML, users can easily create pages containing textual information freely mixed with multimedia content (graphics, audio, and video), as well as the "links" that enable a user to "browse" from page to page across the Internet. The ability to jump between pages is generally referred to as "Web surfing."

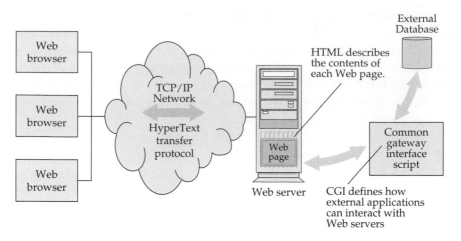

Figure 4.1   The Web Architecture

In addition to static HTML pages where content does not change, the Web technology provides a mechanism for dynamic information to be included in the pages. Examples of dynamic content include stock tickers, sports scores, and news. The Web server in such cases uses a standard interface called the common gateway interface (CGI) to execute a separate program that obtains the dynamic information, formats it into HTML, and forwards it to the Web server (see Fig. 4.1).

Using the CGI method, it is standard practice to include information from many sources such as databases. For instance, in the case of FedEx package tracking application, the customer enters the package ID information into an HTML form on the Web browser. The browser sends the information to a Web server, which then uses the CGI interface to extract the appropriate information from a database and presents the data nicely formatted back to the user. By letting thousands of customers utilize the Web for package tracking, FedEx is saving millions of dollars in labor costs [BW96].

Figure 4.1 shows the architecture for Web clients and Web servers. Components include Web clients, Web servers, HTTP protocol, and applications. These Web components cooperate to provide a seamless transition between today's computing resources and those of tomorrow by transparently integrating information access and exchange within the context of the chosen business application. The basic components have the following characteristics.

Web Clients   Web clients (or browsers) provide a graphical user interface for accessing and displaying content. These programs are available on IBM-compatible PCs, Apple Macintosh computers, UNIX platforms, and other platforms. Web clients typically provide a number of facilities that vary from one Web client to another. The most widely used Web clients are Microsoft's Internet Explorer and Netscape's Navigator.

Web Servers   Web servers are a combination of software and hardware that store documents and other content. The server content is accessed using Web browsers. Web servers are available for a wide range of platforms including IBM PCs, Apple Macintosh computers, UNIX platforms, and a large number of proprietary hosts. The most widely used Web clients are Microsoft's Internet Information Server and Netscape's Communications server.

Hypertext Transport Protocol (HTTP)   HTTP provides the language that allows servers and browsers to communicate. The Web is made up of Internet connections, browsers, and server software, and HTTP provides a way through which various technologies can interoperate together. Each HTTP interaction works in the following way:

1. The browser establishes a connection with the server.
2. The browser issues a request to the server.
3. The server sends a response (a page or graphics).
4. Both the browser and server disconnect and the transaction ends.

Uniform Resource Locator (URL)   Each Web page has its own unique address, called a uniform resource locator (URL). Web browsers use URL addresses to find Web servers. As noted earlier, the power of the Web lies in the ability to connect distributed pages with "hyperlinks," allowing a reader to move between pages by clicking on the hypertext links on a page. For example, Netscape's Web server consists of many pages, each with its own URL, but the starting point, or home page URL, is http://home.netscape.com. Today, the URL is ubiquitous, and is often provided in TV ads as a means of promoting a company's Web site. For instance, when Prudential Securities shows its URL of "http://www.prusec.com/" in an ad, this means that the site is on a Web server with a domain name of "prusec.com."

Hypertext Markup Language (HTML)   HTML is a representation language for hypertext documents containing text, list boxes, and graphics information. While HTML is great for displaying text along with limited graphics, it has many shortcomings that require frequent extensions to the language. In fact, one reason for Netscape's popularity has been the tradition of advancing the language by introducing new extensions. For instance, the most recent HTML addition is the Frames tags, which allow a window to be split into multiple independent panes. Each frame is an independent window-within-the-main-window. Frames lets content authors spruce up their pages with nifty effects. Tags introduced with the early versions of Netscape have been adopted as standard by other browsers, so Netscape keeps others on their toes by upping the ante with several new tags with every new release.

Common Gateway Interface Business applications often require that browsers have the ability to reach out beyond the Web server to other computing environments such as corporate databases. This tunneling (browser → server → CGI script → application) is accomplished through the common gateway interface (CGI).

CGI is the widely used standard interface between Web servers and applications. Server scripts are often written in a variety of computer languages (or scripts) that conform to the CGI standard.

CGI is also used to integrate databases with the Web. Several database companies have developed standard solutions for creating Internet applications using the CGI specification that designates how text is transferred from an HTML form to a back-end program for further processing. For example, Oracle and Sybase make their databases accessible on the Web through sets of server scripts. Since CGI is a technical subject of great importance, an overview is provided later in the next section.

4.3 Interactive Web Applications

As the Web marketplace matures, companies are demanding more sophisticated interactive applications, Web extensions that enable interactivity, and better developmental tools.

Interactive Applications

Interactivity on the Web has evolved through three phases. In the first phase, the Web was a mechanism for sharing static information—technical manuals, papers, software—which were prepared "off-line" and loaded onto a Web server.

The second phase of the Web was driven by a demand for interactive pages, such as forms that users could fill in online. Examples of forms include search forms, user survey forms, and registration forms. If you browse the Web today, you'll notice that several sites have pages that have a high degree of interactivity using various types of forms. Other uses of form-based interaction include pages that display airline or concert schedules, current weather conditions at a location specified by the user, and quotes for specified sets of stocks.

The third phase of the Web has just begun with the emergence of sophisticated scripting languages like Java. With scripting, the Web has progressed to include documents whose content is dynamic or created on-the-fly, in response to user request. This allows Web sites to tailor the content to a particular individual. With these capabilities, the Web becomes a platform for delivering customized applications.

Interactivity and Information Integration

Information integration is the key to developing interactive Web-based applications. The Web provides four distinct forms of integration.

Ability to link data provided by different servers.   Each data item in the Web is addressed by a uniform resource locator (URL). Web documents, expressed in HTML, can contain the URLs of other documents. Browsers typically display these references, called hyperlinks, as special regions called *anchors*. An anchor can be a section of highlighted text or an icon. When the user clicks on an anchor, the browser retrieves the document referenced by the underlying URL. The newly retrieved document can come from a server located across the globe both from the client and from the server that provided the document containing the anchor.

Ability to provide clients with data from diverse sources.   Web servers and Web browsers support this form of integration in different ways. Web servers integrate diverse sources of data by allowing common gateway interface (CGI) programs to run in response to client requests; CGI programs perform general computations including accepting form data, communicating with other computers, and creating dynamic pages. This way, for instance, a Web server can provide clients with data obtained by running transactions on a legacy mainframe system. In such a scenario the Web server acts as a gateway, translating from the new standard for interactive information access (HTTP) to a previous one (3270 terminal protocols).

Ability to encompass new types of data.   The HTTP protocol borrows a design for extensible data typing and type negotiation from the multipurpose Internet mail extensions (MIME) standard. Browsers are designed to support new data types via helper applications that a user can add to the browser. This is how Web browsers deliver audio, video, and PostScript data to users today. The Web is quite prepared for new data types that may become important in the future.

Ability to integrate new helper or plug-in applications.   This extends the Web's capabilities and enhances its functionality. The plug-in architecture that simplifies third-party add-ons was pioneered by Netscape. Plug-ins are add-on programs that let users view flashy animation and graphics, fly through virtual 3-D worlds, and listen to audio broadcasts on the Web—all from within Netscape Navigator.

There are currently more than three dozen plug-ins that literally plug into Netscape browsers and give them more capabilities. For instance, Adobe Systems Inc. has a plug-in that will allow files that support its Acrobat Reader and Page Description Format (PDF) to be read directly from the Netscape browser, while Macromedia's Shockwave allows full-motion animation and video files to run in the Navigator 2.0 browser as well. To install a plug-in, users simply download the program file and run the program's installation routine. While this sounds cumbersome, it is actually very simple and, depending on the size of the files and the speed of the network, may take anywhere from one to ten minutes.

The plug-in concept of browser extension is good because it lets developers mix and match functionality with the specific requirements users may have. For instance, you want to watch a video from Disney Online. If you don't have a video player on your PC, you can download and install a video player plug-in before downloading the actual video. Plug-ins enable better information integration at the browser end. In fact, many argue that part of what makes Netscape products appealing to developers is the concept of plug-in modules.

Web Extensions for Interactive Applications

Publishing static documents on the Web is easy. Creating powerful interactive application functionality to run in a browser environment is another matter.

In this section we examine various types of extensions that are enhancing Web functionality to deliver interactivity. Web extensions are occurring in four dimensions:

Database integration,

Scripting and mobile applets,

Capturing and distributing documents with common look and feel, and

Multimedia Web extensions that include 3-dimensional visualization and audio/video extensions.

Database Integration   Many of the current applications on the Web are adequately served by HTML documents (also called *flat-file information systems*). However, as the sophistication and complexity of Web applications increase, access to databases will be essential. The Web is a complementary, rather than a replacement technology for traditional database management systems (DBMS).

DBMS applications capture, manage, and share an organization's structured data in systems that range from departmental applications to an enterprise-wide data architecture. In contrast to DBMS applications, Web applications capture, manage, and share semistructured information, including documents and graphics, as well as rich data objects such as voice and video. In addition, Web applications take advantage of electronic messaging for document distribution, such as forms routing or workflow applications. However, Web applications are not directly capable of handling transactional systems such as order processing, which require tracking orders, customer account information, product specifications, and many other forms of data that will be immediately accessible to those who need the information.

Consider, for example, how the Web and a DBMS can be used to complement each other and support a corporation's human resources department. Traditionally database HR applications had an internal, data-centric focus, designed to share data and resources solely within a single organization. Web-based HR applications, which are inherently communications-centric, have both an internal and an external focus. The HR database management systems (DBMS) are used to manage low-level highly structured employee and payroll data that includes salary, level, job title, home and office addresses, and phone number for each employee. Web sites, on the other hand, manage the semistructured information relevant to human resources business processes, such as technical manuals, detailed job descriptions, employee reviews, résumés, and corporate communications. Moreover, the Web can be used to manage human resource business processes such as job advertisements, candidate interview scheduling, and distribution of job opportunity notices.

In the context of the HR scenario, the Web serves as an effective vehicle for distributing information managed by the corporate DBMS system, and the Web also acts as a front end that updates detailed data in the DBMS system. The Web server supports applications that automate related processes such as applicant tracking, employee reviews, and education and training. The Web client browser provides a consistent front end to HR and payroll data for all client platforms and locations, and an easy way to access such items as résumés and HR budget analyses. Also, the Web's bulletin board capabilities make it appropriate for such HR tasks as job posting and requisition processing.

Scripting and Mobile Applets   Scripting represents a major paradigm shift in the application development. Scripting is the first step toward making the Web a programming platform. Once application developers can write scripts that will work on the Web, the way we think about and use the Internet will change dramatically. We will see Web pages become more interactive and more dynamic. Perhaps the most widely touted technology for creating dynamic Web pages is Java.

Java is a revolutionary way to add software, or mini-applications called "applets," to the HTML mix. One of Java's purposes is to enable intelligent, client-side processing and event handling to improve interactive performance and functionality. This is accomplished through Java applets—mini-applications that are downloaded from a Web server and run in a browser. Applets, in conjunction with Web browsers designed to support them, can make Web pages perform virtually any task: animation, calculations, input, you name it. A few financial sites are using Java applets to display real-time, constantly updated stock quotes in scrolling banners.

While such improvements are a useful addition to the functionality of the Web, the nature of Java has implications beyond spicing up HTML. Traditional rivals such as Microsoft and Netscape are rushing to embrace the Java standard and incorporate it into their products. Java essentially lets users run computer programs through their browsers, giving those Web sites that support Java an extra added dimension. Some pundits go so far as to predict that Java will upend the world of software, changing the way we use computers.

There are other alternative scripting languages, such as Python, but creating user excitement first gives Java a pretty sizable advantage. Also, don't expect Microsoft to stay out of this fight. Microsoft has previously stated its intention to make its Visual Basic an alternative scripting standard given its market penetration. Visual Basic and Visual C++ each offer programmers the ability to rapidly author applications. In many ways, each of these products could offer the same type of Internet compatibility as Java if the compatible browsers were developed. The advantage of using Microsoft products lies in the existing investment in Graphical User Interface (GUI) development tools and existing software libraries. However, Java's built-in security, object-oriented design, and relatively compact size provide clear advantages over monolithic Visual Basic, which works only in Microsoft Windows, giving it key advantages on the Web.

Capturing Look and Feel   Scripting is not the only area where companies are competing. For example, online publishing is increasing the demand for better-looking Web pages in a way that is currently beyond what HTML can offer. Since HTML is so limited, taking a highly formatted document such as a marketing brochure and posting it on the Web is a real challenge. HTML does not even let you choose the fonts that are displayed on a Web page. These limitations of the HTML have given creators of portable-document products the chance to create new extensions that will give publishers the capability to create more professional-looking documents.

Many publishers are using an alternative format that gives them control over the design of their documents: Adobe's Portable Document Format (PDF). It was originally designed so that a document (anything from a corporate policy memo to a magazine) would look the same way when viewed on just about any computer.

To understand the usefulness of PDF you need to understand the basic idea behind HTML authoring. To create an HTML document, the author tags each piece of text using a word processor or an HTML editor to indicate whether the text is a head, body text, caption, and so on. The Web browser is then able to format the text interactively, that is, using whatever fonts and window size the reader has chosen for the Web browser. On the other hand, Adobe's PDF describes the original document pages, so that an Acrobat viewer can replicate the document exactly as the author produced it, regardless of the fonts or software installed on the viewing system. Another advantage of PDF for many publishers is that PDF documents can be created using any word processing, page layout, or graphics application. To create a PDF document, the publisher simply opens the document and "prints" the entire contents to a single PDF file using the software program's Print command

Acrobat pages have major advantages over HTML documents. Acrobat pages can be highly formatted, and these pages can contain any fonts and graphics in the same way they appear in a publishing product. Acrobat lets users create pages that look more like printed pages, and it is cross-platform in the sense that there are free viewers available for the major hardware platforms. Will PDF penetrate the market? In one word, yes. Adobe already has an agreement with Netscape: Navigator will support Adobe's Acrobat format for viewing portable documents.

Another portable-document manufacturer, Common Ground Software, has recently shipped its Common Ground Web Publishing System. Common Ground's primary advantage lies in its ability to download only particular pages over the Web, while Acrobat still requires users to download the whole document. Either solution will let users see pages that look more like printed pages.

Multimedia Web Extensions   Even with the great interest in the current set of information available on the Web in HTML, software development continues in an effort to make the Web more interactive and to support multimedia with existing Web browsers. Attempts at improving how text and graphics are rendered on the Web is only the beginning. Other software developers are designing new multimedia products and are adapting current ones to address the needs of this new market.

Multimedia Web extensions are occurring in two dimensions: three-dimensional worlds created using virtual reality modeling language (VRML) and point-to-point broadcasting of audio (such as RealAudio), news (such as PointCasting), and video (such as Intercasting [see Chapter 9]).

4.4 Web and Database Integration

Database integration lets Web administrators create Web pages that access a back-end database without writing database queries in languages such as SQL. Web developers can create database solutions such as online product and pricing catalogs, online shopping systems, dynamic document serving, online chat and conferencing, and event registration, among others. Users can search, insert, update, and delete on databases without writing HTML. Why is database integration with the Web critical? Today, many of the applications on the Web are adequately served by simple information structures like HTML. As the sophistication and complexity of Web applications increases, access to relational databases will be essential. Take, for instance, complex search engines (such as Digital's Alta Vista); these applications need the storage power and flexibility provided by DBMS connectivity.

Databases have several advantages over HTML files—increased speed of inquiries, flexibility of queries, the ability to store large amounts of data, and the inclusion of complex data types. All of the information companies wish to provide to their employees and customers can also be made available, without having to change the structure or format of their existing database. In other words, the investment that firms have made over the years is not lost by moving to a Web-based distribution architecture.

Over the years, database applications have become quite sophisticated and it would be stupid to re-invent the wheel again on the Web. For example, databases control concurrent operations, such as immediate updates by using record locking to ensure database integrity and transaction control for applications working with distributed databases. Data replication, along with system and document security and management features, make it possible to appropriately secure and distribute information both within and beyond a single enterprise, so that a Web application can connect an organization with its customers, suppliers, and business partners.

Web Database Products

Like almost everything else about the Web, new database integration products seem to appear on a daily basis. However, the products can be classified into the following broad categories:

gateways provided by database management system (DBMS) vendors to link their own database servers to the Web,

third-party gateways supporting multiple relational DBMSs and other legacy data sources,

text and document databases enhanced to work as back-ends to the Web,

front-end database application development tools enriched with Web access,

Web servers and browsers augmented with database-aware features.

Although these categories cover the majority of products in the marketplace, there are sure to be a few that do not fit neatly into this classification, and new and unexpected variations are bound to emerge rapidly.

HTML Forms and CGI Programs

Application gateways are an important aspect of Web server development. Application gateways are used to integrate the Web with "legacy" applications containing corporate data. Corporate data exists in a variety of databases and files. Some of that data is in other personal databases or spreadsheets on PCs; other data exists in departmental databases, with some on a server and other data on large mainframe systems.

Clearly, database administrators need to provide a gateway to these important data assets of the enterprise. As distributed computing becomes more prevalent, the word "legacy databases" can send shivers down the spines of managers who have yet to make the change to more modern relational databases. These managers are seeking to protect a huge investment in legacy systems (hardware, software, and people) using the common gateway interface (CGI).

In particular, the CGI, a specification for communicating data between Web browsers and executable programs running on a Web server, is changing the nature of integration. A CGI script is a program that negotiates the movement of data between the Web server and an outside application. CGI is used whenever the Web server needs to send or receive data from another application, such as a database. Information on the CGI specification can be found online (at http://hoohoo.ncsa.uiuc.edu/cgi/interface.html).

Figure 4.2 shows how a CGI script can interact with a database management system (DBMS) to pass data into a database and return data from the database to the Web browser as a formatted HTML file. CGI is actually not database-specific because CGI scripts can do almost anything. A typical use of CGI is to pass data, filled in by a user in an HTML form, from the Web server to a database. A call to a CGI script is encoded into an HTML docu-

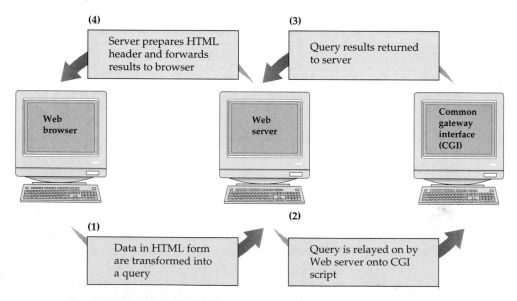

Figure 4.2   Common Gateway Interface in Action

ment, where it usually appears as a hyperlink. Clicking on the link executes the CGI script on the Web server. Data also can be returned to the user's browser via CGI scripts. CGI scripts can receive input parameters, and most return results that may consist of text (a status message at the very least, graphics, or both). Whatever result is returned must be formatted as HTML for display on the browser. Reformating results is therefore a key function of any CGI script. CGI scripts may be written in virtually any high-level language, although C and PERL are the most popular programming languages, since they run on so many platforms.

Practical extraction and report language (PERL) has been a favorite language for CGI scripts because of its string-handling features. PERL is found in UNIX environments where most Web servers originated. However, a number of recent products such as WebSite let developers use other languages like Visual Basic, and they run on Windows NT- and Windows 95-based Web servers.

Most leading DBMS vendors, such as Sybase, released CGI database gateways by late 1995. These Web database integration products promise to shield developers from the tedious details of writing CGI scripts, in much the same way as visual programming environments reduce the need to hand-code repetitive screen handling logic in modern applications. These initial products were typically quick-and-dirty efforts to illustrate what was possible, and developers usually had to do a fair amount of programming to implement solutions. More sophisticated products are replacing or supplementing the original embryonic tool kits.

4.5 Web Software Developmental Tools

Development tool technology for the Internet is in its infancy. However, just as software development requires sophisticated tools to make programming more productive, the delivery of dynamic content on the Web will also require sophisticated tools and techniques.

Web application developers are realizing that choosing the proper tool is critical. Many issues faced by developers during the early days of client/server are being revisited with the Internet, and understanding these issues will help ease the transition to this new model. Internet development tools are still unproven. Reminiscent of the march to client/server, scores of Internet development tools are available in early versions. It is ironic that the most popular tool for many Web developers is a favorite word processor or text editor.

Given the volatile nature of Web technology, developers face difficulty in selecting a tool with long-term viability. Eventually, a handful of tools (such as Sun Microsystems's Java and Progressive Networks' RealAudio technologies) are beginning to emerge from the pack. Currently, there are scores of potential Internet development tools, and it can be difficult to predict which ones will lead the market and which ones will fade away. Will there be a deep pool of trained talent for any particular tool to support projects? Issues of product maturity and longevity are extremely important, and will only be resolved over time.

On a more positive note, advances in scripting languages such as Java, programming interfaces, database technologies, and multimedia extensions are making the development of interactive applications for the Web much easier. However, developers remain hard pressed to find a complete environment that includes database access, interface components, and interactive features. Fortunately, tools required to build database-driven Web applications will mature quickly because they will be based largely on proven technologies from the client/server era.

Need for Better Programming Languages

Historically, programmers have used two classes of tools to develop software applications: third-generation language ("3GL") tools such as COBOL and C++, or fourth-generation language ("4GL") database tools. The 3GL tools have been used for mainframes and for mass-marketed PC products.

These character-oriented languages do not provide an efficient means for developing graphical user interface applications, and programming requires a significant base of skill and experience which typically restricts their use to a small group of professionals. Conversely, the class of tools that has evolved for database applications generally does not allow access to multiple database repositories. They also lack the development capabilities required to build complex enterprise-wide business applications that reach a global audience of employees, customers, and suppliers.

One new language that is becoming very popular in developing Web applications is Java. Java embodies all of the critical elements for a successful Web programming: it is easy to use, it runs on multiple platforms, and it is compact. Additionally, Java solves critical bandwidth and processor bottlenecks through its design and opens a completely new world of interactivity for content developers and end users.

New Programming Language: Java

In 1990, a small team of engineers at Sun Microsystems, headed by James Gosling, started developing software for the consumer electronics market. Initially the team used C++, but the wide variety of hardware architectures used in consumer electronics—coupled with the requirement for robustness—made this problematic. The team therefore developed a new language called "Java" which, it turns out, also addresses many of the issues of software distribution on the Internet.

According to the Java FAQ "the name was chosen during one of several brainstorming sessions held by the Java team. We were aiming to come up with a name that evoked the essence of the technology—liveliness, animation, speed, interactivity, and more. 'Java' was chosen from among many, many suggestions. The name is not an acronym, but rather a reminder of that hot, aromatic stuff that many programmers like to drink lots of" [JFAQ96].

The jury is still out on whether Java is the best possible scripting language. However, what is important is that it is the first of its kind. And this alone gives Java the real possibility of becoming the *de facto* standard, just as the Netscape extensions to HTML have become a standard.

Technically Speaking: What Exactly Is Java?

Java is not a subset of an existing programming language, but a language that was designed from the ground up. In other words, Java is an entirely new programming language that is similar to, but independent of the widely accepted C and C++ languages. According to [JFAQ96], the Java language omits rarely used, poorly understood, and confusing features of C++. The majority of programmers today are conversant in C or C++ and can rapidly (within hours) become productive with Java. Java's rapid acceptance within the inner circles of the Internet community has been driven largely by its elegant design and ease of implementation.

Technically speaking, Java is a simple, object-oriented, multithreaded, garbage-collected, secure, robust, architecture-neutral, portable, high-performance, dynamic language. The language is similar to C and C++ but much simpler. Java programs are compiled into a binary format that can be executed on many platforms without recompilation. This binary format is called *byte code independent*. The language contains mechanisms to verify and execute Java programs in a controlled environment, protecting the user's PC from viruses and other security violations.

Applications programmed in Java essentially become "plug-and-play" objects that can operate on any operating system (platform independent). Basically, Java applets are mini-applications that expand the capabilities of a core Web browser. Using applets, the functionality of the browser is augmented to provide support for specialized applications that range from interactive shopping applications, educational material, and games.

The reasons Java is attractive technically are:

It allows developers to create compact, modular, "plug-and-play" programs called *applets* (or mini-applications) that are portable and reusable.

It allows architecturally neutral applications to be developed, that is, applications that can run on multiple platforms without being recompiled. This means that developers no longer need to "port" code to different platforms.

It lowers the barriers to entry for new and small software developers. For instance, a developer can create a series of "applets" that can be downloaded and run within the user's browser. The result of this can be seen in the wide range of applications that are being developed in the Java language—financial, accounting, games, education, and interactive advertising, to name a few.

Java adds an element of intelligence and computational power to existing Web browser technologies. As stand-alone technologies, today's Web browsers are relatively two-dimensional viewers; they offer little in the way of interactivity or computing power. With Java compatibility, a browser becomes a computer capable of executing software programs and communicating with other computers. More importantly, Java enables content to become active.

Role of Java in Electronic Commerce

Today, Web browsers allow users to manipulate information spread across the Internet as a whole. Web browsers integrate the function of fetching the remote information, figuring out what format it is, and displaying it. These browsers contain detailed, hard-wired knowledge about the many different data types, protocols, and behaviors necessary to navigate the Web.

This hard-wiring of functionality makes extensions in the form of new protocols or modified protocols costly and difficult. Changes will require that the user delete the old browser and re-install a new version. In the current Web environment the browser revision time is often three to six months. For individual users, this might not be a big deal as they can download the new version and install it in a matter of minutes. For a corporate information manager supervising several thousand machines, this incremental revision cycle is stuff that nightmares are made of.

Figure 4.3 presents a view of integrated browsers. It also captures the problem associated with hard-coding functionality, if a user wants to access

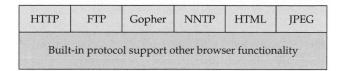

HTTP	FTP	Gopher	NNTP	HTML	JPEG
Built-in protocol support other browser functionality					

Figure 4.3 Integrated Browsers

data on multiple servers each having a proprietary HTML extension as specialized applications are being implemented using proprietary protocols. For instance, many vendors are providing new Web browsers and servers with added capabilities such as billing and security. These capabilities most often take the form of new protocols. Each vendor implements something unique, a new style of security for example, and sells a server and browser that speak this new protocol.

To view these extensions, the user needs have several browsers on her client machine (see Fig. 4.4). Needing several browsers is clumsy and defeats the universal readership purpose that makes the Web so useful. Another problem with this approach is that the user has to decide which browser he or she wants. The decision to go for a particular browser effectively locks the user into a particular environment, denying him or her the necessary flexibility to move around.

This situation can be avoided by using applet-based browsers. Applets are mini-applications that transparently migrate across the network when needed. In other words, there is no such thing as "installing" applets. They are invoked transparently when needed. The advantage is that content developers for the Web do not have to worry about whether some special piece of software is installed in a user's computer; the applet is automatically transported with the requested material. This transparent acquisition

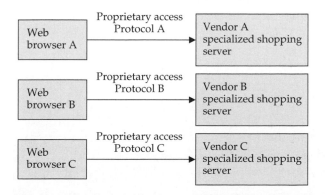

Figure 4.4 Electronic Commerce World without Browser Flexibility

of applications frees content developers from the confines of a limited set of media types and lets them do innovative things.

In other words, we must solve the crucial problem of distributing applet software. In the early days of the Internet, software distribution was not a major problem as most software was written in languages such as ANSI C, which was relatively portable. Then, most programs were distributed with source code, so they could be compiled for the user's preferred operating environment. The exponential growth of the Internet has made the old model impractical as more PCs, Macs, and other non-UNIX machines connect to the Internet. It can no longer be expected that users are technically sophisticated to download and compile software. Also, the heterogeneous nature of the Internet hinders the distribution of software in binary file format. Porting is becoming more difficult, as well. But porting is not the only barrier to distributing software on the Internet. What about security? How many times have you downloaded a binary from a public FTP site and executed it on your machine without worrying about threats to your other files? There are no guarantees that a program won't steal your password or delete a critical file. Even when the software comes from a respected vendor, it can be modified by a clever hacker as it is transported over the Internet.

How Does Java Work?

Figure 4.5 shows the interaction between a browser and server in negotiating for a Java applet. The user clicks on a remote object on the screen. The URL for the object is taken by the browser and the browser retrieves the object from a remote server. The browser then attempts to display the object. It realizes that the format (or type) of the object is something that it does not have the ability to interpret. It then sends another message to the server and fetches the applet suitable for the format in question. The applet executes

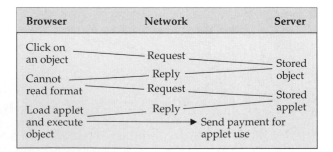

Figure 4.5   Interaction in the Applet World

on the client and displays the retrieved object. All of this interaction is done automatically and behind the scenes. After the applet is fetched, payment must be made for the services rendered.

Using applets, the browser becomes a coordinator of resources, resulting in flexibility and the ability to add new capabilities easily. The result of becoming a coordinator is the ability to exude dynamic behavior for understanding different types of objects. For example, most Web browsers can understand a small set of video formats (typically MPEG). If they see some other type (say QuickTime), they have no way of dealing with it directly.

The applet-based browser, on the other hand, can dynamically install the necessary agent code from the server that has the QuickTime video, allowing it to play the new format. So, if someone invents a new video format, the inventor just has to make sure that a copy of the agent code is installed on the server that contains the video the inventor wants to publish. In the old model of integrated browsers, all the browsers in the world would have to be upgraded to display the new format. The applet-based browser upgrades itself on the fly when it sees this new type.

The dynamic incorporation of applets has special significance to how business is done in electronic commerce environments. With applet-based browsers as a base, vendors can produce and sell exactly the piece that is their added value to what exists and integrate it smoothly with the products of other vendors. This seamless integration creates a final result that is very convenient for the end user, a necessary condition of electronic commerce.

Business Reasons for Using Java

There are clear technical, cost, and marketing advantages to developing applications in Java:

- **Ease of distribution.** Applications developed in Java consist of small components, or objects, that are transmitted from the server to the client transparent to the end user. In essence, Java applications are distributed real-time, on an as-needed basis.

- **Speed of development.** The speed at which Java applications can be developed will both heighten the awareness and popularity of the language. Java lowers the barriers to entry for new software applications.

- **Developer critical mass.** The overwhelming support Java received since its introduction in March 1995 has attracted a large number of developers who have already developed hundreds of applications.

- **Fits the Web paradigm.** Java is platform independent, distributed, compact, and interactive. It embodies the critical elements of success for the new Web-based computing paradigm. Java enables the creation of new applets that are likely to replace many of the "bulk ware" desktop applications that are used today.

- **Third-party support.** Most major tool, database, browser, and application development companies have incorporated Java within their future product plans (including Microsoft, Borland, Oracle, and Netscape).

Independent developers view the emergence of Java as an opportunity to depart from the "Wintel" platform hegemony. Java is a tool that has the potential to dislodge some of the dominant, platform- (or operating system) centric software companies like Microsoft. In essence Java has leveled the playing field for many developers, both large and small.

4.6 Multimedia Web Extensions

The Web is being extended in several directions. The important ones are VRML, RealAudio and Internet/Web-based telephony.

Virtual Reality Modeling Language (VRML)

Virtual reality modeling language (VRML) was developed to extend HTML to three-dimensional worlds. While HTML specifies how two-dimensional documents are represented, VRML describes how three-dimensional environments can be explored and created.

VRML grew out of work done by Silicon Graphics and is now driven by a rapidly growing community that is quickly broadening VRMLs horizons. Many believe that VRML will play a part in the future of the Web because it is more intuitive for users to browse 3-D spaces than to click through hyperlinked 2-D pages.

VRML and Visual Computing   VRML belongs to a category of computing called *visual computing*. The market for visual, interactive computing has grown significantly in recent years for a very good reason: people prefer graphics to text. When it comes to using a PC, playing video games, or navigating through the Web, most users prefer to use intuition instead of logic. Computer users have grown accustomed to graphical user interfaces; the days of text-based commands have gone the way of the horse and buggy.

With the advent of more powerful PCs, consumers have begun to appreciate and expect the benefits that visually oriented applications are providing.

Why then, given its many benefits, has visual computing taken so long to expand beyond the boundaries of scientific applications such as molecular modeling, flight simulation, meteorology, and computer-aided product design? The technology was very expensive initially, marked by few available or affordable platforms and a paucity of software application development. The advent of VRML aims to change the economics of visual computing.

An entire new industry is developing around VRML language based on the assumption that Web sites can attract new users by adding 3-D environments that are fun to explore and by providing a natural way to navigate through the information available on the site. This capability will permit "worlds" where users can roam around and actually explore in the true sense of the word. With the tremendous potential at stake, an all-out war between Netscape and Microsoft is being fought over standards for creating VRML worlds.

What Exactly Is VRML?   VRML is simply a scene representation language that specifies three-dimensional environments on the Web. Similar to HTML, the core Web document representation standard, VRML encodes computer-generated graphics into a compact file format for transportation over networks. VRML allows for much richer interaction and perspective than HTML. When viewing two-dimensional HTML pages, the options are basically limited to jumping from page to page and looking at images from a fixed, predetermined perspective.

When visiting VRML worlds, however, users can freely choose the perspective from which to view the world, just like in the real world. For example, when you walk through a shopping mall, you look around and build a mental map of the place. If someone tells you that you have to turn right at the next store, you can visualize this and get to where you want to go. There is a sense of continuity, and you can see how quickly you progress toward the goal. Sometimes you get lost, but this is part of the experience, and often that is how you discover new stores and new products. Typing the location of a home page and watching the file download onto the PC just isn't the same. The future of the Web clearly lies in letting users navigate unencumbered through 3-D environments, the contents of which are only limited by the imaginations of their creators.

Technically speaking, VRML is an object-oriented 3-D protocol that enables the creation of interactive 3-D environments on the Internet. With VRML, graphics commands and parameters are sent from the server to the client, where they are rendered. Although VRML is interactive in nature, its singular purpose is for creating and displaying 3-D objects and environments. VRML is designed so that users can download and browse through a 3-D scene.

How Does VRML Work?   From the user's perspective, VRML works in the following way. First, the user has to obtain a browser extension (or plug-in) that understands VRML. These extensions are freely downloadable versions that link directly to the Web browser. For instance, Live3D made by Paper Software plugs easily into Netscape Navigator and is automatically invoked whenever a VRML file is downloaded. In fact, Paper Software's WebFX browser was the first Navigator VRML plug-in and remains one of the best. Netscape liked WebFX so much that they decided to buy it. Now called Live3D, it lets users view and navigate through 3-D worlds on the Web. It takes a while to master Live3D, but once accomplished, the effects are stunning.

A VRML file is loaded the same way as an HTML file: either by clicking on a link or typing a file location name and hitting return. VRML files are often compressed to reduce download time. Once the file is downloaded onto the PC, if the VRML browser recognizes the file type, it can automatically parse the compressed file to display the VRML world. Unlike programming languages, VRML does not have to be compiled and run. Rather, VRML files once downloaded by the browser get decompressed, analyzed (parsed), and then displayed.

Based on the speed of the network connection and the size of the file, the loading time can be as little as a few seconds or as much as a couple of minutes. Well-structured VRML files will allow VRML browsers to load the file in pieces, which lets users explore right away while the browser fetches more detailed objects and those that are not currently in the view. As users navigate through the scene, they will notice that some objects are hyperlinked. If they click on them, they will jump either to another VRML world or to another media type such as HTML.

Now that we have seen the user's perspective, let us consider VRML from a developer's perspective. There are three ways to create a VRML world:

Create and edit a VRML text file by hand.

Use a conversion program to convert an existing non-VRML 3-D file to VRML.

Use an authoring package to create models and position them within a world.

VRML is still an evolving technology. Chances are high that even if an authoring tool is used to create the VRML world, developers will need to modify it slightly by hand. Therefore, learning VRML concepts and syntax can be useful.

VRML and Java   VRML 1.0 supports worlds with relatively simple animation. The next generation VRML 2.0, called Moving Worlds, supports complex 3-D animation, simulations, and behaviors by allowing Java and JavaScript programmers to write scripts that act on VRML objects. Fully integrated Java applets can be used to create motion and enable interactivity, and JavaScript allows scripted communication between different objects both inside and outside the 3-D environment.

The Moving Worlds version of VRML enables Web-based applications to include powerful 3-D enhancements that let users visualize database information in real-time; see true 3-D graphics derived from complex spreadsheet data; walk through virtual product showrooms with other online shoppers; participate in multi-player virtual reality games; interact within multimedia chat rooms; collaborate on designs with designers around the world; and study photorealistic 3-D geographies like Jupiter or lunar surfaces. Moving Worlds also enables third-party plug-ins to be used unmodified, adding useful 3-D capabilities to Web-based database, design, and other real-world applications.

RealAudio

Browsing the Web does not have to be just a visual experience. A program called RealAudio from Progressive Networks (www.realaudio.com), allows sound files to be heard as they are being downloaded. Until RealAudio, it was impossible to listen to audio without first downloading the entire sound file; this meant that listening to a ten-minute clip could take nearly half an hour of download time.

RealAudio eliminates the long waiting time associated with multimedia files. Instead of waiting for files to make the journey to the hard drive before playing them, the RealAudio player pops up immediately after the user begins the download, giving instantaneous playback. Unlike other sound formats such as AU, WAV, or AIFF files, which have to download in their entirety before playback, Real Audio files are super-compressed in a special format which ends with .ra or .ram. Regardless of file size, files start playing right away and stream continuously.

RealAudio handles the dilemma of transmitting sound with one of those really obvious solutions that make the rest of the developers wonder why they did not come up with it. Called streaming audio, this technology sacrifices sound quality for convenience (think AM radio with some static). But when it comes to speeches or live broadcasts such as baseball games, the technology suffices.

Elements of RealAudio   Progressive's package consists of three pieces of software: server, encoder, and player. The RealAudio server delivers live and rebroadcast music and audio over the Internet and private TCP/IP networks to computers equipped with the RealAudio Player.

The RealAudio encoder is aimed at multimedia creators, and includes software required to encode all the standard audio format and edit tracks. Basically, the encoder compresses audio into RealAudio format. The encoder can create RealAudio files directly or stream encoded live data to a RealAudio Server for delivery to end users.

The RealAudio player that is located on the user's PC lets users listen to audio CDs and sound clips on the Internet while they are being downloaded. The player includes controls that enable the user to pause and skip around within the audio stream. The RealAudio sound player has been available for quite some time as a separate application and is also available as a plug-in application. The plug-in provides seamless integration with the browser by building controls—forward, rewind, pause, and volume—right into browser's interface. The player software is free, but encoder and server cost money.

How Does RealAudio Work?   In order to cope with the inherent bursty nature of the Internet, RealAudio uses high-compression ratio, combined with buffering at the client end. Each audio stream is compressed using a proprietary linear predictive algorithm and encoded as a fixed-rate 1Kbps data stream. The compression algorithm has been optimized for speech, and the quality of the transmission has been described as of AM-radio–type quality. When audio is requested by the client, the RealAudio Server first sends data at a high rate, to fill the client's buffer, and then throttles back the transmission rate. Decompression takes place on the fly and consequently a PC with at least a fast 80486 is needed to ensure proper playback.

More important than the streaming audio features is the ability to embed network and multimedia scripting commands in the sound without substantially increasing bandwidth requirements. For example, an author can include Web URLs (the pointers that tell a Web browser to connect to a new page) in the audio stream so that, as the narration plays out, the consumer's Web browser turns from page to page, conducting an audiovisual tour of the subject.

Internet and Web-based Telephony

Hitherto a hacker's hobby, the use of microphones and PCs to place phone calls, send faxes, and transmit pager signals over the Internet is emerging as a serious business opportunity. Since the first phone software was crudely hacked together a few years ago as a way to make "free" long-distance calls (free, assuming you have an Internet account, a $3,000 multimedia computer, and someone to call who has compatible software), telephony has become the fastest growing type of service on the Internet.

The Web and Audio   The Web is becoming less "audio" challenged as browser developers are adding better capabilities. For instance, Netscape has already added telephony features, called Cool Talk, to its popular Navigator Web-browser software. Cool Talk allows users to communicate across the Internet with full duplex sound—users can speak and be heard simultaneously. CoolTalk includes a speed dialer, Caller ID functionality, call screening, mute buttons, and an answering machine that records messages and caller information while users are away from the computer.

Separately, Microsoft is planning to embed Internet voice technology into its Windows operating systems and Explorer software. Intel, meanwhile, is adding multimedia extensions to all its future PC microprocessors. Compaq Computer, and other leading PC makers, are building voice capabilities into their machines.

Applications of Technology   Beyond cheap phone calls, the possible applications include:

Shopping on the World Wide Web, where the customer could speak live with a sales agent while viewing product information.

Customer service on the Web, where the customer can speak live to a customer service representative about service issues while working on the computer.

Work-team software that would enable groups working collaboratively on documents via the Internet to converse about the project, too.

Interactive games such as adding voice capabilities to multiplayer computer games like Doom or Quake, so that players could participate vocally.

Technical drawbacks still keep Internet telephony from being a true substitute for the telephone network. And yet, the number of regular Internet telephone users is expected to rise from fewer than 400,000 last year to 16 million by 1999, according to a forecast from the research company International Data Corp. By that year, IDC predicts, Internet telephony could constitute a $500 million market [NY96].

Given the possibilities and market size, some of the biggest telephone companies, whose business might seem threatened by the trend, are studying Internet telephony. All of these companies see potential beyond a few customers saving save a few cents on overseas calls.

4.7 Directories and Search Engines

The proliferation of Web sites presents users with vast amounts of information. Although the Web is renowned for making it easy to access data squirreled away on computers scattered around the Internet, getting to one of these computers requires knowing where to go. With the amount of information increasing rapidly, there is a tremendous need for tools that assist in searching for relevant information.

Users find information among the unstructured multimedia documents scattered around the world in one of two ways. The first, and most serendipitous method, is by clicking on a so-called hot link—a defined word or term in a Web document that automatically launches the reader to whatever cross-indexed source material exists anywhere on the Web.

The more methodical way of moving through the Web is to find the address of a site that seems to have the type of material the person is looking for. But even with this address or URL in hand, the user is restricted to this one Web site's documents or the other sites reached through the hot links embedded in those documents.

The third method is a directory or a search engine that acts as a reference librarian, offering expert guidance through the bewildering stack. A search engine is a program that uses smart agents and information finders to gather information on the Web. For example, by typing the word "IBM" into a search engine, a list of sites containing information about IBM would be provided.

Among the better-known search engines that provide customers with time-saving and cost-cutting services are Yahoo, Lycos, and Alta Vista. We discuss Lycos below because it was among the first to use smart agents to gather documents.

Lycos

Lycos is a search engine based on Lycos Spider Technology. With this technology, Lycos maintains and continually updates a catalog of the Web, keyed off of the most common words appearing on Web home pages.

Lycos's free search tool allows users to access this catalog based on key word searches and "hyperlinks" to applicable home pages.

Lycos makes the following assumption: The problem of information discovery online is very complex and necessitates the use of software agents. While it is impossible to get a completely accurate picture of the number of documents available via the Web, it is clear that it contains millions of documents. It is simply no longer practical for users to wander around online looking for information. As a result, users have to depend on agents in information brokerages (search engines).

If discovering information is a big problem, indexing the entire Web is enormous. Not only must every document be retrieved, but some portion of each document must be stored as a way of summarizing its contents for later retrieval. Managing such a vast amount of information is a problem. If, say, 1/2 kilobyte is saved for each document, the resulting index exceeds several gigabytes.

Alta Vista, another popular search engine, has an index that is over 12 gigabytes. The trade-off becomes one of quality of index versus coverage of documents. Saving more information per document reduces the number of documents that can be covered, and vice versa. This trade-off suggests that a database will be inadequate either in scope or quality.

Clearly, we have a long way to go in developing search engines to solve the resource discovery problem. More work needs to be done in integrating consumer search behavior with agent technology.

4.8 Summary

This chapter described the Web architecture that facilitates electronic commerce by providing a set of tools that, combined, can make interactive applications come to life. The role of the Web browser and server is also discussed. The integration of the Web with corporate databases is discussed in detail. And finally, the evolution of the basic Web architecture in different directions—Java, RealAudio, Internet telephony, and directory systems—is also discussed.

Chapter 5

Firewalls and Transaction Security

Chapter Outline

While corporate presence on the Internet has soared, many companies are simply providing information about themselves—annual reports, product documentation, service information—and have not yet begun to provide full-scale transactions for buying and selling online. This restraint is primarily the result of concern about network and transaction security. Panic-raising articles in the popular press about such security issues as the attack on Netcom, an online access provider, in which hackers bypassed various protections and misappropriated subscriber credit card information, further heighten concern about security, and prevent companies from providing full-scale transactions on public networks.

Likewise, concern over transaction security has made many consumers averse to making payments over the Internet. There is not yet a reliable method of preventing third parties from accessing sensitive financial and personal information (such as credit card numbers or health records) as the information traverses across the Internet. A third-party threat occurs when a hacker, situation, or event has the potential to disrupt data or network resources and incur economic loss. This loss can be in the form of destruction, disclosure, modification of data, denial of service, fraud, waste, or abuse.

In general, security concerns in electronic commerce can be divided into concerns about user authorization, and concerns about data and transaction security. Authorization schemes such as password protection, encrypted smart cards, biometrics (fingerprinting), and firewalls ensure that only valid users and programs have access to information resources such as user accounts, files, and databases. Data and transaction security schemes such as secret-key encryption and public/private-key encryption (see Section 5.3) are used to ensure the privacy, integrity, and confidentiality of business transactions and messages, and are the basis for several online payment systems such as electronic cash and electronic checks.

Network security and data/transaction security must be addressed simultaneously. In much the same way as it is pointless to use an armored truck to transport cash from one bank to another bank and then leave the cash in the middle of the bank lobby, online business/personal information that is protected en route needs to be securely "put in the vault" once it reaches its destination. In order to ensure the safe arrival and storage of information, and to protect it from both internal and external threats, cryptographic methods must be supported by perimeter guards (such as firewalls),

Table 5.1   Internet Security Terms

Term	Definition of Concept
Authentication	A way to verify that message senders are who they say they are.
Integrity	Ensuring that information will not be accidentally or maliciously altered or destroyed.
Reliability	Ensuring that systems will perform consistently and at an acceptable level of quality.
Encryption	A process of making information indecipherable except to those with a decoding key.
Firewall	A filter between a corporate network and the Internet that keeps the corporate network secure from intruders, but allows authenticated corporate users uninhibited access to the Internet.
Spoofing	A way of creating counterfeit packets with private IP (Intranet) addresses in order to gain access to private networks and steal information.
Denial of service	An attack on the information and communications services by a third party that prevents legitimate users from using the infrastructure.

which secure internal computers from Internet access. Managers often assume that encryption is enough to protect a business from possible danger. However, encryption provides transaction security, but does not do much to prevent unauthorized access to computers, information, and databases.

The remainder of this chapter will discuss the managerial and security implications of firewalls, as well as the data encryption techniques that form the cornerstone of electronic commerce.

5.1 Firewalls and Network Security

A firewall is defined as software or hardware that allows only those external users with specific characteristics to access a protected network (or site). Typically, a firewall allows insiders to have full access to services on the outside while granting access from the outside on a selective basis, based on user names and passwords, Internet IP address, or domain name. For example, a vendor could permit entry to its Web site on the firewall only to those users with specific domain names belonging to companies that are in long-term contracts to buy its products.

A firewall works by establishing a barrier between the corporate network (secure network) and the external Internet (untrusted network). This barrier shields vulnerable corporate networks from prying eyes in the public network. A firewall is not simply hardware or software, it is an approach to implementing a security policy that defines the services and access to be permitted to various users. In other words, a firewall implements an access policy by forcing connections to pass through the firewall, where they can be examined and audited.

Firewalls are an important consideration for corporations using the Internet, particularly for those in the financial services industry. In the middle of 1994, Wells Fargo & Co., a bank with an over $50 billion asset base, connected a World Wide Web server to the Internet in order to provide potential customers with new account, credit card, and loan information. To insulate its networks against outside intruders, Wells Fargo installed a firewall called screening external access link (SEAL) [IWA95]. The bank connected to the Internet only after it felt that its firewall was sufficiently impenetrable, thereby providing sufficient protection for its internal business networks, assets, and client confidentiality. As most corporate internal networks operate on the principle of ease of use, firewalls are a necessary shield from possible mischief from external Internet users.

Figure 5.1 illustrates how a firewall controls traffic between internal and external networks by providing a single check point for access control and auditing. As a result, unauthorized Internet hosts cannot directly access

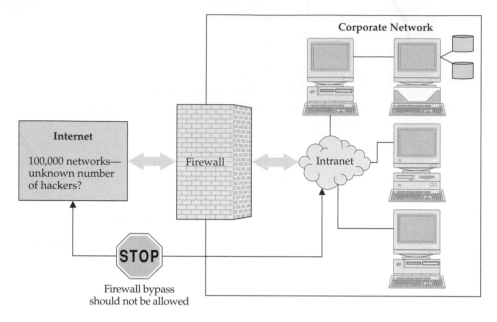

Figure 5.1   Firewall-secured Internet Connection

computers inside the network, but authorized internal users can still use Internet services outside of the network. A firewall system is usually located at a gateway point, such as the place where a site connects to the Internet, but can be located at internal gateways in order to provide protection for a smaller collection of hosts or subnets.

Types of Firewalls

There are several types of firewalls, which offer various levels of security. The most widely used method of firewalling is to place a computer or a router between the network and the Internet, which will then control and monitor all traffic between the outside world and the local network. Numerous variations of firewalls include simple traffic logging systems, IP packet screening routers, hardened firewall hosts, and proxy application gateways.

Simple Traffic Logging Systems   Traffic logging systems are the predominant firewall method used in Web servers. Such systems record all network traffic flowing through the firewall in a file or database for auditing purposes. On most Web servers, an HTTPD log (hypertext transfer protocol daemon), also called *audit log file*, lists every access of files on a given Web site. It records the name of the file accessed, the domain name that the user came in on, the exact second of the access, and number of bytes transmitted.

The content of the audit log on our server: commerce.ssb.rochester.edu is shown in Table 5.2.

Table 5.2 Contents of a Web Server's Audit Log

fission.site.gmu.edu - - [24/Apr/1996:16:29:26 +0100] "GET /cis442/ecomm.ps HTTP/1.0" 200 396881

cba-bkim.unl.edu - - [24/Apr/1996:16:33:08 +0100] "GET /book2.gif HTTP/1.0" 200 20715

inet1.nsc.com - - [24/Apr/1996:16:38:41 +0100] "GET /book1.gif HTTP/1.0" 200 120219

137.158.128.7 - - [24/Apr/1996:16:53:07 +0100] "GET /book.html HTTP/1.0" 200 7775

groa.uct.ac.za - - [24/Apr/1996:16:54:07 +0100] "GET /bank.html HTTP/1.0" 200 6670

By analyzing the audit log of a Web site, managers can answer the following questions: What are the peak demand hours? What directories and pages are most frequently requested? How many times was the home page requested? Does the Web site have any broken content links? What browsers are visitors using? How many requests for product information have been received this week? How does that compare to last week? What type of information is being requested by existing customers? By competitors? By prospective customers? By asking these questions and analyzing their answers, managers can understand traffic patterns and more importantly, customer behavior at a particular site.

IP Packet Screening Routers   The screening router (also called a *packet-filtering gateway*) is the simplest firewall. The screening router operates by filtering information packets that pass through the firewall. Figure 5.2 shows a secure firewall with an IP packet screening router. The firewall router filters incoming packets and permits or denies IP packets based on several screening rules that are programmed into the router and performed automatically. Most frequently used screening rules include:

- **Incoming packet protocol.** Control filtering of network traffic based on protocol (TCP, UDP, ICMP).

- **Destination application to which the packet is routed.** Restrict access to certain applications; target TCP port 80 usually reserved for the Web server application.

- **Known source IP address.** Block access to packets coming from certain IP addresses. For instance, everything coming from a noncorporate site such as an .edu address could be screened and thrown away.

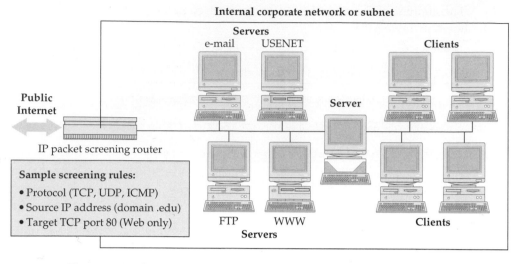

Figure 5.2   Secure Firewall with IP Packet Screening Router

The actual filtering mechanisms vary, but firewalls consist of two mechanisms: one that blocks incoming traffic, and one that permits outgoing traffic. Some firewalls place a greater emphasis on blocking traffic, and others emphasize permitting traffic. Although properly configured routers can block many security holes, they have several disadvantages. First, given the vastly diverse needs of users, it is difficult to determine what type of screening to employ. Second, screening routers are fairly inflexible and do not easily extend to deal with functionality different from that preprogrammed by the vendor. Third, if the screening router is circumvented by a hacker, the rest of the network is open to attack.

For IP packet screening, many firms rely on routers from companies such as Cisco System, which can be programmed with a list of acceptable addresses. Programmable routers cost approximately $3000, a relatively low cost that is attractive to smaller companies. Routers deter casual Internet intruders in much the same way as steering wheel locks such as the Club prevent theft; routers are not full-fledged alarm systems, but act as deterrents.

Hardened Firewall Host   A hardened firewall host is a stripped-down computer (with well-tested resources) that has been configured for increased security. A hardened firewall host requires inside or outside users to connect to the trusted applications on the firewall machine before connecting further. Generally, these firewalls are configured to protect against unauthenticated interactive log-ins from the external world. More than any other mechanism, the hardened firewall host helps prevent unauthorized users from logging onto machines on the network.

In order to create a hardened host, system managers must:

Remove all user accounts except those necessary for operation of the firewall. If users cannot log in to the firewall host, they cannot subvert the security measures.

Remove all noncrucial files and executables, especially network server programs and client programs like FTP and Telnet.

Extend traffic logging and monitoring to check remote access.

Disable IP forwarding to prevent the firewall from forwarding unauthorized packets between the Internet and the enterprise network.

A hardened firewall computer records who has logged onto a system, as well as who has tried to log on but failed. The latter is often a warning sign of an attempted break-in. Through logging, auditing, and sucker traps, companies can tell the difference between a casual knock at the door and a malicious hacker.

In return for increased configuration cost and decreased level of service (because of the fact that an application proxy described in the next subsection needs to be developed for each desired service), the hardened firewall host provides both security and a way to increase auditing capabilities.

Hardened firewall hosts offer specific security advantages:

- **Concentration of security.** All modified software and logging is located on the firewall system rather than distributed on many hosts.

- **Information hiding.** A firewall can "hide" names of internal systems or e-mail addresses, thereby protecting information from outside hosts.

- **Centralized and simplified network services management.** Services such as FTP, e-mail, Gopher, and other similar services are located on the firewall system(s) rather than being maintained on many systems.

There are some contingent problems in the design of current hardened host firewalls because of these advantages, however. In particular, because hardened hosts concentrate security in one spot as opposed to distributing it among systems, a compromise of the firewall could be disastrous to other less-protected systems on the network.

Proxy Application Gateways   Firewalls can also be created through software called a *proxy service*. The host computer running the proxy service is referred to as an *application gateway*. Application gateways sit between the

Internet and a company's internal network and provide middleman services (or proxy services) to users on either side. If a computer user on one company's network wants to talk to a user at another organization, the first user actually talks to the proxy application on the firewall, and the proxy then talks to the remote computer. Similarly, outside hosts talk to internal computers through the proxy on the firewall. The firewall thus serves as a proxy for traffic in both directions, and can support a number of Internet navigation software programs such as the World Wide Web.

An application-level proxy makes a firewall safely permeable for users in an organization, without creating a potential security hole through which hackers can access corporate networks. For example, a user who wants to FTP in or out through the gateway connects to proxy FTP software running on the firewall, which then allows connections to machines on the other side of the gateway.

Proxy servers are often used for caching documents. Caching is the act of storing a document on a local server, enabling it to be presented faster than if it is accessed from the document's original server. For instance, if five hundred America Online users access the same file from Microsoft, it would make sense to cache the document on the AOL firewall and reduce the network traffic by serving the document from the local server for all subsequent requests. The disadvantage of caching from a marketing measurement perspective is that when a document is copied from its original server and stored locally, the user data is blocked from the advertiser. In the printed world, this would be akin to a magazine subscriber making and distributing a thousand copies of a magazine but only counting one reader, leading the publisher to undercount the magazine's circulation and be unaware of its readership's total demographic profile.

How Does the Proxy Method Work?   As an example, consider a Web site that blocks all incoming HTTP connections using a packet filtering router. The router allows HTTP packets to go to one host only, the Web application gateway. A user who wishes to connect inbound to an internal Web site would have to connect first to the application gateway, and then to the destination host, as follows:

Browser first "talks" to the Web server on the application gateway and provides the name of an internal host.

The gateway checks the user's source IP address and accepts or rejects it according to any access criteria in place.

The browser may need to authenticate itself (possibly using a password).

The proxy service creates an HTTP connection between the gateway and the internal host.

The proxy service then passes bytes between the two connections, and the application gateway audits the connection.

Hence, instead of talking directly to external Web servers, each browser request is routed to a user-specified proxy on the firewall. The proxy knows how to get through the firewall. The proxy waits for a request from inside the firewall, forwards the request to the remote server outside the firewall, reads the response, and then returns it to the browser. In the usual case, all browsers within a given subnet use the same proxy.

Advantages and Disadvantages of Proxy Servers   In the case of the Web, the proxy increases security by:

Information hiding, in which the names of internal systems are not known to outside systems; the application gateway is the only host whose name must be made known to outside systems.

Limiting dangerous subsets of the HTTP protocol (a site's security policy may prohibit the use of some HTTP methods); enforcing client and/or server access to designated hosts (an organization has the capability to specify acceptable Web sites).

Robust authentication and logging, in which the application traffic can be pre-authenticated before it reaches internal hosts and can be logged more effectively.

Checking various protocols for well-formed commands.

A significant advantage of proxy gateways is that they allow browser programmers to circumvent the complex networking code necessary to support different firewall protocols, and thereby to concentrate on important client issues. For instance, by using HTTP between the client and proxy, no protocol functionality is lost, since FTP, Gopher, and other Web protocols map well into HTTP methods. This mapping feature is invaluable, for users do not need separate, specially modified FTP, Gopher, and Web clients to get through a firewall; a single Web client with a proxy server handles all the different protocols effectively.

Another advantage is that proxies can manage network functions. For example, proxying allows for the creation of audit trails of client transactions, including client IP address, date and time, byte count, and success

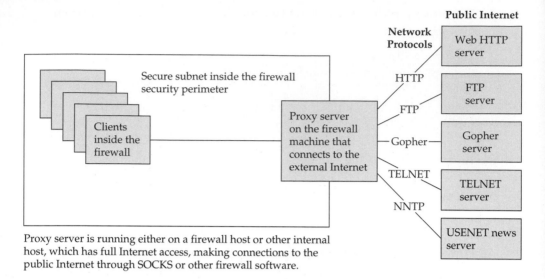

Proxy server is running either on a firewall host or other internal host, which has full Internet access, making connections to the public Internet through SOCKS or other firewall software.

Figure 5.3   Proxy Servers on the World Wide Web

code. Any regular fields and meta-information fields in a transaction can be logged. Proxies can also control access to applications based on browser type, host, and domain.

A disadvantage of proxies and application gateways is that, in the case of client–server protocols such as HTTP, two steps are required to connect inbound or outbound. Some application gateways require modified clients, which can be viewed as a disadvantage or an advantage, depending on whether the modified clients make it easier to use the firewall. Proxy firewalls are poor protection against viruses; as the multiple ways of encoding binary files for transfer over networks, as well as the varied document formats, make it difficult to monitor adequately.

Firewall Security Policies

Firewall protection methods cover a continuum of security concerns from ease of use to paranoia. Administrators with the responsibility of designing, specifying, and implementing or overseeing the installation of a firewall must address a number of management issues before actual installment [IWA94].

Managers must be clear about the security policies of their organizations. For example, managers have to determine whether their company's firewall is in place to deny all services except Internet connection, or to provide a metered and audited method of regulating access to the Internet in a nonthreatening manner. There are various degrees of concern between these positions, and the final firewall decision may be more the result of political and/or financial reasoning than technical or engineering finesse. In short, many corporations and data centers have computing security policies and practices that dictate how data must be protected, and a firewall should be an embodiment of this security policy.

Managers must also be aware of the level of monitoring, redundancy, and control in the functioning of firewalls. Having set a risk level in sync with their security policy, managers must make a checklist of what firewalls should monitor, permit, and deny. For instance, the firewall can control access based on time of day. Organizations might allow employees to run e-mail or FTP at any time, but to read USENET news groups only between 7:00 P.M. and 8:00 A.M. Administrators must determine objectives, combine a needs analysis with a risk assessment, and then sort the requirements into a list to guide firewall implementation.

Firewall policies must be realistic reflections of the level of security in the entire network. For example, if a company restricts access with a firewall, it should require passwords on its internal servers as well. It should also provide regular monitoring for unauthorized modems. For example, if unrestricted modem access is still permitted into a site protected by a firewall, attackers could effectively circumvent the firewall. Further, a site with classified data should not be connected to the Internet in the first place, and/or systems with private data should be isolated from the rest of the corporate network.

Finally, managers need to keep in mind that firewalls are not always impenetrable. During Thanksgiving week 1994, unidentified computer hackers broke through General Electric (GE) Internet security firewalls and accessed proprietary information on GE systems [IWA94]. Major damage was reported, and, as a precaution, GE shut down Internet access for seventy-two hours. This incident sent a shudder through U.S. corporations rushing to implement firewalls and embrace the Internet as a major conduit for electronic commerce. Since then, firewall technology has improved considerably, but thorny management problems concerning security policies have yet to be resolved.

Emerging Firewall Management Issues

The issue that most firms grapple with is the make-or-buy decision. Until recently, few vendors have offered off-the-shelf firewall systems. Hence, in the past, construction of firewalls required a significant amount of corporate time and effort, and most firewalls were handcrafted by site administrators. With more choice in the marketplace, managers need to be careful in selecting a firewall solution and need to evaluate the trade-off between ease of use, ease of administration, and data security.

Frequently, technical design of the firewall is dictated by financial concerns about the costs of buying or implementing a firewall. For example, a complete firewall product may cost anywhere between $0 and $200,000. At the low end, configuring a router will cost staff time. Implementing a high-end firewall with specialized proxy servers might cost several months of programming effort. Managers must also consider the costs of systems management and evaluate firewalls not only in terms of immediate costs, but also in terms of continuing maintenance costs such as support and software upgrades.

Firewalls also present capacity management problems. For instance, in companies that use the Internet a lot, firewalls represent a potential bottleneck, since all connections must pass through the firewall and, in some cases, be examined by the firewall.

Finally, firewalls present content management and control problems. Who manages the information on a firewall? Is it the function of the MIS department, marketing communications, or should it be left to the functional units? This is a tricky problem because for large firms, content management is a function of the marketing communications department, which zealously guards against any effort that may affect the corporate image. In such a scenario, functional units would have to approach marketing communications for clearance and approval before placing anything online. The approval process is bottlenecked and could result in delays of several weeks. In the meantime, the functional units are getting worried because the content is getting dated and would have to be updated the minute it is approved: a classic "Catch 22" situation. Addressing control issues will require serious thinking about delegation of authority, organizational structure, and content management.

5.2 Transaction Security

Transaction security has become a high-profile concern because of the increasing number of merchants trying to spur commerce online. Consumer confidence in the reliability and protection of business transactions against third-party threats must be enhanced before electronic commerce can succeed.

Unsure of security, consumers are unwilling to provide credit card payment information over the Internet. Given the threat of lawsuits and other liability, the mere thought of "sniffer" programs that collect credit card numbers *en masse* is enough to keep merchants from providing online shopping. In order to allay consumer fear and protect the confidential data on public networks, companies are starting to pay greater attention to transaction privacy, authentication, and anonymity.

Table 5.3 lists five "security requirements" that encompass the security needs of electronic commerce [SK95]. Of these, transaction privacy, confidentiality, and integrity are the main barriers to the widespread acceptance of electronic commerce.

Table 5.3 Five Internet Security Requirements

Term	Definition of Concept
Privacy	The ability to control who sees (or cannot see) information and under what terms
Authenticity	The ability to know the identities of communicating parties
Integrity	The assurance that stored or transmitted information is un-altered
Availability	The ability to know when information and communication services will (or will not be) available
Blocking	The ability to block unwanted information or intrusions

Types of Online Transactions

The type of transaction depends on the type of data (or content) being sent across the network. The different categories of data are:

- **Public data.** This type of data has no security restrictions and may be read by anyone. Such data should, however, be protected from unauthorized tampering or modification.

- **Copyright data.** This type of data is copyrighted but not secret. The owner of the data is willing to provide it, but wishes to be paid for it. In order to maximize revenue, security must be tight.

- **Confidential data.** This type of data contains content that is secret, but the existence of the data is not a secret. Such data include bank account statements and personal files.

- **Secret data.** The very existence of this type of data is a secret and must be kept confidential at all times. It is necessary to monitor and log all access and attempted access to secret data.

The fact that there are many different types of Internet transactions makes security difficult. Because of the sensitivity of information being transferred, and in order to protect the consumer from various forms of fraud and misconduct, security and verification are necessary for all types of data.

Requirements for Transaction Security

There are three basic requirements for transaction security:

- **Privacy.** Transactions must be kept private and inviolable in the sense that eavesdroppers cannot understand the message content.

- **Confidentiality.** Traces of the transactions must be expunged from the public network. No intermediary should be allowed to hold copies of the transaction unless authorized to do so.

- **Integrity.** Transactions must not be tampered or interfered with.

Transaction Privacy   Up to now, there have been no real safeguards to ensure that the messages Internet users send and receive are not intercepted, read, or even altered by some unknown interloper. This threat is technically called *unauthorized network monitoring*, or *packet sniffing*.

Sniffer attacks begin when a hacker breaks into a computer and installs a packet sniffing program that monitors the network traffic. The sniffer program watches for certain kinds of network traffic, typically for the first part of sessions that legitimate users initiate to gain access to another system, such as Telnet or FTP sessions. The first part of such sessions contains all the necessary information a sniffer needs to log into other machines, including the log-in ID, password, and user name of the person logging in. In the course of several days, a sniffer can gather information on local users logging into remote machines. Note that one insecure system on a network can expose to intrusion not only other local machines, but also any remote systems to which the users connect.

In one of the most famous sniffing cases to date, two hackers were sentenced for defrauding MCI and other telephone carriers of more than $28 million (U.S.). The hackers had used sniffers to record 50,000 credit card and phone card numbers, and then sold the data to European users who made free long-distance calls using these accounts.

The illegitimate extraction of information from network traffic is nothing new. The problem has been magnified because of the Internet. If the compromised system is on a backbone network, intruders can monitor any transit traffic traversing between nodes on that network. Network monitoring can rapidly expand the number of systems intruders are able to access, with only minimal impact on the systems on which the sniffers are installed, and with no visible impact on the systems being monitored. Users whose accounts and passwords are collected will not be aware that their sessions are being monitored, and subsequent intrusions will happen via legitimate accounts on the compromised machines.

Transaction Confidentiality   The electronic commerce environment must ensure that all message traffic is confidential. After successful delivery to their destination gateways, messages must be removed (expunged) from the public environment, leaving only the accounting record of entry and delivery, including message length, authentication data, and perhaps the audit trail of message transfer agents. All message archiving must be performed in well-protected systems. Provision must be made for the irrevocable emergency destruction of stored, undelivered messages.

Confidentiality is important for transactions involving sensitive data such as credit card numbers, and will become even more important when data, such as employee records and social security numbers, begin traversing the network. Distributed networks and wireless links exacerbate the vulnerability of data communications to interception. Message confidentiality is accomplished using encryption, which secures the communications link between computers.

Transaction Integrity   In order for electronic commerce to succeed, the contents of electronic commerce transactions must remain unmodified during transport between the client and the server. Transmission must be tamper-proof in the sense that no one can add, delete, or modify any part of the message during transit. Unauthorized combining of messages either by intermixing or concatenating during submission, validation, processing, or delivery should not be allowed.

While confidentiality guards against the monitoring of data, mechanisms for integrity must prevent active attacks involving the modification of data while the transaction is in progress. Methods for ensuring information integrity include error detection codes or checksums, sequence numbers, and encryption techniques. Error detection codes or checksums operate on the entire message or selected fields within a message. Sequence numbers prevent reordering, loss, or replaying of messages by an attacker. Encryption techniques can also detect modifications of a message.

5.3 Encryption and Transaction Security

Sensitive information that must travel over public channels (such as the Internet) can be defended by encryption, or secret codes. Although it may sound like the stuff of spy novels, electronic commerce relies heavily on encryption. The goal of encryption is to make it impossible for a hacker who obtains the ciphertext (encrypted information) as it passes on the network to recover the original message. Encryption is the mutation of information in any form (text, video, graphics) into a form readable only with a decryption key. A "key" is a very large number, a string of zeros and ones. Figure 5.6 shows what a key looks like.

There are two main kinds of encryption in common use today. The older and simpler one is called "single-key" or "secret-key" encryption. The more recent method is called "public-key" encryption.

Secret-Key Encryption

Secret-key encryption, also known as *symmetric encryption*, involves the use of a shared key for both encryption by the transmitter and decryption by the receiver. Secret-key encryption works in the following way: Anne wishes to send a purchase order (PO) to Bob in such a way that only Bob can read it. Anne encrypts the PO (the plaintext) with an encryption key and sends the encrypted PO (the ciphertext) to Bob. Encryption scrambles the message, rendering it unreadable to anyone but the intended recipient.

Bob decrypts the ciphertext with the decryption key and reads the PO. Note that in secret-key encryption, the encryption key and decryption key are the same (see Fig. 5.4). The transmitter uses a cryptographic secret "key" to encrypt the message, and the recipient must use the same key to decipher or decrypt it. A widely adopted implementation of secret-key encryption is data encryption standard (DES).

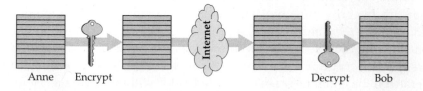

Figure 5.4   Secret-Key Encryption

Although secret-key encryption is useful in many cases, it has significant limitations. All parties must know and trust each other completely, and have in their possession a protected copy of the key. If the transmitter and receiver are in separate sites, they must trust not being overheard during face-to-face meetings or over a public messaging system (a phone system, a postal service) when the secret key is being exchanged. Anyone who overhears or intercepts the key in transit can later use that key to read all encrypted messages.

Since shared keys must be securely distributed to each communicating party, secret-key encryption suffers from the problem of key distribution—generation, transmission, and storage of keys. Secure key distribution is cumbersome in large networks and does not scale well to a business environment where a company deals with thousands of online customers. Further, secret-key encryption is impractical for exchanging messages with a large group of previously unknown parties over a public network. For instance, in order for a merchant to conduct transactions securely with Internet subscribers, each consumer would need a distinct secret key assigned by the merchant and transmitted over a separate secure channel such as a telephone, adding to the overall cost. Hence, given the difficulty of providing secure key management, it is hard to see secret-key encryption becoming a dominant player in electronic commerce.

If secret encryption cannot ensure safe electronic commerce, what can? The solution to widespread open network security is a newer, more sophisticated form of encryption, first developed in the 1970s, known as *public-key encryption*.

Public-Key Encryption

Public-key encryption, also known as *asymmetric encryption*, uses two keys: one key to encrypt the message and a different key to decrypt the message. The two keys are mathematically related so that data encrypted with one key can only be decrypted using the other (see Fig. 5.5).

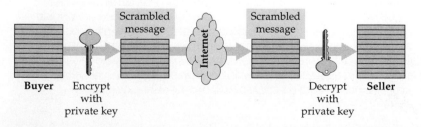

Figure 5.5   Public-Key Encryption

Unlike secret-key encryption, which uses a single key shared by two (or more) parties, public-key encryption uses a pair of keys for each party. One of the two keys is "public" and the other is "private." The public key can be made known to other parties; the private key must be kept confidential and must be known only to its owner. Both keys, however, need to be protected against modification.

The best known public-key encryption algorithm is RSA (named after its inventors Rivest, Shamir, and Adleman). In the RSA method, each participant creates two unique keys, a "public key," which is published in a sort of public directory, and a "private key," which is kept secret. The two keys work together; whatever data one of the keys "locks," only the other can unlock.

For example, if an individual wants to send a snoop-proof e-mail message to a friend, she simply looks up his public key and uses that key to encrypt her text. When the friend receives the e-mail, he uses his private key to convert the encrypted message on his computer screen back to the sender's original message in clear text. Since only the bona fide author of an encrypted message has knowledge of the private key, a successful decryption using the corresponding public key verifies the identity of the author and ensures message integrity. Even if a would-be criminal intercepts the message on its way to the intended recipient, that criminal has no way of deciphering the message without the private key.

Figure 5.6 illustrates what a public key looks like. This long string is actually a number represented in hexadecimal. The computer handles the hard work of manipulating the large numbers used in the math of encrypting and decrypting messages.

Table 5.4 compares secret- and public-key systems. Both types of systems offer advantages and disadvantages. Often, the two are combined to form a hybrid system to exploit the strengths of each method. To determine which type of encryption best meets its needs, an organization first has to identify its security requirements and operating environment. Public-key encryption is particularly useful when the parties wishing to communicate

```
mQCNAivxb7cAAAEEAN7+VovU/NxwQA3xBU24VnaDjeuPS90QTl/9jInwloZ6Qx/R
Rd1OEZWj5ZHPzHwReQvhUndfYFq2yzAmjqGRwDyt6DjZXSkghyCklcDnMWrNOISD
9QjJ1LwJbW5bpK7JEm0JHW2pBjLLaBoHSS9FexGFOAQRmWPUzO9iwsyOoA79AAUR
tB5QZXRlciBNaWRuaWdodCA8cGV0ZXJJAZmNzLm5ldD6JAJUCBRAw4F//hbas87gl
fWEBAULQA/sE5fL3768zk34CiTeIhMGAFZCMDFGsIXGX0xogMTAMtlONP/Hg6xdM
68hhloSmaQdD4gpqq5zNmkj/mh+RbviA7oQNVVDY8DRk1vcuP7Q/z4/RHnox0Erq
zo8vpRFosrbDJrQb46ux2op3kC9QA5Ox4kl44OwMAuP6fqiMsjx4WeC/lyhRH+nJ
=Cc4b
```

Figure 5.6   Example of a Public Key

cannot rely on each other or do not share a common key. This is often the case in online commerce.

Another prominent public-key method being used in online commerce today is called Digital Signatures.

Table 5.4 Comparing Secret-Key and Public-Key Encryption Methods

Features	Secret Key	Public Key
Number of Keys	Single key	Pair of keys
Types of Keys	Key is secret	One key is private, and one key is public
Key Management	Simple but difficult to manage	Need digital certificates and trusted third parties
Relative Speeds	Very fast	Slower
Usage	Used for bulk data encryption	Used for less demanding applications such as en-crypting small documents or to sign messages

Digital Signatures   Digital signatures are implemented using public-key encryption. A digital signature is a cryptographic mechanism that performs a similar function to a written signature. It is used to verify the origin and contents of a message. For example, a recipient of data (such as an e-mail message) can verify who signed the data and that the data was not modified after being signed.

Digital signatures are used for sender authentication. This also means that the originator (the sender of an e-mail message) cannot falsely deny having signed the data. In addition, a digital signature enables the computer to notarize the message, ensuring the recipient that the message has not been forged in transit.

Let us consider the following scenario of a customer, Susan, interacting with a merchant, Online Mart. When Susan orders something from Online Mart, she uses Online Mart's public key to encrypt her confidential information. Online Mart then uses its private key to decrypt the message (only a private key can unlock a document deciphered with a public key); thus the customer knows that only Online Mart received that data. To ensure further security, Susan can enclose a digital signature, encrypted with Susan's private key, which Online Mart could decrypt with Susan's public key and know that only Susan could have sent it. In the other direction,

Online Mart would send confidential information to Susan using Susan's public key, and only Susan could decrypt it using her private key. This scenario shows how digital signatures work in combination with public-key encryption to ensure authentication and privacy.

Technically, How Do Digital Signatures Work?   Data is electronically signed by applying the originator's private key to the data. To increase the speed of the process, the private key is applied to a shorter form of the data, called a "hash" or "message digest," rather than to the entire set of data. The resulting digital signature can be stored or transmitted along with the data. The signature can be verified by any party using the public key of the signer. This feature is very useful, for example, when distributing signed copies of virus-free software. Any recipient can verify that the program remains virus-free. If the signature verifies properly, then the verifier has confidence that the data was not modified after being signed and that the owner of the public key was the signer.

Digital signatures ensure authentication in the following way. In order to digitally sign a document, a user combines her private key and the document and performs a computation on the composite (key+document) in order to generate a unique number called the *digital signature*. For example, when an electronic document, such as an order form with a credit card number, is run through the digital signature process, the output is a unique "fingerprint" of the document. This "fingerprint" is attached to the original message and further encrypted with the signer's private key. If a user is communicating with her bank, she sends the result of the second encryption to her bank. The bank then decrypts the document using her public key, and checks to see if the enclosed message has been tampered with by a third party. To verify the signature, the bank performs a computation involving the original document, the purported digital signature, and the customer's public key. If the results of the computation generate a matching "fingerprint" of the document, the digital signature is verified as genuine; otherwise, the signature may be fraudulent or the message altered.

Digital signatures, variations of which are being explored by several companies, are the basis for secure commerce. A digital signature provides a way to associate the message with the sender, and is the cyberspace equivalent of "signing" for purchases. In this way, consumers can use credit card accounts over the Internet. Interested readers can refer to [SCHN96] for a more detailed mathematical discussion of digital signatures.

Digital Certificates   Authentication is further strengthened by the use of digital certificates. Before two parties, Bob and Alice, use public-key encryption to conduct business, each wants to be sure that the other party is authenticated. Before Bob accepts a message with Alice's digital signature, he wants to be sure that the public key belongs to Alice and not to someone masquerading as Alice on an open network. One way to be sure that the public key belongs to Alice is to receive it over a secure channel directly from Alice. However, in most circumstances this solution is not practical.

An alternative to the use of a secure channel is to use a trusted third party to authenticate that the public key belongs to Alice. Such a party is known as a certificate authority (CA). Once Alice has provided proof of her identity, the certificate authority creates a message containing Alice's name and her public key. This message, known as a certificate, is digitally signed by the certificate authority. It contains owner identification information, as well as a copy of one of the owner's public keys. To get the most benefit, the public key of the certificate authority should be known to as many people as possible. Thus by using one public key (that of a CA) as a trusted third-party means of establishing authentication, disparate parties can engage in electronic commerce with a high degree of trust.

In many ways, digital certificates are the heart of secure electronic transactions. Through the use of a common third party, digital certificates provide an easy and convenient way to ensure that the participants in an electronic commerce transaction can trust each other. For example, in the credit card industry, Visa provides digital certificates to the card-issuing financial institution, and the institution then provides a digital certificate to the cardholder. A similar process takes place for the merchant. At the time of the transaction, each party's software validates both merchant and cardholder before any information is exchanged. The validation takes place by checking the digital certificates that were both issued by an authorized and trusted third party. In short, digital certificates ensure that two computers talking to each other may successfully conduct electronic commerce.

Implementation and Management Issues

This section explores important issues that should be considered when designing, implementing, and integrating encryption to engage in electronic commerce.

Hardware versus Software Implementations   Encryption can be implemented in either hardware or software. Each has its related costs and benefits. The trade-offs among security, cost, simplicity, efficiency, and ease of implementation need to be studied when acquiring security products.

In general, software is less expensive and slower than hardware, although for large applications, hardware may be less expensive. In addition, software is less secure, since it is more easily modified or bypassed than some hardware products.

In many cases, encryption is implemented in a hardware device (such as a card/key entry system), but is controlled by software. This software requires integrity protection to ensure that the hardware device is provided with correct information (controls, data) and is not bypassed. Thus, a hybrid solution of software and hardware is generally provided. Effective security requires the correct management of the entire hybrid solution.

Key Management   All keys need to be protected against modification, and secret keys and private keys need protection against unauthorized disclosure. The proper management of cryptographic keys is essential to the effective use of encryption for security. Key management involves the procedures and protocols, both manual and automated, used throughout the entire life cycle of the keys. This includes the generation, distribution, storage, entry, use, destruction, and archiving of cryptographic keys. Ultimately, the security of information protected by encryption directly depends upon the protection afforded to keys.

With secret-key encryption, the secret key(s) must be securely distributed (safeguarded against unauthorized replacement, modification, and disclosure) to the parties wishing to communicate. Depending on the number and location of users, this task may be difficult. Automated techniques for generating and distributing cryptographic keys can ease overhead costs of key management, but some resources have to be devoted to this task.

Public-key encryption users also have to satisfy certain key management requirements. For example, since a private/public-key pair is associated with (generated or held by) a specific user, it is necessary to link the public part of the key pair to the user. In some cases, the key may be linked to a position or an organization, rather than to an individual user.

In a small community of users, public keys and their "owners" can be strongly bound by simply exchanging public keys. However, business conducted on a larger scale, involving geographically distributed users, necessitates a means for obtaining public keys online with a high degree of confidence in their integrity and binding to individuals. The support for the binding between a key and its owner is generally referred to as a *public-key infrastructure*. This involves support for users being able to enter the community of key holders, generate keys (or have them generated on their behalf), disseminate public keys, revoke keys (in case, for example, of compromise of the private key), and change keys. In addition, it may be necessary to build in time/date stamping and to archive keys for verification of old signatures.

Complying with Export Rules   A number of governments have regulations regarding the import or export of encryption. The U.S. government controls the export of cryptographic implementations because it considers them part of munitions. As a general rule, the U.S. government allows encryption to be used when: the data being encrypted is of a financial nature and the transaction is between known banks; the content of the data is well-defined; the length of the data is limited; and the encryption cannot easily be used for other purposes. The rules governing export can be quite complex, since they consider multiple factors. In addition, encryption is a rapidly changing field, and rules may change from time to time. Questions concerning the export of a particular implementation should be addressed to appropriate legal counsel.

Other Business Issues   Three problems deter widespread acceptance of encryption for public commerce. First, successful encryption requires that all participating parties use the same encryption scheme. Standards that make encryption feasible have to be established within an organization or a cooperating group (such as banks).

Second, the distribution of keys has prevented wider use of encryption, as there is no easy way to distribute the secret key to an unknown person on the network. The only safe way to communicate a key is in person, and even then the distributor must provide a different secret key for each person. Even public-key schemes require a method for key distribution.

The final deterrent to widespread acceptance of encryption is that it is difficult to use. For encryption to flourish, the encryption user interface must be simplified so that an average consumer can easily use the software. Currently, a consumer will not wait more than a few seconds for information access or retrieval. In the future, encryption will be done by fast hardware rather than software.

Legal Issues   As encryption becomes commonplace in the commercial world, employers will face the problem of producing documents that only certain employees can decrypt. Given labor force mobility, a company may be confronted with the task of producing documents encrypted by ex-employees who may not wish to cooperate.

Encryption raises a plethora of legal problems for corporations including: Will courts tolerate the production of pivotal evidence in encrypted form? Will a party's counsel produce information or data without first having it decrypted, leaving the opposing counsel with the task of "cracking" the encryption? On what basis could counsel claim such a data file was irrelevant or privileged? Will the producer have the onus of contacting the ex-employee in the hope that the employee will remember the password necessary for decryption? Will the courts compel individuals to provide their passwords?

Imagine the operational problems if all employees routinely used encryption and changed their passwords regularly, both encouraged practices in security-minded organizations. It may not be unusual, in the years ahead, to find that 100 percent of all electronic mail messages, and perhaps 30 to 50 percent of computer-based documents, are stored in encrypted form [AJL94].

5.4 World Wide Web and Security

For the purposes of electronic commerce, it is important that clients authenticate themselves to servers and that servers authenticate themselves to clients. Whenever a message enters the public Internet for transfer, it must bear some unambiguous identification of the system from which it came. On the network this identification often takes the form of an IP address. Sender authentication is performed at the time a sender submits a message and/or by a gateway system when a message has been delivered to it.

Several software companies and electronic marketplace providers are tackling the issue of secure Web information transfer by developing additional data security measures that involve encryption or digital coding of sensitive data, such as credit card numbers, between the client (user) and server (merchant). The following sections discuss how data encryption is done on the Web using Netscape's Secure Sockets layer, as well as how authentication is ensured.

Netscape's Secure Sockets Layer

Netscape developed Secure Sockets Layer (SSL) to address security concerns about information transferred over the Web. Along with Netscape, other major players in the implementation of SSL include IBM, Microsoft, and Spyglass, all of which are incorporating SSL into their client and server applications.

The Web itself does not encrypt the data sent across it, and anyone who intercepts a Web transmission has complete access to the information contained therein. Through the use of SSL, if a transmission falls into the wrong hands, the information it contains—a credit card number, for example—should be unreadable to anyone other than the sender and receiver.

SSL works in the following way. When a user surfs the Web with the Netscape browser, the browser communicates with Web servers using a language called hypertext transport protocol (HTTP). To download an HTML (hypertext markup language) file of a home page, for example, the browser sends an "HTTP GET" command to the server and the server responds by transmitting the file's contents to the browser. The text of the GET command and the text of the HTML file are sent and received through connections called *sockets*, which enable two remote computers to talk to each other via the Internet. The security problem arises because most of the transmission during the connection is done in the clear (or plaintext), which can be read by almost anyone with access. SSL solves this problem by encrypting HTTP transmissions. Data is automatically encrypted before it is transmitted and then unencrypted on the receiving end. In between, the data is a meaningless jumble of zeros and ones to anyone without the decryption key.

The encryption key that the Netscape browser uses to encode SSL transmissions is generated automatically on a per-session basis from information such as time of day that is gathered at runtime during the transaction. SSL security hinges on the difficulty of unlocking an encrypted message without the key. SSL relies on RC4, a well-known block-encryption algorithm invented by Ron Rivest. RC4 is generally believed to be secure, although the exact details of the algorithm are guarded and have not been subjected to independent scrutiny. For more on RC4 see [SCHN96].

Assuming that the underlying algorithm is mathematically secure, the difficulty of cracking an encrypted SSL message is a function of the key length. If the encryption key is only 8 bits long, for example, messages would be easily decipherable because 8 bits allows only 256 possible keys. A computer could arrive at a solution very quickly simply by trying all 256 keys in a sequential manner (also called brute force method of figuring out the solution). A key containing 512 bits, however, would present a formidable obstacle. With billions of different combinations, a supercomputer capable of testing one million keys per second would require centuries to find the key to the encrypted message.

SSL is far from flawless. Experts have expressed concern about the encryption method. Netscape uses a 40-bit key in the international versions of its browser and servers, as required by the U.S. State Department. The RC4 regulations—named for the RC4 algorithm on which SSL is based—limit the export of products with encryption keys longer than 40 bits. These regulations make Netscape's 128-bit encryption key illegal outside the United States. The now-famous case of a French graduate student and two Berkeley graduate students who cracked an SSL key created some doubt about how secure SSL-based systems are. Microsoft is attempting to correct the perceived shortcomings of SSL with an SSL superset protocol called PCT (private communications technology). PCT will spawn a second key specifically for authentication. The authentication does not fall under the RC4 restrictions, which deal only with bulk encryption. PCT also incorporates a more robust random-number generator than the present generator, which is considered another weak link in SSL's security chain. The random-number generator provides the seed number for generating the encryption key.

S-HTTP (secure hypertext transport protocol) is another important security scheme for the Web that is based on public-key encryption. However, S-HTTP seems to have drawn little support from the Web community because it is limited to dealing specifically with HTTP (Web server) transactions. The other specifications discussed here are designed to work with a variety of Internet server types.

The SSL and S-HTTP Web implementation on the market today provide for confidentiality, integrity, and server authentication, but few offer digital signatures. Digital signatures are needed for customer authentication, and to ensure that the company doing business on the Internet knows who is at the other end. If a customer orders a product and provides a credit card number, it is not always necessary to know who has placed the order, and thus many Internet shopping ventures have proceeded without digital signatures; the credit card number is enough for some companies. Banks, however, will probably want to wait for robust digital signatures. A new protocol called the secure electronic transactions (SET) has recently been developed to provide digital signature capability for financial transactions on the Web (see Chapter 6).

Security and Online Web-based Banking

Security First Network Bank (SFNB) is an online bank that uses a combo of firewalls and encryption to keep consumer deposits and transactions secure. For the business model behind SFNB see Chapter 7.

Security is the primary concern in Web-based banking. Security from loss liability is the first level of consumer protection. Like other banks, deposits at SFNB are FDIC insured, up to applicable limits (generally up to $100,000). Security from "hacker" threat is the second level of consumer protection. SFNB, after seeking the opinions of security experts and becoming convinced that the requisite security technologies currently exist, aligned themselves with Hewlett Packard's subsidiary SecureWare, to develop the security architecture upon which their bank would be built.

Elements of the Security Architecture SecureWare has designed a secure Web platform utilizing a three-tiered security architecture:

Encryption technologies to protect data and ensure privacy as information travels over open networks.

Firewalls and filtering routers to limit access to the system from external networks.

A trusted operating system (Trusted OS running on HP-UX version 10.0), which provides strong access controls that create a virtual lockbox for each customer, protecting against unauthorized tampering with private account information.

Data Encryption Encryption is provided using Netscape's SSL protocol (Secure Sockets Layer)—a protocol for securing data communication across computer networks. SSL is used to provide privacy for the data flowing between the browser and the bank server by providing a secure channel for data transmission. It allows transfer of certificates for authentication procedures and provides message integrity, insuring that the data cannot be altered en route. SFNB is also using public-key encryption to ensure client and server authentication. Under public key cryptography, the bank will issue its customers a public/private key pair. The public key is a widely distributed number, and the private key is known only to its owner. Messages encrypted using the public key can only be decrypted with the private key. Key pairs are the perfect mechanism for mutual authentication, that is, each participant in a transaction can verify the identity of the other before proceeding. Customers can be certain they are transmitting information to the bank and not to a malicious third party. At the same time, the bank is assured that the data it receives is from an authorized customer, not an intruder looking for a way to break in.

Firewalls Firewalls and filtering routers provide SFNB protection from intruders. Each presents an additional barrier between the Internet and the internal bank network. Filtering routers are used to verify the source and destination of each information packet sent to the bank, and filter out all packets not addressed to specific network services. In order to prevent outside users from trying to masquerade as internal sources, the filtering router eliminates any outside packets with an inside source address. Only S-HTTP traffic is allowed to the Bank Server.

Firewalls work like filtering routers, examining each packet of information that is sent across the Internet to the customer service network. The purpose of the firewall is to protect the bank's internal network from outside observation. All traffic to the firewall is filtered through an e-mail proxy, which verifies the source and destination of each information packet, and eliminates any with suspicious attachments or subject lines. The proxy then changes the IP address of the packet to deliver it to the appropriate site within the internal network. This protects inside addresses from outside access.

Trusted Operating System   The bank server runs a trusted operating system, called CMW+, which represents the first commercial implementation of this highly successful platform used for years by the Department of Defense and other high-security government agencies. The trusted operating system acts as a "virtual vault," protecting customer information and funds inside the bank. It uses multilevel technology, and contains privilege and authorization mechanisms that control access to functions and commands. It also contains an audit mechanism that records log-ins and log-outs, use of privilege, access violations, and unsuccessful network connections. This allows quick identification of any suspicious activity.

5.5 Summary

This chapter discussed the security threats electronic commerce transactions face that can result in significant financial and information losses. Threats vary from malicious hackers attempting to crash a system, to threats to data or transaction integrity. An understanding of the various types of threats can assist a security manager in selecting appropriate cost-effective controls to protect valuable information resources. An overview of many of today's common threats presented in this chapter will be useful to mangers studying their own threat environments with a view toward developing solutions specific to their organization.

To ensure security on the Internet, several methods have been developed and deployed. They include: firewalls for perimeter security, authentication of users and servers, encryption, and data integrity. Transaction security is critical; without it, information transmitted over the Internet is susceptible to fraud and other misuse. Information traveling between consumers and remote servers uses a routing process that can extend over many computer systems. Any one of these computer systems represents an intermediary with the potential to access the flow of information between a user and a server. Security is needed to ensure that intermediaries cannot eavesdrop on transactions, or copy/modify data.

However, just having secure transactions is not enough for business. Merchants or sellers must address all Internet security concerns. For example, consumers must be willing to trust the merchant's server with their credit card number before entering into a commercial transaction. Security technology may secure the routes of Internet communication, but it does not protect consumers from people with whom they might choose to do business. The situation is analogous to telling an unknown person the credit card number over the telephone; the consumer may be secure in knowing that no one has overheard the conversation and that the person on the other end works for the company they wish to buy from, but to conduct business the consumer must also be willing to take the extra step and trust the person and the company.

Likewise, online firms must take additional precautions to prevent security breaches. To protect consumer information, they must maintain physical security of their servers and control access to software passwords and private keys. Techniques such as secret and public-key encryption and digital signatures play a crucial role in developing consumer confidence in electronic commerce.

Chapter 6

Electronic Payment Systems

Chapter Outline

Electronic payment is an integral part of electronic commerce. Broadly defined, electronic payment is a financial exchange that takes place online between buyers and sellers. The content of this exchange is usually some form of digital financial instrument (such as encrypted credit card numbers, electronic checks, or digital cash) that is backed by a bank or an intermediary, or by legal tender. Three factors are stimulating interest among financial institutions in electronic payments: decreasing technology costs, reduced operational and processing costs, and increasing online commerce.

The desire to reduce costs is one major reason for the increase in electronic payments. Cash and checks are very expensive to process, and banks are seeking less costly alternatives. It is estimated that approximately 56 percent of consumer transactions in the United States are cash and 29 percent are check. Credits, debits, and other electronic transactions account for about 15 percent of all consumer transactions, and are expected to increase rapidly. Electronic transactions numbered 33 billion in 1993 and are expected to climb to 118 billion by the year 2000. For the same period, paper transactions are forecast to show very modest growth, from 117 billion in

1993 to 135 billion in the year 2000. Banks and retailers want to wean customers away from paper transactions because the processing overhead is both labor intensive and costly.

The crucial issue in electronic commerce revolves around how consumers will pay businesses online for various products and services. Currently, consumers can view an endless variety of products and services offered by vendors on the Internet, but a consistent and secure payment capability does not exist. The solutions proposed to the online payment problem have been *ad hoc* at best. For instance, in one method marketed by CyberCash, users install client software packages, sometimes known as "electronic wallets," on their browsers. This software then communicates with "electronic cash registers" that run on merchants' Web servers. Each vendor's client works with only that vendor's own server software, a rather restrictive scenario. Currently, merchants face the unappealing option of either picking one standard and alienating consumers not subscribing to a standard or needing to support multiple standards, which entails extra time, effort, and money.

Today, the proliferation of incompatible electronic payment schemes has stifled electronic commerce in much the same way the split between Beta and VHS standards stifled the video industry's growth in the 1970s. Banks faced similar problems in off-line commerce in the early nineteenth century. Many banks issued their own notes, and a recurrent problem was the tendency of some institutions to issue more notes than they had gold as backing. Further, getting one bank to honor another's notes was a major problem. Innovations in payment methods involved the creation of new financial instruments that relied on backing from governments or central banks, and gradually came to be used as money. Banks are solving these problems all over again in an online environment.

The goal of online commerce is to develop a small set of payment methods that are widely used by consumers and widely accepted by merchants and banks. This chapter offers a brief examination of the various types of electronic payment systems. It then provides an overview of the business, consumer, and legal implications of electronic payment systems.

6.1 Overview of the Electronic Payment Technology

Electronic payments first emerged with the development of wire transfers. Early wire transfer services such as Western Union enabled an individual to deliver currency to a clerk at one location, who then instructed a clerk at another location to disburse funds to a party at that second location who was able to identify himself as the intended recipient. Cash was delivered to the customer only after identity was established. In this scenario, there was no banking environment; Western Union was a telegraph company. Assurance of payment relied on the financial stability of the firm. Security was provided to the extent that Western Union was a privately controlled transmission facility used to send messages about funds transfer; its lines were not shared with the public, and transactions were private. Authentication was provided only by a signature at the other end of the transmission that verified that the intended party had indeed received the funds.

During the 1960s and early 1970s, private networking technology has enabled the development of alternative electronic funds transfer (EFT) systems. Electronic funds transfer systems have shortened the time of payment instruction transfer between banks, and in the process have reduced float. However, EFT systems have not changed the fundamental structure of the payment system. Many of the so-called payment innovations over the past two decades have been aimed at minimizing banking costs such as reserve requirements, speeding up check clearing, and minimizing fraud. However, the consumer rarely interacted with the early EFT systems. Recent innovations in electronic commerce aim to affect the way consumers deal with payments and appear to be in the direction of a real-time electronic transmission, clearing, and settlement system.

Consumer electronic payment systems are growing rapidly, but the opportunities are scarcely tapped. In the United States, it is estimated that only 3 percent of the $460 billion supermarket industry is transacted on credit or debit cards. Only 1 percent of the $300 billion professional services area is transacted electronically. Less than 12 percent of business at gasoline service stations is electronic and less than 1 percent of fast food restaurants have magstripe readers. The educational market alone is more than $100 billion today, only 6 percent of which is transacted electronically. Even more important is the predicted growth ahead. Consumer payments at the point of sale were $3.6 trillion in 1994, 19 percent of which was on credit and debit cards [FD95].

Recently, several innovations helped to simplify consumer payments. These include:

- **Innovations affecting consumers:** credit and debit cards, automated teller machines (ATMs), stored-value cards, and electronic banking.

- **Innovations enabling online commerce:** digital cash, electronic checks, smart cards (also called electronic purses), and encrypted credit cards.

- **Innovations affecting companies:** the payment mechanisms that banks provide to corporate customers, such as interbank transfers through automated clearing houses (ACHs) that allow companies to pay workers by direct deposit. (The U.S. government can also use direct deposit for social security recipients.)

The rest of this chapter will focus on online consumer-related payments.

The Online Shopping Experience

To understand how electronic payments fit into the shopping experience, consider the following process [SET96]:

> The consumer browses for items. Using a Web browser, consumers view an online catalog on the merchant's World Wide Web page, viewing a catalog supplied by the merchant on a CD-ROM, or looking at a paper catalog.
>
> The consumer selects items to be purchased. He does this by comparing prices and gauging the best value based on brand name, prices, quality, and other variables.
>
> The merchant presents the consumer with an order form containing the list of items, their prices, and total prices, which include shipping, handling, and taxes. This order form may be delivered from the merchant's server to the consumer's PC. Some online merchants may provide the consumer with the ability to negotiate pricing (such as by presenting frequent shopper identification or information about a competitor's pricing).
>
> The consumer selects the means of payment. The different means of payment include digital cash, electronic checks, or credit cards.
>
> The consumer sends the merchant a completed order and a means of payment.
>
> The merchant requests payment authorization from the consumer's bank.
>
> The merchant sends the customer a confirmation of the order shipment and payment.
>
> The merchant ships the goods or performs the requested services as per the order.
>
> The merchant requests payment from the consumer's financial institution.

The ensuing sections focus on the steps where the consumer chooses a electronic payment mechanism as the means of carrying out the transaction.

Limitations of Traditional Payment Instruments

In their present form, traditional payment methods such as checks are not adequate for real-time payment interaction. "Real-time" means that these transactions are triggered and completed when the consumer hits the "pay" button on the Web browser. With real-time payments, a consumer's Web browser delivers payment instructions to a merchant, who forwards those instructions to a network bank. The bank then authenticates the individual and disburses funds to the merchant. The merchant delivers the purchased product upon customer verification.

Off-line payment methods make two fundamental assumptions:

The transacting parties—buyer and seller—will at some time be in each other's physical presence.

There will be a sufficient delay in the payment process for detection of fraud, overdraft, and other problems to be identified and corrected.

These assumptions are not valid for electronic commerce, and thus many of these payment mechanisms are being modified and adapted for the efficient conduct of business over computer networks.

Problems with Traditional Payment Methods   Traditional payment methods do not work online for the following reasons:

- **Lack of convenience.** Traditional payment methods generally require that the consumer leave the online platform and use the telephone or send a check in order to make payment.

- **Lack of security.** In order to make a traditional payment over the Internet, a consumer has to provide card/payment account details and other personal information online. Leaving the Internet and providing the card/payment account details over the telephone and/or by mail also entails security risks.

- **Lack of coverage.** Credit cards only work with signed-up merchants, and do not generally support individual-to-individual or direct business-to-business payment transactions.

- **Lack of eligibility.** Not all potential buyers have suitable credit ratings to allow them access to credit cards and/or checking accounts.

- **Lack of support for microtransactions.** Many payments made over the Internet are of sufficiently low value that the cost of a phone call or letter may be too high of an overhead. The cost of handling these payment methods is often too high for the seller to break even.

To better suit the needs of electronic commerce, several companies are developing entirely new forms of financial instruments such as digital cash, electronic money, and electronic checks. The common element in all these financial instruments is the notion of an electronic token for supporting micropayments.

Micropayments   Micropayments, or small-fee transactions, are the driver behind many of the new electronic token-based methods. Micropayments typically involve nickel-and-dime transactions. For example, if company X charged five cents to download a customer service file "cs123.txt" from its FTP server and 20,000 people chose to do it every day, then X would have $1000 added to its bank account just for that one file. Now assume that there are 1000 files with similar activity. This volume of activity entails $1,000,000 changing hands in one day.

With traditional payment methods, processing even a five-cent transaction could cost a bank as much as $1.00. The overhead is high because the accounting systems of several banks have to be able to respond to a message of the format "transfer five cents from account #1231 of Bank X [the purchaser] to account #5432 of Bank Y [the service provider]." Although the transaction itself is not complex, the surrounding issues of settlement between the payor and payee banks and verification of funds to cover the transaction add to the overall cost.

The potential usefulness of small-money transfers in generating a steady cash flow, combined with the inability of traditional banks to meet this need, has created a vacuum. Some entrepreneurs appear to be moving in to fill the vacuum and to supply a form of electronic token that can be used on the Internet.

Types of Electronic Tokens   An electronic token is a digital analog of various forms of payment backed by a bank or financial institution. The two basic types of tokens are real-time (or pre-paid) tokens and postpaid tokens.

Real-time tokens are exchanged between buyer and seller. Here, users prepay for tokens that serve as currency. Transactions are settled with the exchange of electronic currency. Examples of prepaid payment mechanisms are digital cash, debit cards, and electronic purses that store electronic money (such as Mondex Electronic Money Card).

Settlement or postpaid tokens are used with funds transfer instructions being exchanged between buyer and seller. Examples of postpaid mechanisms are electronic checks (such as NetCheck and NetBill), encrypted credit cards (Web form-based encryption), and third-party authorization mechanisms (such as First Virtual, which is an online intermediary).

Evaluating Various Electronic Token-based Methods   Before examining the specifics of each type of payment instrument, we will discuss the following questions to help us to evaluate the various methods.

What is the nature of the transaction for which the instrument is designed? Some tokens are specifically designed to handle micropayments, or payments for small snippets of information (such as five cents for a file). Some systems target specific niche transactions; others seek more general transactions. The key is to identify the parties involved, the average amounts, and the purchase interaction.

What is the means of settlement used?   Tokens must be backed by cash, credit, electronic bill payments (prearranged and spontaneous), cashier's checks, letters of credit, or wire transfers. Each option incurs trade-offs among transaction speed, risk, and cost. Most transaction settlement methods use credit cards, while others use other tokens for value, effectively creating currencies of dubious liquidity and with interesting tax, risk, and float implications.

What is the payment system's approach to security, anonymity, and authentication?   Electronic tokens vary in the protection of transaction privacy and confidentiality. Encryption can help with authentication, nonrepudiability, and confidentiality of information.

Who assumes what kind of risk at what time?   Tokens might suddenly become worthless because of bank failure leaving customers with currency that nobody will accept. If the system stores value in a smart card, consumers may be exposed to risk as they hold static assets. Further, electronic tokens might be subject to discounting or arbitrage. If the transaction has a long lag time between product delivery and payment to merchants, there is a risk to merchants that buyers will not pay, or to buyers that the vendor will not deliver.

6.2 Electronic or Digital Cash

Electronic or digital cash combines computerized convenience with security and privacy that improve on paper cash. The versatility of digital cash opens up a host of new markets and applications. Digital cash attempts to replace paper cash as the principal payment vehicle in online payments. Although it may be surprising to some, even after thirty years of developments in electronic payment systems, cash is still the most prevalent consumer payment instrument. Cash remains the dominant form of payment for three reasons: lack of consumer trust in the banking system; inefficient clearing and settlement of noncash transactions; and negative real interest rates on bank deposits.

These reasons behind the prevalent use of cash in business transactions indicate the need to re-engineer purchasing processes. In order to displace cash, electronic payment systems need to have some cash-like qualities that current credit and debit cards lack. For example, cash is negotiable, meaning that it can be given or traded to someone else. Cash is legal tender, meaning that the payee is obligated to take it. Cash is a bearer instrument, meaning that possession is proof of ownership. Cash can be held and used by anyone, even those without a bank account. Finally, cash places no risk on the part of the acceptor; the medium is always good.

In comparison to cash, debit and credit cards have a number of limitations. First, credit and debit cards cannot be given away because, technically, they are identification cards owned by the issuer and restricted to one user. Credit and debit cards are not legal tender, given that merchants have the right to refuse to accept them. Nor are credit and debit cards bearer instruments; their usage requires an account relationship and authorization system. Similarly, checks require either personal knowledge of the payer, or a check guarantee system. A really novel electronic payment method needs to do more than recreate the convenience that is offered by credit and debit cards; it needs to create a form of digital cash that has some of the properties of cash.

Properties of Electronic Cash

Any digital cash system must incorporate a few common features. Specifically, digital cash must have the following four properties: monetary value, interoperability, retrievability, and security [KALA96].

Digital cash must have a monetary value; it must be backed by cash (currency), bank-authorized credit, or a bank-certified cashier's check. When digital cash created by one bank is accepted by others, reconciliation must occur without any problems. Without proper bank certification, digital cash carries the risk that when deposited, it might be returned for insufficient funds.

Digital cash must be interoperable, or exchangeable as payment for other digital cash, paper cash, goods or services, lines of credit, deposits in banking accounts, bank notes or obligations, electronic benefits transfers, and the like. Most digital cash proposals use a single bank [MN93]. In practice, not all customers are going to be using the same bank or even be in the same country, and thus multiple banks are necessary for the widespread use of digital cash.

Digital cash must be storable and retrievable. Remote storage and retrieval (such as via a telephone or personal communications device) would allow users to exchange digital cash (withdraw from and deposit into banking accounts) from home or office or while traveling. The cash could be stored on a remote computer's memory, in smart cards, or on other easily transported standard or special-purpose devices. As it might be easy to create and store counterfeit cash in a computer, it is preferable to store cash on an unalterable dedicated device. This device should have a suitable interface to facilitate personal authentication using passwords or other means, and a display for viewing the card's contents.

Digital cash should not be easy to copy or tamper with while it is being exchanged. It should be possible to prevent or detect duplication and double-spending of digital cash. Double spending, the electronic equivalent of bouncing a check, is a particularly tricky issue [DFN88]. For instance, a consumer could use the same digital cash simultaneously to buy items in Japan, India, and England. It is particularly difficult to prevent double-spending if multiple banks are involved in the transactions. For this reason, most systems rely on post-fact detection and punishment.

Digital Cash in Action

Digital cash is based on cryptographic systems called "digital signatures" (see Chapter 5). This method involves a pair of numeric keys (very large integers or numbers) that work in tandem: one for locking (or encryption), and the other for unlocking (or decryption). Messages encoded with one numeric key can only be decoded with the other numeric key. The encryption key is kept private and the decryption key is made public.

By supplying all customers (buyers and sellers) with its public key, a bank enables customers to decode any message (or currency) encoded with the bank's private key. If decryption by a customer yields a recognizable message, the customer can be confident that the bank encoded it. Over the past two decades, digital signatures have been as secure as the mathematics involved, and have proved to be more resistant to forgery than handwritten signatures. Before digital cash can be used to buy products or services, it must be procured from a currency server.

Purchasing Digital Cash from Currency Servers   The purchase of digital cash from an online currency server (or bank) involves two steps: the establishment of an account, and the maintenance of sufficient money in the account to back any purchases. Some customers might prefer to purchase digital cash with paper currency, either to maintain anonymity, or because they do not have bank accounts.

Currently, most digital cash systems require that customers have an account with a central online bank. This requirement is restrictive for international use and multicurrency transactions; customers should be able to access and pay for foreign services as well as local services. To support global access, digital cash must be available in multiple currencies backed by multiple banks. A service provider in one country could then accept tokens of various currencies from users in many different countries, redeem them with their issuers, and have the funds transferred back to banks in the local country. A possible solution is to form an association of online banks that would serve as a clearinghouse.

Once the account has been established, consumers use the digital cash software on the computer to generate a random number, which serves as the "note." In exchange for money debited from the customer's account, the bank uses its private key to digitally sign the note for the amount requested, and transmits the note back to the customer. In effect, the network currency server is issuing a "bank note," with a serial number and a dollar amount. Through its digital signature, the bank commits itself to back that note with its face value in real dollars.

This method of note generation is very secure, as neither the customer (payer) nor the merchant (payee) can counterfeit the bank's digital signature. Payer and payee can verify that the payment is valid, since each knows the bank's public key. The bank is protected against forgery, the payee is protected against the bank's refusal to honor a legitimate note, and the user is protected against false accusations and invasion of privacy.

How does this process of note generation work in practice? In the case of DigiCash, a company that implemented digital cash systems, every customer has an account at a digital bank. Using that account, people can withdraw and deposit digital cash. When a digital cash withdrawal is made, the digital cash user's PC calculates how many digital coins of what denominations are needed to pay the requested amount. The result of these calculations is sent to the digital bank. The bank debits the client's account for the same amount. The authenticated cash is sent back to the user. The serial numbers plus the bank's digital signatures are now digital coins, and their value is guaranteed by the bank.

Using the Digital Currency   Once the tokens are purchased, the digital cash software on the customer's PC stores digital money undersigned by a bank. The user can spend the digital money at any shop accepting digital cash, without having to open an account or having to transmit credit card numbers. As soon as the customer wants to make a payment, the software collects and transfers the necessary amount from the stored tokens.

Two types of payment transactions are possible: bilateral and trilateral. Typically, transactions involving cash are bilateral or two-party (buyer and seller) transactions, in which the merchant checks the veracity of the note's digital signature by using the bank's public key. If satisfied with the payment, the merchant stores the digital currency on her machine and later deposits it in the bank to redeem the face value of the note. Transactions involving financial instruments other than cash are usually trilateral or three-party (buyer, seller, and bank) transactions, in which the "notes" are sent to the merchant, who immediately sends them directly to the digital bank. The bank verifies the validity of these "notes" and ensures that they have not been spent before. The bank then credits the merchant's account.

In many business situations, bilateral transaction is not feasible because of the potential for double-spending. To detect double-spending, banks compare the notes received from the merchant against a database of spent notes. Like paper currency, digital cash is identifiable by serial numbers. In order to be able to detect double-spending, "notes" have to be registered in some form so that all "notes" issued globally can be uniquely identified. However, it is difficult to match notes with a central registry online. For banks, which handle high volumes of micropayments, this verification method is cumbersome and time consuming. In addition, the need to monitor notes forces banks to carry extra overhead because of constant checking and security logs.

6.3 Electronic Checks

Electronic checks are designed to accommodate the many individuals and entities that might prefer to pay on credit or through some mechanism other than cash. Electronic checks are modeled on paper checks, except that they are initiated electronically, use digital signatures for signing and endorsing, and require the use of digital certificates to authenticate the payer, the payer's bank, and bank account. The security/authentication aspects of digital checks are supported via digital signatures using public-key cryptography.

Ideally, electronic checks will facilitate new online services by: allowing new payment flows (the payee can verify funds availability at the payer's bank); enhancing security at each step of the transaction through automatic validation of the electronic signature by each party (payee and banks); and facilitating payment integration with widely used EDI-based electronic ordering and billing processes.

Electronic checks are delivered either by direct transmission using telephone lines, or by public networks such as the Internet. Electronic check payments (deposits) are gathered by banks and cleared through existing banking channels, such as automated clearing houses (ACH) networks. This integration of the existing banking infrastructure with public networks provides an implementation and acceptance path for banking, industry, and consumers to build on existing check processing facilities.

Benefits of Electronic Checks

Electronic checks have the following advantages:

Electronic checks work in the same way as traditional checks, thus simplifying customer education. By retaining the basic characteristics and flexibility of paper checks while enhancing the functionality, electronic checks can be easily understood and readily adopted.

Electronic checks are well suited for clearing micropayments; the conventional cryptography of electronic checks makes them easier to process than systems based on public-key cryptography (like digital cash). The payee and the payee's and payer's banks can authenticate checks through the use of public-key certificates. Digital signatures can also be validated automatically.

Electronic checks can serve corporate markets. Firms can use electronic checks to complete payments over the networks in a more cost-effective manner than present alternatives. Further, since the contents of a check can be attached to the trading partner's remittance information, the electronic check will easily integrate with EDI applications, such as accounts receivable.

Electronic checks create float, and the availability of float is an important requirement for commerce. The third-party accounting server can earn revenue by charging the buyer or seller a transaction fee or a flat rate fee, or it can act as a bank and provide deposit accounts and make money from the deposit account pool.

Electronic check technology links public networks to the financial payments and bank clearing networks, leveraging the access of public networks with the existing financial payments infrastructure.

Electronic Checks in Action

The electronic check process works in the following way:

Electronic check users must register with a third-party account server before they are able to write electronic checks. The account server also acts as a billing service. The registration procedure can vary depending on the particular account server, and may require a credit card or a bank account to back the checks.

Once registered, a consumer can then contact a seller of goods and services.

Using e-mail or other transport methods, the buyer sends an electronic check to the seller for a certain amount of money.

When deposited, the check authorizes the transfer of account balances from the account against which the check was drawn to the account to which the check was deposited.

As noted earlier, the electronic check was created to work in much the same way as a conventional paper check. An account holder will issue an electronic document that contains the name of the payer, the name of the payer's financial institution, the payer's account number, the name of the payee, and the amount of the check. Most of the information is in a nonencrypted form. Like a paper check, an electronic check will bear the digital equivalent of a signature. Further, again like a paper check, an e-check must be endorsed by the payee, using another electronic signature, before the check can be paid. Properly signed and endorsed checks can be electronically exchanged between financial institutions through electronic clearinghouses, with the institutions using these endorsed checks as tender to settle accounts.

NetCheck: A Prototype Electronic Check System

Clifford Neumann of the University of Southern California developed a prototype electronic check system called "NetCheck." NetCheck provides "accounting server" software that allows organizations to set up their own in-house, online "banks," which would accept paper checks or credit card payments in exchange for crediting a customer's NetCheck account. Such accounting servers will enable large organizations to pay bills and settle accounts with their own banks, in effect integrating their own internal accounting systems with those of the external financial institutions.

NetCheck works in the following manner. When the payee receives an electronic check, the payee presents it to the accounting server for verification and payment. The accounting server verifies the digital signature on the check. The payer's digital "signature" is used to create an order to a bank computer that authorizes fund transfer to the payee's bank. Figure 6.1 illustrates a check encashment scenario where a payer receives a bill/invoice from a payee, issues an electronic check, and sends it to the payee. The payee presents it directly to the accounting server for authentication. The accounting server verifies the check and notifies the payee, and then sends instructions to the payee's bank to debit money from the payer's account.

An interesting aspect of the NetCheck system is that it can be used as a resource management tool on Intranets, a form of internal cash. With the advent of Intranets, companies are looking at electronic payment technology as a crucial element of internal resource management. For instance, a company can provide digital money to its employees and charge for using the various networks, servers, and databases in order to ensure fair resource allocation. Each user in the organization could be given an account and be billed for his use of various resources, a measure that would allow organizations to use accounting mechanisms to manage resources more effectively. Also, with increased cross-functional activities, payment and settlement could become an integral part of Intranet-based commerce, where departments exchange goods and services among themselves. Such resource management will become important in the future as corporate networks become more congested.

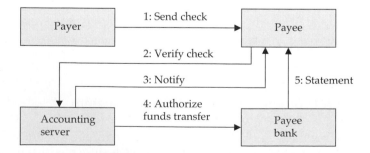

Figure 6.1   Check Encashment Process

Electronic Check Project

The Financial Services Technology Consortium (FSTC) is developing a prototype electronic check system. The FSTC is a consortium of members who come from the banking industry, financial service industry, banking associations, the computer and communications industry, and various governmental and research institutions. The goal is to develop a system that can work independently of the hardware, software, and financial service provider.

The electronic check project is directed at providing a safe, secure means of providing electronic check payment over online networks, such as the Internet, that is extensible to other forms of account-based payment, such as debit card and funds/money transfer. It is tied to bank accounts and existing clearing and payment systems. The electronic check project is designed for use at point of sale (POS), over phones, and through other emerging and existing consumer devices, as well as PCs over the Internet. It is based on the electronic analog to paper checks. Two parties can transact directly online over public communications (such as e-mail and the Web). Like a check, it does not require prior relationship between payor and payee.

The electronic check uses public-key cryptography to allow an individual to electronically issue and digitally sign a payment instruction, such as a check, and to transmit it over public networks, where it can be verified by the recipient as being a legitimate authorization from an authentic account that has not been altered. It is based on standards, and uses tamper-resistant hardware (PCMCIA card and/or Smart Cards) to add additional security/protection against fraud. In order for someone to make a fraudulent payment, he must not only know the customer's password, but also must possess the card. This card also allows for portability. Customers can transact anywhere. They do not need to own a PC; transactions can take place over any PC or device (kiosk, telephone) equipped to read their card. Electronic checking thus supports the notion of universal access.

Figure 6.1 illustrates the basic concept behind the electronic check. In this scenario, a purchase was paid for by electronic check using standard Internet browser and server hardware/software. The customer digitally signed the payment instructions, including remittance information, using a hardware electronic checkbook. The digitally signed check electronically transmitted to the merchant, where it was verified, electronically endorsed, and electronically delivered to the recipient's bank for collection. The bank then effected the actual transfer of funds between banks and bank accounts through an existing clearing and settlement network, in this case the ACH (automated clearinghouse network).

FSTC plans to initiate some pilot projects, in an effort to further test the security and interoperability of the concept, to refine the design, to test customer acceptance, and to demonstrate the business value of this payment mechanism.

6.4 Online Credit Card–Based Systems

Credit card payment negotiation involves two steps: The merchant presents the customer with product/service price, order confirmation and status, delivery notifications, and payment options accepted by the merchant; and the buyer presents the merchant with payment choice and associated information in a secure manner. As of yet, there is no standard way of sending secure payment instructions over the Web. Currently, consumers can "shop"—look at content and read product descriptions—in the Web environment, but have to go off-line in order to use their credit cards to actually make their purchases.

Recently, several companies, including CyberCash, VISA, and First Virtual, have implemented payment systems. Different vendors have lined up behind different proposed security measures, each fighting to be the dominant standard. As vendors continue to wage security standards battles, it is perfectly reasonable for consumers to be cautious about making online purchases. Until consumers feel as comfortable using their credit cards online as they do over the telephone, Web-based commerce will languish rather than flourish.

The different payment schemes require customers to set up special accounts, and/or buy or download and install special software for their personal computers. However, not all banks can handle different payment systems. In order to avoid losing customers by selecting one payment method over another, some merchants sidestep the confusion caused by multiple payment standards by verifying credit card transactions manually. They take credit card numbers over the Internet, and then, at the end of the day, batch the verification process. If there is a problem, they send e-mail to the customers informing them of the problem.

Safe credit card–based commerce will not be possible until security standards are in place. Security standards ensure the negotiation of payment schemes and protocols, and the safe transport of payment instructions. Microsoft/VISA and Netscape/Verifone contend that they can vastly simplify the payment process by developing software for both banks and merchants. The bank software would allow banks to use their existing computer systems to verify and process encrypted credit cards coming from the online world. The merchant software would allow merchants to buy one single package integrated with a Web server that serves as a storefront and payment system. The customer can simply continue to use his or her current browser to interact with the electronic storefront.

Types of Credit Card Payments

Credit card–based payments can be divided into three categories:

- **Payments using plain credit card details.** The easiest method of credit card payment is the exchange of unencrypted credit cards over a public network such as telephone lines or the Internet. The low level of security inherent in the design of the Internet makes this method problematic (any hacker can read a credit card number, and there are programs that scan the Internet traffic for credit card numbers and send the numbers to their programmers). Authentication is also a significant problem, and the vendor is usually responsible for ensuring that the person using the credit card is its owner.

- **Payments using encrypted credit card details.** Even if credit card details are encrypted before they are sent over the Internet, there are still certain factors to consider before sending them out. One such factor is the cost of a credit card transaction itself, which might prohibit low-value payments (micropayments).

- **Payments using third-party verification.** One solution to security and verification problems is the introduction of a third party to collect and approve payments from one client to another.

Payments Using Encrypted Credit Card Details   Encryption is initiated when credit card information is entered into a browser or other electronic commerce device and sent securely over the network from buyer to seller as an encrypted message. This practice, however, does not meet important requirements for an adequate financial system, such as nonrefutability, speed, safety, privacy, and security.

To make a credit card transaction truly secure and nonrefutable, the following sequence of steps must occur before actual goods, services, or funds flow:

1. A customer presents his or her credit card information (along with an authentic signature or other information such as mother's maiden name) securely to the merchant.

2. The merchant validates the customer's identity as the owner of the credit card account.

3. The merchant relays the credit card charge information and digital nature to his or her bank or online credit card processor.

4. The bank or processing party relays the information to the customer's bank for authorization approval.

5. The customer's bank returns the credit card data, charge authentication, and authorization to the merchant.

One company that has implemented the preceding process is CyberCash (www.cybercash.com). CyberCash transactions move between three separate software programs: one program that resides on the consumer's PC (called a wallet), one that operates as part of the merchant server, and one that operates within the CyberCash servers. The process works in the following manner: The consumer selects items for purchase and fills out the merchant's order form, complete with necessary shipping information. The merchant server presents an invoice to the consumer and requests payment. The consumer is given the option to launch the CyberCash Wallet, a software program that does the encryption, if they already have it. When the consumer clicks on the "PAY" button, the CyberCash software on the merchant server sends a special message to the consumer's PC that awakens the CyberCash Wallet. The consumer simply chooses which credit card to pay with and clicks on it. The rest of the process is a series of encrypted automatic messages that travel between the three parties on the Internet and the conventional credit card networks that are connected directly to the CyberCash servers. Since the CyberCash Wallet is a separate piece of software, the consumer can use virtually any browser to shop at a merchant on the Web.

CyberCash can also be used for micropayments, that is, people pay small change—usually a nickel or a dime—as they click on icons, which could be information or files. The process is an offshoot of CyberCash's Wallet technology. Currently, users download free Wallet software to their PC and load it up electronically with a credit card cash advance. The plan for micropayments is to create a "small change" version, which would dip from a checking account as well as a credit card. After selecting a game to play or item to buy, an invoice comes on screen. The consumer clicks on a Pay button, and a transaction is encrypted that transfers money out of a coin purse icon and into the vendor's account, which is set up on a CyberCash server. CyberCash will make its money by selling the technology as well as by offering payment authentication and aggregation services. The company believes it can process payments as low as ten cents.

Payments Using Third-Party Verification: First Virtual   The "Internet Payment System" was formed by First Virtual Holdings and gets around the credit card security problem by ensuring that the credit card number never travels over the Internet. The fully operational system relies on existing mechanisms to enable the buying and selling of information (as opposed to goods or services) via the Internet. It is most easily thought of as a conduit, linking credit cards, banks, processing agents, and the Internet. Internet users need not make any additional hardware or software purchases in order to make use of this payment system. Information sellers and buyers only need an Internet mailbox and a First Virtual account. First Virtual (FV) makes servers available to sellers lacking the computer capacity or warehouse Internet servers to handle their sales directly.

The following seven-step process captures the essence of the FV system.

1. The consumer acquires an account number by filling out a registration form, which gives FV a customer profile that is backed by a traditional financial instrument such as a credit card.

2. To purchase an article, product, or other information online, the consumer requests the item from the merchant by quoting her FV account number. The purchase can take place in one of two ways: The consumer can automatically authorize the "merchant" via browser settings to access her FV account and bill her, or she can type in the account information.

3. The merchant contacts the First Virtual payment server with the customer's account number.

4. The First Virtual payment server verifies the customer's account number for the vendor and checks for sufficient funds.

5. The First Virtual payment server sends an electronic message to the buyer. This message could be an automatic WWW form, or a simple e-mail. The buyer responds to the form or e-mail in one of three ways: Yes, I agree to pay; No, I will not pay; or Fraud, I never asked for this.

6. If the First Virtual payment server gets a Yes from the customer, the merchant is informed and the customer is allowed to download the material immediately.

7. First Virtual will not debit the buyer's account until it receives confirmation of purchase completion. Buyers who receive information or a product and decline to pay may have their accounts suspended.

Merchants advertise their wares on a "First Virtual Infohaus," similar to a public mall where anyone can rent space to store and sell data. The infohaus also serves as a distribution center and clearinghouse for all billing and accounting functions, and it is where First Virtual verifies each transaction in a closed-loop confirmation system. Confidential credit card data is stored in an off-site system not linked to the Internet.

Merchants pay First Virtual a one-time registration fee of $10.00. For each transaction, merchants pay First Virtual a $.29 fee and 2 percent of the charged amount. Each time a payment is made to their account, sellers also pay a $1.00 processing fee. The start-up cost for consumers is $2.00. There are no membership fees for either side.

Secure Electronic Transactions (SET)

Secure electronic transactions is a protocol for encrypted credit card payment transfers. Announced in February, 1996, by VISA and MasterCard, SET establishes a single technical standard for protecting payment card purchases made over the Internet and other open networks. Participants in the SET consortium include Microsoft, Netscape, GTE, IBM, SAIC, Terisa Systems, and Verisign. SET is based on public-key encryption and authentication technology from RSA Data Security. The objectives of payment security are to: provide authentication of cardholders, merchants, and acquirers; provide confidentiality of payment data; preserve the integrity of payment data; and define the algorithms and protocols necessary for these security services.

Why Do We Need SET?   One of the benefits of the Internet is that it enables users to tap into information around the clock, from just about anywhere in the world. However, it does pose some practical drawbacks. The potential for fraud and deception is far greater online. When the other "person" is merely a blip on a computer screen, it is difficult to determine whether or not they hold a valid account. And how can a "real" merchant feel comfortable accepting a credit card account number without some form of identification? It is also difficult to trust a merchant you have never actually seen. After all, the merchant's "store" may exist only on a remote hard drive. In order to combat fraud there has been increasing focus on authentication on the Web. Web authentication requires the user to prove his or her identity for each requested service. Various vendors in the e-commerce market are attempting to provide an authentication method that is easy to use, secure, reliable, and scalable. Third-party authentication services must exist within a distributed network environment in which a sender cannot be trusted to identify him- or herself correctly to a receiver. In short, authentication plays an important role in the implementation of business transaction security.

What Features Does SET Specify?   The following objectives are addressed by SET specifications: confidentiality of information, integrity of data, consumer account authentication, merchant authentication, and interoperability.

Confidentiality of information. To facilitate and encourage financial transactions, it will be necessary for merchants and banks to assure consumers that their payment information is safe and accessible only by the intended recipient. Therefore, credit card account and payment information must be secured as it travels across the network, preventing interception of account numbers and expiration dates by unauthorized individuals. SET provides confidentiality by the use of message encryption.

Integrity of information. SET ensures that message content is not altered during the transmission between originator and recipient. Payment information sent from consumers to merchants includes order information, personal data, and payment instructions. If any component is altered in transit, the transaction will not be processed accurately. In order to eliminate this potential source of fraud and/or error, SET provides the means to ensure that the contents of all order and payment messages received match the contents of messages sent. Information integrity is ensured by the use of digital signatures.

Consumer account authentication. Merchants need a way to verify that a consumer is a legitimate user of a valid account number. Digital signatures and digital certificates ensure consumer account authentication by providing a mechanism that links a consumer to a specific account number. SET designates a third party called a *certificate authority* to authenticate the sender and receiver.

Merchant authentication. The SET specifications provide a way for consumers to confirm that a merchant has a relationship with a financial institution that allows that merchant to accept bank card payments. Merchant authentication is ensured by the use of digital signatures and merchant certificates.

Interoperability. The SET specifications must be applicable on a variety of hardware and software platforms, and must not prefer one over another. Any consumer with compliant software must be able to communicate with any merchant software that also meets the defined standard. Interoperability is ensured by the use of standard protocols and message formats.

For the technical underpinnings of the SET standard, please see the latest information published on VISA's Web site, http://www.visa.com/.

6.5 Other Emerging Financial Instruments

Several other electronic payment systems are currently being prototyped and tested. These include debit cards, electronic benefit transfer cards, and smart cards.

Debit Cards at the Point of Sale (POS)

The fastest growing number of electronic transactions today are debit card point-of-sale transactions. Such a transaction occurs when a customer uses a debit card to make a purchase from a merchant (supermarket, gas station, convenience store, or some other store that accepts such cards instead of using cash, check, or credit card).

The transaction works much like a credit card transaction. For example, a customer gives an ATM card to the merchant for the purchase. The merchant swipes the card through a transaction terminal, which reads the information; the customer enters his personal identification number (PIN); and the terminal routes the transaction through the ATM network back to the customer's bank for authorization against the customer's demand deposit account. The funds, once approved, are transferred from the customer's bank to the merchant's bank.

These transactions occur within the banking system, and safety of payment is assured. The third-party processors who provide services for merchants are also examined by the federal regulators for system integrity. Both the consumer and the merchant maintain bank accounts, and the funds are transmitted inter-bank within the payment system. Authentication is provided by the use of the digital signature or PIN numbers, just as it is at ATMs. Further, PINs are sent through the system in an encrypted form, and the PIN pads and terminals are tamper-proof. Dedicated lines are also often used for transmission, particularly by larger merchants.

Debit Cards and Electronic Benefits Transfer

Debit cards are being used extensively for electronic benefits transfer (EBT). Electronic benefits transfer uses debit cards for the electronic delivery of benefits and entitlements to individuals who otherwise may not have bank accounts. In an EBT system, recipients access their benefits in the same way that consumers use debit cards to access their bank accounts electronically: the card is inserted into or swiped through a card reader and the cardholder must enter a PIN associated with that card. The benefit recipient can then access his or her benefits to make a purchase or obtain cash. For example, food stamp purchases are charged against the participant's allotment, and other purchases or cash distributions are charged against the participant's cash assistance program allotment.

Benefits that can be delivered via EBT generally fall into three categories: federally funded, but state administered benefits (such as food stamps, Aid to Families with Dependent Children programs); state-funded and state-administered benefits (such as general assistance, heating assistance, refugee assistance, and supplemental or emergency payments); and benefits that are both federally funded and federally administered (such as Social Security and Veterans benefits).

Through EBT, existing networks and technologies can provide benefit recipients with online access to their funds at POS devices and ATMs. In an EBT process, no paper changes hands, except for the receipt printed for the purchaser by the POS device or the ATM. Recipients can access cash through any number of establishments, including grocers, drugstores, and financial institutions, as well as ATMs. Certain cash payments can also be facilitated by installing POS devices in housing authority and utility company offices to accept rent and bill payments.

Electronic benefits transfer has several advantages over paper-based, benefit distribution systems. First, EBT is less costly. Currently, many recipients of federal and state benefits must pay significant fees (three or more dollars) to cash their checks. EBT systems are designed to provide no-cost or low-cost access methods.

Second, EBT is more convenient than paper methods. EBT eliminates the need to carry food stamp coupons, stand in long lines to cash checks, or accept the entire benefit amount at one time. EBT programs also provide recipients with toll-free customer service lines and multilingual support to handle questions or problems. EBT is safer than cash or coupons, which can be lost or stolen. In EBT, benefits are stored electronically, and can be used only when needed and in the amounts required. Recipients control all access to their benefits through their cards and PINs. They can also deactivate lost or stolen cards immediately and request a replacement card by a toll-free phone call.

Third, EBT is convenient for retailers. It eliminates the time-consuming task of handling food stamp coupons, making grocery checkout procedures faster and easier. By eliminating checks and coupons, EBT reduces losses associated with theft, forgery, and fraud.

Finally, EBT is convenient for the government. Its inherent audit and tracking advantages enhance investigations into suspicious conduct by retailers. EBT improves benefit program management by creating an audit trail and record of benefit usage, ensuring that programs are working properly and effectively.

Smart Cards

Smart cards, also called *stored value cards*, use magnetic stripe technology or integrated circuit chips to store customer-specific information, including electronic money. The cards can be used to purchase goods or services, store information, control access to accounts, and perform many other functions.

Smart cards offer clear benefits to both merchants and consumers. They reduce cash-handling expenses and losses caused by fraud, expedite customer transactions at the checkout counter, and enhance consumer convenience and safety. In addition, many state and federal governments are considering stored value cards as an efficient option for dispersing government entitlements. Other private sector institutions market stored value products to transit riders, university students, telephone customers, vending customers, and retail customers.

One successful use of stored value cards is by New York's Metropolitan Transportation Authority (MTA). The MTA is the largest transportation agency in the United States and, through its subsidiaries and affiliates, operates the New York City subway and public bus system, the Long Island Railroad and Metro-North commuter rail systems, and nine tolled intrastate bridges and tunnels. These facilities serve four million customers each workday. In 1994, the MTA began the operation of an automated fare-collection system based on a plastic card with a magnetic stripe. The MetroCard is either swiped through a card reader at subway stations or dipped into a farebox on buses where the fare is decremented. All 3,600 MTA buses became operational in 1996. The full complement of 467 subway stations is expected to be operational by mid-1997. By 1999, the MTA anticipates more than 1.2 billion electronic fare collection transactions a year on subway and bus lines.

The management challenges created by smart card payment systems are formidable. Institutions such as the MTA have made a considerable investment in the stored value card processing network, and to get a good return on investment must identify new and innovative ways to achieve additional operating efficiencies and value. For example, many commuters in the New York area use two or three different mass transit systems to get to and from work. Each of these systems bears the expense of maintaining its own proprietary network. In addition, the customer ends up having to manage two or three different fare media, and make two or three times as many fare purchase transactions. New regional initiatives will be necessary to integrate the multiple networks, and to make it cost-effective and possible to implement a regionwide transportation fare payment system that will link all of the transit providers in that region.

The Federal Reserve recently created a Payments System Research Group to define the key public policy issues related to the evolution of the smart card payments system. Some of the questions being studied include: When is an account deposit insured? Is the account still insured when the value has been loaded on a smart card? Is the value on a smart card considered cash? Is a smart card more like a traveler's check or a credit card?

One reason for the success of stored value cards is that their application focus is narrow and they build upon existing infrastructure such as: credit, debit, and ATM cards; funds-clearing and settlement mechanisms; regional and national ATM/POS networks; and retail, corporate, and government customer relationships. It remains to be seen how the integration between smart cards and online commerce will take place.

6.6 Consumer, Legal, and Business Issues

The consumer, assisted and at times cheered on by the press and politicians, can exert considerable influence in the development of payment systems. The key consumer issues associated with payment systems include:

Consumer protection from fraud arising from efficiency in record keeping.

Transaction privacy and safety.

Competitive pricing of payment services to ensure equal access to all consumers.

Right to choice of institutions and payment methods.

Record Keeping and Proof of Payment   For obvious reasons, virtually all electronic payment systems need to be able to keep automatic records. From a technical standpoint, this is no problem for electronic systems. Credit and debit cards keep automatic records. An automatic record is an after-the-fact transcription of what happened, created without any explicit effort by the transaction parties. Automatic records are: available for permanent storage; accessible and traceable; held within a payment system database; and capable of providing data to the payment maker, the bank, or monetary authorities.

Once information has been captured electronically, it is easy and cheap to keep; it might even be more costly to throw it away than to keep it. For example, in many transaction-processing systems, old or blocked accounts are never purged and old transaction histories can be kept forever on magnetic tapes. Since electronic transactions are intangible by their very nature and a record is the only way to resolve later disputes, it might be a useful general rule of payment dynamics and banking technology to never discard any data.

However, the need for record keeping for purposes of risk management conflicts with the transaction anonymity of cash. One can say that anonymity exists today only because cash is a very old concept, invented long before the computer and networks gave us the ability to track all transactions. While a certain segment of the payment-making public will always desire transaction anonymity, it can be argued that anonymity runs counter to the public welfare because tax evasion, smuggling, and/or money laundering possibilities exist. The anonymity issue raises the question of whether electronic payments should happen without an automatic record feature.

Many payments systems currently being implemented are naive in terms of audit abilities. For instance, the Mondex electronic purse touts equivalence with cash, but its electronic wallets are designed to hold automatic records of the card's last twenty transactions with a built-in statement. Further, card-reading terminals, machines, or telephones could all maintain records of all transactions and it is probable that they ultimately will. With these records, the balance on any smart card could be reconstructed after the fact, allowing for additional protection against loss or theft.

In sum, anonymity is an issue that will have to be addressed through regulation covering consumer protection in electronic transactions. There is considerable debate on this point. An anonymous payment system without automatic record keeping will be difficult for bankers and governments to accept. Were regulation to apply, each transaction would have to be reported, meaning it would appear on an account statement, making mistakes and disputes easier to resolve. However, customers might feel that such record keeping is an invasion of privacy, resulting in slower than expected adoption of electronic payment systems.

Managing Information Privacy   The electronic payment system must ensure and maintain privacy. Every time one purchases goods using a credit card, subscribes to a magazine, or accesses a server, that information goes into a database somewhere. All payment details of a consumer can be easily aggregated: where they buy, when they buy, and what they buy. Furthermore, all these records can be linked so that they constitute in effect a single dossier. This dossier would reflect what items were bought, and where and when they were bought. This violates one of the unspoken laws of doing business: that the privacy of customers should be protected as much as possible.

Privacy must be maintained against eavesdroppers on the network and against unauthorized insiders. The users must be assured that they cannot be easily duped, swindled, or falsely implicated in a fraudulent transaction. This protection must apply throughout the whole process by which a good is purchased and delivered. For many types of transactions, trusted third-party agents will be needed who can vouch for the authenticity and good faith of the involved parties.

Risk Management　One of the perennial problems of any payment system is the inadvertent shifting of credit and liquidity risks through "timing gaps" in the exchange of assets. Such gaps create float (interest-free loans) and lead to credit and liquidity risk. Two major risks in the operation of the payment systems are: fraud and credit risk, each of which requires attention. Dealing with fraud requires improvements in the security framework. Curtailing credit risk requires devising procedures to constrict or moderate credit and reduce float.

Credit or systemic risk is a major concern in settlement systems since the failure of a bank to settle its net position could lead to a chain reaction of bank failures. The digital central bank must develop policies to deal with this possibility. Various alternative policies exist. A digital central bank guarantee on settlement removes the insolvency test from the system, since banks will more readily assume credit risks from other banks than from merchants or customers.

On the other hand, without such guarantees, the development of clearing and settlement systems and money markets may be impeded. A middle road is also possible, for example, setting controls on bank exposures (bilateral or multilateral) and requiring collateral. If the central bank does not guarantee settlement, it must define, at least internally, the conditions and terms for extending liquidity to banks in connection with settlement.

6.7 Summary

In this chapter we discussed various types of electronic payment schemes that are emerging. Consumer acceptance of electronic payment initiatives may be slow. Many people were skeptical about direct deposit when it was first available. It took consumers twenty years to get accustomed to using ATMs.

It is also possible to underestimate the potential of new developments. The introduction of credit cards was downplayed by arguments that: no one wanted them, they could never replace cash, and no retailers would accept them. Early consumer response to ATMs was also entirely negative. In fact, the banks introduced ATMs to steer the less wealthy away from teller windows. These examples go to show that one must be a little skeptical when listening to those who claim that there is no merit or public interest in using new payment methods. Quite often, consumers express indifference to something new simply because they do not comprehend what it is or what it can do for them.

In order to keep a sense of proportion of what is possible and what may happen, it is prudent to examine the key consumer, legal, and business issues that will affect the pace of payment systems change. However, the biggest question revolves around consumer behavior and acceptance: how customers will take to a paperless and cashless world. It may be too early to know the pace and extent of consumer acceptance. Twenty-five years ago, industry "experts" were predicting the extinction of checks by the 1990s—the so-called checkless society. Instead, we have seen check volumes continue to rise.

Chapter 7

Electronic Commerce and Banking

Chapter Outline

"Banking is vital to a healthy economy. Banks are not" [AS95]. This quote succinctly captures the structural and operational tumult occurring in the financial services industry. Banking as a business can be subdivided into five broad types: retail, domestic wholesale, international wholesale, investment, and trust. Of all these types, retail and investment banking are most affected by online technological innovations and are the ones that stand to profit most from electronic commerce.

The role of electronic commerce in banking is multifaceted—impacted by changes in technology, rapid deregulation of many parts of finance, the emergence of new banking institutions, and basic economic restructuring. Given these environmental changes, banks are reassessing their cost and profit structures. Many banks feel that in order to be profitable they need to reduce operating expenses and maintain strict cost control. This philosophy is evident in the many mergers and acquisitions occurring in the banking industry. The challenge behind bank restructuring lies in adequately operationalizing the notion of cost control.

Technology is the predominant solution for controlling costs. Banks are increasingly turning toward technology to help reduce operating costs and

still provide adequate customer service. Innovation and technology are becoming the key differentiators in the financial services business. Advances
in networking, processing, and decision analytics have allowed institutions
to lower service costs. Technology has also accelerated the pace of product
innovation. For example, sophisticated arbitrage instruments like deriva-
tives are changing the nature of investment banking. The Securities and
Exchange Commission's decision to allow Spring Street Brewery to trade its
stock online may also fundamentally change investment banking by disin-
termediating the traditional role of underwriting.

Technology is enabling the development of new products and services.
For example, technology is capable of replacing or expediting tedious financial exercises like check writing, filing taxes, and transferring funds.
Although large businesses have automated these tasks, many small businesses and most households still do them manually. This is not surprising;
large businesses have been undergoing computerization for more than
thirty years, whereas PCs have been entering households in significant
numbers only in the last few years.

Technology is changing the interaction between banks and consumers.
In particular, technological innovations have enabled the following capabilities: online delivery of bank brochures and marketing information; electronic access to bank statements; ability to request the transfer of funds
between accounts; electronic bill payment and presentment; ability to use
multiple financial software products with "memory" (thus eliminating the
need to re-enter the same data); online payments—encrypted credit cards
for transferring payment instructions between merchant, bank, customer;
and finally, micropayments (or nickel-and-dime transactions using electronic cash and electronic checks). These online capabilities increase the facility and speed of retail banking. ˩ᵢₘᵢₜₐₜᵢₒₙ

However, new technology is a double-edged sword. While it enables
banks to be more competitive through huge investments, it also enables
new competition from fast-moving, nonbanking firms. This trend can be
seen in the area of online payments, where recent innovations have provided an opportunity for nonbanks to break into the banking business,
threatening the banking stronghold on one of the last key services provided
by banks. The present nature of online payments is a clear indication that if
the banking industry fails to meet the demand for new products, there are
many industries that are both willing and able to fill the void.

Technology also creates problems in the product development life-cycle. In the past banks had the luxury of long roll-out periods because successful investment in retail banking required a large monetary
commitment for product development. This financial requirement pre-

vented new participants from entering the market and was a key determinant of success. This is no longer the case. Instead of a single institution doing everything, technology allows the creation of a "virtual financial institution" made up of firms, each contributing the best-of-breed software or products to the overall product. In this new "virtual model," banks compete with the twelve-to-eighteen-month product development times of companies like Intuit or Netscape, which have product life-cycle times of only six to nine months.

Clearly, the impetus for drastic change in the banking industry does not come from forces within banking; it is from competitive pressure outside the industry. It is important to determine the origins of this competition as well as to ask three questions more relevant to managers: What are the dimensions of nonbank financial services competition? What is the role of the Web, Internet, and electronic commerce in this competition? How can financial institutions effectively leverage the "legacy" information infrastructure to thwart nonbank competition? This chapter addresses these questions and presents an overview of changing dynamics in the banking industry that, together with technological changes, are creating the need to rethink the existing paradigm of financial services.

7.1 Changing Dynamics in the Banking Industry

In recent years, there has been a major change in the way banks strive for increased profitability. In the past, the banking industry was chiefly concerned with asset quality and capitalization; if the bank was performing well along these two dimensions, then the bank would likely be profitable. Today, performing well on asset quality and capitalization is not enough. Banks need to find new ways to increase revenues in a "mature market" for most traditional banking services, particularly consumer credit. A thorough understanding of this competitive environment is needed before banks can determine their online strategy.

Five distinct factors contribute to the new competitive environment:

changing consumer needs driven by online commerce,

optimization of branch networks in order to reduce costs,

changing demographic trends and potential new consumer markets,

cross-industry competition caused by deregulation, and

new online financial products.

Changing Consumer Needs

Consumer requirements have changed substantially in the last decade. Customers want to access account-related information, download account data for use with personal finance software products, transfer funds between accounts, and pay bills electronically. Of course, along with these services, banks must be able to supply/guarantee the privacy and confidentiality that customers demand, which is not a trivial matter to implement on the part of the banks.

Many consumer requirements are based on a simple premise: customers and financial institutions both seek closer and more multifaceted relationships with one another. Customers want to be able to bank at their convenience, including over the weekend or late at night. Bankers want more stable and long-term relationships with their customers.

From the bank's perspective, developing and maintaining this relationship is difficult. Although financial products are essentially information products and financial institutions are highly automated, there is a gulf between automated information and the bank's ability to reach the consumer in a unified way. This gulf is filled with established methods, such as branches, postage and mail, advertising, and people on telephones. These methods can be costly and impersonal. Electronic banking provides a method of communication that will enable the bank customer to be reached, served, and sold products and services in their homes and offices whenever it is convenient for them—twenty-four hours a day, seven days a week.

Cost Reduction

Since 1984, the banking industry has been consolidating at a rapid pace. The central goal of most mergers is to reduce operating costs. During the decade 1984–1994, the number of banks in the United States fell by 27 percent. A recent survey found that of the 13,000 banks and thrifts operating today, only between 6,000 and 9,000 institutions will be operating by the year 2000. The reason for this reduction is evident from the economics of existing delivery channels. In general, brick and mortar branches cost at least $1.5 million each. Online technology can deliver services far more economically than these existing methods, as the infrastructure costs such as PCs are shared with the consumer.

As banks merge to reduce their operating costs, they are obviously growing in size. However, even their increased size is dwarfed by many of their new competitors. Consider the following: Merrill Lynch manages over $500 billion in financial assets, and expects to top $1 trillion by the end of the decade. Merrill Lynch also manages more retirement funds—$71 billion worth—than the 100 largest banks combined. Likewise, assets managed by the Fidelity Group in the United States have grown from $4 billion in 1972 to $40 billion in 1985, and up to $400 billion in 1994 [KURT95].

Similarly, the top issuer of credit cards in the United States is not a bank but rather Dean Witter (Discover Card) [KURT95]. The GM and Ford finance companies offer more installment financing to their customers than most banks. If banks are going to compete with these larger competitors, they are going to have to address their traditional banking overhead structures, as well as their existing retail strategies. Providing online financial services can address both these needs.

Demographic Trends

Consumers are increasingly careful about their personal finances. Social, demographic, and economic changes have altered the way Americans value their time and money. Americans spend more time working than ever before, and therefore place a higher premium on their leisure time. Thus, they are a very receptive audience for time-saving products and services. In addition, the reduced level of job security and the need to plan for the future has heightened concern over personal debt, retirement planning, tax planning, and saving for college.

A culmination of these consumer concerns can be seen in the trend of customer purchase of investment services like mutual funds, annuities, and trust services. For the last decade, investment products have been the fastest growing industry in the United States. Since 1989, bank deposits have grown 8 percent, while mutual funds grew 63 percent. Further increases are expected in investment product services where the potential growth is enormous.

Baby boomers are one of the primary reasons for this increasing demand. Between 1948 and 1963 an average of 4.4 million babies were born each year. Today we have 77 million baby boomers driving our economy, and they represent only part of the economic picture. The United States also has 44 million retirees who have savings and incomes and who need financial advice, counsel, and products. These two groups comprise a market of over 100 million potential investment product clients.

The companies that take advantage of this opportunity by targeting the appropriate customers with appropriate products and services will have a lasting competitive advantage. As it provides convenience and the ability to customize products and services on a mass level, electronic delivery of these products and services will be one of the key means of achieving this advantage.

Regulatory Reform

Banks occupy a unique strategic position as they act as intermediaries in re-distributing capital from areas of excess to areas of scarcity. This role has made financial services a closely watched and regulated industry, as government is interested in the control and stability of this redistribution. Recent years have brought about far-reaching regulatory changes that have removed many of the competitive protections banks enjoyed for a long time. The ability to provide complete financial services is necessary if commercial banks are to survive increasing competition from mutual funds, brokerage firms, and insurance companies. The passage of the Interstate Banking Bill in 1994 has created new opportunities for banks to serve customers across state lines—from accepting a deposit in any branch to combining all of a consumer's banking products into one total relationship, regardless of where the customer is located.

A bill pending in Congress will dismantle the Glass-Steagall Act, part of the Banking Act of 1933, passed during the Great Depression. At that time, the government decided that it was necessary to dilute the concentration of financial power in America. Toward this end, the Glass-Steagall Act was drafted to force the separation of commercial and investment banking. Reform of the Act is expected to allow investment banks to broaden their product lines.

The Glass-Steagall Act is considered outdated for three reasons. The Act prevents corporations, state and local government enterprises, and other borrowers from realizing the cost, efficiency, and revenue benefits that would result from greater competition among providers of financial services. At the international level, it works against fair competition; U.S. companies, lenders as well as borrowers, are hobbled by restraints that do not inhibit their foreign counterparts. More importantly, the Act blocks the opportunity for retail banks to acquire brokerage institutions and investment banks. It is expected that these brokerage institutions and investment banks will be vulnerable to mergers and acquisitions in the next ten years as few of them have the capital to succeed on their own.

Technology-based Financial Services Products

The growing importance of computer technology is another factor complicating predictions about the future structure of banking. Some observers believe that additional development of electronic cash, such as smart cards, could stimulate further banking consolidation. They point to the fact that the start-up costs associated with electronic payments technologies can be high, in part because electronic cash requires large investments in computer software and other resources to establish a network of secure electronic transactions. Such large fixed costs have led these observers to warn that a few financial services providers—those with the resources to absorb those costs—could come to dominate the payments system.

In contrast, the development of electronic banking might actually increase competition in banking markets and lower bank operating costs. Electronic banking offers an inexpensive alternative to branching to expand a bank's customer base, and many banks are using electronic banking to increase service to their customers. Many banks have started Web sites on the Internet, and many plan to offer banking services over the Internet. Some banks are already offering certain banking services over the telephone. Smart cards and other forms of electronic cash could be the key to consumer acceptance of home banking, eventually allowing banks to reduce the number of their physical branches.

7.2 Home Banking History

The recent hyperbole around home banking is not simply the latest Wall Street fad. Financial institutions were interested in turning the home banking concept into a reality as early as 1970. Many banks invested millions of dollars in research and development, certain that home banking was going to take off. In October 1981, *The American Banker* had a set of articles promoting the virtues of home banking. In answer to the question: "Will home banking be a major force in the market by 1985?," an executive vice president of First Interstate Bank replied, "Absolutely! And I want to be there."

The most popular approach of the 1970s was home banking via a touch-tone telephone, which enabled customers to check account balances, transfer funds, and pay bills. With telephone banking, customers use a numeric password on a push-button telephone to access banking services. As most people have telephones, the telephone was believed to be the ideal home banking technology. Despite the initial optimism, results were very disappointing. The telephone was an awkward technology for home banking, since there is no visual verification, which is important to customers. Also, touch-tone phones were not common in the 1970s.

In the 1980s, cable television also was considered as a possible medium for home banking. Although this approach solved the graphic limitations dilemma of the telephone, it had other drawbacks. The primary obstacle was that the necessary two-way cable was virtually nonexistent, as only a small percentage of Americans had two-way cable TV. Since the PC has both visual display and two-way communication, it has been considered a leading contender for the home banking medium.

During the 1980s and early 1990s, several banks offered home banking services and invested hundreds of millions of dollars in home banking. Just like the telephone and the cable systems of the 1970s and early 1980s, home banking from a PC was initially a failure: the absence of a critical mass of PCs and a PC-friendly population stunted the growth of the concept and resulted in the failure of efforts such as Chemical Bank's Pronto System.

Why Will It Be Different This Time?

There are several factors that lead us to believe that home banking has a good chance at success this time.

Consumers Up the Learning Curve   Consumers are becoming increasingly computer-literate and are able to interact more fluently with their online financial service providers. Over the years, consumers have demonstrated a high level of acceptance of basic electronic services. The banking industry expects that PCs will eventually replace ATMs and POS terminals as the crucial method of consumer–bank interfacing. However, the use of technology is not just restricted to ordinary consumer–bank interface (or retail banking). Evidence indicates that banks and software companies are beginning to find a receptive audience among PC users wanting to simplify bill paying, checkbook balancing, and tax-related tasks.

Increasing Consumer Awareness   Advertising about and media attention to online banking have never been stronger. Mainstream magazines are increasing the amount of coverage given to computer-related topics. As a result, consumers are increasingly aware of alternatives to traditional branch banking. As consumers become aware of alternatives, they are going to demand more. Banks that fail to meet expectations face the possibility of mass exodus.

Large Base of Installed PCs   Finally, there is a critical mass of PC-using households with modems. For a long time, home banking was a classic "chicken or egg" problem; without a large enough sample of potential users, there was no urgency for financial institutions to provide services. Conversely, without a wide array of services, there was little consumer interest. This problem is resolving itself. Today there are more than 30 million PCs in American homes, and, for the first time in history, consumers are now spending more on PCs than TV sets. Modem penetration into households is a key issue for home banking, as online services require a modem. Clearly the technology exists to make home banking a reality. Whether it will happen via the Internet, a proprietary service, or both is yet to be determined, but the home banking infrastructure is in place.

The Alternative Is Too Expensive   Last year, 30 billion checks were processed in the United States. The cost associated with writing, mailing, and processing these checks is staggering. The typical firm spends $9.00 per customer (in processing and infrastructure overhead) in order to receive payment for services rendered. Moreover, the process begins and ends on a computer system, albeit with numerous steps in between. That is, the end-points of the process are already automated but the intermediary steps are not. The current system is becoming too costly, inefficient, and susceptible to fraud. Sooner or later this complicated payment structure will need to be changed.

Fierce Competition   While home banking offers a great deal of promise, it also carries above-average risk. First and foremost, the likely competitors for home banking customers (Intuit, Microsoft, Charles Schwab, and AT&T) are faster moving and better capitalized than most banks. Given the potential profitability and strategic importance of home banking, competition is likely to intensify. Second, while we believe in the promise of home banking and think that consumers are ready to adopt the service, it may be years before anyone makes money in home banking because of the enormous up-front investment required. However, those who do not make the investment to build the service infrastructure today are taking a huge risk as well as risking their ability to compete at all in the banking world of tomorrow.

7.4 Home Banking Implementation Approaches

Pushed by growing consumer demand and the fear of losing market share, banks are investing heavily in home banking technology. Collaborating with hardware, software, telecommunications, and other companies, banks are introducing new ways for consumers to access their account balances, transfer funds, pay bills, and buy goods and services without using cash, mailing a check, or leaving home. The four major categories of home banking (in historical order) are:

- **Proprietary bank dial-up services.** A home banking service, in combination with a PC and modem, lets the bank become an electronic gateway to customers' accounts, enabling them to transfer funds or pay bills directly to creditors' accounts.

- **Off-the-shelf home finance software.** This category is a key player in cementing relationships between current customers and helping banks gain new customers. Examples include Intuit's Quicken, Microsoft Money, and Bank of America's MECA software. This software market is attracting interest from banks as it has steady revenue streams by way of upgrades and the sale of related products and services.

- **Online services-based banking.** This category allows banks to set up retail branches on subscriber-based online services such as Prodigy, CompuServe, and America Online.

- **World Wide Web-based banking.** This category of home banking allows banks to bypass subscriber-based online services and reach the customer's browser directly through the World Wide Web. The advantages of this model are the flexibility at the back-end to adapt to new online transaction processing models facilitated by electronic commerce and the elimination of the constricting intermediary (or online service).

In contrast to packaged software, which offers a limited set of services, the online and WWW approach offers further opportunities. As consumers buy more and more in cyberspace using credit cards, debit cards, and newer financial instruments such as electronic cash or electronic checks, they need software products to manage these electronic transactions and reconcile them with other off-line transactions. In the future, an increasing number of paper-based, manual financial tasks may be performed electronically on machines such as PCs, handheld digital computing devices, interactive televisions, and interactive telephones, and the banking software must have the capabilities to facilitate these tasks.

Home Banking Using Bank's Proprietary Software

Online banking was first introduced in the early 1980s and New York was the hotbed of home banking. Four of the city's major banks (CitiBank, Chase Manhattan, Chemical, and Manufacturers Hanover) offered home banking services. Chemical introduced its Pronto home banking services for individuals, and Pronto Business Banker for small businesses in 1983. Its individual customers paid $12 a month for the dial-up service, which allowed them to maintain electronic checkbook registers and personal budgets, see account balances and activity (including cleared checks), transfer funds among checking and savings accounts, and—best of all—make electronic payments to some 17,000 merchants. In addition to home banking, users could obtain stock quotations for an additional per-minute charge. Two years later, Chemical teamed up with AT&T in a joint venture called Covidea. Despite the muscle of the two large home banking partners, Pronto failed to attract enough customers to break even and was abandoned in 1989.

Other banks had similar problems. CitiCorp also had a difficult time selling its personal computer-based home banking system, Direct Access. Chase Manhattan had a PC banking service called Spectrum. Spectrum offered two tiers of service: one costing $10 a month for private customers, and another costing $50 a month for business users, plus dial-up charges in each case. According to their brochure, business users paid more because they received additional services such as the ability to make money transfers and higher levels of security.

Similar to other bank offerings, Banc One offered two products: Channel 2000 and Applause. Channel 2000 was a trial personal computer-based home banking system available to about 200 customers that was well received. Applause, a personal computer-based home banking system modeled after Channel 2000, attracted fewer than 1,000 subscribers. The trial was abandoned before the end of the decade as the service could not attract the critical mass of about 5,000 users that would let the bank break even. Almost all of the banks discovered that it would be very difficult for any one bank to attract enough customers to make a home banking system pay for itself (in other words, to achieve economies of scale).

Online banking has been plagued by poor implementation since the early 1980s. In a scathing critique, the Yankee Group [YG87] cites Bank of America's Home Banking as an example of this poor implementation. That service, it says, "was designed initially to operate entirely online on their central processor, with difficult sign-on procedures, slowly drawing graphics at 300 baud for each single entry screen, and such slow response time has to be confusing and cause errors." This service later evolved into a menu-driven service with no graphics that operated at either 300 or 1,200 baud accessible from any personal computer via Tymnet. It took a few more years before users could use the Dollars & Sense financial management software to integrate personal finance with online banking activities. Given this gradual evolution, consumers who initially used the service and left could not be coaxed back into using it again.

Most home banking services were anything but easy to use. They worked at 300 baud and later 1200 baud, and had complex menus that reflect more about the way the bank keeps its books than the way consumers spend their money (see Fig. 7.1). Typically, the services were designed to run on the most basic PC possible (Pronto, for instance, was geared to the Atari 400), so they turned even the most powerful PC into a dumb terminal. They nearly lobotomized the user with mind-numbing repetitions of menus

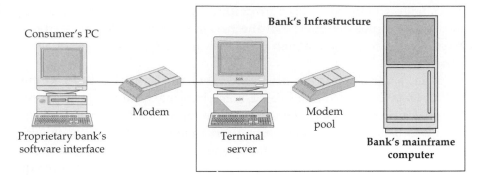

Figure 7.1 Proprietary Software Method

and torturous verification procedures, which, combined with the crawl of remote communications to the bank's mainframes, made home banking seem extremely slow and even painful to use.

Banking via the PC Using Dial-Up Software

The main companies that are working to develop home banking software are Intuit, the maker of Quicken; Microsoft, the maker of Microsoft Money; Bank of America and NationsBank, who acquired Meca's Managing Your Money software from H&R Block; and ADP, which acquired Peachtree Software. In this section, we will examine Intuit in detail, as it is the leader among home banking software companies and exemplifies the overall strategy in this area.

Intuit   Intuit is the leading provider of home and small business financial software, supplies, and services for PC users. It pioneered computerized personal finance management with the introduction of the Quicken program in October 1984. Intuit has consistently been in the forefront of new online financial services, launching bill payment services in 1990, IntelliCharge credit card services in 1993, and Quicken Quotes, a portfolio price update service, in 1994. In recent years the company benefited from both the personal computer boom and its giving consumers a diverse product breadth and a software bundle (or suite) focus, including offerings on personal finance, small business finance, financial planning, tax preparation, and bill payment and transactions.

Since its introduction, Quicken has been enhanced and upgraded several times. Quicken allows users to organize, understand, and manage their personal finances. Designed to look and work like a checkbook, Quicken provides users with a method for recording and categorizing their financial transactions. Once entered, the financial information can be analyzed and displayed using a set of reports and graphs. Quicken also allows users to reconcile their bank accounts, and track credit card purchases, investments, cash, and other assets and liabilities. It enables users to make payments by printing computer checks or by initiating electronic payments via modem. Several factors, including good design, affordable pricing, and the availability of new features and services, have contributed to Quicken's success.

As a complement to its personal financial software products, Intuit offers value-added services such as online banking, bill payment, and credit management that further automate users' financial transactions. Online banking is a new feature of Quicken 5 for Windows, which was released in the first quarter of fiscal 1996. Intuit's online banking services, in conjunction with the services of Intuit's financial institution partners, allow users to download and automatically categorize savings and loan account activity, brokerage activity, and charge account activity, thereby reducing data entry and providing an easily accessible view of their financial portfolio.

How it works.   Customers will sign up with a local bank, and then use the Quicken software to get the desired information. The software will dial a local number using AT&T's 950 access service. (The 950 service covers 90 to 95 percent of the country, and users simply dial 950-1ATT.) Online connections between the financial institutions and Quicken users are the responsibility of Intuit's subsidiary, National Payment Clearinghouse, Inc., a privately held provider of automated bill payment services, which changed its name to Intuit Services Corporation (ISC) in 1993. ISC gets Internet access from Concentric Network Corporation, which has over 200 local points of presence (POPs). ISC also currently provides the online banking and bill payment services for users of Microsoft Money. ISC was recently sold by Intuit to CheckFree.

Intuit Services Corporation is basically an intermediary between Quicken software and financial services. Figure 7.2 illustrates the structure of this network. ISC's network design is what is known as "burst and disconnect," which simply means that the user will get the requested information quickly and then log off of the system. This strategy allows for a maximum number of users in a short period of time. In contrast, services like America Online or CompuServe earn money by keeping the customer on line and billing for time spent. These traditional online services have a lot of menus and graphics that take time to traverse.

Intuit sells specific information and wants users on- and off-line quickly. ISC was also designed from the bottom up with security in mind; the network employs the RSA method of security. Intuit's banking partners down-

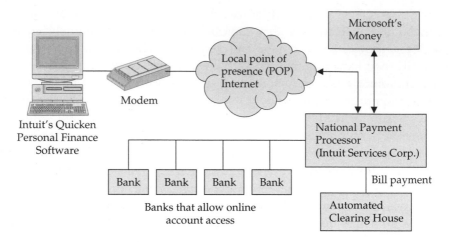

Figure 7.2   Intuit Services Corporation Architecture

load all the relevant banking information (such as bank balances and statements) to Intuit's servers (ISC). The banks send information for every customer signed up for the service. When a customer requests information, the Quicken software dials the ISC servers in Downers Grove, Illinois. Since the data has already been transmitted to ISC, the requested information is simply downloaded to the local Quicken user. The total online time is about 15 seconds.

While the banks will transfer data in batch mode once a day, this is not practical for credit card processors like American Express. Users want to check on recent transactions and want real-time data. For instance, in the case of American Express, ISC will simply pass the customer request on to American Express. The requested statement information is then passed back to ISC and to the Quicken customer. Currently, American Express is Intuit's only partner set up to handle real-time data transmissions. The banks work in batch mode, but over time, many of the banking partners will have to move to real-time mode.

Online banking enables users to check current account balances, transfer funds between accounts, determine the clearance of given transactions, and reconcile accounts. Each financial institution sets its own fees for online banking services charged to their customers. The compensation Intuit receives from the financial institutions is based on that institution's consumer usage.

Bill payment.   Online bill payment enables users to pay bills by transmitting payment instructions via modem. Bill payment works differently from the other banking services. If, for example, a Quicken user needed to pay three bills—Bell Atlantic, Macy's, and Fred's Auto Repair—the user would open Quicken and type the names of the payees and the amounts, and then hit transmit. The Quicken software then dials ISC, which looks at each payee and determines the correct method to handle the transaction. The first bill, Bell Atlantic, is tied to the Federal Reserve's automated clearing house (ACH) network. Thus, the bill is paid electronically using the ACH system, and this happens almost immediately. The bill is cleared at midnight Central Time.

In the case of the second bill, Macy's, which is not tied to the Federal Reserve ACH system, Intuit will print a physical check, batch it with other Macy's payments, and then express mail it. In the third instance of Fred's Auto Repair, or any individual payee that is not likely to have multiple incoming checks, Intuit will print a check and mail it. These payments take only a few seconds to process. The network then informs the local Quicken user how long each bill will take to clear and sends back a confirmation number. The next time the user goes to pay the bill, the software will tell the user how much time it will take for the bill to arrive.

This service is offered both through financial institution partners as well as directly from Intuit. Again, each financial institution sets its own prices for online bill payment services, and Intuit receives compensation from the financial institution based on consumers' usage. For its customers who do not bank at a partner institution, Intuit provides an online bill payment service for a monthly fee of around $5.95 per month for twenty bill payment transactions.

Prognosis for Intuit.   Intuit believes that it can enhance its competitive position by extending its business into the emerging electronic commerce market. In its annual report, the company defines electronic commerce as "electronically-enabled financial transactions and electronically-enabled marketing and sales of financial products." Through its Automated Financial Services division, Intuit works with financial institutions to offer a number of online services, including online banking, electronic bill payment, online tools for evaluating stocks, and IntelliCharge credit card services, that extend the capabilities of Intuit's software products and increases the automation of financial tasks. Intuit Services Corporation, Intuit's new electronic financial services operational center, delivers the online services to Quicken customers and bank partners, and also provides the services enabling financial institutions to connect to users of Quicken and Microsoft Money. The company is evaluating additional opportunities related to electronic commerce, and has begun to invest significant resources to develop and acquire products and services for this market.

Intuit is well positioned to exploit the online banking wave with a diversified set of products. Reasons that make Intuit a formidable competitor include:

- **Multiplatform strength.** Unlike some of its competitors who have concentrated solely on the Windows market, Intuit established itself as the personal finance software leader for the DOS, Windows, and Macintosh platforms.

- **New revenue opportunities.** Intuit is developing both new software products and electronic services that complement its main products, Quicken and QuickBooks.

- **Recurring revenue opportunities.** By offering services such as electronic credit card statement delivery, and supplies such as checks, invoices and envelopes, Intuit adds to the attractiveness of its software products. These additional services pave the way for new revenue opportunities with relatively more stable revenue streams than those commonly associated with packaged software.

In addition to the prospects of benefiting from the strong PC growth among consumers and small businesses, Intuit is in a strong position to benefit from strategic alliances with financial institutions.

Banking via Online Services

Although personal finance software allows people to manage their money, it only represents half of the information management equation. No matter which software package is used to manage accounts, information gets managed twice—once by the consumer and once by the bank. If the consumer uses personal finance software, then both the consumer and the bank are responsible for maintaining systems; unfortunately, these systems do not communicate with one another, thus giving new meaning to double-entry bookkeeping. For example, a consumer enters data once into his system and transfers this information to paper in the form of a check, only to have the bank then transfer it from paper back into electronic form.

Unfortunately, off-the-shelf personal finance software cannot bridge the communications gap or reduce the duplication of effort described above. But a few "home banking" systems that can help are beginning to take hold. In combination with a PC and modem, these home banking services let the bank become an electronic gateway, reducing the monthly paper chase of bills and checks.

CitiBank and Prodigy   To understand the more contemporary online banking services, we look at CitiBank and Prodigy. Prodigy has been providing home banking to consumers since 1988, and has relationships with more banks than any commercial online service.

To expand the attractiveness of its online banking services, in 1996 CitiBank began offering Prodigy subscribers a free and direct link to its electronic home banking service. Access to CitiBank is available to Prodigy subscribers at no extra fee throughout the New York metropolitan area. The agreement represents the first time that CitiBank has expanded access to its proprietary PC Banking service through a commercial online service. To encourage CitiBank customers to try online banking through Prodigy, free Prodigy software will be made available at local CitiBank branches. CitiBanking on Prodigy offers a full range of banking services. Customers can check their account balances, transfer money between accounts, pay bills electronically, review their CitiBank credit card account, and buy and sell stock through CitiCorp Investment Services. CitiBank and Prodigy allow customers to explore the wide array of services using an interactive, hands-on demonstration.

Figure 7.3 presents the online services banking architecture.

Intuit and America Online   On November 13, 1995, Intuit announced an agreement with America Online (AOL) in which AOL will offer Intuit's home banking services to its 4 million-member customer base. AOL users

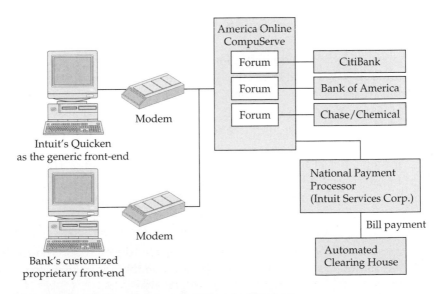

Figure 7.3   Online Services Banking Architecture

will not need to use off-the-shelf Quicken software to access the banking services. Rather, Intuit will build a Quicken-like application into America Online that will have the basic banking functionality of transferring funds, paying bills, downloading bank statements, and checking account balances. The banking service is provided through Intuit's banking subsidiary, Intuit Services Corporation, the same entity that links Quicken to Intuit's twenty-one banking partners. In order to use this service, AOL customers will have to have an account with one of Intuit's partner banks. The service was launched in the middle of 1996.

Customers of this service do not have to pay AOL any additional fees, and the payment to Intuit is structured the same as when the customer chooses to use Quicken without AOL. The financial institutions charge the customer a fee for the banking services (though some banks have opted to not charge customers); money is then paid back to Intuit. One can think of the AOL relationship as another access point to Intuit Services Corporation. A customer can walk into a bank and the bank can offer the customer three home banking choices: Quicken, Microsoft Money, or AOL. All three use the Intuit back-end payment service (Intuit Services Corporation).

In sum, this offering gives customers more choices for home banking. Clearly, Intuit wants to get the banking service into as many hands as possible as quickly as possible. AOL customers are a preselected group of potential early adopters; they already have modems and are users of online services. The more customers that sign up for AOL, the more financial institutions will enter the home banking arena, bringing with them more potential customers.

Banking via the Web: Security First Network Bank

With the explosive growth in Internet use, banking via the World Wide Web will undoubtedly catch on quickly. The goal of this approach to banking is to provide superior customer service and convenience in a secure electronic environment. The competitors in this segment are banks that are setting up Web sites, and firms like Intuit that can easily transport their product to the Internet.

How is Internet banking different from online banking? This is an important question and the answer is often misunderstood. Banking on the Internet is not the same as banking via online services. Internet banking means that:

Consumers do not have to purchase any additional software (the Web browser is sufficient), store any data on their computer, back up any information, or wait months for new versions and upgrades, since all transactions occur on a secure server over the Internet.

Consumers can conduct banking anywhere as long as they have a computer (not necessarily their own computer) and a modem—whether at home, at the office, or in a place outside the United States. Banking via online services is restrictive in that the consumer has to install a software package onto her computer. This limits the customer to banking only from that computer, making a call to access a separate network, working with a separate software company, and banking during limited hours of operation.

Consumers can download account information into their own choice of programs rather than following the dictates of the service provider.

Internet banking allows banks to break out of the hegemony of software developers. If bank customers (end users) install personal financial management software on their PCs, these customers become direct customers of software firms. By controlling the software interface, software firms such as Intuit can control the kinds of transactions end users make and with whom these transactions occur. By maintaining a direct relationship with end users via the Web, banks can offer additional services and provide a personal feel to the interface, without seeking the cooperation of a software company.

If banks choose to offer home banking via personal financial management software, they lose control over the end user interface and the relationship they have with customers. This loss of control has tremendous long-term implications. The software industry history offers compelling proof of the importance of organizations having a direct relationship with consumers. In the early 1980s, IBM decided that operating systems were not central to IBM business strategy. As a result, IBM licensed DOS from a small software company called Microsoft. IBM called this operating system PC-DOS and allowed Microsoft to market this same operating system to competing computer manufacturers under the name of MS-DOS. IBM's seal of approval made DOS an industry standard. However, IBM was unable to move the industry to a new operating system called OS/2 in the late 1980s because Microsoft controlled the customer relationship and was able to convert most end-users to Windows. For banks, too, losing control over the interface could have dire consequences.

Intuit's Internet Strategy   Intuit realizes that the Web could be a big factor in home banking and is working to provide a version of Quicken that uses the capabilities of the Web. The future success of Intuit lies in the ability to integrate its software with different systems from several institutions. New software features allow users to integrate Quicken with Web browsers such as Netscape Navigator and Internet access module. For example, a single click on one of Quicken's banking screens lets the user connect to the Internet, launch Navigator, and go directly to a site dealing with banks on the Web.

Today, Quicken can store a wealth of information, but that information is static. Intuit plans to use the Internet as an extension of the core products. If a user wants information about a topic and it is not available on the CD-ROM, the product can dial the Intuit Web page where there will be additional financial information. The information will range from stock information to advice, to technical support. "Surfing" the Net requires a browser, and Intuit has opted to bundle the market leader Netscape Navigator with its Quicken for '96.

The difference between Intuit's service offering on Netscape and its offering on ISC is that confidential information will be handled through ISC, and the Internet will be for browsing and obtaining general information. This separation will remain until Internet security issues are resolved. The Internet also may help Intuit to sell more software. For instance, a user working on a tax return can be alerted to the availability of a state tax program from within the software. The user can download the software and unlock it with a code from Intuit after supplying a credit card number separately. Intuit believes that the Internet is a great way for the company to offer superior customer support. The company has designed a system in which customers use the Internet to reach Intuit's customer service facility.

Intuit will provide free access to the Web using a third-party provider, Concentric Network Corporation. The concept of this free access is that any time a customer needs help, he or she can, from within the software, dial the Net and access the Intuit Web page, where help is available. If the user wants to browse Internet sites other than Intuit's, then the customer must pay a fee. Concentric is charging $1.95 a month for one hour of access, which is competitive with other access providers.

Security, which is a crucial component of Internet banking, is handled in one of two ways, depending on whether the network in question is public or private. For a private network, Quicken contains a communications module that connects directly to customers' financial institutions for the transmission of confidential data and financial transactions. For a public network, all such transactions are secured by end-to-end encryption utilizing RSA's Public-Key encryption technology combined with triple DES (see KALA96).

Security will be invisible to users because these transactions are performed from within Quicken; the communications will happen in the background and the information will be seamlessly integrated into the user's Quicken files. For interactive access to the information available on the Internet, Quicken users will have integrated access to the security mechanisms built into the Netscape Navigator. In addition, Intuit is working with Netscape and others to encourage the development and availability of secure protocols for electronic commerce such as Secure Electronic Transactions.

Security First Network Bank   The first Internet bank to provide electronic banking services to Internet users was Security First Network Bank, SFNB (see Fig. 7.4 and http://www.sfnb.com). In an effort to help expand Internet banking, SFNB made its software available for licensing to other financial institutions. Security First Network Bank had to cross many regulatory challenges before getting permission from the regulators to become a Web bank.

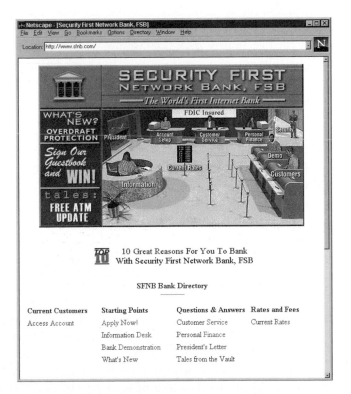

Figure 7.4   The Home Page of Security First Network Bank on the Internet

Before going online, Cardinal Bancshares, the holding company for SFNB, applied to the Office of Thrift Supervision (OTS) in September 1994 for approval to change the business plan of their subsidiary, First Federal Savings Bank of Pineville, Kentucky, to include banking on the Internet. The application also requested that the bank's name be changed to Security First Network Bank. After a careful review and a detailed analysis of the security architecture, the OTS granted approval on May 8, 1995, and SFNB went on-line on October 18, 1995 [JM96].

Structure of SFNB operations.   Security First Network Bank is composed of two distinct units. The first is the Information Server, the area potential customers use to learn about the bank and its services. Once a customer decides to open an account, he or she uses a secure registration form to send an encrypted message to the Bank Server, which contains the actual banking applications. Using information provided on the registration form, the bank verifies the account information and creates a new account for the customer. An account creation package, containing the user name and password needed to access the account, is sent to the customer through the U.S. mail. This package may eventually include a personal authentication device such as a smart card or floppy disk containing an encrypted private key and certificate. Customers communicate with the bank using their WWW browser. Each transaction a customer sends to the bank is encrypted to protect the information as it travels over the network. The bank server receives the transaction, decrypts the message, and performs the service requested.

The information and bank servers reside in a client/server environment on an HP 9000 Model 715 server. This server works as the bank's main Web server, and runs the bank application client software. The database server is an HP 9000 Model K200 server, housing a single processor board and filled with 128 MB RAM, 10 GB RAID, and several communications boards [HP96].

What are the different types of products?   Security First Network Bank is attempting to innovate and set the pace for online Internet banking by introducing certificates of deposit, money market accounts, and joint checking accounts. To attract customers, SFNB offers the highest interest yields available in the country for money market accounts and CDs. In addition, SFNB is offering joint accounts, full personal financial reports, and check imaging. The joint accounts allow multiple parties to access account information from various locations. For example, a parent may open a joint checking account with a child living away from home during college. Using the World Wide Web, both the parent and the student can access and manage account information online from their respective locations. Check imaging allows Internet banking customers to actually view scanned images of their checks online the day after they clear the bank.

Security First Network Bank expects to strengthen its ties to consumers by selling more services, and thus making it more difficult for customers to switch. By brokering new financial services, banks can become one-stop shops for upscale customers. Most importantly, they can significantly increase fee income.

How does SFNB plan to make money?   The goal is to develop a business model that is far more efficient than traditional banking models. With the Internet, SFNB has a "footprint" that spans the entire United States, with a network operations center located in Atlanta along with a banking office in Pineville, Kentucky. A traditional bank would need to have fully staffed branches all over the country to achieve the same reach. As a result of operating exclusively online, they expect their operating costs to be far lower than a traditional bank, and hope to pass the savings on to their customers. Subject to regulatory approval, SFNB plans to offer brokerage, insurance, loans, and other financial services. Although SFNB intends to generate fee revenue for these services, their goal is to set lower fees than those currently available to consumers [JM96].

7.4 Open versus Closed Models

While it is clear that electronic commerce and electronic banking are inevitable, the technology models for providing these services may not yet be fully understood by the banking industry at large. Two technology models of online banking are open and closed systems. Briefly, in an open system, content changes can occur easily because of the use of standard technology and components. For instance, a banking interface developed around the Web is an open system that is easy to customize to a bank's changing needs. On the other hand, a closed system is one in which the changes are difficult since everything is proprietary. For example, a banking interface developed around a package such as Intuit's Quicken cannot be modified unless the vendor distributes a new version of its software.

Banks need to be familiar with both these models when offering products and services online. With the high level of customer interest in PC banking and the emergence of the Internet as a vehicle for doing business, many banks have announced plans to offer Internet banking services. A handful of banks have already set up home pages on the Internet to provide existing and potential customers with information about upcoming services. However, with the exception of SFNB, few banks are offering any actual banking transaction services, as they do not yet have the necessary technology or expertise.

Internet banking differs from traditional PC banking in several ways. Typically, the bank provides the customer with an application software program that operates on the customer's PC. The customer then dials into the bank via modem, downloads data, and operates the programs that are resident on his PC. The customer is able to send the bank a batch of requests, such as transfers between accounts. Any software upgrade has to be incorporated into new releases and redistributed to the customer, and as more functionality is added to the software, more and more space and speed are required from the customer's computer.

With Internet banking, on the other hand, there are potential customers who already have all the software they need. All that is required is a web browser since the actual banking software resides on the bank's server in the form of the bank's home page. The banking software can be updated at any moment with new information, such as new prices or products, without having to send anything to the customer; it can also continue to expand and become more sophisticated without becoming difficult for the customer to operate.

With traditional PC banking interactions, if the customer has more than one account or other financial products, the data is downloaded from multiple sources and then plugged into the appropriate places in the software. A bank server on the Internet, however, can perform this function for the customer and provide an integrated snapshot of the customer's financial portfolio. In the case of Internet banking, it becomes much easier for the bank to outsource a product such as a brokerage account and have that information appear on a customer's bank statement as if it were an internal bank product.

Another difference between the two models is that in the PC banking model, although the customer can work on his or her finances off-line and then make a quick call to download new data, this call would involve a long-distance or 1-800 call for customers outside a metro calling area. Banking with a browser, on the other hand, involves a continuous, interactive session, initiated by a local telephone call to a local access provider or online service.

An open system such as the Web offers two additional key benefits: control of the user interface and intermediation. With an open system, such as the application designed for SFNB, the bank designs the user interface and is therefore able to incorporate its own "look and feel." This authority allows the bank to enhance its brand awareness and maintain direct access to its customers. The open system also allows banks to offer an expanded array of financial services and to choose their business partners when offering additional services such as brokerage accounts and mutual funds—all of which lead to stronger customer relationships and increased revenue.

In a closed system using proprietary financial management software such as Quicken, the software firm acts as intermediary between the bank and its customers. In managing the customer relationship, the software provider controls the interface design, thus diminishing and even eliminating any reference to the bank itself. The software provider also controls the selection of financial providers and determines the choice of services and the availability of those services.

7.5 Management Issues in Online Banking

The challenge facing the banking industry is whether management has the creativity and vision to harness the technology and provide customers with new financial products necessary to satisfy their continually changing financial needs. Banks must deliver high quality products at the customers' convenience with high-tech, high-touch personal and affordable service. In order to achieve this, management has to balance the five key values that increasingly drive customers' banking decisions: simplicity, customized service, convenience, quality, and price.

Online banking will realize its full potential when the following key elements fall into place:

The development of an interesting portfolio of products and services that are attractive to customers and sufficiently differentiated from competitors.

The creation of online financial supply chains to manage the shift from banks as gatekeeper models to banks as gateways.

The emergence of low-cost interactive access terminals for the home as well as affordable interactive home information services.

The identification of new market segments with untapped needs such as the willingness to pay for the convenience of remote banking.

The establishment of good customer service on the part of banks. The fact that technology increases the ease of switching from one bank to another means that banks that do not offer superior customer service may see low levels of customer loyalty.

The development of effective back-office systems that can support sophisticated retail interfaces.

However, banks that attempt to master all of the above elements before offering online banking services may be least likely to reap the rewards. As online banking is initially attractive to a wealthy segment of the population, the banks that move first will increase their share of the most profitable customers.

Differentiating Products and Services

The characteristics that will differentiate winners from losers in the competitive online banking industry are: being willing to take risk in terms of being a first mover, making strategic decisions about whether to partner with a software provider, making strategic decisions about the products and services offered online, and exploiting the service attributes that build customer retention for profitable customers.

Strategic decision making needs to take into account the changing market structure. Intuit and other vendors see a growing demand for their products and are cleverly setting themselves up as intermediaries in the personal finance marketplace. In other words, Intuit is setting up an interface between desktop software (Quicken) and a third-party network processor that will serve as a switch to any bank that wants to participate in home banking. Similarly, Microsoft wants Microsoft Money to serve as the front-end for customers doing banking over the Internet. Microsoft and Intuit would charge banks for each time a customer comes through the third-party processor's switch.

To offset the increasing power of companies like Microsoft and Intuit, some banks are forming cooperative partnerships with banking-software companies, while others are writing their own software. Banks are wary of letting another party control the interface, even if such an opportunity appears convenient and economical at the outset. Banks fear that once customers set up Microsoft or Intuit software, it would be easier to change the bank than to change the software because banks all look the same to a Quicken user and thus would be viewed as providing interchangeable services. A particular bank would have no way to differentiate itself from the others, no way to add new products to their offering, and would build no brand identity with those customers doing banking over the Internet.

The alternative is for banks to bypass these software intermediaries and provide customers with bank-developed software. The problem with this approach is that banks are not very good at developing consumer software and they do not have the resources in terms of software expertise to continually improve it. However, a positive outcome of developing internal expertise is that banks can position themselves to react to competition and consumer trends.

Banks may find their current customers switching from branch banking to PC banking, allowing a more efficient use of the bank's resources. An appropriate strategy must include methods to prevent customers from migrating to banks with competing online offerings. The ultimate market leaders will be those who enhance their image as customer-driven banks, even with those customers who do not use home banking.

Managing Financial Supply Chains

Today, banks are no longer gatekeepers but gateways to financial products (see Fig. 7.5). In the old gatekeeper model, the bank functioned as an inhibiting intermediary that restricted a customer's set of product choices. In the new gateway model, the bank functions as a flexible intermediary that provides access to an entire spectrum of products and delivery channels. Some of the products—insurance, entertainment, travel, investment management—may not even originate from the bank but from a third-party provider. The bank acts as a gateway and provides its customers with access to value-added service providers anywhere in the world.

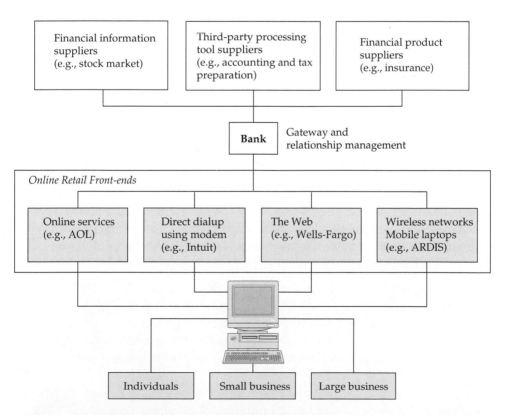

Figure 7.5 Emerging Financial Supply Chains

Banks and other financial services firms are not the only institutions acting on the gateway model. Online technology allows software companies like Intuit and Microsoft to become gateways also. The challenge to banks is real: most software firms are used to product life cycles of twelve to eighteen months. It takes banks years to develop and deploy new products. Although the current focus of these software companies is primarily on developing gateways for financial transactions and simple account management tasks, the threat to banks is imminent, as the software company model can be extended to include other types of financial products.

Thanks to deregulation, financial institutions are now able to offer a wider variety of financial services. However, if financial institutions choose to let software companies control their relationships with end users, the software companies can determine which business partners in the financial supply chains banks can choose. In fact, a savvy brokerage provider would rather negotiate with a personal finance software company than with a bank. Signing a deal with Intuit or Microsoft would mean that the processor would gain access to all Bank1, Bank2, and Bank3 end users. Signing a deal with Bank1 would mean that the processor would only have access to Bank1's customers. Clearly, the design of financial supply chain relationships is a matter of great importance.

To attempt to gain advantage in this potentially lucrative market, banks are following three strategies:

Investing an unprecedented amount of capital in building information architectures, technology infrastructures, and online banking products/services that will counter the threat from nonbanks and fundamentally change the way banks service retail customers.

Seeking partners in the online financial supply chain that links customers, intermediaries, banks, and third-party service providers. With partnerships in place, banks expect to provide much better value than the disjointed chains that predominate today. These financial supply chains seek to provide the best price and value to the end customer (where the battle for the market share is ultimately won or lost).

Moving from a product-dominated (mass production) model to a customer-centered (mass customization) model. The objective is to capture customer loyalty by providing an ever-increasing number of consumers with the luxury of more convenient, customer-centered (relationship) services that until now have been available only to major accounts.

Probably the single greatest challenge facing banks is the lack of holistic strategy by the management toward pursuing these objectives.

Pricing Issues in Online Banking

Perhaps the single most important issue driving consumer acceptance of online banking is pricing. Home banking services can be expensive to implement and operate, yet consumers are rarely willing to pay much more than $10 or $15 per month for this service. Once online, a user confronts high connect charges, high subscription fees, or both. Data have shown repeatedly since 1986 that PC owners do have an interest in home banking services, but they are very price-sensitive, with large drops in consumer interest when prices go above $10 per month [YG87].

Pricing affects online banking at three levels: initial software pricing, financial product pricing, and usage pricing.

- **Initial software pricing.** In order to gain market share and achieve a critical mass of customers, banks and other software companies will bundle their respective personal finance products with new PCs. This is not just a variation of the old "give away the razors, make money on the blades" marketing approach; it is a reformation of the way in which software and networks are tightly linked or loosely coupled in ways that create far greater flexibility in pricing for market share as well as in pricing for profit.

- **Financial product pricing.** The pricing of financial products has to balance three major costs. The first are developmental costs, which include costs associated with the design, implementation, testing, and commercialization of a financial product. The second set of costs are marketing costs, which include costs of launching the new product and maintaining it throughout its initial stage. Finally, there are support costs, which include the costs of providing and delivering the product and maintaining it via back-office systems.

- **Usage pricing.** This type of pricing is based on the bank's volume of transactions. Companies offering these services must provide incentives, such as low fees, to attract customers to the service. Ultimately, the marketplace dictates the equilibrium prices. If the target audience perceives the cost of new products as being too high, they will resist adopting them.

Banks need to balance a number of objectives when establishing pricing strategies. For example, when CitiBank dropped all fees for electronic banking services in 1995, its objective was to achieve market penetration among both existing and future customers. This strategy is based on the premise that market share and long-term profitability are correlated. Pricing can also be used as a behavior modification mechanism. For example, First Chicago penalizes customers who use tellers by charging them $3.00 each time they use a teller for a transaction that could have been performed at an ATM [AS95]. Clearly, pricing is a complex issue that has both long-term implications in terms of cost recovery and profitability, and short-term implications in terms of market penetration.

Marketing Issues: Attracting Customers

The benefits of online banking are often not made clear to the potential user. Consumer questions include: How is balancing the checking account online superior to doing it on paper? Is paying bills online superior to the familiar process of writing checks? Where is the consumer gaining value? Perhaps the answers to these questions are not clear to the bankers themselves. Regardless of how a bank chooses to answer these questions, it is clear that banks make a mistake trying to sell online banking services on the basis of convenience. While short-term convenience is important, consumers want the long-term ability to control and organize their finances more than they want convenience.

Banks must also look beyond home consumers for online banking consumers. The rapidly growing use of personal computers by small businesses provides a solid opportunity for banks to build a profitable base of small businesses until a broader consumer market evolves. There are millions of small businesses with annual sales ranging from $250,000 to $5 million. Many of these firms have PCs and modems. New services like interactive cash management services could generate significant revenues for banks. Industry studies indicate that 20 percent of small businesses are immediate prospects for online banking and are willing to pay more than individual consumers for the service—up to $100 a month. Thus, banks have the opportunity to tap into this market segment.

Marketing Issues: Keeping Customers

Keeping customers (or customer loyalty) requires the following:

1. Banks must switch the costs of moving from one software platform to another to keep customers from moving. Customers are increasingly familiar with using technology to access bank accounts and to handle financial affairs, and this familiarity increases interest in additional services and increases switching costs.

2. Banks must provide integrated services. The oft-cited time squeeze on consumers—long commutes, heavy workload, family obligations, household management—is pushing consumers toward integrated ser-

vices that can speed up financial procedures. These integrated services contribute to cementing the customer relationship.

3. Banks can realize the positive cost implications for the long-term value of building customer loyalty. In the online world, there is not a big cost difference between serving one customer and serving 100,000 customers.

Clearly, marketers must also work on building a loyal customer base not only in order to maintain the existing base, but also in order to be attractive to potential customers.

Back-Office Support for Online Banking

Although banks are making great strides in developing the front-end interface, there needs to be a great deal of thought put into the re-engineering of back-office operations and systems. Back-office operations technology is often a crucial and misunderstood element of online banking.

Figure 7.6 shows a model where a bank's system interfaces with the third party transaction processor Intuit Services, which provides a common interface for Microsoft Money and Intuit's Quicken transactions. The inter-

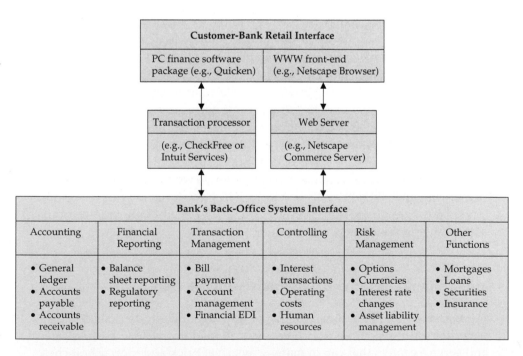

Figure 7.6 The Elements of the Back-Office Interface

esting questions raised by this model are: If a customer pays a bill by Quicken in the morning, can the result of that transaction be seen that evening when he attempts to balance his checkbook? Or can a customer call a bank customer service representative to put a stop-request on a payment the same day it was initiated? Or can a customer who transfers money by PC see that transaction when she goes to the ATM later that day? The answer to these questions for many banks is "no" and the reason is that existing back-office systems were not meant to work in real-time.

In addition to the real-time difficulties, online banking is further complicated because most existing back-office systems are batch-oriented. For instance, if $300 is withdrawn from an account at an ATM machine, the account balance will not be changed until the next day. The delay results from the fact that the third-party transaction processors post these transactions by automated clearinghouse in batches in order to accommodate economies of scale. Until banks and other payment processor systems go real-time, there will be a timing disorientation between PC service and the bank's pay-by-phone, telephone, branch, and ATM services, which are all posted in real-time to the bank's host computer. This problem is further exacerbated when banks try to integrate product lines.

Figure 7.6 illustrates the complex structure of back-office systems. The complexity arises from the fact that each of the modules (such as Accounting and Financial Reporting) in large banks may be on separate mainframe systems. With electronic commerce, banks will have to find ways of integrating the information stored in these mainframe databases. This integration will require a fundamental change in the database design and architecture, with information integration as the goal.

Managers often think of back-office systems and operations as a subordinate function that should respond to their needs and desires and go quietly about handling all the boring details and back-office drudgeries that a manager should not have to worry about. This attitude may have its roots in the historic role of clerks, whose job was to support the manager. For too long, operations functions in banks have been viewed as cost centers with a vague customer linkage. This thinking will have to change to reflect the strategic nature of back-office systems and will need bank-wide commitment to keep up with new demands.

Integrating Telephone Call Centers with the Web

A increasing number of big banks are committing millions of dollars to convert their dull telephone call center operations into beefed-up cross-sales and service centers that can in many ways rival brick and mortar branches.

Technologically sophisticated banks such as NationsBank, Keycorp, and Barnett Banks have made the restructuring of call centers one of their biggest priorities.

Call center investments are not trivial. According to *The American Banker* [AB96], the cost of building a telephone call center is approximately $3.5 million for technology and facilities and another $5.5 million for the hiring of 250 to 300 customer service representatives whose annual salary is between $18,500 and $24,500. The operational costs are also quite high. According to the ABA's 1995 Retail Banking Survey Report, it cost the banks an average of 24 cents to handle a telephone inquiry via automated voice response, $1.82 if a call center representative did the work, and $2.93 if a representative in a branch answered the call.

Call centers have evolved from a necessity to become a strategic differentiator for banks; the questions facing bankers are: How can we make call centers more effective for a lower cost? How can banks get more bang for the technology buck? Banks need to ask themselves: Are we investing wisely in continuing the buildup of telephone call centers or are we simply blindly following the trend set by other banks? These questions are important given the scale of investment and the emergence of new channels such as the Web.

Call center integration takes two forms. The first, and simplest, is integration of telephone call centers with other online services. Customers should be able to go from a Web application to a service representative with all the screens they accessed transferred to the representative. This kind of integration has been common for three years between service representatives and voice-response-unit applications. There is no reason why the same cannot be done on the Internet.

Second, the application should be integrated with Intranet sites. This kind of integration provides a powerful platform for providing customer service. For a financial software vendor, there is always some issue with a related product that needs research. Customers should be able to pop from a help screen in the primary application to Frequently Asked Questions (FAQs).

Through hotlinks, a Web application can go from site to site gathering that information. This speeds the decision process without the need for human intervention. Between voice response units, Web applications, and other forms of electronic business, banks must constantly examine their use of customer service resources. This does not mean banks should force customers to use a service channel they do not want. But customers can be sold on the benefits of one channel over another, allowing banks to adjust costs and meet customer expectations.

This reallocation will drive an additional round of consolidation in the call center industry. Call centers have experienced round after round of technological advances. The automatic call distributor, voice response unit, and computer–telephone integration have been used to build and continually improve a sophisticated customer service model. The Web and Internet will provide the much-awaited final automation link. Banks should be ready to accept this change and start focusing on how to make the best use of the existing infrastructure.

Finally, we must not forget the fact that technology must be integrated with call center processes. Call center processes have evolved to withstand efficiently the repeated rigors of high call volumes. Fluctuating volumes demand processes that minimize waste. Likewise, online call centers must balance infrastructure costs and customer satisfaction. With process control as their focus, operationally excellent call centers have the potential to drive growth and retention of the customer base through fast and efficient response. Those that focus on customer intimacy can attract and retain customers by crafting experiences that cater to the needs and preferences of their various market segments, down to individual clients.

7.6 Summary

This chapter discussed reasons why online banking is picking up steam, the technology behind online banking, and the management challenges that need to be addressed. The momentum of online banking has picked up considerably recently and we expect it to accelerate in the future for three reasons:

> Banks now have a variety of technological means to initiate online banking programs without incurring the investments needed to develop their own systems. The reach and delivery capability of computer networks such as the Internet far exceeds any proprietary bank network ever built, and makes it continually easier for customers to manage their money anywhere, anytime.

> Banks understand the need to separate the content (financial product) from the distribution channel (the branch). Attempting to provide both is similar to movie companies (content producers) owning their own theaters (distribution channels). Clearly, the traditional model of integrated delivery has outlived its usefulness and needs to be thought through again.

> Banks recognize the potential benefits of early entry into what will inevitably be an important but crowded market. To avoid being left behind, banks are going directly to the market with online banking programs, rather than running lengthy pilot tests with focus groups.

If banks do not offer online banking services, affluent customers will be stolen away by software companies, online access services, brokerages, or global entertainment companies. In addition to wanting to protect their existing franchises, banks hope online banking will win them new business. However, few managers have a clear vision of tomorrow's banking environment. In fact, few banks have strategic plans in place that anticipate the future of electronic banking. The challenge for the banking industry lies in creating the right atmosphere and providing the right incentives for consumers to use personal computers regularly for banking, and in making sure that they provide attractive and affordable services.

Chapter 8

Electronic Commerce and Retailing

Chapter Outline

"Americans will love shopping for their underwear in their underwear" [QVC94]. This statement, although a wee bit crude, sums up the potential of online shopping. Retailing is expected to change with the rapid development of new online sales and distribution channels that literally can be used from anywhere, anytime—from work, school, a hotel, car, or airplane. These developments should impact retailing as much as the advent of strip malls, catalog retailing, and TV-based home shopping.

Almost every retailer is reevaluating every aspect of its operation from customer service to advertising, merchandising to store design, and logistics to order fulfillment. Furthermore, reacting to the pressure of retailers, suppliers are assessing technology-based solutions to drive down costs (labor, delivery, and production) and become more efficient producers of goods.

Online channels such as online services and the Web are also impacting traditional retail business models. In the traditional model, the customer went to the store and located the product. In the online model, the retailer seeks out the customer. The success of catalog retailers demonstrates that a significant portion of consumers have embraced the reverse model: the retailer going to the consumer.

217

However, retailers need to consider the following issues in developing a business model:

- **Product/content issues:** What kind of products are suited for online retailing?

- **Software interface issues:** What kind of features will constitute an effective interface? What features make it easy to find and select items for online purchase?

- **Process issues:** What are the specific steps in the shopping process from a consumer's perspective? What kind of processes should companies develop to fulfill orders efficiently?

- **Pricing issues:** How much will consumers be willing to pay for convenience?

- **Payment issues:** What payment methods would consumers use for online purchases?

- **Market penetration issues:** Would an online channel be popular with consumers? How long will such a system take to attract a critical mass and become profitable?

Understanding these issues will help companies formulate a merchandising strategy—and build a merchandising mindset—from what they sell to how they sell it; from pricing to timing; from product development to sourcing; from their choices of electronic media to how they integrate them; and from customer payment alternatives to shipping procedures. We need critical analysis of these questions in order to maintain the proper perspective on online retailing. The potential is serious, but so are the problems that lie ahead.

Before examining the implications of changing consumer behavior and online retailing in the existing retail business, let us step back for a moment and ask the question: Why should retailers consider the online environment as a way of doing business? The answer lies in understanding the market changes that affect retailing and that will continue to affect it in the future.

8.1 Changing Retail Industry Dynamics

Important factors affecting the retailing industry dynamics are:

Overbuilding and excess supply.

Changes in consumer demographics, with more premium placed on efficient use of time.

Changes in consumer behavior, with less focus on brand name and more on lowest prices.

Technology improvements that provide greater convenience and more information than traditional retailing.

Overbuilding and Excess Capacity

With online retailing, constraints of time and space disappear. There is no bricks and mortar storefront to worry about, no critical locations. This new way of retailing can severely affect companies that have invested in expansion and adding capacity. It is important to understand the trouble traditional retailers will face if online retailing takes off.

The 1980s was a period of overexpansion and turmoil for retailers. By the end of the decade, complaints about excessive retail space were being voiced. Profits were declining and control of operating expenses became a paramount management objective. Retailers reduced staff and minimized merchandising in order to enhance profits. Sales growth and market share development were given second priority behind profit enhancement.

In the 1990s, companies are under pressure to grow and produce profit. An important measurement of profit gains is gross margin per square foot. For many retailers, this number is either growing slowly or declining, partially reflecting a less favorable product mix and more competition. Inadequate productivity, both per worker and per unit of space, is also reducing profit margins. Overbuilding also resulted in a growing shortage of low-cost, entry-level workers for the retail industry. The shortage of entry-level workers means that retailers are using undertrained workers who are less able to empathize with shopper needs—leading to a perception that retailers in general and shopping centers in particular are unable or unwilling to provide quality service.

Clearly, with crowded domestic markets and competition constantly grinding away at operating profit, new ways of retailing are being explored by forward-thinking companies such as Wal-Mart.

Demographic Changes

Shopping patterns are beginning to change with the increase of time-strapped, two-career couples and the aging of America. Value and time management are the consumer concerns driving interest in online retailing. Recent retail data shows a decline in the amount of time Americans are spending in shopping malls [EDR95]. The suggested reasons vary: time constraints, safety concerns, and growing frustration with the lack of courteous service and insufficient product information. Understanding the implications of time constraints on consumer shopping behavior is important as they portend the trends to come. For instance, Americans have openly embraced shopping channels like QVC and Home Shopping Network and retailers like CUC International.

Today's time-strapped shoppers have less time and want better values, fewer hassles, and more options. Today, a shopping trip requires a consumer to decide what he or she or the family needs, brave the traffic on the way to a store, hunt for parking, find and select items for purchase, take them to a checkout, wait in line, pay for the items, sometimes bag them, and carry them back home. It can be a hassle and a lot of work, so most working professionals have learned to dread shopping trips. As technology improves, it may not be long before driving to the store gives way to online shopping with home delivery as provided by Peapod (see Section 8.3).

In contrast, there is a growing segment of the population for whom time constraints are less of a problem. The demographic outlook in the United States is for an increasing share of older shoppers (age 50 and above) who prefer shopping at stores rather than online. However, the product mix offered by many department stores and malls is increasingly out of touch with the aging population and does not reflect the shift in purchasing power. Also, with the aging of the population, there is evidence to indicate a shift in consumer interest away from material goods and toward experiences, such as travel and recreation. In addition, as people get older, they tend to become more frugal.

Retailers will need to concentrate on value by offering new product mixes. By this we mean a product mix that includes not only merchandise but also bundles in entertainment and "recreational" shopping with movie theaters, restaurants, bookstores, libraries, and community meeting facilities. This sort of change is already occurring in bookstore design (such as Borders Bookstores and Barnes and Noble), which include a variety of facilities such as coffee shops. However, building shopping malls based on these new business models is a risky venture and requires huge investments.

Consumer Behavior

Consumer behavior is more volatile than ever before, and companies need new ways of responding to consumer needs and satisfying demand. According to one survey, the typical consumer spent only four hours a month in a shopping mall in 1990 versus ten hours in 1985, and sales per square foot dropped. Specialty retailing—power centers, discount malls, discount stores, and catalog shopping—has become one solution for closely monitoring consumer trends and reacting to them quickly. All of these alternatives have one thing in common: they provide consumers with a very large selection of producers priced with deep discounts.

Consumers are no longer as influenced by brand names as they used to be. The emergence of the value shopper is changing retailing. Today, the shopper is less willing to pay the premium for the brand name and much more attentive to quality and value. The decline in gross margins is the first evidence of the impact of that change, reflecting lower initial markups and more discriminating shoppers in that segment. Clearly, retailers that are focused on providing value—the best price, service, and selection—regardless of the brand name will be successful. The real differentiating characteristic for retailers will be in their ability to define what the broad or niche consumer segment is looking for, identifying characteristics of customers in each target segment, and learning how to bundle products and package brands so that they become the preferred choice for online customers.

Technology Improvements in Electronic Retailing

Today, electronic retailing is still far from being a competitive threat to more traditional store retailing (see Table 8.1), but it is becoming increasingly attractive as technology and applications improve, and retailers gain experience.

Table 8.1 Traditional Retail Outlets

Type of Outlet	Definition and Examples
Shopping malls and department stores	These include under one roof general merchandise, drug stores, and groceries.
Supercenters	These consist of three or more anchor stores with a total leasable area between 200,000 and 700,000 square feet.
Factory outlet mall	These primarily stock name-brand manufacturers' items. These are growing in stature and popularity as well. Like power centers, factory outlet malls are also gaining market share at the expense of shopping malls.
Warehouse clubs	These are retailers offering common consumer products at near wholesale prices when purchased in bulk quantities. Examples include Wal-Mart's Sam's Club, Price/Costco, and BJ's Wholesale.
Mail order and catalog shopping	These are retailers offering all kinds of products that can be ordered over the phone. The goods are often delivered within forty-eight hours.

Three dominant forms of electronic retailing channels are: television retailing, CD-ROM retailing, and online service-based retailing, in which we include Web-based retailing.

Television Retailing   Television retailing grossed an estimated $3.2 billion in 1994. One of the pioneers in this area is Home Shopping Network, Inc. (HSN), which began broadcasting electronic retailing to a small, local audience in 1982. Three years later they took this still unproven idea national—and made it work. Today, HSN is a television-based retail, entertainment company, and online retailer (owns Internet Shopping Network), with coast-to-coast customers and annual sales of $1+ billion.

The breadth and reach of TV retailing are amazing. In 1994, HSN reached 65.8 million television households throughout the United States. These households received the signals via cable, broadcast, and satellite dish, twenty-four hours a day, seven days a week. Unlike online audiences, which tend to be predominantly affluent and well educated (net annual income is estimated at $60,000–$80,000), the target audience for television retailing is moderate income households and mostly women.

How does it work? The TV retail marketing and programming are divided into segments that are televised live, with a show host who presents the merchandise and conveys information relating to the product, including price, quality, features, and benefits. Show hosts engage callers in on-air discussions regarding the currently featured product or the caller's previous experience with the company's products. Viewers place orders for products by calling a toll-free telephone number. Generally, merchandise is delivered to customers within seven to ten business days of placing an order. The purchased item may be returned within thirty days for a full refund of the purchase price, including the original shipping and handling charges.

The success of television shopping is the result of the effective utilization of electronic media for capturing the power and influence of celebrity and the magic of showmanship, and bringing them to bear on a sale. In its annual report, the Home Shopping Network states that a celebrity can debut a line of jewelry on HSN and sell more than $2 million in a single weekend. Of course, there's another advantage to television retailing. When customer interest, which is monitored by the number of calls being received, begins to wane, the retailer knows it instantly and can simply move on to the next product.

More recently, infomercials have become a crucial retailing topic. The infomercial has become a new and interesting way to retail specialty products. Modern filming techniques and ingenuity make it possible to create high-quality, cost-efficient, and entertaining documentaries that sell. This coincides with the television viewing public's appetite for information. Infomercials are an especially logical medium since retailers have the opportunity to economically test and evaluate a product through mass channels such as television retailing before committing major capital resources to infomercial production.

CD-ROM–based Shopping   Relatively inexpensive to produce and distribute ($2 per disk), CD-ROMs represent a cost-effective alternative to traditional print catalogs. A key advantage is that they can be produced at a much lower cost than paper catalogs by spreading the cost among many retailers on a single CD. Retailers can create their own disk at a cost of between $10,000 and $50,000, or participate in a multiple marketer disk for a fee of between $1,000 and $2,500 per megabyte of display space.

The crucial business ideas behind catalogs is threefold: build name and brand recognition for the stores and manufacturers; help determine store expansion plans by using the catalog as a prospecting tool; and develop inventory control mechanisms that reduce excess capacity by creating alternative distribution avenues.

Why is the CD-ROM-based catalog market growing? CD-ROM catalogs are basically a new twist on traditional print catalogs. A CD-ROM catalog has multimedia capability and can enable a merchant to add sound, photos, and full-motion video to a product presentation. An apparel merchant can, for example, present merchandise by showing a model walking down a runway. Furthermore, CD-ROMs can be interactive, enabling the customer to pick and choose which merchandise categories to view, or which full motion video to run. With digital technology bringing high-resolution graphics to computer screens, interactivity has become a cost-efficient, as well as visually superior, medium for showing products. Also, the increase in the number of PCs with CD-ROM players is boosting this market.

However, there are several disadvantages to the medium, the most obvious being that not everyone has a CD-ROM drive. Consumers are not comfortable with this shopping method because the CD-ROM is a static medium, meaning that once a disc is created it cannot be updated, whereas other online-based methods allow continuous updating. To address the static media criticism, the CD-ROM-based catalog business is undergoing major changes. Soon many catalogs will offer online ordering, which will increase the functionality of CD-ROM catalogs and provide the opportunity for retailers to grow prospect mailing lists. Improvements in networking will allow the company whose catalog is on the CD to take advantage of a network connection and allow the consumer to go online or pay for the products using credit cards.

Online-based Shopping   The burgeoning online marketplace has enticed more and more retailers to offer their wares online. Online retailers can be divided into four distinct groups:

Retailers that operate off-line stores, getting their feet wet with online storefronts.

Retailers such as catalogers who are concerned with the new Web-based methods of catalog retailing.

"New age" retailers that do not currently operate retail businesses, but they understand how this new medium can revolutionize shopping.

Manufacturers exploring the potential to go "direct to consumers."

Retailing via online services has been around for a while. Online service providers such as CompuServe and America Online (AOL), offer twenty-four-hour access to their own shopping environments. These online malls can be very effective. For instance, when Home Shopping Network (HSN) launched its retail outlet on Prodigy in late 1994, subscribers purchased the entire inventory of cookware and jewelry in only a few days. Another example can be found in the music business, Tower Records. Tower jumped online in June 1995, when it put a store up on AOL. In December 1995, the Tower's AOL store registered almost $200,000 in sales, exceeding Tower's expectations in terms of sales.

More recently, retailers are increasingly looking toward the Web as a retail outlet because of its reach, constant innovation, and low cost. Numerous retailers are developing programs to deliver online shopping to Internet users twenty-four hours a day, seven days a week. Orders are shipped the next day, but can be processed as quickly as within fifteen minutes. Initially, retailing on the Web was more focused on marketing and less on order taking. However, as companies gain experience and learn from their mistakes, they are beginning to study consumer habits, define trends, purchase and develop products to fit a plan, support plans with merchandising ideas, and turn consumer statistics into long-term customer relationships.

The intriguing aspect of online retailing is the emergence of companies that only exist online, like The Electronic Newsstand, Amazon.com, Pawws, and E*Trade. The brief history of E*Trade Securities illustrates what the new paradigm is all about. E*Trade has advantages that few Internet companies can claim: profits and operating history. E*Trade started accepting stock trades on a Web page. The impact on the business could be seen within two months: about 10 percent of its trades came through the Web. The ability to be online made pricing more competitive. E*Trade charges $14.95 for a listed market order. These are unheard of prices in the brokerage industry.

The success of this firm indicates that there is a significant market potential online waiting to be tapped into.

8.2 Online Retailing Success Stories

Peapod, CUC International, and Virtual Vineyards help to explain the intricacies of online retailing.

Online Retailing: Peapod's Experience

Peapod, based in Evanston, Illinois, is using the online medium for food retailing services. Founded in 1989 by two brothers, Peapod (http://www.peapod.com/) is a member of an online grocery/drugstore shopping and delivery service that already has thousands of customers in the Chicago, San Francisco, and Boston areas.

Peapod was founded on the idea that people do not want to go to the grocery store. Peapod has an online database of over 25,000 grocery and drugstore items, and allows comparison shopping based on price, nutritional content, fat, or calories. Other features include electronic coupons, retailer preferred customer discounts, and other benefits like recipes, tips, and information. Peapod membership also allows users to use the shopping and home delivery service. Peapod has a staff of professional shoppers, produce specialists, and delivery people who fulfill the order.

How Does It Work?   Peapod provides customers with home shopping services via PC. Customers need to buy a software application that enables them to access Peapod's database through an online computer service. Peapod initially had a DOS-based system with graphics. They introduced a new version of the software in 1995—a Windows platform in which product pictures are available.

Using the PC, a consumer can access all of the items in a grocery store and drug store. Peapod customers create their own grocery aisles in their own virtual store. Customers can request a list of items by category (cereals), by item (Frosted Flakes), by brand (Kellogg's), or even by what is on sale in the store on a given day. Within categories, they can choose to have the items arranged alphabetically by brand or sorted by lowest cost per ounce, package size, unit price, or nutritional value. Customers also can create repeated-use shopping lists (baby items, barbecue needs, and the like). Peapod's back office is linked with the mainframe databases of the supermarkets at which it shops for its customers (Jewel in Chicago and Safeway in San Francisco), allowing it to provide the supermarkets' stockkeeping units and shelf prices electronically to its customers.

Once consumers have made a selection, they can then give specific shopping instructions, such as "substitute with same calories," or "red grapes only." They can click on the "Comment" button and type in any extra information they would like the Peapod shopper to know. At any time during the order, a consumer can subtotal the amount purchased, or access the "Help" screen for immediate assistance.

Online ordering is simple: users double-click on the Peapod icon and then enter their user IDs and passwords. On verification, users get access to a whole grocery store and drug store of items. Before the actual purchase of an item, users can view images of it and the nutritional content as well. The system allows users to sort items by various criteria like price, price/unit, total calories, fat, protein, carbohydrates, and cholesterol. With these features, Peapod aims to target the health and fitness conscious consumer who chooses foods tailored to specific dietary needs. There are also search features to help locate a particular item. A "Find Item" option at the top of the screen lets users search either by brand name or product type.

When users have finished shopping, they click on "Done" and the order is electronically routed to Peapod. During the transaction closing process, users need to choose a delivery time within a 90-minute slot. Pinpoint delivery (within a 30-minute window) can be selected for a small additional charge. Payment can be made by check, charge, or Peapod Electronic Payment.

Eighty-five to ninety percent of Peapod's orders come in via computer; the rest are faxed or phoned. Peapod orders are taken centrally, and then faxed to the stores. The store gets a printout with the order, the delivery address, and instructions for getting there. Each order is filled by a Peapod employee, who shops the aisles of the store. The employee pays for the groceries, often at special Peapod counters in the back of the store. The order is then taken to a holding area in the supermarket, where the appropriate items are kept cold or frozen until the deliverer picks up a set of orders and takes them to the customers within their 90-minute preselected windows. At each stage—ordering, shopping, holding, and delivery—the processes are tailored to provide personalized service at a relatively low cost.

If a customer has a problem, he or she can call Membership Services, and a service representative will try to resolve the matter. Peapod treats each call as an opportunity to learn (and remember) each customer's preferences and to figure out what the company can do to improve service as a whole. For example, service representatives found that some customers were receiving five bags of grapefruits when they really wanted only five grapefruits. In response, Peapod began asking customers to confirm orders in which order-entry errors may occur.

Peapod members are charged actual shelf prices, plus a monthly service fee, a per-order charge of $5.00 plus 5 percent of the order amount. Customers are willing to pay these extra charges for convenience and because Peapod provides a lower cost shopping experience for the consumer. Consumers save money—despite the extra overhead—because they use more coupons, do better comparison shopping, and buy fewer impulse items than they would if they shopped at a real supermarket. Reducing impulse purchases is important when you consider that 80 percent of the items purchased in a grocery store are impulse items—nonplanned purchases. In addition, consumers save time and have more control because they can shop from home or work whenever they want.

What Is the Business Model?   Rather than automating the trip to a retail store, as other online providers are doing, Peapod is using interactive technology to change the shopping experience altogether. Indeed, the formula for Peapod's success is the busy American lifestyle. The homes it delivers to cut across many demographics. The one thing these demographics have in common is they have better things to do than grocery shop. Still, if it were not for well-managed logistics, these customers would be back in the stores in a second. The behind-the-scenes logistics are central to what Peapod is all about; Peapod has to make sure the orders get to the stores and that they are shopped correctly.

How does Peapod compete with traditional retailers? Traditional retailers make money from the suppliers. They provide access to customers and make their money by buying on deals, volume discounts, and getting coop advertising. Peapod makes all of its money on the customers it serves; it is a mass customizer. It creates the supply chain after identifying a specific demand from a specific customer, and it feeds off the existing infrastructure to do it.

However, existing retailers do have some advantages. An important, though subtle, advantage enjoyed by food retailers is the shopper's resistance to switching food stores because of familiarity with the shelf locations of products purchased. It is also inconvenient for consumers to relearn dozens of product locations at a new store. The online environment must offer significant advantages to overcome shopper inertia and induce trial, let alone continued, patronage.

Is Peapod a competitor to the retail grocer? Not really. Peapod's strategy has been to partner with the retailer rather than compete directly. A lot of credibility comes with the name of the retailer in its individual market. Peapod can help grocers expand into places that might not otherwise be practical from a capital investment standpoint. However, it is quite possible that in the future Peapod may be tempted to compete with grocers by emulating certain aspects of their warehousing. Why? As these new retail formats emerge, and once Peapod gains enough customers, Peapod will be tempted to say it is costing a lot to go to the store and pick the product off the shelf. To avoid the overhead Peapod could have its own warehouse. As soon as Peapod does that it is likely to fall into the same traps as the retailers, such as having an overflow warehouse when something is available on a deal or buying products before there is actual need.

How does Peapod profit from online customer interaction? Peapod has found that every customer interaction is a learning opportunity. At the end of each shopping interaction, it asks the customer, "How did we do on the last order?" Peapod gets feedback on almost 35 percent of orders; most companies consider a 10 percent response rate to customer-satisfaction surveys to be a good one. Consumer feedback allows Peapod to institute a variety of changes and options, including providing nutritional information, making deliveries within a half-hour window (for an additional $4.95) rather than the usual 90-minute window, accepting detailed requests (such as three ripe and three unripe tomatoes), and delivering alcoholic beverages. Peapod also views delivery as another learning opportunity about customers' preferences. It asks employees to find out where customers would like the groceries left when they are not at home and other details that may enhance the relationship. Peapod fills out an "interaction record" for every delivery to track those preferences as well as service metrics, such as the time of the delivery.

Clearly, Peapod stands as a testament to the power of new ideas in retailing. The service, which has 15,000 customers, has a customer-retention rate of more than 80 percent. However, with competition heating up from other entrants, Peapod has to find new ways to be efficient in order to make money in a low-margin business.

CUC International

CUC, a direct marketing powerhouse, was a sizzling initial public offering (IPO) a few years ago when Morgan Stanley took it public on little more than a concept—that you could build a billion-dollar business with no inventory (stockless dealer), no stores, and few employees.

CUC was born in 1973 when its founder, Walter Forbes, anticipated a world of online consumers. He originally launched the company as Comp-U-Card International, a service for computer-based shoppers. The home-PC scheme did not work, so Forbes remade CUC into a telephone-based shopping club. Key products sold to individual members include: shopping (dubbed "Shoppers Advantage"); travel ("Travelers Advantage"); auto ("Autovantage"); and dining ("Premier Dining"). Members pay $49 a year to join each club.

Over the past two decades, CUC has evolved from its original format to a broad-based membership services company that provides its subscribers with a variety of services ranging from discount shopping to credit card enhancement packages.

How Does It Work? Most of CUC's more than 40 million members reach CUC through a toll-free telephone number. Several hundred thousand members connect through a computer online service such as CompuServe (CUC has been on CompuServe for more than a decade) or America Online and more recently through the Web. A Web presence allows CUC to both reduce its costs and increase its reach. In September 1995, Shoppers Advantage opened for business on the Web (http://www.cuc.com) with its database of more than 250,000 brand-name, discount-priced products. In the next several months, CUC intends to add many of its other membership-based services to the Web. Interactivity provides significant economic benefits to CUC. Specifically, CUC has found that on-line members generate:

Higher renewal rates (above the corporate average of 70 percent).

Higher usage rates.

Lower operating costs (reduced customer service requirements since much of the information the customer requires is available online).

At the core of CUC is a series of product databases stored on a cluster of minicomputers. Each week, vendors transmit, via dial-up connections, some 40,000 changes in product features and prices. CUC also has direct access to information about inventory levels at its key vendors, enabling CUC to anticipate when customers' orders will be filled. To put the supporting catalog infrastructure in perspective, it is useful to understand how challenging the demands on the system can be. According to industry sources, J.C. Penney's catalog operation in the fourth quarter of 1993 had to answer 9 million phone calls in its telemarketing centers in the three-week period prior to Christmas. On peak days, the system had to handle over 500,000 calls each day. The distribution centers had to process 1.2 million units a day, and on peak days, shipped out 3,000 tons of merchandise [IW94].

Without question, the computer age has allowed CUC not only to exist, but also to thrive. Through its database of customers, merchandise, and vendors, and its sophisticated telemarketing operation, CUC processes a high volume of orders. With its close, paying connections to credit card issuers, such as CitiBank, AT&T, Sears, and Texaco, and to regional banks, CUC offers the issuer an additional revenue stream on the credit card holders and bank accounts. In return, CUC harvests those companies' lists through its direct-marketing effort with its varied services tailored to consumer buying trends.

What Is the Revenue Model?   CUC's revenues are derived principally from membership fees. This distinction from other consumer marketers (which make money on product sales) has enabled CUC to continually lower merchandise margins to maintain pricing that is comparable to competing retail formats. The average annual fees range from $8 to $89.

CUC's business is divided into three segments: individual, wholesale, and discount. CUC's members are solicited through direct marketing (individual and wholesale members) and through direct sales (discount members). Individual memberships differ from wholesale and discount memberships in that the marketing cost associated with obtaining the member is borne by CUC. Wholesale revenues are generally derived from individual services (such as discount shopping) sold on a third-party basis to banks and credit unions as checking account enhancements. Discount revenues accrue from memberships that include discount coupon membership programs (coupon books offering members discounts at a variety of local and national service providers), fund-raising programs, and local merchant discounts sold door-to-door.

CUC's sales force enlists financial institutions, retailers, oil companies, and credit unions to market CUC services to their customers. The corporate client derives commission revenues from each new or renewing membership sold and achieves competitive differentiation by offering more feature-laden credit cards.

What Is the Business Model?   CUC is an information intermediary that reduces a consumer's search cost. CUC is taking advantage of the fact that the catalog industry is highly fragmented. It is estimated that there may be as many as 7,000 different catalogs being published. Over the past few years there has been a consolidation in the catalog industry, and this will continue as economic factors make it more difficult for the smaller catalog companies to compete. Traditional catalog firms are facing rising production expenses as postage, paper, and printing costs increase. Although some changes can be made to offset a portion of these price increases, they cannot be absorbed without retail price increases. These increases will pressure the smaller catalog companies the most, as they do not have the size or the deep pockets to absorb these costs.

The online medium is one of the few service delivery channels where costs are coming down. Online companies such as CUC have significant advantages, given their size and ability to consolidate information. With high fixed costs (due to technology investments), improving customer response rates, order fulfillment rates, and transaction volume can lead to significant increases in profit.

The key to continued success is having the capital to invest in distribution capabilities and new technologies. In February 1996, CUC announced deals to buy Davidson & Associates Inc. for $ 1.14 billion and Sierra On-Line Inc. for $ 1.06 billion. These purchases allow CUC to broaden the product offerings to include entertainment and educational content. The reasons for these acquisitions are as follows: First, CUC strongly believes that the expanding PC and interactive platforms worldwide are how consumers will access information and conduct commerce. Second, education and entertainment are among the fastest growing areas of consumer spending, and Davidson and Sierra On-Line are preeminent in these sectors. Their products are well suited for penetration of the PC and Internet into consumers' homes. These acquisitions will enable CUC to explore the membership model in the education and entertainment areas. CUC also acquired Rent Net, which offers nationwide apartment rental information on the Internet. By combining local maps, color pictures, and timely information, Rent Net's software enables consumers to simplify and improve the way they search for apartments. In short, CUC is relying on technology and content improvements to raise the barrier for competition and solidify its position.

Wine on the Web: Virtual Vineyards

Virtual Vineyards (http://www.virtualvin.com) is an online retailer that caters to the needs of a niche audience, wine lovers who want to buy wine over the Internet.

How Does It Work?   Virtual Vineyards launched its online wine Web marketplace using Netscape's Commerce Server, which allows merchants to build and maintain servers on the Internet so they can actually bill customers. Wells Fargo Bank (San Francisco) authorizes and processes the credit card payments. Virtual Vineyards (VV) lists the different wines and prices from each participating winery, as well as a summary of information and tasting charts. Pricing for wines starts at $10. Users are offered a 10 percent discount when they order by the case.

Once a selection is made, customers input their selection with the encrypted credit card payment information, which is electronically transmitted to Wells Fargo Bank. The bank transfers the money from the customer's credit card account over Wells Fargo's private electronic network. On payment, Virtual Vineyards fulfills the order from its warehouses.

Virtual Vineyards has developed an integrated marketing program that includes outbound communications, sales follow-up, and direct mail and electronic mail campaigns to support transactions on the Web site.

What Is the Business Model?   Virtual Vineyards is a retailer whose model is based on transactions that depend on impulse purchasing behavior. Virtual Vineyards picked a perfect niche market. Most people do not know much about wines, but would like to. But once online, people can learn how to describe wine tastes, wine terms, what foods work with what wines, and ultimately order online.

Virtual Vineyards makes money by receiving a percentage of each wine sale. Interestingly, because of the commerce clause in the U.S. Constitution, wineries do not pay Virtual Vineyards to participate in its online retail store. The clause states that liquor or wine stores cannot receive payment to retail alcoholic beverages.

Virtual Vineyards serves a special need for small wineries, which are typically run by two or three people with minuscule marketing budgets and minimal time to keep up with orders. The potential of companies like Virtual Vineyards lies in the ability to bring somewhat specialized and esoteric information to people in an economical way. Ordinarily, the wine purchase experience can only be done piecemeal: research wines, visit one winery at a time, and take a wine-tasting class. Services like Virtual Vineyards make the complicated process easier to navigate.

Web-based Travel Agencies

The Web has made an impressive foray into the travel business—hotel booking, car rentals, and airline tickets. Table 8.2 summarizes the issues in the travel business.

Making a reservation or purchasing an airline ticket is usually a time-consuming and frustrating process for the traveler and an increasingly costly one for the ticket provider. In order to make decisions, travelers are demanding more and more travel information and services while insisting on lower rates, which increase costs for travel agencies while reducing revenues.

Table 8.2 Summarizing the Implementation Issues

Business Problem	Reach new customers with low overhead.
	Reduce expense of booking hotel rooms and issuing airline tickets.
	Provide nice GUI interface to hotel and airline information.
Solution	Use the Web and Internet to reduce overhead by giving consumers the ability to book hotel rooms and purchase airline tickets.
Requirements	Interface internal systems with the World Wide Web, dial-in, and telnet access.
	Send airline tickets overnight after they are purchased.
Benefits	Expect competitive advantage via: up-to-date information, reduced support overhead, and customer empowerment.

There is a rapidly growing group of travelers who prefer to make their own travel arrangements online anytime from anywhere they might be and not depend on the business hours of a travel agency nor the problems of phone communication. This group of travelers includes those using corporate travel agencies and the 30 percent of air travel not purchased through the travel agency community. Giving personal access to airline reservations and tickets would tap into a rapidly growing group of travel consumers while dramatically reducing the costs of producing an air ticket.

Prior to 1993, U.S. travel agencies' business was primarily corporate travel (90 percent) under great margin and competitive pressure from much larger travel agencies. In 1993, they began active development of an online air reservation and ticketing system designed to capture part of the air travel market not using travel agencies and those travelers who want the ease and convenience of an easy-to-use self-booking system. In April 1994, they began allowing dial-in connections to the service, offering a text-based modem connection. In November 1994, they added telnet session connections through the Internet. This service quickly became very popular, adding 20,000 subscribers in the first three months of availability. In June 1995, they added World Wide Web access to the service.

As online competition grows fiercer, travel agencies are confronting new challenges. The trend is toward specialization and customization in both sales and purchasing, pumping even more resources into the competitive struggle, calling for better ways of meeting customer needs, and developing new business models. Take, for instance, the intermediation model. If the agent is an intermediary to airlines, hotels, and car rentals, the business model seems to be a good one: the agent gets a cut of each transaction, and the companies pay for that cut out of their savings in the cost of sales they do not incur online (ticket printing and mailing; brick and mortar for retail outlets). But that is in theory. We will have to see how this business model plays out over time.

8.3 Mercantile Models from the Consumer's Perspective

It is important to realize that ordering products simply by pushing a "BUY" button on a Web page is inherently complex and is not likely for all types of products or services—despite the promises and hype. However, although each consumer has a distinct way of doing business, some generalizations can be made about the way consumers do shopping. These generalizations (or mercantile models) are essential for understanding consumer dynamics. Mercantile models formalize the interaction between consumers and merchants. These models create consistency and increase consumer convenience by eliminating the need to figure out a new business process for every single vendor. Without a common process for managing and completing transactions, electronic commerce will be entangled in a mesh of bilateral *ad hoc* mechanisms that are specific to each company doing business online. For instance, the online medium works well for delivering product information and providing a forum for discussing product merits and drawbacks.

But, try actually ordering something over the Web. In most cases, consumers will be bounced back to some low-tech apparatus like a fax machine or a telephone. Mercantile processes need to be reengineered to facilitate as much of the entire loop—preliminary customer interaction, order entry and processing, order fulfillment, and post-sales customer service—online as possible.

Mercantile models can be developed from two perspectives: consumer and retailer. From the consumer side, the mercantile model specifies the sequence of activities a shopper takes in purchasing a product or service. Understanding this sequence of steps is important for developing electronic commerce software. From the retailer side, the mercantile model defines the order management cycle, which specifies the activities within an organization that must take place in fulfilling the customer's order. The order management process is discussed in Chapter 10.

Distinct Phases of a Consumer Mercantile Model

Consumer mercantile activities can be grouped into three phases: prepurchase preparation, purchase consummation, and postpurchase interaction (see Fig. 8.1):

The prepurchase preparation phase includes search and discovery for a set of products in the larger information space capable of meeting customer requirements and product selection from the smaller set of products based on attribute comparison.

The purchase consummation phase specifies the flow of information and documents associated with purchasing and negotiation with merchants for suitable terms, such as price, availability, and delivery dates; and electronic payment mechanisms that integrate payment into the purchasing process.

The postpurchase interaction phase includes customer service and support to address customer complaints, product returns, and product defects.

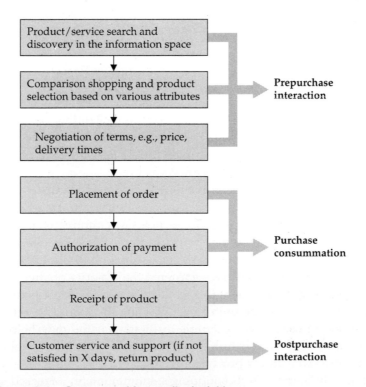

Figure 8.1   Consumer Mercantile Activities

Before considering each of the consumer purchasing phases in detail, let us first elaborate on the various types of consumers found in the online marketplace and the different types of purchasing behavior.

Types of Consumers   In general, consumers can be categorized into three types:

Impulsive buyers, who purchase products quickly;

Patient buyers, who purchase products after making some comparisons; and

Analytical buyers, who do substantial research before making the decision to purchase products or services.

An understanding of the consumer type allows us to delve deeper into what motivates various types of shopping (impulse purchasing, compulsive shopping, window shopping, or browsing). Consumer behavior, which has a profound impact on the way online systems are developed, can be viewed in terms of two questions: Why is the consumer shopping and What is in it for the consumer? As these questions imply, an online shopping experience can be valuable (accomplishing something), or valueless (simply browsing), "fun" or a "chore."

Marketing researchers over the years have categorized shopping experiences into two dimensions: utilitarian, carrying out a shopping activity "to achieve a goal" or "complete a task"; and hedonic, carrying out a shopping activity because "it is fun and I love it." An understanding of hedonic and utilitarian shopping can provide insight into many electronic commerce consumption behaviors that are normally not taken into account in the design and layout of electronic marketplaces.

Utilitarian behavior has often been portrayed as task-related and rational, implying that a product is purchased in a deliberate and efficient manner. It is conceivable that a purchase is not a key motivator in utilitarian behavior. For example, value may result from a consumer collecting information to get some ideas and prices on various possibilities. In general, shopping's utilitarian aspects have garnered the majority of attention in the design of online systems. The utilitarian dimension is often equated with a work mentality and may be useful in explaining the "chore aspect of shopping" alluded to earlier. For example, utilitarian value may help explain why few consumers browse through online stores, which most feel is an arduous and time-consuming process.

Hedonic shopping reflects shopping's entertainment, increased arousal, heightened involvement, perceived freedom, fantasy fulfillment, and escapism. In other words, people buy so they can shop, not shop so they can buy. The purchase of products may be incidental to the entire experience of shopping. Hedonic value is more subjective than its utilitarian counterpart. It is also difficult to quantify benefits from fun and playfulness rather than from task completion.

The hedonic aspect of shopping has not been explored much in online environments although it makes up a large part of consumer shopping behavior. Furthermore, vicarious consumption through technology like virtual reality can provide hedonic value by allowing a consumer to enjoy a product's benefits without purchasing it. Consumers may also receive hedonic value through bargain perceptions. Some people like to hunt for bargains, and *discovering* a really cheap bargain alone can provide increased sensory involvement and excitement.

Types of Purchases   Marketing researchers have isolated several types of purchasing behavior:

Specifically planned purchases, where the need was recognized on entering the store and the shopper bought the exact item planned.

Generally planned purchases, where the need was recognized, but the shopper decided in-store on the actual manufacturer of the item to satisfy the need.

Reminder purchases, where the shopper was reminded of the need by some store influence. This shopper is influenced by in-store advertisements and can substitute products readily.

Entirely unplanned purchases, where the need was not recognized upon entering the store.

While the key role of the in-store influences on purchasing behavior is indisputable, very little is known about what influences purchasing online.

Prepurchase Preparation

Many business models being designed for the Web assume a direct or one-to-one correspondence between predisposition to purchase and actual purchase. These models assume that electronic commerce could flourish simply by establishing the inclination to purchase a product by creating attractive Web pages for that product. These models fail to acknowledge that one must create an environment that addresses the multiple steps a consumer goes through in the prepurchase phase: deliberation, comparison, and negotiation.

Prepurchase Deliberation   Any major consumer purchase involves some amount of prepurchase deliberation, the extent of which is likely to vary across individuals, products, and purchase situations. Purchase deliberation is defined as the elapsed time between a consumer's first thinking about buying and the actual purchase itself. Information search should constitute the major part of the duration, but comparison of alternatives and price negotiation would be included in the continually evolving information search and deliberation process.

During deliberation consumers are watchful for new information regarding variables that are important for the purchase decision process. For example, the purchase of a new car involves an appreciable time lag between the initiation of the information search process and the decision. Unlike the purchase of food, an impulse purchase, purchasing a car involves gathering information as well as monitoring changing conditions (an unexpected increase in income, the existence of a promotional sale). These changing conditions can either speed up the purchase decision or encourage the consumer to postpone the purchase decision in some fashion (because prices encountered were too high).

Deliberation is much shorter in the case of impulse/unplanned purchasing. But, understanding how it works is no less important. It is estimated that impulse buying (or unplanned purchasing) accounts for a third of total purchasing in nonelectronic markets. In fact, in grocery sectors, impulse buying is in the region of one half or more of total purchases.

The answers to several important questions about the purchase deliberation process can shape the way online shopping environments are designed and created:

How much time are buyers allocating and spending on their purchasing decisions with respect to various products?

What factors account for the differences in consumer decision time?

What technology can be used or designed to reduce decision time?

What shopping environment keeps customers happy and wanting to return?

Information on customer characteristics associated with reduced purchase deliberation times can be quite valuable when attempting to target market segments properly. This important element of the mercantile process has been difficult to address online because of certain technological limitations such as lack of sensory touch, poor user interfaces, low quality monitors, and lack of three-dimensional exploratory shopping experiences.

Prepurchase Comparison and Negotiation Process　In many cases, comparisons of various attributes are necessary preconditions to purchasing decisions. In the context of attribute comparison, search can be further classified along two additional dimensions:

> Consumer search, which is defined as the degree of care, perception, and effort directed toward obtaining data or information related to an individual's purchase decision problem; and

> Organization search, which is defined as a process through which an organization adapts to such changes in its external environment as new suppliers, new products, and new services.

The consumer search process.　Most consumer search is focused on price comparison. In many markets, consumers show a healthy respect for price as an indicator of quality—and by this suggest that to compete on price alone may well be an unnecessarily dangerous and inevitably damaging strategy. For instance, it is often said that consumers are largely unaware of the price of staple food and so are insensitive to moderate price changes. Aggressive price promotion often leads to a greater price awareness among consumers, reducing the retailers' ability to push prices back up. Retailers are aware of this and often avoid price wars on certain food categories. Likewise, in the online marketplace, retailers have to be careful not to engage in short-term price wars that could prove detrimental to the well-being of the overall retail industry.

The Internet is changing the dynamics of price comparison. The *Financial Times* [FT96] quotes a German wholesale and foreign trade association that claimed that companies were losing lucrative niche markets because the Internet made it easier to compare prices. The value of the Internet in finding the cheapest price of a product or service could become even more pronounced if "intelligent agents"—software capable of conducting an exhaustive search on behalf of the user—automate the process. In general, technology poses a management challenge when it reduces search cost, which could lead to unstable and intensely competitive pricing. The tendency in this situation is for companies to set the prices of their products more on cost than on the value to consumers.

The comparison of attributes has been the focus of much research, primarily in the area of economics. The emphasis was on understanding outcomes or results rather than on the specific nature of the underlying comparative processes. In online markets, the outcomes may be identical to those obtained in off-line markets, but the process of reaching them is significantly different. While the nature of comparative behavior is undocumented and not well understood, it is crucial in the development of consumer–retail interfaces.

The organizational search process.   Organizational search is designed to balance the cost of acquiring information with the benefits of improved final decisions. The search process can be characterized in terms of the overall effort made by the buyer to obtain information from the external environment and in terms of the overall duration, or the length of time between the first initiation of information-gathering activities and the time when all of the information considered necessary to make a decision has been collected. The organizational search process is determined in part by market characteristics (such as pace of change and technological complexity) and by certain aspects of a firm's present buying situation (switching costs and prior experience). Together, these dimensions impose a series of demands on the search process used.

Certain forces may represent disincentives to organizational search. For example, organizational buyers often have strong vendor relationships based on prior purchases of a particular product. Such vendor relationships may involve nontrivial levels of switching costs that represent a disincentive for buyers to search outside the established vendor portfolio and may result in constrained search processes. Furthermore, strong vendor relationships may constrain buyers' search processes indirectly by insulating them from market information. As a consequence, buyers with strong vendor relationships may perceive less change to be taking place and hence have a low incentive to engage in searches.

The rate of information change in the marketplace imposes additional demands on a firm's search process. Although change can be argued in a general sense to constitute uncertainty, its particular time-dependent nature may create needs above and beyond the traditional information needs. Under rapidly changing market conditions, acquired information is time-critical and tends to have a shorter lifetime. That is, information about a product received today may be relatively less valuable tomorrow to the extent that the product's features or underlying technology is improving quickly. For a buyer, the implication of fast-paced change may be a disincentive to prolong a search process. In cost-benefit terms, fast-paced change implies that distinct benefits are associated with search effort, yet costs are associated with prolonging the process. Firms may respond to high-paced information change by constraining search process time.

Purchase Consummation

After identifying the products to be purchased, the buyer and seller must interact in some way to actually carry out the mercantile transaction. A *mercantile transaction* is defined as the exchange of information between the buyer and seller followed by the necessary payment. Depending on the payment model mutually agreed on, they may interact by exchanging currency that is backed by a third party (a central bank) or by transferring authorizations for a credit billing organization (VISA, MasterCard).

A single mercantile model will not be sufficient to meet the needs of everyone. Just as there are multiple mercantile models in the off-line world, it is quite possible that multiple mercantile models will coexist online. In very general terms, a simple mercantile protocol would require the following transactions:

The buyer contacts the vendor to purchase a product or service. This dialogue might be interactive online—the Web, e-mail, or off-line via a catalog and telephone.

The vendor states the price.

The buyer and vendor may or may not engage in negotiation.

If satisfied, the buyer authorizes payment to the vendor with an encrypted payment containing a digital signature for the agreed price.

The vendor contacts his or her billing service to verify the encrypted payment details.

The billing service decrypts the payment details and checks the buyer's account balance or credit and puts a hold on the amount of transfer. (The billing service may need to interact with the buyer's bank.)

The billing service gives the vendor the "green light" to deliver the product and sends a standardized message giving details of the transaction (such as authorization number) for the merchant's records.

On notification of adequate funds to cover the financial transaction, the vendor delivers the goods to the buyer or, in the case of information purchase, provides a cryptokey to unlock the file.

On receiving the goods, the buyer signs and delivers the receipt. The vendor then tells the billing service to complete the transaction.

At the end of the billing cycle, the buyer receives a list of transactions. The buyer can then deny certain transactions or complain about overbilling. Suitable audit or customer service actions are then initiated depending on the payment scheme.

The software framework for implementing the above sequence of steps, shown in Fig. 8.2, allows for common ways of creating and updating content, shopping interfaces, and credit card authorization and payment. This

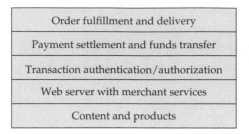

Figure 8.2   Software Framework for Purchase Consummation

framework combines all of the software tools needed to create and run an online store ("front office") with complete "back-office" customer support and transaction management services.

One such software framework is the Microsoft merchant solution, built on Windows NT and the Internet Information Server. Microsoft's retailing solution contains a merchant server and a workbench that includes a set of tools enabling flexible store design, product display, customer profiling, and decision support. The solution will also enable credit card authorization using the Secure Electronic Transaction protocol to transfer information between merchants and suppliers and between merchants and customers, and interoperability with third party vendors and existing information systems. For the client side, Microsoft is developing a shopping utility that will be a standard part of the Windows operating system. The shopping utility will allow merchants to develop customized, branded online retailing systems, while ensuring that the mercantile processes are always the same for the consumer. In addition, Microsoft promises to make available programming interfaces so that solution providers, independent software vendors, and other third parties can build merchandising applications and solutions.

The rationale for a merchant server is simple. It is fairly costly and laborious for merchants to conduct electronic commerce because they have to custom-develop applications on secure Web servers, rely on third parties to build a Web site, and maintain the system—all of which can cost anywhere from tens of thousands to hundreds of thousands of dollars. And even after spending that kind of money, merchants still have not addressed some of the most important aspects of transacting business online, such as automated customer service and online soft goods fulfillment and calculation of shipping fees. Vendors such as OpenMarket have noticed this gap and have developed solutions such as Merchant Solution, which enables merchants to get themselves up and running on the Web for a fraction of what they would pay to do it all themselves.

Postpurchase Interaction

Postpurchase interaction plays an important role in all elements of a company's profit equation: customer value, price, and cost. As long as there is payment for services, there will be refunds, disputes, and other service issues that need to be considered. Returns and claims, crucial parts of the purchasing process, impact administrative costs, scrap and transportation expenses, and customer relations. In the ongoing relationship with the customer, this step can produce heated disagreements; every interaction becomes a zero-sum game that either the company or the customer wins.

It is estimated that every time a customer returns a product or disputes a purchase, it costs the retailer at least $25–50. When a customer has online access to the full record of his transaction, many of his questions can be answered. However, most companies design their mercantile processes for one-way merchandise flow: outbound to the customer. That means that returns and claims must flow upstream, against the current, creating logistical messes and transactional snarls and dissatisfied customers.

Postpurchase service can affect customer satisfaction and company profitability for years because of the information conveyed and intimacy involved. In most companies, the postpurchase service people are not linked to any marketing operation, internal product-development effort, or quality assurance team. An effective electronic commerce environment must take advantage of emerging Intranet architectures for information distribution, such as account activity and account statements to facilitate postpurchase interaction (see Chapter 11).

8.4 Management Challenges in Online Retailing

While changes in retailing may be driven by technology, managerial vision is required for successful implementation. Traditionally, retailing has been a low-tech environment in which retailing executives often relegated technology issues to back-room operators. These managers are most at risk, as they do not have a clue that a major revolution has begun. Most of them have never used a computer (or had to), never been on an online service, and do not know what the Internet is or what it can do. The winners will be the players who understand how to leverage the unique capabilities of the online medium to effectively meet the changing needs of the consumer.

While the technology required to implement online retailing is maturing, many management issues remain unanswered. No one really knows yet how to build and run a successful, mass-market online mall. The sales medium is new, the technology is new, and retailers have a lot to learn about tricky technology, customer behavior, and management issues. But one thing is clear: For online retailing to succeed, online technology must complement management and operational strategy.

Some immediate strategic questions that need to be addressed include: How can the company generate "pull" forces that attract people to the online store? How can the company leverage on established brand names? How can the company utilize features of a product or service to signal value or quality to an online customer? These questions and others in Table 8.3 will dictate the shape and structure of online retailing in the coming decade.

Table 8.3 Management Issues in Online Retailing

Retail Advertising and Marketing Issues	*Retail Operations Issues*	*Retail Management Issues*
Advertising and segmentation	Merchandising and inventory management (buying and handling merchandise)	Location (trade area) analysis and decision making (site selection)
Product display and positioning		
Brand and category management (establishing and sustaining an image)	Retail management information systems collection (POS)	Retail organization and human resource management
	Retail SKU decision support	Retailing policies, practices, procedures, and planning
Pricing	Customer service quality	Financial dimensions of managing operations
Promotion and Incentives		

Come Up with a Retailing Strategy

Strategy is needed to address the whole retail process. The steps involved in retailing strategy include: prospecting for potential customers, qualifying a customer, learning the customer's needs, understanding the customer's purchasing process, selecting the presentation to be made, making the presentation, adapting the presentation based on customer reaction, handling objections, negotiating with the customer, closing the sale, and building an ongoing relationship through service. Each of these steps needs to be rethought and reexamined in the online environment.

Strategy also deals with stimulating demand. Retailers have not learned how to stimulate online demand, something that will become increasingly important. To stimulate demand, retailers must get out ahead of consumers by anticipating shifting attitudes and lifestyles, and must use marketing methods that trigger traffic and sales. Marketing triggers need to resonate with the targeted consumer, which today simply cannot be everyone. Retailers need to find a unique voice and image. Words, images and merchandise connected to lifestyle and consumer trends can stimulate demand, even in this difficult climate.

A good retail strategy can have a telling impact on the marketplace. One example is the supercenter concept being promoted by Wal-Mart that has been called the new retailing phenomenon in the 1990s. Through its convenient one-stop shopping format, large selection, and low prices, supercenters are growing faster than any of the major retail formats in the United States. The supercenter addresses the needs of today's consumer—lack of free time and appetite for low prices—with the benefits of economies of scale. Industry analysts predict that the supercenter will be to the 1990s what shopping malls were to the 1960s, discount stores were to the 1970s, and specialty stores were to the 1980s.

To understand the size and layout of a supercenter, consider SuperTarget in Omaha, Nebraska. SuperTarget is a 192,000-square-foot, 64-checkout format, which includes a 62,000-square-foot supermarket and a 125,000-square-foot discount general merchandise section. Supercenters provide companies with a means to increase sales in a maturing discount store industry. It has been reported that by adding a supermarket to the traditional discount store, sales of general merchandise have increased by an estimated 25 to 30 percent. The synergies of supermarket and general merchandise departments, with the potential for cross-shopping, allow for greater sales than either as stand-alone entities. Supercenters have created pressure on suppliers profits and forced traditional outlets to either respond or shut down. In short, online retailing is desperately in need of new retailing strategies like the "supercenter."

Manage Channel Conflict

How will manufacturers move toward the online environment without alienating their current distribution partners? All firms use a channel of distribution to get their products or services into the hands of the customer or consumer. For instance, Seattle-based Online Interactive (OLI) made a pact with Microsoft to distribute twenty-five of the software maker's products via the Internet. Here, OLI is the reseller, which can create channel conflict: Some of OLI's customers are value-added resellers (VARs) and some are VARs' end-user customers. The online advantage is apparent when one compares lost margins with instant access and the resulting increase in customer satisfaction.

The online economy threatens the existence of "middlemen," such as distributors, brokers, and wholesalers. Signs of this first appeared several years ago when Wal-Mart began requiring its vendors to communicate information about products and orders directly via EDI. In doing so, Wal-Mart cut the manufacturers' sales representatives, traditionally the source of those product updates, out of the process. Unless distributors address the threat posed by online retailing to their existing business models, they could be the real losers in online retailing.

Learn to Price Online Products/Services

Pricing has not been receiving the attention it deserves in the online marketplace. There are two types of pricing in the online marketplace: access pricing and product pricing. Access pricing is analogous to stores charging people money just for the right to enter and shop. In the off-line world, customers would probably revolt and the stores would end up declaring bankruptcy in a matter of weeks. But that is essentially what every online store and mall in cyberspace is asking consumers to do: pay charges to their Internet access provider.

Research has shown that consumers will pay few, if any, incremental dollars to use new untested services, and retailers cannot expect consumers to pay significant "access" charges to buy products from their homes. It is unlikely that retailers will achieve a critical mass of people shopping in virtual stores until it is at least equal in cost to the alternatives.

The "access charge" model is being attacked by some forward-thinking retailers. They are providing two sources of entry: via the Web or using their direct dial-up Windows software—at absolutely no cost as the merchant picks up the access charges. Clearly, some value shifting or cost shifting will have to take place to reduce the burden on the consumer; otherwise the store will be bypassed. In today's retail world, up to 20 percent of a product price actually pays for store-related costs, so if the store is physically removed from the equation, retailers have a 20 percent margin to pay for enabling technologies, delivery, and other costs.

Deliver a Satisfying Shopping Experience

It is true that by being online there's no traffic hassle, no waiting in line, and no wasting time in sales pitches, but will the consumer be able to find the products he or she wants quickly, make selections, and enjoy the whole process? Management needs to learn how to make a monitor or Web page deliver a satisfying shopping experience. The challenge is to build technology that entices consumers and helps them find their way through the virtual maze.

Some retailers have attempted to address this complex problem. A few years ago, J.C. Penney experimented with an interactive television called Telaction that allowed them to get to about 100,000 households in the Chicago area. Consumers used their touchtone telephone as a keypad, and through cable television could navigate their way through a virtual mall. This mall had about forty different stores. Catalogers and other direct marketers were among the first to join. One of the important lessons learned was that the transition from merchandising through the pages of a catalog into merchandising in an interactive multimedia environment is not easy. One cannot just take the pictures out of a catalog and put them on a TV screen. The merchandising rules must change.

Online retailers often find that they are dealing with a different set of customers than they had expected, or with customer attitudes that are incompatible with this new market. Many firms discovered that the limited product selections and canned presentations that work on television do not appeal to the individuals who are using PCs. Consumer interface needs to include text, graphics, simulated 3-D, and actual virtual reality. For example, eshop Plaza has designed the shopping experience from the customer's point of view. The visual interface shows a simulated 3-D view of a plaza that is genuinely pleasant, appealing, and easy to navigate. eshop is reacting to the fact that shoppers want a more exciting experience than flipping pages of a catalog on the screen.

Interactive free-flowing and low-cost information dictates instead a business model that includes unlimited selection, prices close to cost, and two-way communication capability. How firms implement this model will define their future. The most successful retailers will be those who use the new media capabilities to reach consumers and let them shop the way they wanted.

Design the Layout of an Online Store

Creating a virtual store that consumers will like is not easy. The virtual store will have to have a great impact on the consumer's value equation. To significantly alter consumer buying behavior, virtual retailing will have to provide better, faster, cheaper, or more entertaining shopping experiences.

The layout of the store also depends on manufacturer incentives to retailers such as slotting allowances. Slotting allowances are lump-sum advance payments made by manufacturers to retailers for stocking their new products. In exchange for a slotting allowance, the retailer makes an agreement with the manufacturer to place the product in a high-traffic area for promotional purposes. Slotting allowances can be used by retailers to determine how to design their user interface, namely, what products appear visually closer to customers, and also what products are found when search criteria are specified.

The layout of the store also depends on how sophisticated user interfaces become. Several research groups are working on capturing 3-D images of every product in the store. Their notion is that consumers want to find something familiar. They will want to see a store laid out the way stores today are, with aisles and shelves with products on them. Consumers will be able to "walk" the aisles of this store on their screens, pick a box off the shelf, rotate it around to read the side label and look for a special offer, put it back on the shelf, or put it into the basket.

Another thing users will be able to do in a virtual store is put themselves in the picture. For instance, when Anne is shopping for clothes, Anne will actually be able to see how a garment looks on her before buying it. Anne will be able to see the representation of the garment on the screen, then bring a representation of herself into the picture and actually try it on. In fact, Levi's is already using technology that allows shoppers to see how pants will look without actually trying them on.

Manage Brands

Online brand management is a new and exciting area of retail management. Retailers know that consumers adopt a brand, and make it part of their lifestyle; they remain loyal and purchase the brand again and again. The adoption decision is preceded by a number of other steps: unaware, aware, interested, knowledgeable, positive attitude, experience, trial, repeat, and adoption.

Purchase behavior in electronic markets differs from traditional retail settings in two ways. First, a retailer is concerned with simply inducing purchase through the use of marketing mix variables (retail and/or manufacturer rebates, list price discounts, trade-in allowances). Second, a retailer is interested in inducing purchase now, rather than later. Thus online coupon books and other tools likely to induce a consumer to make decisions quickly can have important implications on the purchasing process.

In electronic markets, in contrast, retailers currently have limited understanding of the marketing variables effective in inducing purchases. Also, the issue of information dissemination is a major problem. If retailers create coupon books, how do they get them to the online customer without flooding the network with junk mail? To solve both problems, a better understanding of brand management in conjunction with online consumer behavior is imperative.

Create the Right Incentives

The right incentive can influence consumer acceptance. However, incentive design for online retail markets is fairly new and not well understood. The question here is: How can coupons, discounts, or other incentives be used by online merchants to build and retain shopper loyalty? For instance, Tower Records offers an online coupon good for $3 off all CDs priced $12.99 and above, and $2 off all CDs priced $9.99 to $11.99. That is better than a 20 percent discount. However, existing incentive mechanisms are often very simple and their effectiveness is not clear.

Incentives are so basic to traditional retailing that one can only marvel at the myopia among some online retailers that technology can conquer all. Retailers need to think about different incentive strategies for different types of online products/services. For instance, how do you influence consumers to download a file? By charging a low price, by offering value, or by offering frequent flyer miles. One may argue that these are basic questions that have been addressed in regular retailing. That might be the case, but online retailing is subtly different on many planes and requires merchants to rethink their incentive mechanisms.

8.5 Summary

In this chapter we discussed how the world of retailing is evolving. Is it too late for retailers not doing online retailing? By no means. Traditional retailers that combine current market shares, rapid expansion, focused culture, productivity, technology, and cost leadership will continue to be successful in the next decade. You will certainly see retailers do something in the online area in a much more aggressive fashion—when they need to. This model for electronic commerce is young and is still experimental, and needs to mature and make itself much more user friendly.

Finally, it remains to be seen how profitable online retailing actually becomes. Many experts feel that the added convenience and value provided by online retailing will facilitate acceptance. The elimination of bricks and mortar could result in sharply decreased prices for a wide variety of goods that consumers purchase today. Similarly, the potential for delivering merchandise and marketing messages through the online medium is substantial because such a medium would further enhance the convenience factor of shopping at home and having the product shipped there.

Chapter 9

Electronic Commerce and Online Publishing

Chapter Outline

The Web may have blossomed because of peer-to-peer publishing, but judging from recent product offerings, there is an enormous groundswell of interest among both commercial and corporate publishers in the Web. For instance, it was reported that, in less than three months, the *Wall Street Journal* Interactive Edition attracted 500,000 registered readers on the Web, and that number is growing by some 3,000 readers per day. Also, the electronic edition has attracted more than thirty advertisers paying to reach this audience [WALL96].

Initially, growth in the online publishing marketplace was driven by the potential of new interactive technologies and applications. The promise of new interactive publishing captured the imagination of both content providers and the public. However, from 1993 to 1995 much of online publishing was inhibited by a lack of business purpose. At that time, the content creation side of online publishing was dominated by techno-savvy individuals who were not experienced at selling and who did not understand the business of publishing. In addition, there were publishing companies who took a "Just Get Me on the Web!" approach, failing to define the business purposes driving their online presence.

As the initial euphoria wore off, publishers realized that simply having a presence on the Web did not guarantee profits. They discovered that offering exciting technology without compelling content is insufficient to capture market share. These firms are learning that the best way to capture consumers' attention is to develop a business model that allows the company to offer unique and valuable information, programming, and services. This content, no matter how it is delivered, must be packaged so that it provides more value than alternative sources of information. The key is to identify what the customer wants and finds interesting and to avoid being distracted by new technologies. Publishers need to pay more attention to their core competency of packaging and delivering content and making money online. These are tricky but necessary conditions to successful online publishing.

Many online publishing pioneers have gone up the technology curve and are confronting tough management questions such as how to gain market share and how to be profitable sooner than later. Some of these firms have invested tens of millions of dollars in people, equipment, and marketing, and they have not yet turned a profit. Some of the sites employ hundreds of people, with millions of dollars in payroll alone. Many early pioneers invested a huge amount of money into brand building, marketing, and content, but they have not been able to figure out which business model works best for making money.

Online publishers are developing new business models to charge customers directly and convince them that such charges are justified. As more and more firms begin to offer online content, they are being forced to adjust to new customer attitudes regarding pricing. Publishers currently finance their businesses by offering advertisers mass markets for delivering their message in return for large advertising fees. The public has been trained to think that the news, information, and entertainment they receive should be subsidized or nearly free and that advertisers will pay the bill. This approach may not be viable in the online medium when mass markets are replaced by customers selecting their information and delivery methods. For instance, early experiments with online subscriber-based services have not been very successful. Today, common wisdom states that consumers are not eager to pay for online content, although several initiatives described in Section 9.3 will give that theory a test.

The early online publishing pioneers are trying to accomplish a difficult feat. Newspaper and magazine publishers, some of the first to stake their claims on the Internet, are tinkering with new advertising models for their fledgling Web sites. In general, mainstream advertisers have been skittish about pumping money into a medium with an audience whose size and habits are nearly impossible to figure out. As a result of relatively low ad revenues, none of the Web publishers have turned a profit. While ad revenues are not coming close to covering expenses now, they could grow substantially in coming years as the traffic increases and brand names become established. Brand development is important because every time a user sits in front of a Web browser, she needs to make a decision about where to go. The better the brand, the more likely it is to pop up in the consumer's mind. We examine advertising issues in Section 9.4.

Another key issue in online publishing relates to digital copyrights. Effective technological protection mechanisms are vital to ensuring the availability of quality content online. Today, publishers such as Addison-Wesley only offer catalogs or sample selections of works available online. They do not and cannot offer more because in an environment where the culture and technology provide so little protection for the rights of content producers, there is too great a risk to their intellectual property. The Internet makes it extremely easy to copy, retransmit, and alter works without the permission of the copyright holder. Moreover, the digital world has no international boundaries, and policing is impossible since the levels of protections and sanctions against infringement vary widely in countries across the globe, which makes the risk even greater. Clearly, without effective protection, publishers are not willing to risk their investment and hard work. We examine digital copyright protection in Section 9.5.

9.1 Why Online Publishing?

Online publishing evolved out of public funding associated with the aerospace and medical research programs of the late 1960s. Lockheed's DIALOG (later sold to Knight-Ridder for $353 million in 1988) and System Development Corporation's ORBIT services became operational in 1972 with a limited set of databases. These databases were the result of a technology switch made by most of the major publishers from manual typesetting and printing to computer-assisted photocomposition.

Although early photocomposition units were unable to offer much variety in the typeface used, the attraction for publishers lay in the generation of a digitally encoded magnetic tape as part of the production process. Not only were such tapes inexpensive to duplicate, but they also enabled the creation of a central database from which a series of online services could be provided. Other technical developments that impacted online publishing include remote access and dial-up database systems, improved magnetic storage devices, improved telecommunications networks, and the availability of low-cost terminals.

More recently the emergence of the Internet and Web have played a large role in bringing online publishing from a niche target audience to a mass audience. Some of the reasons for the dramatic and sudden increase in the interest of publishers, advertisers, and content providers in the Web include:

> Widespread adoption of the Web, combined with rapidly evolving technology, makes it possible to meet time-to-market requirements that were unimaginable even a few years ago.

> Much of the investment in infrastructure has been made by others: Internet access providers, hardware companies, and various software developers. Huge investments in advance of uncertain returns are not necessary.

> The Web allows new ways of targeting and reaching customers. This also coincides with publishers' desires to migrate from talking to large numbers of customers in a mass market to working with smaller target groups.

> There are no gatekeepers on the Web. The egos and financial interests of those running powerful multiple-system cable television operators (MSOs), huge media conglomerates, television networks, and group broadcasters play less of a role in publishing and advertising plans executed on the Web than they do in conventional media.

The publishing community's rapid movement toward the Web seems to have caught the advertising world by surprise. Advertising is an industry that has been relatively untouched by technology. Major advertising agencies have been notoriously resistant to change in the past, and their reaction to advertising on interactive media has been no exception. Edwin Artzt, then CEO of Procter & Gamble, in a 1994 speech at the annual meeting of the American Association of Advertising Agencies, warned the agencies that they would become less relevant to their clients unless and until they embraced the new media.

Needless to say, the shift in the publishing world has brought forward a massive flow of commentary, forecasts, and philosophical and sociological musings, as well as road maps of the future for investors and other interested parties. These debates can be categorized into three main areas. On one side are technical issues:

> How to improve and enforce copyright protection?

> How to create compelling content using the available technology?

> How to conduct financial transactions for individual articles (micropayments)?

On the other side are management issues:

How to create an organization for online publishing?

How to select business models that ensure success in different segments of online publishing?

How to satisfy online customers and keep them loyal?

In the middle is the more philosophical debate on what exactly is meant by online publishing. Online publishing can be viewed in two ways:

As the activity of disseminating information (which scholars have done for thousands of years and the purpose for which the Web was invented).

As the activity of publishing for sale. In order to realize revenue from their information, publishers package their product as a bundled commodity rather than disjointed information.

There is a fundamental difference between information and commodities. A commodity such as a digital book needs to be sold in volume in order to generate revenue, so publishers must keep their material from spreading freely all over the planet. On the other hand, the value of information is not lost when it is sold because the contents are not limited by their medium of expression.

Online Publishing Strategies

As with any new development, there are generally three strategies for publishing companies to consider:

- **Early movers.** These are highly skilled independent publishers with existing access to such key capabilities as direct marketing and order fulfillment. These publishers have the capacity to derive the highest benefits from new media as their learning curves are much shorter than others, and they already have many of the necessary resources at hand.

- **Watchers.** These are large publishing companies that employ scale-sensitive economics. They are unlikely to view online publishing as a sufficiently attractive channel until costs fall and distribution widens. This category includes publishers of unbranded or less distinctive content who cannot attract a sufficiently large initial consumer franchise, as well as focused publishers in categories not easily suited for the online medium.

- **Testers.** These are the majority of publishers that face either attractiveness and/or skill challenges. Gathered here are many multicategory and specialty publishers who are competing successfully in traditional markets, who are uncertain who will win in the online marketplace, and who neither need nor want to make a choice now. Testers also include branded general publishers with robust consumer franchises and attractive distribution channels already in place. For this group, the online medium appears to be an alternative.

In general, publishers are educating themselves about the potential opportunities without committing themselves to any one position. Those with strong brand images and existing consumer franchises may choose to postpone entry until they find viable service providers and distributors. Publishers such as the *Wall Street Journal* and *New York Times* are taking part in targeted tests and pilot projects aimed at learning what online publishing has to offer, building required skills, and exploring the attractiveness of potential channels. These tests often include a skill-building program as well as an early warning system so that a company can quickly identify and react to changes within the industry or economy.

Content, incentives, service, quality, and price will not be enough to compete in this new environment. Speed of delivery, bundling of products, and diversity of choice also become critical success factors. Publishers will have to innovate constantly and challenge present concepts if this form of commerce is to become widely accepted and popular. Winning in online publishing will entail developing new skills in areas such as tailored advertising, order processing and fulfillment, and customer service as well as relearning the fundamental principles concerning why people subscribe.

9.2 Online Publishing Approaches

There are four contrasting content publishing approaches.

- **The online archive approach.** This is new to the Web, but is a logical extension of the trends in electronic delivery over the past several years.

- **The new medium approach.** This is more controversial and more difficult to implement, but also more exciting.

- **The publishing intermediation approach.** This is an online extension of the third-party publisher role off-line.

- **The dynamic and just-in-time approach.** In this approach, content is assembled in real-time and transmitted in the format best suited to the user's tastes and preferences.

The Online Archive Approach The online archive approach (including bibliographic databases and full-text search/retrieval services) is one that appeals to corporate publishers and, to some extent, commercial publishers (such as academic or journal publishers) who have an existing digital archive that they want to deliver over the Web as well as on paper, CD-ROM, or other media.

The most prevalent example of online archive approach is library catalogs and bibliographic databases. Most libraries have replaced traditional card catalogs with sophisticated electronic online bibliographic databases offering an incredible range of functions. At revenues of over $1 billion a year, bibliographic databases represent a sizable chunk of the online database market. An example of a bibliographic database is MEDLINE, developed by the National Library of Medicine (NLM), which caters to an increasing number of physicians who rely on online medical databases to keep up to date with the latest developments and literature. The spread of PCs has enabled physicians to directly search databases used only by librarians in the past. MEDLINE and other medical databases are available free of charge on the Internet.

The online archive approach is also being used by niche publishers such as Ziff-Davis, which began its venture into electronic publishing in 1985 with a bulletin board system for readers of PC Magazine. That bulletin board evolved in 1988 to become PC MagNet on CompuServe, which quickly grew in popularity. In 1991, Ziff-Davis created the ZD Net subscription service on CompuServe to provide a service supporting online versions of all its publications. Members of the ZD Net/CompuServe edition have access to several features, including the ZD Net University series of comprehensive online "continuing education" courses, sophisticated online forums with top industry personalities, and a comprehensive database of past articles. In addition to its successful CompuServe subscription service, the ZD Net Web Edition (http://www.zdnet.com) logs access by more than 700,000 Internet hosts each month and is reportedly showing a profit.

The New Medium Approach The new medium approach (including real-time news delivery, personalized news delivery, and edutainment) aims to create new material for the Web—to treat the Web as its own medium, one deserving its own material. This approach will have the most appeal to commercial print publishers, such as magazines, that view the Web as an alternative, not a replacement, for print publications. For example, *Wired* magazine sees very little crossover in content between its magazine and its HotWired venture. Some writers may write for both media, but separate content streams will be developed for each medium.

This approach currently has some teething problems because of technological limitations. For instance, the formatting limitations of the Web are frustrating at the moment, but with technological advancements they will soon be forgotten. The frustrations are more than offset by the excitement of the interactivity the Web offers; its model is both broadcasting and conversation at the same time. With online publishing there may be a well-known starting point, but with no controlling gatekeeper, the subsequent value-added improvisation from readers makes each online magazine a unique experience.

Even if the technology constraints were overcome, the expectations of the Web are so different from print media that new content, written for a Web audience, must be created. It quickly becomes apparent that under this model, the old paradigms do not work. The publisher gives up not only its brand name, but its intellectual content, too—once the information is out there, it is no longer owned. Faced with that model, all a publisher can do is "be the first with the most interesting stuff," an approach that HotWired is taking in its attempt to create a place where readers can see what the world has to say on a minute-by-minute basis.

The Publishing Intermediation Approach   The publishing intermediation approach (including online directories) exploits new service opportunities for intermediaries. For example, in the growing market for educational material such as coursepacks and other customized books, companies offering material owned by more than one publisher face the daunting task of obtaining permissions. New organizations that specialize in the management of copyright clearance are emerging as key players.

Online directories are important for several reasons. Companies and consumers interested in conducting electronic commerce often struggle to navigate the Internet to create an electronic marketplace. Once on that sprawling network, they are having trouble finding other companies, products, and services. The success of Yahoo's initial public offering (IPO) underscores the importance of online directories. Yahoo (which stands for Yet Another Hierarchical Officious Oracle) was created in 1994 by David Filo and Jerry Yang, two Stanford University electrical engineering PhD students who began by simply compiling lists of their favorite Web sites. It went on to become one of the most popular means of navigating around the Internet. Yahoo is the first place millions of Internet users go when they try to find their way around the rapidly growing Internet. At one time, Yahoo was getting about 6 million visitors per day, which made it the second most active Web site next to Netscape's home page.

Clearly, there will be a demand for intermediation because there will always be a need for a good directory to help people locate goods, services, and products. The future is bright for the publishing intermediaries who offer ease of operation, speed, and detailed information.

The Dynamic and Just-in-Time Publishing Approach   Online content is no longer static information. Content can now be created in real-time and transmitted on the fly in the format best suited to the user's location, tastes, and preferences. More importantly, the content engine recognizes repeat visitors to a site and configures the Web pages to match the individual's known preferences. For example, a publisher planning to deploy a large product catalog will no longer have to author and update each individual Web page. Instead, the elements of each page—text, graphics, video, and sound—are stored separately in a database and used to create individualized pages on the fly as each user browses the site. The page content can be further customized to reflect which Web browser is being used, the user's geographic location, and modem speed.

Another way of looking at dynamic publishing is that it is just-in-time publishing. That is, the stories, applets, and content flow into the computer just as consumers need them, and then self-destruct after usage. A six-story subscription to *SportsWorld* might cost 99 cents. Pictures of your favorite actor might go for $1.99. Want to buy a round in a cyber adventure game? How about a quarter? However, there is one question that constrains this vision: How can payments be collected on a product that costs a nickel or dime? So who cares if it costs 15 cents or more to process the transaction? Businesses do, and to satisfy the small-amount transaction market need, "micropayments" are essential.

A number of micropayment schemes are emerging. The world of online entertainment—specifically "pay-for-play" outlets being developed by Sony, Sierra On-Line, and others—could serve as the best model for everyone else [PCW96]. Clearly publishers and developers should be thinking about low-value payments, but it is still too early for most companies to deploy. For micropayments to work, transaction costs must be very small (around 10 cents), and they are nowhere near that yet. What is more, the proposed schemes vary widely and many kinks in the micropayment puzzle have to be worked out.

Having discussed the various types of online publishing paradigms, we turn now to the specifics of each paradigm.

Full-Text and Bibliographic Databases

This part of the online publishing industry represents one of the fastest growing publishing sectors. These databases contain trade publications and newspapers. There are more news transcripts, professional journals, magazines, loose-leaf services, and newswires going online every month. In full-text electronic publishing, several brand names dominate: LEXIS/NEXIS, DIALOG, Dow Jones, and NewsNet. Of these LEXIS/NEXIS is the most famous.

LEXIS/NEXIS   Launched in 1973, LEXIS provides the full text of U.S. legislation and court proceedings as well as United Kingdom and French law and statutes; NEXIS provides text of news, magazines, newsletters, and journals and other information sources. Combined, they include the full text of more than 100 million documents, ranging from Supreme Court decisions to international business, scientific, and financial information. These databases are supposed to have more than a quarter of a million customers around the world. Mead estimates that more than 10,000 customers dial into their databases every day in search of answers. In fact, the electronic publishing arm of Mead grew from $6 million in 1968 to an estimated market value of $1.6 billion in 1994, when it was bought by Elsevier and Reed International.

LEXIS is used by many students, large law firms, law libraries, financial institutions, and government agencies. LEXIS has become the norm in legal research; law students are given a free subscription as an introduction to the service. NEXIS also has a broad spectrum of users, with the news media and researchers—academic and professional—being the largest user categories.

Academic LEXIS/NEXIS users are usually students with an insatiable thirst for information. Its usage is growing rapidly, especially among researchers and students who need access to its vast up-to-date database to do research. The company expects the business or professional user to remain the primary user of information services, however. How is it used by professionals? Take, for instance, CNN and other news organizations that often get hot leads and need to get the background information for the story right away. Since they do not have all the necessary information themselves, they contract with companies such as Mead to do the research for a story, which requires searching for the information and packaging it in terms of a report. LEXIS/NEXIS was in the news in September 1996 when one of its offers, "P-Trak," was rumored to be making available consumer information that was confidential.

Securities and Exchange Commission (SEC) EDGAR Database   Access to corporate documents, such as annual reports which describe financial well-being, is fast becoming a major online publishing market. One of the best known of this category on the Internet is the Securities and Exchange Commission (SEC) EDGAR, arguably the world's most valuable collection of financial data. EDGAR (electronic data gathering, analysis, and retrieval) is an experimental database designed to automate the estimated 12 million pages of financial documents that public U.S. companies are required to file each year. The primary users of these filings are the financial and investor community, brokerage houses, law firms, and institutional investors.

The SEC (http://www.sec.gov/) began studying methods to automate its filing process in the early 1980s, out of concern that someday the agency would be swamped by the ever-growing flood of paper. EDGAR was designed to speed up not only the collection but also the dissemination of data to the public. Under the older, paper-based system, accessing the documents can take more than a week, although people who visit SEC headquarters in Washington, D.C., can get them within a day or two if they place an order in advance and camp out in a reference room. In 1994, EDGAR was made available on the Internet thanks to a National Science Foundation (NSF) grant and the efforts of a few consumer groups.

Easy Internet access to EDGAR has fundamentally transformed a business that was closed, costly, and profitable into an open, inexpensive, and competitive market. For instance, an EDGAR document downloaded from the Web costs nothing, in contrast to a paper copy of the same document (which would cost more than $50 from a leading SEC data vendor, Disclosure). Previously, Wall Street brokerage firms, corporate lawyers, and others are estimated to have paid $250 million a year to be wired into this information. Also, before EDGAR, it took up to six weeks to get documents entered and transmitted electronically. Currently, about 4,000 companies are on the system, and approximately 15,000 publicly traded companies are expected to be phased in by 1997. These companies file more than 100,000 reports with the SEC every year.

What Lies Ahead?   Full-text services play an important role in the legal, medical, and education industries. The future of full-text publishers lies in their ability to create products to suit different customer needs. To meet the needs of the busy professional, sophisticated information research facilities have to be developed. The individual user, for the intermediate term, is likely to be limited to college students who do not want or need information research in a packaged form and, most important, cannot (or are not willing to) pay for the more expensive services. Unlike the business user with deep pockets, an individual or a small business requires flexible pricing.

The main complaint about full-text services is their high price. Ignoring the vast market of users who cannot afford the expensive services represents a market gap that needs to be filled with low-cost providers. This weakness is being exploited by CompuServe, America Online, and online service providers teaming up with content providers to offer news, magazines (such as the *New York Times* and *Time*), and online stock market information. We will have to wait and see which companies step in to offer competitive pricing to services similar to those offered by LEXIS/NEXIS. The next step of the competitive battle lies in acquiring customers on the Internet.

Personalized and Customized News

News on-demand is in essence a personalized electronic news magazine that delivers customer-selected information on a customer-specified schedule. These types of services deliver a large variety of news and information sources in real time to PCs and workstations; they automatically monitor and filter the news; and they alert the users to stories of interest to them.

Why Is News Delivery an Important Market?   Today, news is among the top three reasons users connect their PCs to the Internet. Organizations that traditionally specialized in this activity, namely newspapers, have reached a key moment in their history—and the newspaper executives, managers, and editors know it. Far-sighted news executives no longer define their mission by the limitations and constraints of ink and paper. Recognizing that readership trends are slowly declining and that technology will change the way information is delivered and accessed, the news industry is moving to decrease its reliance on cash flow from paper-based segments. Instead, companies have come to depend more on electronic publishing and news on-demand services.

The advantages of news on-demand do not stop with rapid dissemination of information. News cries out for hypertext and other forms of linking, grouping, and classification that are not possible on paper. Although hypertext (text that contains easily followed links to other text and other media) has been discussed a great deal, serious hypertext applications in the news sector have been few in number.

Already, several companies are collaborating to define and develop a system that can deliver hyperlinked news on-demand to corporate and financial services professionals. The service combines video, audio, text, and graphics in a format that permits browsing, searching, and user-notification on breaking news. These systems will attempt to deliver late-breaking news with minimal delays. Users are able to retrieve the information they need at any time. One such system is PointCasting (see Section 9.3).

Requirements of Dynamic News Delivery   All news on-demand applications have a number of "dynamic" requirements that distinguish them from conventional "static" multimedia publishing efforts:

- **Time-critical alerts.** The timeliness of the information is paramount. For instance, when a news story matching a user's personal profile arrives, the user needs to be notified by a visual and audio alert, even if the user is then working in another application.

- **Delivery control.** Because several gigabytes of information are generated every day, the information provider must be able to target each news story to a particular group of authorized subscribers and monitor the delivery.

- **Aging and archival.** Certain stories are discarded at the end of the day, while others are retained for several months. Some information may even be archived permanently.

- **Dynamic user preferences.** Users have ever-changing information needs and must be able to vary their "interest profiles" at any time. The information must be coded and categorized by the provider for maximum retrieval flexibility.

Fundamental to real-time news delivery is the concept of personalization, a package of news and advertising tightly tailored and customized to the wants and needs of individual readers and advertisers and made available across the whole spectrum of consumer devices (like a waiter or waitress who knows what you want even before you order it). To meet the needs of personalization, real-time news publishers must understand and gain expertise in the information packaging business, which has traditionally been the purview of the news media. News media strength stems largely from its unrivaled ability to package and present a vast amount of information in a compact format.

Business Information and News Delivery

The market for business information services is undergoing significant change, driven by growth in the amount of available information, increasingly competitive industry environments, and increased requirements to improve the quality and timeliness of the information businesses receive. It is estimated that businesses and organizations in the United States spent over $28 billion in 1994 on business information services.

The decentralization of decision making and accountability in large organizations has created a need for the widespread distribution of business information to workers across a number of disciplines and at different levels within the organization. At the same time, the accelerating pace of business activity has created a need for business information to be more current, timely, and easy to access and use. While the demand for business information has created a profusion of information sources, including online services and Web sites, these sources by themselves have not addressed the need for that information to be readily available to workers on the desktop systems that they use every day.

Traditional electronic information sources often require stand-alone proprietary hardware systems and are typically accessed by centralized, specially trained library personnel who pass the information on to the workers who request it. This approach makes access to information relatively costly and time-consuming, discourages widespread use of an organization's electronic information resources, and fails to provide immediate notice of important breaking news. Consequently, traditional approaches to accessing electronic information are not well suited to meeting workers' needs.

Traditional electronic information sources also have not generally taken advantage of the large investment in LAN infrastructure. While the major investment in LAN infrastructure by large organizations has connected workers to each other and allowed them to communicate and work together through e-mail, groupware, and other client/server applications, to date it has not been used effectively to connect them to external information sources. As a result, the demand for organizations to widely distribute customized news on a timely basis to workers who need it has not been satisfied.

Edutainment = Education + Entertainment

Edutainment—a combination of entertainment, education, and games—combines interactive learning products with an entertaining format. Once dismissed as a fad, this category has taken on a new level of importance as a result of successful products created by such companies as Brøderbund, Electronic Arts, and Software Toolworks. Because they prefer to emphasize the educational experience of their products, some developers of edutainment titles take exception to being included in the same category as video games. However, this software niche utilizes technology similar to that used in games. Many products are available with photorealistic images, full-motion film clips, digitized voices, and sound.

An important quality of edutainment systems is that they engage users in an interactive learning experience that mixes video, graphics, music, voice narration, and text. Their goal is to control the learning experience so that a student becomes an active rather than a passive learner. Edutainment programs are designed for specific age groups and cover a range of subjects including mathematics, reading, early learning, writing, history, and geography. The degree to which edutainment software actually teaches literary, numerical, and science skills has not been determined; however, parents (the purchasers) prefer that their children's software have some educational component—and the consumer is always right.

Interestingly, the use of the online medium as an edutainment distribution channel has been minimally exploited. It is a well-known fact that interactive role-playing games such as MUD (Multi-user Dungeons) are played by millions of people online. Games such as ID Software's Doom, Doom II, and Heretic are examples of very successful games that were initially distributed on the Internet. So many copies of these games have been sold that ID software developers have become quite wealthy. Clearly, a business opportunity exists; the challenge is to create a strategy for developing, distributing, and supporting online edutainment.

9.3 Online Publishing Success Stories

There are several types of publishers on the Web. They range from big players like Time Warner's *Pathfinder*, *HotWired*, Disney Online, and others, to home-brewed productions like specialized newsletters that may be a one-person operation. There is a middle ground—companies offering professional quality content without the resources of a Time Inc. Examples of companies in the middle include Songline Studios, which publishes *Web Review*, a publication about the Web.

To examine the challenges in managing various types of online publishing firms, it is imperative that we look at the experience of a few companies that are already delivering content electronically. We look at PointCast Inc., an online personalized news delivery system; Time Inc.'s *Pathfinder*, an online magazine; Disney Online, an edutainment publisher; and then a promising new technology called Intercasting that enables the integration of TV signals and data streams. We describe the business model being used and challenging management issues that are being tackled.

PointCasting

Hardly a day goes by without yet another company announcing plans for a new technology that promises to jump-start electronic publishing on the Web. One such company is PointCast, Inc. with their unique technology called PointCasting. PointCasting, or one-to-one custom news delivery, is the ability to deliver breaking news according to the interests of each individual user. Unlike "broadcasting," "pointcasting" only delivers the information specified by the user.

How Is Pointcasting Different from Web Publishing?   PointCasting can be distinguished from the information offerings of individual news providers because it integrates the newswires from a number of competitive sources into a single, comprehensive service offering. It is different from online systems because it is implemented on customer LANs and PCs where news can be distributed to all users at a fixed, predictable cost. Unlike traditional online services, which require users to dial out and pull information when they think of it, PointCasting automatically pushes news to users on their own PCs.

PointCasting is made possible by combining the aspects of traditional broadcasting—in which top stories are researched, identified, and delivered to audiences by news professionals—with the personalization options offered by the PointCast Network (PCN). The PointCast Network represents the natural marriage of broadcast and the PC. It combines the power of the Internet with the convenience of broadcast news to give users current, personalized news and information without wasting valuable time searching, surfing, and sifting through the Internet.

What is available on the PointCast Network? The network features six "channels": News, Companies, Industries, Weather, Sports, and Lifestyles. Subscribers can customize the news they want to read; industries, companies and sports they want to follow; business, international, and political news; stock quotes from any U.S. stock exchange; sports news; weather reports and maps; entertainment news and more from various sources, such as Reuters, S&P Comstock's stock ticker, SportsTicker, AccuWeather, and Variety. Additional content for the network will be provided by special-interest publishers and regional media partners, offering local news to viewers.

How Does PointCast Work?　PointCast's SmartScreen technology automatically begins running the PointCast Network when a user's computer is not in use, turning a static screen saver into a dynamic medium. Now, instead of looking at a screen saver while talking on the phone, users can view current headlines, stock quotes, and sports scores on their screen. To obtain the full story on any topic, the viewer simply clicks on the headline. Viewers can also choose to activate PCN at their convenience, such as periodic updates every three hours. The PCN service is available free to anyone with Internet access, but requires PointCast's special software (which also is free for download).

The PointCast Network consists of a two components: (1) a central broadcast facility at PointCast's headquarters in Cupertino, California, and (2) PointCast client software, which displays news on each viewer's computer screen. Companies that want to broadcast internal news can use PointCast I-Server. PointCast I-Server resides behind a corporation's firewall and acts as a local broadcast facility for corporate Intranets. It extends the capabilities of the PointCast Network to enable companies to broadcast internal news alongside public channels, which include News, Industries, Weather, Sports, and more. Instead of exploring company Web sites or sifting through e-mail messages to read company news and updates, employees can now view up-to-the minute company news broadcasts throughout the day directly on their individual computer screens. This ensures that important company information—such as employee benefits announcements, sales updates, or upcoming events—is widely seen and read.

Time Warner's *Pathfinder*

Time Warner is one of the world's leading media and entertainment companies, with interests in magazine and book publishing, recorded music and music publishing, filmed entertainment, broadcasting, theme parks, cable television, and cable television programming. Time Warner's *Pathfinder* site (http://www.pathfinder. com/) is one of the most popular venues on the World Wide Web. *Pathfinder* is the centerpiece of Time Warner New Media, a division created in 1992 to catapult the $7.4 billion company into the interactive age. Launched in October 1994, it offers 90 online features, although the vast majority are versions of Time Warner magazines. It has garnered high praise, even from competitors.

Time Warner's *Pathfinder* site, along with *HotWired* and Knight Ridder's *Mercury Center*, an offshoot of the San Jose *Mercury News*, were the Web publishing pioneers. All three opened operations in late 1994, when most consumers had never heard of the Web. These online pioneers take advantage of the fact that magazines have access to the same information as newspapers and differentiate themselves by being more creative in both information presentation and reporting/packaging to capture the reader's attention. Customers love the format and style of reporting of magazines; they seem to feel that they deliver information more effectively than newspapers.

Why do consumers consider magazines effective? The answer is convenience because of the tailoring of content to niche/focused markets and credibility because of the reputation for accurate reporting. Credibility comes from two sources: good editorial content constantly defined and redefined by feedback from the marketplace, and the impression of an unbiased atmosphere that is free of external influence. Credibility allows the consumer to develop trust in the value of information. In the long term, trust saves consumers time and money by reducing the search cost.

What Is the Available Content?   *Pathfinder* contains online versions of Time Warner magazines, *People, Sports Illustrated, Money, Fortune, Entertainment Weekly*, and others such as the *Netly News*—a daily look at the latest trends on the Web. Furthermore, the service offers continually updated stock quotes, sports scores, and technology news. *Pathfinder's* visitors can read the same stories and features found in the printed versions.

Online magazines such as *Pathfinder* are ideally suited for information gathering and packaging. Editorial packaging comes from interacting with readers and getting marketplace feedback from advertisers. Unlike many other online newspapers, where updates are pulled unedited from third-party wire services, *Pathfinder* editors work around the clock to identify and tailor the most relevant information. *Pathfinder* also markets Reuters News. Reuters receives both subscription revenue paid by *Pathfinder* for use of the news service, and a share of advertising dollars generated from Time Warner's selling of ad space on the Reuters news pages.

What Is the Revenue Model?   Given the wide variety of content available, *Pathfinder* attracts legions of users every week, estimated at an average of 27 million "hits," or communications contacts, a week. That's enough usage to convince advertisers that it is worth paying $30,000 for a three-month run.

Pathfinder foresees two revenue streams:

- **Subscription fees for magazine content.** Pathfinder expects subscriptions to account for 50 percent of revenues eventually. It also hopes to make money distributing its content to other entities, for instance, via an international distribution deal with companies such as Hong Kong Telecom.

- **Classified and other advertising.** In 1995, *Pathfinder* took in nearly $2.5 million in advertising sales. Time Warner expects the ad revenues to triple in 1996.

In the early phase of Web publishing, the revenue model relied purely on advertisements. However, the advertiser-supported model is not really covering costs for online publications, and *Pathfinder*, which requires a dedicated staff of editorial, design, production, and technical resources, is expensive to produce. In the end, however, online publishers cannot keep giving content away. Clearly, the best approach is a hybrid—generating revenue based on a mix of subscription fees and advertising revenue. However, there is limited understanding of the pitfalls of building a Web-based subscription-based magazine. This is something that will have to be addressed in the near future.

What Are the Management Challenges?   Clearly the equation (Profit = Revenue – Costs), needs to be examined carefully by management. So far, it has cost Time Warner an estimated $15 to $25 million and returned only one-tenth of that in revenues. If the site could double its business it might be able to cover payroll this year, but that does not account for equipment, overhead, and other expenses. Clearly, managing rapid growth is quite a challenge.

Given the amount of traffic that *Pathfinder* is receiving, it is clear that electronic publishing is a real business, but what is not clear yet is how to generate profits. In less than two years, *Pathfinder* has amassed at least 100 full-time staffers and payroll expenses of at least $6 million. *Pathfinder* could conceivably cover payroll, but that is just part of the equation. The departure of talent such as Pathfinder's editor and creative genius, James Kinsella, is raising doubts about whether a giant corporation such as Time Warner can ever make such a new media venture work [CB96].

Management of firms such as Time Warner that are entering new markets must be forward thinking and must not apply traditional models such as cost-benefit analysis. Improved information management and customer service, and the ability to reach new markets are difficult to measure. If a firm is overly concerned with immediate returns or short-term margin improvements, it may cripple its potential for long-term benefits by incompletely implementing electronic publishing applications, or choosing not to implement them at all. Instead of focusing on increasing profits in the short term, firms need to view their participation in the online marketplace as an opportunity to gain a competitive advantage.

Disney Online

Edutainment purveyors like Disney have high hopes for their online progeny, particularly in terms of new revenue opportunities. It costs well over $1 million to establish and maintain an excellent Web site. But this investment has intangible benefits such as free advertising in terms of magazine articles and positive word-of-mouth among users.

Disney.com is the first in a series of family Web products from Disney Online, a Disney Interactive division founded in September 1995. Filled with games, puzzles, stories, and software, Disney.com is the one place where Disney aficionados of all ages can experience the full breadth of Disney's offerings, including movies, television, publishing, music, retail stores, and of course, the famous Disney theme parks. For example, guests can visit the Walt Disney World site and find a wealth of information about park attractions, travel arrangements, tour information, and accommodations. Guests can also visit Walt Disney Pictures to play an interactive game or download movie clips from recent releases.

To accommodate varying modem speeds and each guest's personal preference, each page of Disney.com can be viewed either in color (high bandwidth) or in black and white (low bandwidth). Viewing the site in black and white can speed up navigation through the Disney.com site, while maintaining the graphical style. However, creation of content that is appropriate for both low- and high-speed connections is both tricky and costly.

What Is the Business Model?   Disney's challenge is to develop an online presence geared toward the market of kids aged four-to-eighteen years and their parents. Audience estimates from Jupiter Communications, which publishes a monthly Digital Kids Report, claim that by 2000 there will be 15 million consumers under age eighteen using Web-based or online services consistently. While that number hardly competes with the existing market for licensed toys, books, and entertainment products, it is an audience worth grabbing.

Marketing, of course, is the cornerstone of the site's business plan. Disney's online projects are designed both to promote existing Disney products and to develop and market new services profitably. Marketing to kids can take several forms. For example, a child clicking on the Kellogg's Clubhouse site on the Web can enter a "rec room," where they are greeted by cartoon characters Snap, Crackle, and Pop. Depending on where the child clicks, the characters offer to display a recipe; send an e-mail greeting from Snap, Crackle, or Pop; or help the child send a Kellogg's greeting card to a friend through e-mail.

Disney is creating the right incentives for the cybertot marketplace. For instance, a child may be invited to play a computer game, join a club, or enter a contest, but to do so, the child will have to answer a series of questions—presented as a sort of game—asking how old the child is, how old his or her siblings are, the last movie they saw, what their parents do, or what toys they like. At Pepsi's Website, completing such questions enters a child in a contest to win a trip to Florida. At Microsoft Network's Splash Kids play area, a portable CD player is the prize.

Also to continuously attract kids, it is important to keep content fresh. It is reported that Disney Online is vigilant about eliminating stale content. System designers monitor how many "hits" each page gets and how much time individuals spend on a particular attraction; low-rated areas are cut every week [OCR96].

What Are the Management Challenges?   The big challenge is: How to build a steady revenue stream? Disney sees that linking with complementary sites could result in extra revenue. For instance, Disney could charge to link to a package-goods marketer. An example is the virtual Kellogg's Clubhouse at the Kellogg's Co. site (http://www.kelloggs.com). This direction in terms of complementary contracting also requires that marketers measure traffic. The links must enhance the potential to influence kids' brand choices.

The second challenge is: How to find a winning business strategy? Disney, like others, is experimenting with a variety of strategies. For instance, the next step in Disney's online strategy is family.com, an advertising-supported, parent-information service on the Web. Care must always be taken to make sure that the strategy is coherent and the various sites complement each other. That is often hard to do because of the multiple organizations involved that may have different agenda and hence appear to be pulling in different directions.

The third challenge is: How to walk the fine line between marketing and invasion of privacy? Firms like Disney see the "lucrative cybertot category" as a new market. But parents are concerned that Disney is brainwashing their children with well-designed Web "playgrounds" that are nothing more than elaborate ads. Firms like Disney that are marketing to kids need to be very careful for two reasons: (a) invasion of children's privacy by overtly—or covertly—gathering and recording information about children's online habits and personal likes and dislikes; and (b) unfair and deceptive advertising that allows children to play with product characters for hours with no warning that the site is only an advertisement with no educational content. It remains to be seen how these issues play out.

The fourth challenge is: How to sell rather than advertise merchandise? Today, online merchandising and development of children's licensed products at Disney Online are still in their infancy. Currently, online sites are used more often to promote kids' entertainment, rather than to sell products. But the potential of the market is mind-boggling. Evidence of this can be seen in the immensely popular Toy Story site, which has already received over 21 million hits to date. Then, with the click of a mouse, guests will soon be able to look for the ideal gift from an online catalog at The Disney Store site. Clearly, given the choice between a piece of plastic or figurine (physical world) and an interactive environment with characters, the winner will be the one that engages over a long period of time.

The final challenge is: How to measure the effectiveness of the site? Today, site effectiveness is gauged by how many visitors have looked at what on a Web site. But the impact of this content is not easy to gauge. For instance, the Toy Story site helped kids get a taste of the film, but did it make more people go to the film? The linkage between cause and effect is much harder to determine.

Integrating TV and Data Streams: Intercasting

Intercast technology enables the integration of video (TV signals) and data streams (HTML documents). It represents the true convergence of the computer and television by linking the Internet and television on home PCs. For example, an advertiser can send down three "pages" of information related to its ad, along with the television commercial. The user can browse these three pages at his leisure. The advertiser may also embed within these pages a hyperlink back to the advertiser's Web site on the Internet. By clicking on this hyperlink, the user will be connected to the advertiser's Web site via the modem back-channel.

How Does Intercasting Work?   Intercast technology uses one-way broadcast communications to broadcast TV programming and related Web pages to a PC. Embedded in these broadcast Web pages are hyperlinks to additional Web pages, some of which have already been broadcast and stored on the user's local hard disk, and some of which are on the Web. PCs equipped with Intercast technology will be able to extract Web pages and other data inserted onto a standard television signal.

Users of Intercast technology-equipped PCs can watch TV on one part of their PC monitor screen and simultaneously interact with broadcast Web pages presented in the remaining screen area. What kind of browser is necessary for viewing Intercast content? The Intercast Web browser can be used like any other Web browser for accessing sites on the Web, and it can also receive Web pages broadcast to the user's hard disk using Intercast technology. These broadcast Web pages will be cached and retrieved from the hard drive. When a user follows a link from a broadcast Web page out of the cache to the Web, the browser will connect the user to his Internet service provider. At that point, it functions as any other Web browser. In other words, using a modem and any direct Internet connection, PCs with Intercast technology will be able to move transparently between Web pages sent with the television broadcast signal and those on related Internet sites.

Intercast content will be created with HTML, the language of the Web, and will include hyperlinks to related information on the Internet. For instance, a breaking news story could be linked to additional information on the geography or historical background of the event. A music video could air, with Web pages featuring concert dates and hyperlinks to fan club information on the Web. Sports programs, like the Olympics, could provide broadcast Web pages with information on individual athletes and live, continuous statistics on the athlete, the game, and/or the league. A fashion program could be accompanied by broadcast Web pages allowing the viewer to purchase highlighted apparel instantaneously.

Intercasting at Work   CNN is exploring the use of Intercast in CNN at Work, a service that delivers real-time news video and text to desktop computers in a business environment. Intercast will allow CNN to progress toward a well-integrated video and text news service. CNN aims to use Intercast to deliver financial data with video footage. What do traders, analysts, and fund managers want to see in the video window? Reuters has done a considerable amount of market research to answer this question. They found that customers would be willing to pay a price premium for real-time cross-referenced price, text, and video material, with other retrieval facilities. Through their research, Reuters found that users want more than just general news: this is already available every twenty minutes on rolling news channels such as CNN, albeit without cross-reference search and retrieval facilities. Market professionals want to see financial events coverage alongside general news. Footage of the Federal Reserve Chairman addressing a key congressional committee adds most value for forex, money, or equities market traders, allowing them to read the body language as well as the text of the official announcements. A database of video interviews with company chief executives will add value for equity followers, giving a quick feel for management personalities and strategy.

The provision of information is not enough. The client software must provide the necessary flexibility to manipulate data on site, enabling CNN to differentiate its service. For instance, the software needs to support "drag and drop" with "cross-referencing" between applications. For example, the analyst or fund manager will link real-time prices and graphics into their own word processing or spreadsheet packages. Taking this a stage further, video files will be integrated with user applications, which is useful for integrating with presentation software.

What Are the Implications of Intercasting?   With the customers in control, advertisers using Intercasting have to rethink what to sell, how to sell it, and how to attract customers' attention. News of the future will have to deliver clever interactive advertisements or infomercials that entice viewers to "experience" test-driving a car, the look and feel of a new line of designer clothes, or a view from the suite reserved on a cruise ship. In other words,

ncept of advertising on the Web and broadcast media such as televi-
is probably going to merge to create one entity that can be customized
the fly to the medium of delivery.

9.4 Advertising and Online Publishing

With the intention of attracting advertising dollars, magazines and newspapers have also set up sites on the Web. Many online periodicals include traditional advertisements as well as icons, which display an advertiser's logo and,
when clicked with a mouse, send a user across the Web to the advertiser's
Web site. Among periodicals that have gone from print to online advertising
with some degree of advertising success are: Knight-Ridder's *San Jose Mercury
News* newspaper, which reportedly charges $100 per day for an advertisement,
and magazines such as *HotWired*, *Playboy*, and *People*, which reportedly charge
$30,000–$45,000 per quarter for an advertiser to place an icon in the periodical.
Promotions are also common. In many cases, advertisers ask site visitors to
provide their names and addresses in exchange for a product discount.

Advertising spending is expected to increase for five reasons.

Shorter access times. As more bandwidth becomes available, users will
spend a larger proportion of their time on Web sites and a smaller proportion waiting to access them. With more time available to draw users' attention, advertisers should be willing to pay more per user to place their icons
in online periodicals. Shorter access times also enable increasingly complex
graphics to be placed on Web sites, without requiring additional access
time. This should draw to the Web advertisers who may have been concerned that the current graphical quality was insufficient for displaying
their products. With more advertisers, advertising rates should rise.

Reduced access fees. New Internet users will be attracted by reduced access fees, with part of the reduction covered by advertisers. The cost of the
access fee itself can be shared by an advertiser if, for example, the advertiser
pays for the access time used when accessing online yellow pages.

Increasingly convenient access to information. As the amount of information online increases, it should be increasingly important for advertisers to
get users to their sites quickly, leading them to pay more for placement in
online periodicals.

Increasingly valuable information.   Product descriptions can be enhanced through online advertising. With more information available, the decision to purchase should be easier and more purchases should occur (assuming the product is desirable). This should boost the appeal of the Web and increase the rates that advertisers could be charged for placing their icons in an online periodical.

Better measurement of advertising effectiveness.   Product advertising is far more effective if it leads to a purchase. If online advertising encourages users to shift a portion of their purchases to the Web, then companies may pay far more to advertise. However, a measurement system will not be useful until: (1) an online publisher can use it to determine advertising rates and the appeal of its articles, and (2) an advertiser can use it to justify the cost of promoting a Web site, maintaining a Web site, and placing a site-linked icon in an online page.

Despite the popularity of advertising on Web sites, few publishers have attempted to measure how many advertising dollars are being spent. There are three reasons for this:

The market is too small to justify the cost of measuring its size.

There is not a clear definition of what advertising expenses should be counted. Spending can be the amount that advertisers pay other Web sites such as periodicals and games to display their icons or product offerings.

The market is changing too rapidly to develop an effective means of measurement.

Effective measurement of online advertising is taking center stage. It was reported in *MediaWeek* [MW96] that Procter & Gamble was ready to spend some of its $3.3 billion ad budget to advertise on various Web sites. However, the packaged-goods giant told the online publishing community that it will compensate the ad banners it buys only on a "click-through" basis. In other words, standard impressions—delivered when an Internet surfer sees an ad banner but does not click on it to connect to a Web site— are considered to have no value by P&G. The anticipated P&G strategy, a sharp departure from the industry standard which measures hits (see Table 9.1), has sent a shiver down the spine of many ad sales executives. The concern was that other advertisers will follow P&G's lead.

Table 9.1 Vocabulary for Web Advertising Measurement

Hit	An entry into the log file of a Web server, generated by every request for a file made to that server. The number of hits has no predictable relation to the number of visitors to a Web site because, for example, a single page with ten small icons will register ten hits in the log file for each icon.
Qualified Hits	Hits that deliver information to a user. This excludes such things as error messages and redirects and does not indicate the number of visitors.
Visit	The gross number of occasions on which a user looked up the site. This is a sequence of hits made by one user at a site within a set period of time. It does not indicate whether visitors are digging into the site's content or just skimming.
Unique Users	The number of individuals who visit a site within a specific period of time. It is calculated by recording some form of user registration or identification. Most Web sites are not equipped with this feature.
Standard Impressions	The number of times an Internet surfer sees an ad banner but does not click on it to connect to the advertiser's Web site.
AdClicks	The number of times users "click" on an in-line ad (commonly called a "banner") within a certain period of time. It does not measure effectiveness of an ad.

Why is this a radical departure? Only about 10 percent of Web surfers currently click on ad banners. Because Web advertising rates generally are determined by the size of a site's overall audience—the method used in pricing television and print advertising units—P&G's proposed "click-through" model is expected to generate considerably less revenue for Web sites.

The demand for coming up with credible measurement methods is strong. *Inside Media* [IMD95] reported that the vice president of General Motors' North American marketing and advertising stated he was "terribly distressed about the lack of attention that [Web site] measurement has been given." Let us then give "measurement" some attention.

An Online Publishing Missing Piece: Measurement

Currently, the ability to measure the effectiveness of online advertising is at a fairly immature state. With traditional advertising, it is difficult to determine whether the amount spent on a specific ad will be covered by the sales and profits generated by it. On the Web, this should be easier because users leave an electronic trail of where they came from, what they did at a site, and whether they purchased a product. If technology can be developed for viewing the trail easily, then advertisers should find it easier to justify the cost of their advertising. The only danger is that as reluctant as advertisers are to pay for ads online, they may eliminate their spending entirely if they discover that sales are insufficient; however, the electronic trail may enable advertisers to identify and correct problems with their advertising.

In our opinion, no significant amount of advertising dollars will flow to the Web until a credible, third-party audience measurement device is in place to provide a currency for the investments. Many, particularly those from the technology side of the equation, have missed this key point. Virtually all of the investment in advertising on the Web to date has come from research and development, market research, strategic, and/or corporate seed money budgets. These budgets are measured in hundreds of thousands of dollars, rather than the tens and hundreds of millions of dollars flowing through traditional media budgets. When advertising on the Web becomes measurable, it will stop being a fringe medium.

For Web sites, the only measurement-related information that most advertisers and online periodicals can receive consists of the number of files accessed on the site. This number is referred to as an "access" or a "hit." The number of hits for an online magazine is roughly analogous to the number of times each of the pages is viewed in a printed magazine. For example, if an online magazine has a separate file for each of its 100 pages and each page was visited four times per week, the magazine could state that it gets 400 hits per week. The problem with using hits as a measurement such as circulation is that all 400 hits could have come from the same user, from two users viewing every other page, or from 400 different users viewing only one page each. The electronic trail that provides the number of hits could be analyzed further to get a circulation-like number known as the number of "visitors," but this capability is not at an acceptable level for most advertisers.

There is now an increasing demand to move away from counting hits and to move toward breakdowns based on reach and frequency, with measures done by a third party. As yet there is no standard format for this. There has been an evolution in measuring Web advertising from counting "hits" at a site, which initially was the most commonly used traffic measure, to some more suitable advertising measures. Six different measurements have been proposed (see Table 9.1).

Many companies are working on products that sound sensible and are being tested by impressive lists of partners, but whose discussion is beyond the scope of this book. Among the companies and products are the Interactive Information Index, Digital Planet's NetCount, Interactive Media Works' sample-NET, Internet Profile's I/COUNT, and WebTrack's Webstat Verification Service. These products offer a means of measuring the number of visitors to a Web site; however, these products and others can also be used for market research and site-visit auditing.

9.5 Digital Copyrights and Electronic Publishing

Intellectual property rights (copyrights, trademarks, and licenses) is an important asset possessed by the publishers in their respective markets. Protecting intellectual property rights and collecting dues from online users is proving to be quite challenging. The scope and magnitude of the problem is clear. The potential of online copyright infringement vastly surpasses the damage that can be inflicted with a photocopy machine. Anyone with a computer can make and distribute countless copies of anything digital, be it a book, a TV or computer program, or a piece of music. Even worse, the digital version can be sent to friends or even a bulletin board system (BBS) for downloading by anyone with a modem.

Advances in technology have raised the stakes considerably. Today, virtually any work can be "digitized," archived, and used in the digital format. This increases the ease and speed with which a work can be reproduced, the quality of the copies, the ability to manipulate and change the work, and the speed with which copies (authorized and unauthorized) can be "delivered" to the public. Works also can be combined with other works into a single medium, such as a CD-ROM, causing a blurring of the traditional content lines. The establishment of high-speed networking makes it possible for one individual, with a few key strokes, to deliver perfect copies of digitized works to scores of other individuals.

In short, the emergence of the Internet is dramatically changing how consumers and businesses deal in information and entertainment products and services; as well as how works are created, owned, distributed, reproduced, displayed, performed, licensed, managed, presented, organized, sold, accessed, used, and stored. All of this has led to a clarion call for changes in the copyright law.

The stakes are high. Owners of copyrights are not willing to put their interests at risk if appropriate protections are not in place to permit them to set and enforce the terms and conditions under which their works are made available online. Likewise, the public will not use the services available and create the market necessary for online publishing's success unless access to a wide variety of works is provided under equitable and reasonable terms and conditions, and unless the integrity of those works is assured.

Online Copyright Protection Methods

Unauthorized access to published content can be restricted by two methods:

Restricting access to the source of the work. This includes controlling Web server access or controlling individual document access.

Restricting manipulation of the electronic file containing the work.

Controlling Web Server Access   Nearly all information providers, including commercial online services such as America Online and dial-up private bulletin boards, not only control access to their systems but also vary it depending on the information a user wishes to access; that is, access to certain data is conditioned on paying a higher fee, and having greater access rights. Some information providers on the Internet grant full unrestricted access to all the information contained on their servers, so that anyone can access any data stored on the servers. Other information providers restrict access to users with accounts or grant only limited access to unregistered users. For example, a user can often log on to an FTP server as an "anonymous" user (a user for whom no account has been created in advance), but access through anonymous FTP is limited to certain data.

Controlling server access may be used as one of the first levels of protection for the works stored on it. Access to servers can vary from completely uncontrolled access (the full contents of the server are accessible without restriction), to partially controlled access (unrestricted access is granted to only certain data on the server), to completely controlled access (no uncontrolled access in any form is permitted). Access control is effected through user identification and authentication procedures (log-in name and password) that deny access to unauthorized users of a server or to particular information on a server. But access control does not preclude copies from being made once this initial layer of protection is passed.

Controlling Document Access   A second level of control can be exerted
through measures tied to the electronic file containing the work. One type
of restriction can be implemented through "rendering" or "viewing" software. Such systems require

> A proprietary or unique file format that can be read only by certain
> software and that is developed or controlled by the information
> provider; or

> Software that incorporates both a "control" measure to prevent viewing
> or use of a work without authorization from the information provider
> and "manipulation" functions to permit the user to view or use the
> work.

Another method of access restriction is encryption. Encryption technologies can be used to deny access to a work in a usable form. File encryption simply converts a file from a viewable file format such as a word
processor document to a scrambled format. The user can obtain authorization from the publisher in the form of an appropriate password or "key,"
which is required to "decrypt" the file and restore it to its original format.

Controlling Use of the Work   Hardware and/or software placed in personal computers can provide protection against unauthorized uses of copyrighted works. For instance, the Audio Home Recording Act requires
circuitry in digital audio recording devices and digital audio interface devices that controls serial copying. Based on the information it reads, the
hardware circuitry will either permit unrestricted copying, permit copying
but label the copies it makes with codes to restrict further copying, or disal-
low copying. The serial copy management system implemented by this circuitry allows unlimited first-generation copying—digital reproduction of
originals—but prevents further digital copying using those reproductions.

Controlling use of a published work can be implemented through hardware, software, or both. For example, files containing works can include instructions used solely to govern or control distribution of the work. This
information might be placed in the "header" section of a file or another part
of the file. In conjunction with receiving hardware or software, the copyright information can be used to limit what can be done with the original or
a copy of the file containing the work. It can limit the use of the file to
read/view only. It can also limit the number of times the work can be retrieved, opened, duplicated, or printed. For the technical details the reader
is referred to [COPY95].

Implementing Electronic Contracts Software-based systems for tracking and monitoring uses of copyrighted works are being developed by publishers. Software-based systems may be used to implement licensing of rights and metering of use. A combination of access controls, encryption technologies, and digital signatures can be used by copyright owners to protect, license, and authenticate information. These security measures must be carefully designed and implemented to ensure that they protect the copyrighted works and are not defeated.

Information included in files can be used to inform the user about ownership of rights in a work and authorized uses of it. For instance, information can be stored in the header of a file regarding authorship, copyright ownership, date of creation or last modification, and terms and conditions of authorized uses. It can also support search and retrieval based on bibliographic records. Electronic licenses may be used in connection with information sold. Providers may inform the user that a certain action—the entering of a password, for instance, to gain access to the service or a particular work, or merely the use of the service—will be considered acceptance of the terms and conditions of the electronic license.

The Library of Congress's Electronic Copyright Management System is active in copyright management. They are implementing a system that has three distinct components: (1) a registration and recording system, (2) a digital library system with affiliated repositories of copyrighted works, and (3) a rights management system. The system will serve as a testing area to gain experience with the technology, identify issues, develop a prototype of appropriate standards, and serve as a working prototype if full deployment is pursued later.

In sum, protection and management methods must be based on nonproprietary technologies, given that they have broad usefulness. Furthermore, if the systems developed are too cumbersome or complicated to use, consumers may reject works protected under them. Whether various measures are useful in protecting copyrighted works, however, the ultimate judge will be the marketplace.

Online Liability for Copyright Infringement The question exists as to who is liable for copyright infringement on digital networks. There are differences of opinion as to the extent to which online service providers should be liable for infringing materials delivered over their systems. On the one hand, an argument could be made that where an entity does nothing more than provide communications facilities through which flow thousands of messages, it should not be liable to the full extent of the law if those transmissions contain infringing content. On the other hand, online service providers are also publishers, and they have a responsibility to take affirmative steps to discourage infringement. For instance, some providers already automatically warn subscribers who are about to post information via their services on an Internet newsgroup to avoid violations of "netiquette" (or the general rules of conduct on the Internet). They also urge subscribers to obey accepted, informal norms of behavior and also copyright law.

The courts are just beginning to grapple with the application of the intellectual property laws in the new electronic world of bulletin boards, e-mail, Internet, and online information services. If the law of contributory infringement and vicarious liability is strictly applied to companies providing interactive services, companies will be discouraged from providing such services or building the infrastructure because of the enormous risks of liability. The result might be an online world that only allows users to view data, not to engage in two-way interactive communications that allow the uploading and manipulating of data. Moreover, such a standard for liability might also force online service providers to restrict access only to companies and individuals willing and financially able to indemnify themselves if their activities result in copyright infringements on their systems.

9.6 Summary

This chapter examined how the growing interest in online media and a squeeze on consumers' time are forcing publishers to reappraise their traditional markets. Publishers are seeking to exploit the strengths of the online media: low-cost ubiquitous access, time and place independence, and ease of distribution.

The information industry is engaged in a debate over what effects online publishing will have on print publications. Electronic publishing is mostly being used to supplement rather than supplant demand for printed products, but inroads by these online media are becoming more evident every day. Gains by the electronic media are well perceived by leading publishers, several of whom have established facilities to produce electronic materials such as online databases and online magazines for their customers.

However, many management challenges need to be overcome. Foremost is the profit question: How can an online presence be turned into a profitable one? What kind of business model would result in the most revenue? The second issue is the measurement issue: How effective is the site? How can advertisers be charged fairly?

Many publishers are also wary because of the lack of adequate copyright protection. Most publishers have defined the task of building copyright protection as primarily technical. How can the protections they have in today's print environment be mapped onto the online environment? Current efforts range from encryption with decoder devices for paid subscribers and information usage meters on add-in circuit boards, to sophisticated document headers that, much like the late unlamented copy protection schemes of many software vendors, would monitor how and how often the text was being used.

Chapter 10

Intranets and Supply-Chain Management

Chapter Outline

One of the most exciting trends today is the use of the World Wide Web and Intranets in managing the supply chain. A supply chain is essentially a business process that links manufacturers, retailers, customers, and suppliers in the form of a "chain" to develop and deliver products as one "virtual" organization of pooled skills and resources. The objective is to obtain benefits by streamlining the movement of manufactured goods from the production line into the customer's hands, by providing early notice of demand fluctuations and coordination of business processes across a number of cooperating organizations.

In the last decade, many industries have developed initiatives to implement supply chains. Initiatives like just-in-time, quick response, efficient consumer response, vendor managed inventory, and continuous replenishment all have the same goal: to manage the supply chain effectively. Clearly, the issues that companies face in managing the supply chain today are the same as those faced in the past. What has changed is the need to quickly share and disseminate information across the supply chain. Some companies are already doing so with electronic data interchange (EDI), but this is only a tiny fraction of what is feasible. In our opinion, the impact of the Web and associated technological developments on supply-chain management applications is an issue of great import that cannot be ignored.

The integration of electronic commerce and supply-chain management (SCM) is changing the way businesses work internally and work with each other. Companies are no longer looking at SCM purely from an efficiency or cost reduction perspective, but instead are focusing on the outcomes of better SCM—superior customer service, growth, and revenue enhancement—as a way of setting themselves apart from the competition. This trend parallels the shift in business model most firms are adopting in the 1990s from an internal, process/efficiency-driven focus to a more customer value/benefits-driven focus.

The movement toward customer value represents an understanding that staying alive and being profitable takes a lot more than trimming costs and improving operational efficiency here and there. It requires understanding customer needs, and then creating and delivering products/services based on customer needs. Business success depends on the ability to react to the changing needs of customers while meeting the costs of customer demands. Costs are often highly correlated to the uncertainty in the supply chain. Uncertainty is created by global supply and sourcing, unpredictable demand, fluctuating pricing strategies, shorter product life cycles, and decreasing brand loyalty. To manage this uncertainty, a new class of software called *enterprise integration* or *supply-chain software applications* is coming into existence.

Software that supports SCM has become a multibillion-dollar market. Corresponding to this trend, managers are gaining new responsibility for software buying/implementation decisions that go beyond the bread and butter applications: payroll, order entry, and accounting systems. Today, managers are facing the tough task of selecting—and integrating—finance, manufacturing, logistics, and other SCM modules. These modules will not only efficiently exchange and process work, but also protect and capitalize on existing investments. In order to make the right choices, managers need to understand the growing interplay between SCM and electronic commerce.

In this chapter, we begin by outlining the fundamentals behind SCM. Then, we explain the basic difference between push versus pull supply chains and between static and dynamic supply chains. Any discussion of SCM would remain theoretical if a real-world case were not studied. To make the discussion of supply chains more practical, the use of SCM in the retail industry is detailed. Software requirements for managing the retail supply chains are then reviewed. This leads us into a discussion of the supply-chain software industry, and its evolution as the Web and Intranets take center stage in application development. In the subsequent chapters, we will delve into the key elements of SCM, namely sales, marketing, and customer service (Chapter 11), manufacturing and logistics (Chapter 12), and financial control systems (Chapter 13).

10.1 Supply-Chain Management Fundamentals

Supply-chain management is the center of a major business revolution to get products to market faster and at lower costs.

What Exactly Is a Supply Chain?   A supply chain is a collection of interdependent steps that, when followed, accomplish a certain objective such as meeting customer requirements. The supply chain is gaining prominence as manufacturers control less of the speed at which products are manufactured and distributed. The main reasons for decreasing manufacturing control are the parity across the board in product quality and price wars with the emergence of global competition.

With customers increasingly calling the shots, manufacturers are scrambling to meet customer demands for options/styles/features, quick order fulfillment, and fast delivery. Meeting customers' specific demands for product delivery has emerged as an opportunity for competitive advantage. Clearly the hypothesis is that firms that manage their supply chains will be more successful in the global marketplace.

What Is Supply-Chain Management?   Supply-chain management is a generic term that encompasses the coordination of order generation, order taking, and order fulfillment/distribution of products, services, or information. Interdependencies in the supply chain create an "extended enterprise" that reaches far beyond the manufacturing facility. Material suppliers, channel supply partners (wholesalers/distributors and retailers), and customers themselves are all key players in supply-chain management.

The complex nature of SCM is considered equal parts art (presentation, sales techniques, and service) and science (forecasting, data analysis, sourcing, margins, and distribution). However, SCM is more than just a bag of tools or a method for linking disparate information systems. It is a methodology that requires a new way of thinking and a holistic view of the supply chain from start to finish.

Is Supply-Chain Management a New Concept?   The concept of SCM is not new—it has evolved over the past twenty-five years. In the 1970s, businesses focused on very specific functions in the supply chain. They wanted to improve manufacturing, or they were focused on sales and marketing or on distribution. With the advent of the 1980s, businesses realized that integrating all facets of their enterprise could increase productivity and margins. In the 1990s, business realized that product excellence alone fails to guarantee success. In fact, customers expect many services, including the prompt delivery of products to precise locations, with near-perfect on-time delivery and physical quality.

In order to fulfill these new requirements, companies understand that they need to address information integration issues, that is, the flow of information between and within organizations. For instance, information integration means that customer orders, inventory levels, purchase orders, and other key information must flow automatically from one business function to another. In this new business model, competition is no longer simply viewed as company versus company, but as supply chain versus supply chain. Hence, the ability to manage the different models of SCM becomes crucial.

Pull versus Push Supply-Chain Models

In recent years, the trend toward more efficient operations has accelerated as technology transforms consumer choice, and consumer choice in turn affects corporate strategy. The consumer need-based business model is forcing a fundamental shift from a traditional manufacturing push-based model (also called build-to-stock) to a pull-based model (build-to-order).

This shift in the business model is captured in Fig. 10.1, which shows the push versus pull models of SCM in a retail environment. In the more traditional "push" model, the merchandise is pushed into the customer's hands. In the "pull" model, the customer actually initiates the supply chain. This is also called a *demand-driven model*.

The "pull" concept is both simple and compelling. As the customer moves through the supermarket check-out, the scanner picks up the exact details of her purchases. These transactions are used to trigger product deliveries from the distribution depots. Further data aggregations at the distribution depots are signaled back to the manufacturers preparing their next deliveries to replenish the depot. The manufacturers' production programs are simultaneously updated to take account of the delivery schedules, and their purchasing schedules are adjusted accordingly, so that the raw material suppliers alter their own delivery plans. Often, all this happens before the customer has signed her credit-card slip and left the store.

The pull model dictates a need for: (1) supporting increased variability (product variants); (2) reduced lead times; (3) improved quality and lower unit cost; (4) operational excellence; and (5) comprehensive performance measures for control purposes. The pull factors shaping supply chains are

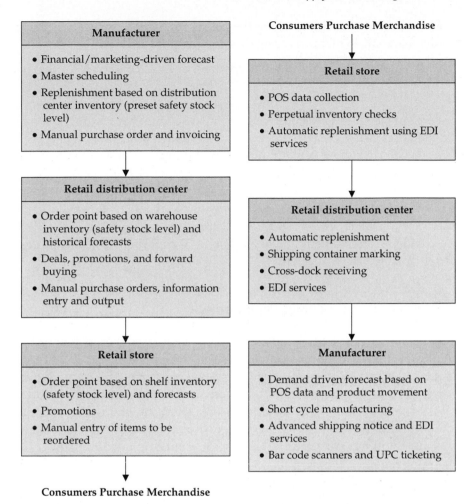

Figure 10.1   Push-based Supply Chain versus Pull-based Supply Chain

exerting tremendous pressure on business strategy. Instead of trying to gain a competitive advantage on the basis of quality or price, companies are seeking to gain an edge through their ability to deliver the right product in the right amount at the right time.

However, few companies understand how to manage "pull" supply chains optimally. The reason for this is quite simple. Effective SCM requires firms to:

Gather customer demand requirements quickly and accurately;

Make the best choices about how they can meet those requirements at the lowest possible cost;

Make informed decisions along the entire supply chain, from procuring raw materials to manufacturing/assembling products; and

Distribute finished goods to the consumer and collect the requisite payment.

Performing these four steps well and in sync with one another is easier said than done. Today, the supply chain is like a football team in which each player refuses to cooperate with the others and kicks or passes the ball in a random direction. Also, magnifying the problem is the fact that every player has a manager screaming directions or plays at him.

To resolve this chaotic situation, supply-chain managers have to accomplish three things: (1) provide a unified action plan to all the players; (2) enable communication among the players; and (3) coordinate the players and prod them in the right direction.

Elements of Supply-Chain Management

At the highest level, SCM crystallizes into three key processes: planning, execution, and performance measurement. The common theme in all three is the need to optimize processes that extend beyond narrow functional areas, taking into account the needs of the customer. This view is reinforced by trends in recent years, where there has been a shift from a purely functional view to a more process-oriented view. To take a more process-oriented view, firms must shift from one-time transactions to shared online processes.

Planning Systems   Planning systems focus on having the right product at the right place and at the right time. These systems facilitate order taking and information gathering from the customer and orchestrate the flow of information along the entire supply chain, from initial order to raw material procurement to final consumption. This requires understanding demand—what customers want, when they want it, and where they want it—and is fundamental to successfully managing all parts of the supply chain. For instance, by using point-of-sale (POS) data gathered at the retail terminal, actual demand can be communicated throughout the supply chain—directly from the retailer to the distributor, the manufacturer, the raw materials supplier, and the transportation provider.

For several years, planning systems involving demand forecasting and replenishment have been moving away from a model that "pushes" the product out to the market to a model that "pulls" the product. This is based on the assumption that nothing happens until there is consumer demand. Consumer demand triggers order movement up the supply chain to the raw material supplier and then initiates the movement of product back down the chain to the retailer. Ideally, the movement of information would be paperless and shared throughout the entire pipeline. Manufacturing would use demand information to drive its manufacturing schedule and the procurement of raw material. Only when the entire supply chain is driven by the consumer's purchase will inventory be removed from the pipeline and not just pushed back up the supply chain.

To support "pull"-based models, planning systems need to support three goals: to gather information about consumer demand effectively; to accommodate fluctuations in demand; and to use demand information for inventory investment, including safety stock, inventory turns, and replenishment frequency. This involves integrating into one seamless solution the processes of (1) order generation and planning, which helps anticipate customer demand through market forecasting; and (2) order taking and entry, which feeds replenishment planning; this incorporates distribution requirements planning (DRP), vendor managed inventory (VMI) and continuous replenishment planning (CRP) (see Chapter 11).

Execution Systems   Execution systems facilitate the physical movement of goods and services through a supply chain. This focus traditionally includes some application-based systems such as (customer) order fulfillment, inventory control, and manufacturing and logistics (see Chapter 12). Execution systems focus on operational efficiency, which entails finding new ways to streamline and automate day-to-day business operations to reduce costs and improve productivity. The first step toward improving operational efficiency is to upgrade key business applications to a single, integrated system that can run the entire business. This enables firms to efficiently move their products through the supply chain.

The need for cross-functional integration has become a central theme of execution systems. Over the years, companies have discovered that optimizing across functions often leads to better results than optimizing locally within a function. For instance, the goal of maximizing production capacity utilization is often at odds with inventory minimization. This forces firms to make trade-offs between customer service, inventory, and manufacturing costs to make the best use of available resources—people, equipment, and materials. Hence, execution systems attempt to ensure that order fulfillment, procurement, manufacturing, and distribution management are integrated to enhance the supply-chain coordination.

Performance Measurement Systems   Performance measurement process keeps track of the health of the supply chain. This is necessary in order to make more informed decisions and respond to changing market conditions. Here, accounting and financial management systems are the real focal point. These applications utilize electronic commerce tools such as data warehousing to allow for effective information auditing and analysis. But this has proven easier said than done. Most operational business systems and traditional reporting tools are designed for transaction processing; they are not designed for easy access to information for decision support purposes.

Companies are addressing the problem of information access by developing integrated data warehouses (see Chapter 13). A data warehouse also provides tools for analyzing data. A data warehouse allows managers to perform analyses of business information without impacting the performance of the operational systems. For example, in retail market trend analysis, managers many want to analyze sales revenue by country, by region, by sales representative, or by product line. After viewing the various segments, managers may also want to analyze sales revenue by state over time in order to better understand seasonal fluctuations. This type of business analysis involves enormous amounts of statistical computation.

Another interesting trend in performance measurement is the movement toward more proactive analysis using Web-based software agents. Agents are programs that act on the behalf of users. They are very useful in an environment with gigabytes of data. With so much information available, it is important to prioritize the information to which management must pay attention. After all, everyone in the organization has a different view of which business events require particular attention or action. Software agents let users set their own criteria for sifting through information. For example, accountants may want notification of improper transactions, salespeople may want notification of new leads, material planners may require low inventory warnings, and purchasing agents may need notification if any invoices matched to their purchase orders are placed on hold. Software agents can help managers proactively monitor their business operations and immediately respond to key business events.

Integrating Functions in a Supply Chain

Supply-chain management takes isolated business functions—marketing, materials management, purchasing, manufacturing, and distribution—and allows them to function in tandem (see Fig. 10.2). This is not limited to an individual company, but across all firms in a supply chain—from supplier through to the customer.

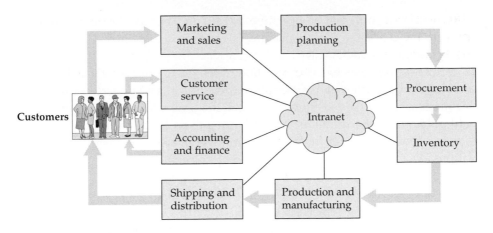

Figure 10.2 Intranet Linking Supply-Chain Functions

The key functions in supply-chain management are:

Managing information about demand to enable a better understanding of the markets and customer needs. By drawing on data from customer service as well as sales support and other functional systems, companies can funnel information gathered in customer facing operations to manage proactively. This aspect of the supply chain is called the *customer asset management* function (see Chapter 11).

Managing the flow of physical goods from suppliers. This aspect of the supply chain is known as *integrated logistics*, and includes production planning, procurement, and inventory management (see Chapter 12).

Managing the manufacturing process to ensure low production costs. This aspect of the supply chain is known as *agile manufacturing* (see Chapter 12).

Managing the financial flows with suppliers and customers through financial intermediaries. This aspect of the supply chain is known as *financial and accounting management* (see Chapter 13).

Coordination of processes and integration of data are common in all of the above supply-chain functions. Often, competitive advantage is gained by integrating supply-chain activities at a lower cost than competitors. As a company begins to conceptualize itself as a complex network of business processes, it becomes clear that the supply-chain processes extend beyond the boundaries of any one building, any one corporation, or any one country. Coordination of activities and management of supply-chain relationships can be a source of competitive advantage and can bring additional value to the customer. Supply-chain coordination is also known as *workflow management* (see Chapter 13).

However, the effective orchestration of the basic premise (more integration is better for all) requires that all participants align key technology and business process goals to eliminate waste, maximize long-term profits, and add value to final consumers. This alignment can be daunting, as companies are challenged with finding ways to meet ever-rising customer expectations at a manageable cost. To do so, companies must identify which parts of their supply chain are not competitive, understand which customer needs are not being met, establish improvement goals, and rapidly implement necessary improvements.

The need for effective chemistry of business applications often conflicts with today's intense competitive pressures that require a fast response. Unfortunately, most business development efforts cannot keep up. They take too long to install, and once installed take too long to adapt to the ever-changing environment. The movement toward modular software as exemplified by client/server computing is a promising new direction for supply-chain application development. If implemented properly, modular applications let firms upgrade business processes. Firms can deploy them quickly, change them as needed, and always use the latest technology to drive state-of-the-art business processes. This trend toward modularity is the key driver behind the Web, Intranets, and application packages.

To understand how the different elements of SCM fit together, we will look at the application of the technique in retailing.

10.2 Managing Retail Supply Chains

The U.S. general merchandise retail industry accounts for revenues over $1.5 trillion, with approximately 1,000 retailers recording sales in excess of $80 million [QRS95]. As competitive pressures within the industry have intensified, retailers have focused increasingly on the importance of efficient merchandise management to improve their financial performance.

There are two axioms by which retailers live and die: merchandise has to be "on trend" and it must be in-stock. Failure to manage merchandise to meet customer demand results in lost sales and ultimately leads to obsolescence and bankruptcy. It is estimated that inefficiencies such as inadequate information, excess inventories, and slow communications between vendor and retailers have cost over $25 billion in lost revenues each year [QRS95].

Merchandise management is a complex problem. For example, the average department store carries more than one million stockkeeping units

("SKUs") at a time, each unique in terms of product style, size, and color. Each retailer's SKUs are produced by hundreds of vendors. These vendors are required to manage rapid production and accurate delivery of ordered goods to multiple retail locations.

To address these issues, many retailers are learning how to utilize sophisticated systems to manage "on-trend" and "in-stock" execution strategies. Retailers have developed strategies for optimizing selection and availability while minimizing absolute inventory levels. These strategies are known collectively in the industry as "quick response merchandise management" and are intended to improve the efficiency of the retail demand chain. The participants in the demand chain are actively pursuing ways to optimize the flow of merchandise by improving procurement, inventory, and distribution management.

Successful retailing, whether in a store or online, is about demand or SCM. Retail SCM is crucial: It influences the bought-in price per unit, it gives management the ability to maximize the initial level of mark-up (through ability to secure further stock), and it minimizes markdowns (by raising the open-to-buy level). The last two also rely on shorter lead times, which in turn are dependent on level of system integration. Many retailers have shown consistent gross margin improvements from a tighter and more rapid flow of information between retailer and manufacturer (for example, Wal-Mart and Proctor & Gamble). The true benefit of managing the demand chain is more accurately measured in how well these systems allow large institutions to operate as small nimble (or agile) entrepreneurs.

Managing the retail supply chain is crucial to the success of all retailers. Before going further, let us define what is meant by a *retail supply chain*. Essentially, a retail supply chain is a number of independent activities which, working together, transfer goods from their point of origin to the final customer. Although the SCM concept is common for all retailers, each retailer will implement this in a different way. Variations are the result of retailers' specific needs and the demands placed on them by the marketplace and their customers.

Now that we know *what* a retail supply chain is, we need to ask: Where does the retail supply chain originate? The retail supply chain is essentially captured in the order management cycle (OMC) shown in Fig. 10.3.

The Order Management Cycle (OMC)

The typical OMC includes seven distinct activities, although overlaps may occur. The actual details of OMC vary from industry to industry and may differ for individual products and services.

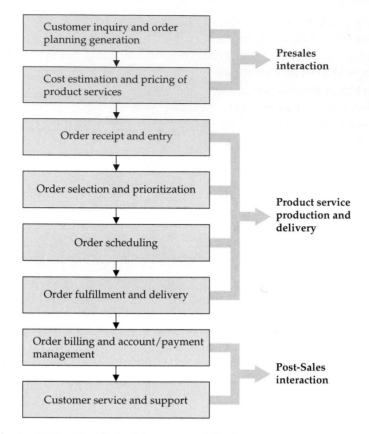

Figure 10.3 The Order Management Cycle

Order Planning and Order Generation Supply-chain management begins long before an actual order is placed by the customer. What happens in
the first step, order planning, actually shows how and why a lack of integrated operations can cripple a company: Those farthest from the customer
often make crucial decisions. For example, the people close to the customer,
either in the sales force or in marketing, develop a sales forecast. At the
same time, a group in manufacturing drafts a capacity plan that specifies
how much money will be spent, how many people will be hired, and how
much inventory will be created. The production planners often develop the
final forecast used to hire workers and build inventory. A lack of internal
communication can cause what is produced to differ significantly from
what is actually needed.

Order planning leads into order generation. Orders are generated in a
number of ways in the online environment. The sales force broadcasts ads
(direct marketing) and sends personalized e-mail to customers (cold calls).
Regardless of the specific marketing approach, the process is almost always

the same: sales and marketing worry about order generation, and the other functions stay out of the way. Little coordination takes place across functional boundaries. This is changing now. Software exists today that allows sales representatives to custom-configure products for their customers. These tools simultaneously integrate the order into the engineering and manufacturing processes.

Online Cost Estimation and Pricing   Pricing is the bridge between customer needs and company capabilities. Good pricing strategies can reduce the pressure on gross margins. Unfortunately, pricing is not well understood. David Ogilvy, a marketing guru, once said: "Pricing is guesswork. It is usually assumed that marketers use scientific methods to determine the price of their products. Nothing could be further from the truth." [OGIL96]

Pricing is crucial online as it provides a method for order flow management. For instance, customers may have specific requirements (color, size) or want expedited delivery. To deal with customized requests, companies need to think of order-based pricing. Yet, most companies do not understand how to execute order-based pricing in online markets. Pricing at the individual order level depends on understanding the value to the customer that is generated by each order, evaluating the cost of filling each order and instituting a system that enables the company to price each order based on its value and cost.

There are often problems with the way pricing decisions are made. Pricing decisions are politically charged compromises, not thoughtful implementations of a coherent strategy. Often, battles erupt between engineers who do the estimation, accountants who tabulate costs, management members who oversee pricing, and the sales representatives who actually quote a price. Each group questions the goals of the others. On one side, the finance division is usually keen to set prices so that they cover costs and achieve their profit objectives. On the other, the marketing and sales staff want prices set low enough to achieve their sales objectives. Meanwhile, of course, the customer waits for the bid or quote, unattended.

Another common obstacle to effective pricing is inadequate analysis of data. Many businesses fail to explore the concept of price elasticity, or how a price change will affect the quantity sold. The airline industry has been quite effective in exploiting price elasticity with their yield management systems.

Effective data analysis enables retail merchandise markdown planning. With the use of trend analysis tools, retailers can better evaluate results against the plans and can analyze the potential elimination of excess inventory. Retailers are also looking at ways they can track the price of merchandise from the day it was bought until the day it was sold. Product tracking provides a guide to the timing of merchandise markdown and will impact gross margins.

While order-based pricing is difficult work that requires meticulous thinking and deliberate execution, the potential for greater profits is simply worth the effort.

Order Receipt and Entry   After an acceptable price quote, the customer enters the order receipt and entry phase of OMC. Traditionally, this was under the purview of departments variously titled customer service, order entry, the inside sales desk, or customer liaison. These departments are staffed by customer service representatives who are in constant contact with customers (see Chapter 11).

Order entry requires an interface to inventory systems. To serve the customer properly, a company must inform a customer right away when an item ordered is sold out—not with a rain check or back-order notice several days later. On the other hand, if the item is in stock, a company must assign that piece to the customer and remove it from available inventory. Otherwise, the company will have a disappointed customer who knows he or she does not have to put up with such problems and seeks alternative sources of products.

Linking inventory with order-taking systems requires database integration. Generally, when consumers access a Web page and place an order, their order should be sent to a customer service representative who confirms the order's correctness and is able to verify various inventory levels for order fulfillment. Clearly, a lot of behind-the-scenes process planning needs to occur before companies even create a Web page for order taking.

Order Selection and Prioritization   Customer service representatives are also often responsible for choosing which orders to accept and which to decline. In fact, not all customer orders are created equal; some are simply better for the business than others. In particular, the desirable orders are those that fit the company's capabilities and offer healthy profits. These orders fall into the "sweet spot" region, which represents a convergence of customer demand and high customer satisfaction, which in turn translates into customer loyalty.

Another completely ignored issue concerns the importance of order selection and prioritization. Companies that put effort into order selection and link it to their business strategy stand to make more money, regardless of production capacity. In addition, companies can make gains by the way they handle order prioritization—that is, how they decide which orders to execute faster. These decisions are usually made not by top executives who articulate corporate strategy, but by staff who have no idea what that strategy is. While customer service reps decide which order gets filled when, they often determine which order gets lost in limbo. In sum, there is little recognition of the importance that should be placed on order selection and prioritization in electronic commerce.

Order Scheduling   During the order scheduling phase the prioritized orders get slotted into an actual production or operational sequence. This task is difficult because the different functional departments—sales, marketing, customer service, operations, or production—may have conflicting goals, compensation systems, and organizational imperatives: Production people seek to minimize equipment changeovers, while marketing and customer service reps argue for special service for special customers. And if the operations staff schedule orders unilaterally, both customers and their reps are completely excluded from the process. Communication between the functions is often nonexistent, with customer service reporting to sales and physically separated from production scheduling, which reports to manufacturing or operations. The result is lack of interdepartmental coordination.

Order Fulfillment and Distribution   While the details vary from industry to industry, the fulfillment and distribution activities have become increasingly complex. Order fulfillment involves multiple functions and locations: Different parts of an order may be created in different manufacturing facilities and merged at yet another site, or orders may be manufactured in one location, warehoused in a second, and installed in a third. The more complicated the task, the more coordination required across the organization. And the more coordination required, the greater the chance that the order is delayed.

In a competitive environment, order fulfillment is becoming more and more important in the eyes of the customer. Take for instance, TV home shopping. As a leader in the lucrative TV home shopping marketplace, QVC offers potential customers the convenience of viewing merchandise on their television screen and calling a toll-free number to place their orders. QVC learned that just offering shopping services directly to the home via the television is not enough to compete against traditional stores. The valuable lesson: Retailing is not just about selling, but excelling at order fulfillment. A retailing service that is not supported by supply-chain processes—efficient merchandise ordering and delivery processes, and reliable customer service—will not prosper.

As online retailing becomes more prominent, there is one question that needs to be addressed: What will happen to existing fulfillment and distribution methods? The answer: Demand for warehouses to store products and vehicles to transport them will change dramatically.

Some companies are already anticipating the demand changes in transportation and distribution. Federal Express (FedEx) launched a new organization, Federal Express Logistics Services, to outsource telemarketing, warehousing, and transportation services from nontraditional retailers such as catalog companies, cable TV shopping channels, and online services. The goal is to provide "virtual fulfillment" services. The idea behind the program is to eliminate unnecessary legs in the transportation process. Take the example of a computer manufacturer whose systems—motherboard, power supply, printer, and monitors—are all manufactured at different sites. What FedEx would do in this case is ship all components from their points of origin to a customer's home or business without first consolidating the order or storing it at a warehouse. FedEx would track the items and move them so that all components arrive at the destination simultaneously. In essence, Federal Express is remaking itself from a pure transportation company to a distribution company. The make-over allows Federal Express to leverage its expertise in automated logistics systems and funnel business to its core service: shipping products.

Order Billing and Account/Payment Management   After the order has been fulfilled and delivered, billing is typically handled by the finance staff, who view their job as getting the bill out efficiently and collecting quickly. In other words, the billing function is designed to serve the needs and interests of the company, not the customer. Often customers do not understand the bill they receive, or they believe it contains inaccuracies. The bill may not be inaccurate, but it is usually constructed in a way more convenient for the billing department than for the customer.

Software Interfaces in Order Fulfillment

Little has been written or documented about the nature of software in the order management process. One of the major obstacles preventing electronic commerce from coming into its own is the haphazard and nonstandard manner in which transactional technologies have been developed. Without the comfort of a familiar standard to fall back on, a critical mass of merchants and consumers have not shown the willingness to take the risk.

The software for managing retail supply chains must interface with three different entities: manufacturers, retailers (we include distributors here also), and consumers (see Fig. 10.4). The key function of the software is twofold: (a) facilitate moving information about consumer demand patterns up the supply chain to the manufacturers, and (b) facilitate moving the product efficiently from supplier through to customer.

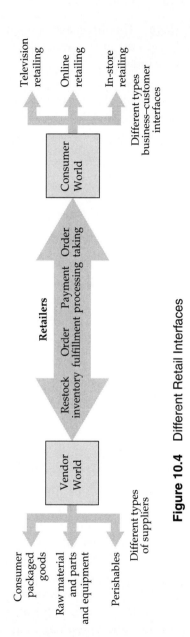

Figure 10.4 Different Retail Interfaces

The supply-chain software has three distinct modules: customer-retailer interface, retailer-supplier interface, and retail management interface.

Customer-Retailer Interface   This interface is a set of systems that manage the marketing, sales, and customer service interaction. The customer-retailer interface typically includes:

- **Store operations**—includes all systems installed and administered within the four walls of the store: POS (customer checkout, price management/labeling); and in-store processing (labor management and shelf management).

- **Customer service**—includes electronic marketing, streamlined checkout, product visualization, gift registry, employee training, in-store shopper tracking, telephone/order entry assistance, customer service center, and 1-800 service.

In the customer-retailer interface, electronic commerce entails linking online order forms or POS systems at the cash register with back-office systems to supply precise data on the sale of individual products. The replacement of cash registers with POS terminals made possible automatic price look-up and merchandise tracking. These capabilities, and the rapid spread of bar coding, soon led to the retail industry's adoption of a standardized product identification, numbering, and communication format. Known as the universal product code, or UPC, this standard has greatly increased the efficiency with which retailers and vendors can mark, track, and exchange product information.

Retailer-Supplier Interface   This interface includes a set of systems concerned with moving the product efficiently from supplier through to customer. The objective of this interface is to provide high customer service levels while minimizing stock holding and reducing wastage (food past its sell-by date) or mark-downs (end-of-season sales of clothing). The retailer-supplier interface also includes under its purview decisions regarding the optimum quantities and location for stock and then ordering, storing, and moving it. Responsibility for different aspects of the supply chain may fall under a single logistics department or may be spread between functions such as purchasing, distribution, and operations. This generally includes:

- **Purchasing**—deciding order quantities, placing orders with suppliers, and communicating with suppliers.

- **Inventory management**—deciding the right quantities of stock to have at each location.

- **Stock control**—tracking the movement and storage of products.

- **Stock movement**—receiving, checking, storing, picking, and dispatching goods.

- **Distribution operations**—planning and managing the operation of warehouses and transport fleets.

Successful implementation of the retailer-supplier interface is dependent on close cooperation between the retailer and suppliers. To achieve information integration, the retailer often needs to account for a dominant percentage of a supplier's sales; hence, the increasing use of the term "partnership" to describe SCM. This increased cooperation has led, logically, to an increasing reliance on a few key suppliers and the consolidation of the supplier base, or at least plans to move in that direction.

The growth of partnership and advances in data communications fostered the use of computers for the electronic transmission of transaction documents, including purchase orders, invoices, and shipping instructions. Such paperless transactions are widely referred to as electronic data interchange or EDI. EDI has benefited retailers by lowering costs, reducing errors, and improving the timeliness of the merchandise ordering process (see Chapter 12).

Retail Management Interface   This interface is a set of systems for planning and controlling all business processes within the organization, such as finance and accounting, and human resource management (see Chapter 13). Some specific activities include:

- **Business intelligence or merchandise planning**—includes category management, vendor profitability analysis, clearance markdown planning, promotion planning/analysis, and space planning.

- **Micromarketing**—includes advertising analysis, target marketing, geographic information systems, promotion effectiveness, customer category management, and loyalty programs.

- **Brand management**—includes efficient product introduction packaging and design, promotion planning/analysis and advertising.

The above activities are quite information-intensive. Take, for instance, merchandise planning, which helps the retailer to make balanced decisions in order to minimize lost sales and mark-downs, therefore maximizing margins. The merchandise planner needs the following inputs to develop a plan: actual sales data, the company business plan, and information about existing items within departments. Additional information is required regarding decision parameters such as: which lines to stock in each store, how many of each line to order, the retail price of the line, when to request delivery, and in which quantity from the supplier.

The merchandise planner is also responsible for planning the layout of each store, deciding how the merchandise will be displayed and the floor space that lines will occupy. This enables the retailer to coordinate the merchandise mix of each store before any buying decisions are made, and then constantly re-evaluate those decisions as the sales period progresses.

What Is Missing?   Ideally, electronic commerce should provide retailers with an integrated system for planning and controlling all business processes in the supply chain stretching from suppliers to consumers. This is easier said than done. The demand for more effective integration is giving rise to new software requirements. Implementing efficient supply chains requires a software architecture that integrates conventional stand-alone application software systems into a "well-oiled" machine. Integration of various functional systems provides maximum value when application software is integrated into networked operations, both within and between enterprises. This is facilitated if an "open Intranet architecture" allows the applications software and user interfaces to be distributed via a client-server protocol across many different types of computers.

How well a company performs depends on the integration of these modules. The goal is to tightly link applications to improve staff efficiency and thus unleash a major potential for boosting productivity. Development and maintenance of such software requires a great deal of innovative energy that exceeds the staff resources of most individual retailing operations.

Understanding how to operationalize and implement retail supply chains using technology has remained an art form for a very long time. This is changing with integrated SCM software packages.

10.3 Supply-Chain Application Software

Application software is computer programs that capture, represent, distribute, and apply knowledge to solve specific functional problems. Applications software can be divided into horizontal and vertical categories. Horizontal or "cross-industry" applications include financial and manufacturing software, all of which use generic functionality across all industries (accounting and human resources are common to most market segments). Table 10.1 outlines the five major functional areas in horizontal applications software.

In contrast, vertical applications automate tasks that are specific to individual market segments. For example, a vertical application would track the Food and Drug Administration's rigorous pharmaceutical application process for a drug company, maintaining proper paperwork procedures throughout the convoluted process; an Intel in the electronics industry could track the production of its Pentium chips from order to delivery. Other major vertical applications markets include financial services/insurance, health care, government, and education.

The dominant players in the horizontal and vertical marketplaces are SAP (a German firm), Oracle, PeopleSoft, and Baan (a Dutch firm). Application software can, of course, be deployed on a variety of platforms but, typically, in the current environment it is deployed on a variety of mid-range platforms manufactured by many different hardware vendors including DEC, Hewlett Packard, and IBM.

Table 10.1 Elements of Supply-Chain Management Software

Major Functional Areas	*Set of Key Activities in Each Functional Area*
Manufacturing	Engineering and product configuration, production planning and cost management, production execution, and quality management
Logistics	Purchasing and order management, distribution, inventory, and warehousing
Financials	General ledger, payables and receivables, billing, budgets and asset management
Marketing	Advertising, sales, order management, customer service and support, and market research and strategy
HRMS	Payroll management, time and labor management, benefits administration, and pension administration

Software for Supply-Chain Management

The basic idea behind application software is to provide the corporate customer with efficient standard software, which avoids the need to develop expensive individual solutions requiring a significant degree of maintenance. For purposes of comparison: instead of being an expensive "made-to-measure" suit, the customer can purchase "off-the-peg" clothing that fits just as well after minor alterations, but is considerably cheaper and easier to adapt to changes in requirements. In the case of application software, the standard solution during installation is adapted as much as possible to the needs of the company.

Application software makes possible the compilation, processing, and linking of data from all company divisions. Decision makers receive more rapid and more comprehensive information, they can plan more precisely, and thus they can optimize operating processes. The basic modules include:

Accounting (bookkeeping, cost accounting, controlling, calculations).

Logistics (production planning, stock control, distribution, purchasing, quality control).

Personnel systems (administration of personnel data, salaries, personnel planning).

Basic functions, which incorporate general applications supplied with all software modules (graphic user interface, documentation, archiving).

Customized programming tools, which customers can use to create their own applications or to develop enhancements to the standard software. The tools support the modular construction method, that is, the customer may buy only individual modules (such as bookkeeping) or sections of useful packages.

The strength of the application software lies in its ability to integrate various company divisions; that is, data from production, distribution, and accounting are exchanged and linked up. This is very different from other traditional software systems that were used in isolation in specific functional areas, like in the accounting or human resources departments. This was in keeping with the development of standard software, which in the early 1970s was designed from a narrow perspective. Implementation was application-focused. First came financial accounting, then materials management, and later sales, production, and marketing. This approach meant that the full value-added potential came only after implementation of the last application.

Function-oriented business structures cemented this approach until internal pressure for innovation and two major trends broke down the rigid interfaces between functional areas: new, more productive software/hardware platforms for client/server computing and the use of new, process-integrated business solutions called mega-packages. Configuring these packaged solutions is the key to a flexible and maintainable solution that enables companies to be more responsive and flexible to customers and market changes; it also cuts out unnecessary layers and gives more decision-making power to managers.

Recent Trends in Application Software

The early 1990s approach to SCM, in which companies redesign business processes before considering the technology solution, negates many of the benefits of the new generation of application software. These traditional methods of SCM aim to redesign processes in an idealized form and in too much detail. Software packages then usually require extensive modification to support the new design. Not only does this take time and money, but it also detracts from the intrinsic value of the package, adds to the risks, and reduces the system's life-span because upgrades become virtually impossible to apply.

The more recent approach to SCM advocated by software companies such as SAP and PeopleSoft (which we call packaged SCM) is a benefits-focused approach that encourages companies to redesign business processes to complement and exploit the capabilities of the chosen package. Proponents of packaged software say that it offers two key advantages over traditional SCM. First, organizations are able to save time and effort in modeling processes, since a wide range of process options are already detailed and documented by the supplier. Second, packaged SCM allows early prototyping, leading to visible progress and rapid delivery of benefits with minimal tailoring of the package.

The use of packaged SCM software by companies is increasing. The main reason for this is that it is difficult for companies to adapt their own, often badly documented software developments to a rapidly changing environment. In addition, MIS departments have not been able to handle the demand that is coming from organizational restructuring and cross-functional integration. In addition, companies are beginning to change their way of thinking in the wake of extensive restructuring in the last few years. While in the past software had to be adapted where possible to existing corporate procedures—which was often difficult, if not totally impossible—companies are now trying to organize themselves (and improve) around the available software. Last but not least, software has become much more flexible and can offer more functions.

Resistance to packaged software sometimes emerges when organizations believe a package supplier could never have a good appreciation of their business process needs. In reality, however, the best package suppliers accumulate solutions based on the needs and best practices of a wide range of organizations. This means that they represent a distillation of knowledge and experience that is beyond the resources of most companies individually.

What Is the Business Model?

The business model and competitive positioning of packaged application software providers focus on:

1. Leveraging reengineering cycles with flexible and easy-to-implement technology—Customers are increasingly basing their application vendor selection on the total costs of deployment, not just license fees.

2. Partnering to expand market presence—Most vendors are working closely with systems integrators and consultants to expand the distribution channel for their company's products.

3. Evolving technology ahead of competition—Client/server architectures, workflow, intelligent software agents, and electronic commerce facilities have begun to appear in the software providers feature set. We believe that agility in incorporating emerging technologies before the competition is a key competitive differentiator.

4. Securing leadership in key verticals—Most vendors are targeting vertical industries such as automotive, food/beverage, industrial projects, and electronics to further penetrate these markets with customized solutions.

In general, the application software firms offer a variety of products in each of these broad functional areas (modules), and the modules can then be linked together. The modules can be tightly or loosely integrated and they can run off of one or several database files with greater or lesser degrees of integration. For each of the major models, the application software firms offer a variety of optional features from which the customer can pick and choose, which are automated—blended into their solution in an automated fashion.

Most modules can be configured to address the customer's objectives, or "tailored." Tailoring is best described as predefined customization. The customer is allowed to select from a menu of choices that helps them address the look and feel of the system as it will be used in their environment. The resulting system looks like it was configured uniquely for that customer, but it is in fact based on off-the-shelf packaged software at packaged software prices easily maintainable and supportable by the client.

Understanding the Application Software Architecture

The initial efforts attempted to overhaul mainframe legacy systems to provide the greater ease of use and accessibility users had come to demand at the desktop. These systems are typically of the two-tiered application architecture, also known as "fat client." While definitely offering easier-to-use interfaces, these early client/server systems did not fully exploit the strengths of either of the two platforms they attempted to blend.

A more mature technology marketplace is now turning to a component-oriented, distributed architecture known as "three-tiered" client/server. Three-tiered systems bring the power of desktop and server hardware together, along with the speed of advanced enterprise networks, to create highly modularized and efficient computing solutions.

In effect, client/server concepts have freed businesses to use multiple independent technologies as appropriate for their unique needs without sacrificing communication and information sharing. The three-tiered application architecture consists of three distinct layers, or tiers, of software logic:

- **User services**—the front-end client that communicates with the user through a graphical user interface. A code at the user services level calls upon an application-services tier to provide business functionality.

- **Application services**—a collection of services enforces business rules, processes information, and manages transactions. Application services may reside on the client, the server or both.

- **Data services**—decision-independent data is made available to the application services tier for processing. This is typically accomplished through a database management system, usually a relational database (RDBMS).

Client/server computing uses the power of both desktop and server machines. In so doing, it raises questions about what application functionality should run on the client and what should run on servers.

The two-tiered client/server approach places all the application functionality on the client. The client, in turn, communicates over a network with an RDBMS. While this approach works well for many departmental applications, enterprise-wide applications can encounter performance and control problems when all application processing is placed on the client.

Three-tiered applications can substantially increase client/server performance by partitioning the application functionality so that some portion runs on the client while other portions run on one or more servers.

10.4 Future of Supply-Chain Software

Despite its promise, supply-chain application software implementation is accompanied by the confusion and misconception that is inherent in any new technology and business method. The questions range from:

What is the technology best suited for SCM?

How can the costs involved and return on investment be estimated?

What are the key design issues in developing an information architecture?

How can technology and management issues be aligned to gain the maximum value?

Of these, the most pressing question facing companies is: What is the right technology that protects investment in a changing environment? The answer appears to lie in network-centric computing—Intranets and the Web.

Intranets and Network-Centric Computing

Even as businesses implement two- or three-tier client/server systems, a new computing paradigm is quickly emerging. Whether it is called network-centric computing, Intranets, or distributed objects, the aim is to provide more highly configurable, more fault-tolerant, more scalable, and more easily used solutions for enterprises than traditional client/server systems have been able to deliver.

Demand for Intranets—corporate networks fenced in with firewalls with a smattering of internal Web servers that provide a robust client/server architecture—is booming as businesses worldwide seek to replace their aging "legacy" information systems with better architectures.

The goal of Intranets—using the Internet and electronic commerce concepts for internal corporate usage—is to enable more "open" integrated systems where marketing, distribution, manufacturing, and financial management functions all communicate with each other to achieve a common objective. The degree of integration and the specific activities that are integrated are dependent on the firm's infrastructure and the industry in which the firm operates.

Intranets built around the Web are proving to be useful as they enable the creation of applications that have a high degree of business-process integration while, at the same time, allowing decoupling of software functionality so that cross-platform applications are a reality. For users, a Web-based solution insulates from the underlying technology. Users do not have to know the nuts and bolts of the network to access data, run reports, and use applications.

For developers, the Web's platform-neutral design speeds application development, deployment, and modification. In most cases, applications are built and customized with reusable business objects—"check credit authorization" and such—not programming code. The emergence of the reusable architecture, coupled with increasingly difficult, expensive maintenance of "legacy" mainframe applications, has accelerated the growth in Intranet development.

The Web does not lock business into a prescribed configuration. System administrators can configure the system to meet the needs of the business, no matter how often those needs may change. They can add platforms, databases, new technologies, and users as necessary without worrying about bringing the business to a grinding halt. Table 10.2 summarizes the salient reasons why Intranets are useful.

Table 10.2 Summarizing the Business Reasons for Intranets

Business Problem	Expand access to information while controlling costs.
	Reduce complex and expensive maintenance/support of custom client/server software on thousands of client systems.
	Reduce multiple end user interfaces which result in confusion.
Solution	Integrate business application access using World Wide Web technology.
Requirements	Small amount of code on client workstation.
	Custom code on Web servers only.
	Low bandwidth needed for end users.
Benefits	Easier management with expanded supports for client platforms.
	Minimizes space required on client systems.
	Requires no special client code.
	Position for mobile access.

Intranets and Application Software

The primary driver of Intranets will continue to be business process re-engineering, where global deployment of operations, increasing mobility in the workplace, the aftermath of mergers and downsizing, and a competitive environment for information technology are forcing large companies to look at all aspects of their application deployment to gain competitive advantage. This, in turn, is forcing data and applications to move closer to and become more accessible to decision makers throughout the enterprise.

From a business side, Intranets take center stage in implementing SCM as companies are faced with a growing list of software products to serve different needs and applications. Managers are anxious not to be tied into any one system that might be obsolete in five years' time. This fear was superbly captured by Bernie, a character in the Doonesbury cartoon strip, "I went out to lunch, and when I got back the whole industry had changed"—explaining why his company had suddenly hit trouble. The need for flexibility is precisely the reason why managers are looking toward Intranets.

Intranet-based SCM applications fall into the category of what would be considered mission-critical business applications. They are the types of systems that companies use to run their business: take their customer orders and order management; plan their distribution of inventory and forecasting of demand for their products; schedule their production and manufacturing processes; account for all of these transactions; and, basically, manage the flow of materials from customer-order management all the way through the accounting process.

The Intranet-based supply-chain software philosophy stresses the enterprise, rather than any functional unit. Increasingly, these applications must be "workflow enabled"; that is, they must be able to support the underlying business processes that create, manage, and use information. This is in contrast to technologies such as networking, electronic mail, EDI, and groupware that have redefined many aspects of corporate information systems. At the same time, these rapidly evolving technologies have created islands of automation that undermine the integrity of the overall enterprise information system.

Impact of the Web on Application Software

The current trend is to create interfaces for the user between the application software (such as SAP's R/3 product) and the Web, either on the Internet or Intranet. The Web is an ideal front end that works with a number of applications, connects to the application through the Internet or an Intranet, and is not limited to the archaic constraints usually placed by strange quirks of application software.

Web front ends can be easily integrated into a three-tier client/server architecture because processing in three-tier systems is separated from results presentation. This allows the results to be transmitted via the Internet or Intranet. The integration of Web applications will not cause any significant shift in the market positions of individual suppliers in the short term. However, since the Internet is likely to have a significant impact on economic life in the longer term, suppliers with poor or no Internet interfaces could lose market share.

The Web approach allows developers to build common application front ends with reusable software components that will run in multiple client/server environments. A developer can build a front end, or visual component once, and reuse that visual component in many different applications and many different user environments. In a traditional approach, developers would need to know how to communicate with SAP or PeopleSoft using their native protocol. For instance, with the Web approach, a developer could build a customer service inquiry screen and use it in a desktop application. Then, without making any changes to the code, he could place it inside a Web browser.

The advantage of this approach is quite significant. If developers build an application that needs to access SAP, it would be the same process as if users were accessing Baan or PeopleSoft. End users do not need to learn three separate technologies to access three different systems. The Web approach allows access to all three of those systems through a common interface.

The key benefit is that the technology enables casual users to periodically access these applications. The GUIs on existing application systems are not particularly intuitive for somebody not trained on the use of that GUI. In addition, there are costly licensing and training issues involved in putting somebody on an application system as a full-blown user. Those end users who only access the system once a week or once a month need not incur the training or licensing cost to give them access to the system. The Web enables corporations to selectively expose and extend certain transactions to a new user community, through an intuitive interface. It does not require a proprietary client on the desktop.

Elaborating on the Intranet Architecture

Competitive pressures lead to an intense challenge for companies to improve their business while reducing the strain on corporate information systems. In light of these demands, Intranets take on increasing importance as well as a new role in the development, deployment, and management of applications and resources.

Unfortunately, many firms are still based on rigid functional structures (such as purchasing, personnel, and production). Correspondingly, software development sought largely isolated solutions to the problems of the various divisions. From the point of view of the whole company this led to less than optimal and inflexible software solutions. To solve this problem, managers are beginning to connect their companies' disparate software functions with the Intranet in order to streamline business processes.

Intranet applications rest on several layers of infrastructure. A layered architecture allows companies to combine applications, tools, and databases in a coordinated approach. The layered approach also allows companies to offer application enhancements at each layer.

Why is a layered framework useful? Information systems managers and developers today often have to manage incompatible systems, brought in at various times to do very different tasks. The data formats usually differ, and the connectivity issues involved are inherently complex. Achieving a high level of integration requires the capabilities of multiple software products to communicate and cooperate in data exchange and process hand-offs. These demands require Intranets to go beyond their traditional "lowest common denominator" role of electronic mail to more complex functions such as:

Simplify access to the multiple databases, applications, platforms, and objects common in today's organizations.

Integrate existing systems easily with new technology as it emerges.

Improve the scalability, performance, and reliability of today's client/server applications.

Provide the flexibility to partition applications between different computers and platforms.

Simplify administration of the distributed environment by supporting proprietary as well as industry standard management solutions.

However, the movement toward Intranets is not a panacea. Firms might fail to integrate their supply-chain strategies for a number of reasons, among them a lack of system and information integration resulting from fragmented supply-chain responsibilities. Hence, in neglecting to align Intranets and the concept of SCM, firms might be missing an opportunity to cut costs and boost service quality.

What Remains to Be Done?

Technology alone does not solve all problems. To successfully manage today's complex supply chains, managers need to carefully interface and coordinate business functions, processes, and the technology that link the various components of the organization to its customers and suppliers.

Coordination becomes crucial as the supply chain crosses functional boundaries. For instance, if customer orders consist of multiple products that are supplied by different divisions, the company often uses an integrating (or merging) center. Obviously, tight coordination among suppliers is important as the customer is often given a target date. Unfortunately, arbitrarily generated target dates that do not consider existing backlogs in the supplying divisions can be problematic. As a result, target dates are often missed, resulting in unhappy customers.

Lack of coordination results in excessive delays, and ultimately, poor customer service. At the same time, inventory builds up at the merging center. Another consequence of poor coordination is that some divisions expedite deliveries. These products sit in the merging center for weeks until the last product comes in. In many cases, organizational barriers—differences in objectives and performance metrics, disagreements on inventory ownership, and lack of incentives to commit resources—rather than technology may inhibit coordination.

10.5 Summary

This chapter discussed the emerging management philosophy called *supply-chain management* (SCM). SCM refers to the integration of the internal and external partners on the supply and process chains to get orders from customers, raw materials from suppliers, and finished products to end user.

SCM enables companies to avoid the vagaries of the marketplace by improved stock management techniques and better distribution management. This requires cooperative relationships that stem from interfirm linkages with upstream and downstream suppliers and consumers to create very positive win-win situations. Effective management of interfirm linkages in the supply chain can add value in numerous ways: lower cost, improved quality, faster speed of delivery, improved support, and stronger competitive positioning.

Also discussed was how Intranet-based electronic commerce technology and supply-chain functions are becoming intertwined as the walls between functional structures (such as purchasing, personnel, and production) are dismantled. Correspondingly, software development that provided isolated solutions to the problems of the various divisions is a thing of the past. The focus today is on the optimization of integrated processes that extend beyond particular divisions, taking account of the customer's wishes.

Whether a company seeks to simply connect two different systems or to combine all its systems into a single, enterprise-wide computing resource, it needs Intranet technology that enables the exchange and linking of data from all areas of the company. For firms, the Intranet environment offers the promise of a new approach to better address certain business requirements. Many firms see Intranet computing as highly complementary to their activities on the public Internet. Aside from the complementary interplay, what matters most are the Intranet's implications and benefits in managing supply chains.

Chapter 11

Intranets and Customer Asset Management

Chapter Outline

11.1 Why Customer Asset Management?

11.2 Online Sales Force Automation

11.3 Online Customer Service and Support

11.4 Technology and Marketing Strategy

11.5 Summary

Conventional SCM systems focus on basic operations but ignore a key point; that is, most "pull" supply chains are customer demand driven. In the "pull" model, customer satisfaction depends on effectively linking the customer information-gathering front line (sales and customer service) to the upstream functions (manufacturing and distribution). To facilitate smoother information flow, new Web-enabled approaches are displacing traditional stand-alone sales force automation and customer support implementations.

In parallel to the technological changes, a new customer interaction strategy, Customer Asset Management, is being employed by companies seeking to increase revenue and competitive advantage. Basically, Customer Asset Management is the integration of the front-line activities in a supply chain—namely sales, market intelligence gathering, and customer service—to act in a coordinated manner rather than pulling in different directions.

Customer Asset Management is based on the premise that customers are the most valuable asset of any business. Each interaction is viewed as critical and must add value. You might immediately ask: What is new here?

The importance of attracting, pleasing, and keeping customers is as old as the notion of marketing itself. What is new, however, is the use of technology for the active management of a firm's current (or installed) customer base as a strategic asset. The goal is to use technology to add value to every customer interaction and produce revenue growth.

Companies are embracing Customer Asset Management as a revenue growth strategy that maximizes the value of customer relationships. Indeed, many recent so-called marketing revolutions are reflections of this more basic shift in perspective. Such revolutions include "zero defections" loyalty, relationship marketing, direct marketing, interactive marketing, database marketing, and mass customization. Interest in these marketing initiatives has expanded from niche industries (such as catalog, credit, and financial services) to consumer durables, nondurables, and manufacturing.

A result of this trend is a change in the way customer information systems are built from stand-alone systems that create islands of information to an integrated suite of software applications that provide a comprehensive view of each customer. Unlike traditional sales force automation (SFA) systems, which only address the sales process, Customer Asset Management systems enable tracking of customers through the entire customer life cycle, from initial marketing to customer service.

However, developing integrated systems requires a substantial financial investment in many cases, and often success relies on sophisticated technology, business processes, and multifunctional cooperation. Since specific Customer Asset Management systems can bring such large financial returns, their details are also highly proprietary, and companies can find themselves reinventing the wheel rather than building well-grounded principles.

This chapter will examine in some detail the leading practices in Customer Asset Management and also the application of electronic commerce to its successful implementation in organizations. The chapter will be organized around four major components of Customer Asset Management:

Online sales force automation—contact management, activity management, opportunity management, call reporting, lead tracking, order entry and support, customer contact, and telemarketing (see Section 11.2);

Online customer service and support—account management, maintenance/help desk services, and field service applications (see Section 11.3);

Market intelligence—competitor intelligence, trend analysis, and supplier management (see Section 11.4); and

Marketing management—performance analysis, marketing planning, sales forecasting, and human resource management (see Section 11.4).

Before discussing how Customer Asset Management can be managed effectively, it may be helpful to describe in more detail what Customer Asset Management means to leading practitioners and why it represents a major change in perspective on marketing activities.

11.1 Why Customer Asset Management?

The benefits of managing customers as strategic assets include creating more loyal customers, who are less inclined to shop around or buy on price; more efficient, effective, and highly targeted communications programs; retention of profitable customers; and more focused development of new products. It is also, for many managers, a change that causes substantial anxiety and frustration.

The case for managing customers as strategic assets rests on four conditions, only some of which may be met in some industries [FT95].

First, current customers are a predictable source of future sales. Understandably, expected future sales from the current customer base often form the starting point for a plan to meet sales targets, with customer acquisition efforts established to close the gap between the two.

Second, customers can be segmented in terms of future sales potential (their "asset value") based on their history to date. Research has found that sales history is more effective in segmenting customers than many demographic factors. Realization of the importance of sales history accounts for the efforts to create databases that capture the customer's transaction history. With knowledge of customer history, the ability to anticipate future trends makes it natural to view each individual as an "asset" of the corporation. Sales history is also useful in developing promotions.

Third, customers, like every other asset, are subject to depreciation. Why? Like other assets, customer attrition is a fact of life. For example, in online services customer attrition is called *churn* and is often factored into profitability. The factors that affect customer retention/attrition patterns include: customers tiring of existing services, customers dissatisfied with the service, and customers finding a better price elsewhere. More importantly, this attrition is often predictable, especially with the knowledge of transaction history. Customer asset/depreciation perspectives have become so widely accepted that they are now standard accounting practice in the United States.

And finally, customers can be bought and sold. An explicit valuation of future sales potential from specific customer groups is increasingly an important component of merger and acquisition decisions. For example, the recent merger of two large banks (Wells Fargo and First Interstate) represents the combination of customer bases whose sales potential is to be realized with a smaller and more efficient corporate infrastructure.

In short, customers often have an asset value that can be evaluated reliably, especially with the availability of detailed transaction history information. Next, let us consider some of the challenges in implementing an asset-based perspective.

Challenges in Implementing Customer Asset Management

Companies implementing Customer Asset Management systems face two major challenges. First, the information needed to describe, track, and capture the customer as part of an asset base can be difficult or expensive to gather. Further, the benefits are not obvious until that long, costly process is completed. Second, the active management of customer assets typically requires an unprecedented degree of coordination across various customer-facing functions.

The first challenge can be overcome by changing the cost economics for data acquisition and management (for example, using the Web and Intranets); by developing better software designed specifically for managing marketing-oriented customer databases (for example, data warehousing technology); by creating opportunities to partner with other companies (including those downstream in the channel of distribution) to share information of mutual benefit; and by inventing incentives for consumers who wish to facilitate the collection of this information.

The second challenge, related to coordination of the company's information systems and its marketing programs, can be overcome by increasing cross-functional interaction in companies, including cross-functional integration, and pushing responsibility for customer orientation beyond the marketing function to include manufacturing and R&D. These functions provide an underutilized and overlooked focal point for improving the efficiency of the supply chains.

Customer Asset Management and Supply Chains

Before going further, let us clarify why Customer Asset Management is important in the context of supply-chain management. It is estimated that marketing and sales costs average 15 to 35 percent of total costs. This means that the price a product can command is less a reflection of raw materials and labor than of marketing-related services like selecting appropriate product features, determining the product mix, and ensuring product availability and delivery.

Increasing marketing productivity even a small amount can have a great impact on both fixed costs and variable costs. Lower fixed costs mean lower break-even points. So, a given percentage increase in sales produces a correspondingly larger increase in operating profits. Meanwhile, lower variable costs mean that every sale contributes more to the bottom line.

Clearly, investments in front-line systems—marketing, sales, and customer service—hold tremendous potential for supply-chain productivity improvements. For instance, the Web allows firms to gather critical pieces of information from the consumer questions and suggestions. These customer contacts are important as they help firms turn out consistent, quality products by alerting the company when something goes out of kilter somewhere in their complex operations. Customer contacts can also serve as a source of new product ideas.

Despite the proven worth of customer interaction, companies have been relatively slow in automating any part of their marketing and sales functions. Even fewer appear to understand the strategic benefits that can accrue from applying technology to the marketing and sales; most early adopters have automated as a matter of faith rather than as part of a strategy for gaining competitive advantage. A better approach begins with an understanding of what marketing and sales automation can do, how it works, and how it can be implemented.

11.2 Online Sales Force Automation

The sales function is critical for the success of any business. As businesses strive to address online business opportunities, the sales force is faced with complexities never before experienced, such as intense product or service differentiation, increasing configurations and new specifications for products, improved customer service, and reduced operating costs. By streamlining the information flow between customers and companies, businesses are seeking to eliminate sales order mistakes and the resulting rework, increasing productivity. The result is reduced order fulfillment costs and dramatically shortened delivery cycles.

What Is Sales Force Automation?

Sales force automation satisfies two basic functions: (a) to support the sales person in the field; and (b) to integrate sales activity into a corporate information structure to improve overall corporate efficiency and coordination with other business-critical functions.

In the context of supporting the sales person in the field, sales force automation (SFA) means different things to different sales people. To some, SFA is synonymous with contact managers: personal computer-based applications used to collect data on customer leads and to maintain records of customer visits, phone calls, and correspondence.

To others, SFA is synonymous with opportunity management. An opportunity management system consists of a database application that is used to store data on customer prospects, a marketing encyclopedia offering a content-searchable catalog of marketing literature and other information for review or communication to sales representatives or customers, and a sales and marketing process model that is used to interpret field data and predict when, and for how much, sales may occur.

What are the business reasons for sales automation? Many factors contribute to an increasing number of companies' interest in sales automation. Among the most compelling reasons is the cost of sales. An average sales call costs several hundred dollars—a lot more in some companies. Replacing a dissatisfied customer costs far more than that.

As companies attempt to do more with less, they rely on "virtual offices" to reduce real estate and support costs and look for ways to increase each salesperson's productivity. Still others seek the competitive advantage that automation can provide. Ultimately, the objective is to remove boundaries and to bring the customer closer to the company. The goal is to energize sales by easily gathering potential leads and then transferring qualified leads to the sales force. Too often, the inability to act quickly means a lost opportunity.

Elements of Online Sales Automation

In general, sales force automation systems include: customer account management, direct sales, telemarketing, direct mail, literature fulfillment, advertising, customer service, dealers, and distributors, all of which offer opportunities for efficiency improvements.

Let us delve into some features of a fully integrated sales automation system in which centrally located employees as well as a remote sales force work from a distributed database of customers and prospects. Information and work flows in all directions. Marketing may integrate marketing programs and distribute and track leads. Management may access sales activity and utilize the database to make strategic decisions about the market.

Elements of such a sales automation system include:

- **Salesperson productivity tools**—planning and reporting of sales calls, reporting of expenses, entering orders, checking inventory and order status, managing distributors, tracking leads, and managing accounts. In addition, mobile salespeople can reduce sales lead times by requesting product specifications, sending product samples, and updating forecasts directly from their laptop computers.

- **Online telemarketing**—targeting qualified prospects, managing demand creation, processing responses, providing literature fulfillment, and tracking sales campaigns' effectiveness. This requires tracking and forwarding qualified leads to the sales teams for immediate action; ranking prospects; and prompting scripts (sales, customer service, and support).

- **Direct mail and fulfillment**—merging, cleaning, and maintaining mailing lists; tracking and forwarding leads; customizing letters, envelopes, and labels; generating "picking lists" for literature; and managing literature inventory.

- **Sales and marketing management**—providing automated sales management reports (sales forecasts, sales activity, forecasts versus actuals, and so on); designing and managing sales territories; and analyzing marketing and sales programs by such criteria as territory, product, customer, price, and channel.

- **Sales force compensation management**—sales management has difficulty with accurate forecasts, visibility into sales productivity, and accurately compensating employees for their accomplishments. The problem is further complicated when firms have global sales teams. Managers need to be able to track market activity through pipeline versus forecast reporting and develop incentive compensation solutions for various selling channels.

- **Sales process management**—the most important factor in any sales automation system is the sales process. Automating a bad process leads to more chaos. The sales process must be analyzed for problems, and the system should be designed to address these problems. Some examples of problems include: Will sales be able to more effectively bring resources to bear on the best prospects? Can the loop between sales, customer service, operations, and the customer be closed? Can the sales force be proactive while minimizing associated sales support costs? These issues must be addressed and incorporated into the system.

Online sales automation systems can automate the work of a single salesperson, a single marketing activity like direct mail, or a company's entire marketing and sales operation. These systems combine direct selling, distributor relationships, telemarketing, and direct mail to: generate, qualify, rank-order, distribute, and track sales leads; fill prospects' requests for product and price information; update customer and prospect files; provide sales and technical product support by telephone; and automate order entry and sales reporting.

Intranets and Sales Automation

The Intranet-enabled sales automation framework has multiple benefits. First, it helps bridge the "islands of information" that can exist within a company, especially within sales and marketing. Intranets are an important tool for augmenting sales productivity as they provide a single point of access to all essential information on customers, prospects, products, marketing programs, and marketing channels. Some existing systems supplement the essentials with industry data (growth rates, entries, exits, and regulatory trends) and data on competitors (products, pricing, sales trends, and market shares).

Second, the availability of interactive Web monitoring software and intelligent agents makes it possible to build a "smart" solution that delivers vital, specific sales intelligence directly to the desktop of each sales representative, instead of mounds of general information. These intelligent agents make direct sales and direct marketing more efficient by automating highly repetitive support tasks, like answering requests for product literature and writing letters, and by reducing the time salespeople spend on nonselling tasks, like scheduling sales calls, compiling sales reports, generating proposals and bids, and entering orders.

Third, Intranets can also be used for electronic publishing, to educate and inform sales representatives and make the selling process more proactive by providing all the information and tools necessary to close the sale on-site at a customer location. Using Intranets as a publishing medium offers an inexpensive, easy-to-use, easily updated alternative to paper-based, LAN-based, and CD-ROM-based documentation systems. Also, Intranets remove the obstacles inherent with publishing information in multiplatform environments.

And finally, once the Intranet-based solution is in place, companies find it possible to extend information sharing beyond the boundaries of the enterprise, to outside parties critical to the sales effort. The collection and analysis of marketing information improves the timeliness and quality of marketing and sales executives' decision making. Organizations can extend marketing and sales intelligence to distributors, third-party partners, or even customers.

Table 11.1 indicates some of the benefits of using Intranet technology.

Table 11.1   Benefits of the Intranet for Sales

Shorten the sales cycle through prequalification of prospects.

Increase revenue through targeted marketing.

Automate the management and qualification of Web leads.

Capture all customer information directly into sales database.

Enhance order management with access to data on pricing, promotions, availability, production schedules, export regulations, carriers, and transportation schedules.

Intranets and a Mobile Sales Force   The ability to act quickly often implies that the sales force is mobile. No longer do sales people have to be in the office or logged onto a LAN system in order to do their work. The recent trend in sales automation is toward solutions designed to serve the unique needs of remote or mobile user populations—those whose jobs limit their ability to be connected while they work—is reaching critical mass.

Many of the components necessary to ignite this remote access market are in place. Many companies are giving their sales force customer sales data via laptop computers. For example, Xerox launched a "virtual office" program, in which sales representatives receive computer equipment and training and a shove out of the office door. The idea was to get sales reps to spend more time in the field where they can be in touch with the customers. Sales mobility provides a way to better understand and meet customer needs throughout the enterprise.

However, to be effective, a mobile sales force needs integrated back-office systems. These systems provide account managers with access to data on pricing, promotions, availability, production schedules, export regulations, carriers, and transportation schedules. However, such systems are still on the drawing boards of many firms.

Integrating the Web with Contact Management   Many organizations have set up Web sites for customer contact. The goal now is to seamlessly integrate the Web front-end with the existing sales process to achieve better productivity. For instance, leads are collected from an organization's Internet Web site, and then sorted and automatically e-mailed to the appropriate sales person. With the click of a mouse, these leads are transferred directly into the sales database. Automatic e-mail notifications are sent to the prospects, acknowledging their Web site request. Table 11.2 lists the requirements of customer contact systems.

The architecture of such a system would have two components: a server module and the client module on the sales team's PCs or laptops. The process is initiated when a prospect fills out an HTML form on a Web page. An automatic customized reply e-mail is sent to the prospect, acknowledging their Web site inquiry. The server automatically sorts the prospect's entry based on customized, predetermined distribution rules. Distribution criteria can be based on territories, states, product interest, or any other fields on the client designed forms. The sales team then receives lead notifications as messages in their electronic mailboxes and the data is stored as file attachments to the messages.

Upon receipt of their e-mail, the sales people execute the client programs on their PCs or laptops which automatically load the information into the correct database. For easy data entry, the client software is configurable so that the software matches fields from a Web form to fields in the database. By providing seamless integration between the Web and contact management software, the system distributes leads quickly and automatically, saving an organization time and resources. By reducing the sales cycle and eliminating redundant data entry, the Intranet architecture improves the return on investment.

Table 11.2 Contact Management Requirements

Track and manage prospect targeting, direct marketing campaigns, response measurement, and prospect qualification.

Apply target profiles to lists to identify prospects.

Assign leads based on product type, regions, territories, or markets.

Share access to information among headquarters staff, field locations, and channel partners to support team selling.

Pull all information about an opportunity into a single consolidated view to facilitate complex sales.

Assist in quote preparation based on customer sales history and expected purchases.

Intranets and Target Marketing   In the area of direct marketing, Intranets help hone the efficiency of customer contacts. The Intranet interface adds value to the customer interchange by automating the process of qualifying leads from an external Web home page. Used in conjunction with other applications, the Intranet enables the integration of the Web as an interactive marketing forum to become an input to the sales and marketing processes within the company. For example, a system for the telemarketing function can schedule and dial calls based on the prospect's priority, prompt the telemarketer with a sales script, and automatically update customer files.

How does this work? The external Web page enables a prospective customer to simply register her interest level and information directly into the home page. The lead is then automatically assigned to the appropriate inside telesales representative, and a follow-up task and assignment are immediately sent off. As the representative starts to work with the lead, all the relevant information has been captured, including the customer's name, address, company, industry, and referral source—even their interest level and any general information. All of the vital qualifying information can be immediately put into use, increasing productivity of the sales force and ultimately shortening the sales cycle.

In companies with many channels, proper use of the distributed database helps to track and coordinate all marketing activity. The database typically includes: (1) all customer contacts, whether by mail, phone, direct salesperson, or national account manager; (2) the status of all sales efforts; (3) the origins of all leads; (4) all leads that are being qualified internally and by whom, and all leads that have been forwarded to distributors; (5) all customers who decided to buy; (6) what and when they purchased; and (7) any incentives or promotions that helped close the deal. Coordination of information through this system prevents independent marketing groups from pursuing the same customers with conflicting promotions.

The information in sales databases is different from manufacturing- or production-related data. Rather than focusing on products (What was the cost to produce each unit? How many units were made, sold, and shipped?), the sales database is customer driven. Whenever marketing or sales activities are performed, the database captures information that answers questions about customers and their needs. Who were the prospects? What were their interests? How were these interests generated? Which sales or marketing personnel performed which tasks? When were the tasks performed? Which follow-up tasks are required and when? Did any sales result? Gradually the database becomes a rich source of marketing and sales information, enabling management to track marketing activities and measure the results of marketing programs.

Intranets enable access to the central database, thereby providing salespeople and direct marketers with information to improve the quality of the contact, whether it is by mail, by telephone, or in person. Many financial services firms use the Web to handle account inquiries. While responding to a customer's request or query, the system updates the customer's profile information and attempts to cross-sell other financial products. Table 11.3 lists the requirements that are being met with Intranet-based applications.

Table 11.3 Coordination Requirements

Provide individualized lead and contact management through automatically updated to-do lists, ticklers, and follow-up lists.

Drive leads to closure while tracking all the decision makers, even if they are distributed over multiple sites.

Automatically escalate action requests and notify appropriate people when deal status changes.

Generate forecasts, including product, territory, regional, national, and worldwide reports.

Generate lost business reports to support analysis of product/market needs.

Publishing Dynamic Sales Information   The sales environment changes constantly, as promotions and price lists are updated and leads and competitive information become available. Hence, it is important to keep everyone on the same page. Intranets have proven that they are the ideal medium for facilitating effective business communications. They provide universal access to dynamic, up-to-the-minute sales intelligence for both connected and disconnected mobile users throughout the enterprise. Table 11.4 summarizes the business problem and the characteristics of a solution.

There are several difficulties inherent with building and maintaining dynamic sales information and providing access to mobile users in order to foster more effective business communications. Managing and administering the system, as well as controlling content and keeping it up-to-date can be an overwhelming challenge, especially in large enterprises that have huge quantities of sales materials in a variety of formats and media. It is also important to constantly bring in real-time data and updates from outside information sources. The most critical challenge is providing the same level of system access and the most up-to-date information to mobile users who can only occasionally connect up to the system.

The Intranet is designed to overcome these obstacles and ensure that businesses can provide pertinent, up-to-date business intelligence to both connected and mobile users and ultimately have a significant positive impact on sales and marketing productivity. Most importantly, the Web lets sales representatives organize and personalize their view of the corporate sales "encyclopedia" and be alerted when critical new information arrives. Programs called *intelligent agents* can be designed to seek out and deliver vital intelligence on the competitors, customers, or topics of specific interest to each individual sales representative.

Table 11.4   Summarizing the Implementation Challenges

Business Problem	Timely and low-cost distribution of information.
	Need to reduce cycle time for filling orders.
Solution	Use World Wide Web to publish and solicit content.
	Automate processes using Intranets and enable electronic sales via the Web.
Requirements	Interface internal order management systems with the Web.
Benefits	Low-cost medium with fast turnaround.
	Enables world wide electronic sales.
	Automates internal business processes.

What Are the Management Issues?

Creation of an integrated sales database is an astute management investment. The database chronicles every one of a company's marketing and sales activities, from advertising that generates leads to direct mail and telephone qualification of the leads, to closing the first sale—all the way through the life of each account. It enables marketing and sales management to relate marketing actions with marketplace results.

The goal of using Intranets is to reduce marketing inertia by streamlining the implementation of pricing and promotional programs. As marketing managers become accustomed to these systems, they find new uses for them, like analyzing and modeling the buying behavior of prospects and customers. Account histories also improve management's ability to devise and implement account management policies based on profits. By linking orders, services delivered, and prices paid with the actual costs of lead generation, pre-selling, closing, distribution, and post-sale support, Intranets furnish the tools for analyzing and adjusting the marketing mix.

Finally, management must institute policies that coordinate and direct sales resources toward the highest priority prospects and customers. In this context, management must understand that the technology resources are employed to further corporate goals rather than the goals of individual marketing or sales groups. While this may sound like something obvious, research shows that optimizing marketing resources is much more easily said than done. Often, salespeople routinely discard hundreds of sales leads, making little or no effort to evaluate or review them. In essence, they are dissipating the resources that generated these leads—budgets for advertising, trade shows, public relations, and other communications media.

Efficiencies gained through automation and improved marketing management are interdependent and reinforcing. Automation drives the collection of more complete customer and marketplace information, and more informed decision making targets marketing and sales activities where they are most effective. In this way, marketers get a bigger payoff from low-cost, low-impact selling methods like direct mail and catalogs, as databases customize the timing and content of mass-marketing campaigns. At the same time, high-cost, high-impact selling methods, like personal selling and national account management, become more efficient as information systems perform routine sales support tasks, reduce nonselling time, and synchronize the use of these resources.

11.3 Online Customer Service and Support

Ask any forward-thinking business executive to name her company's most valuable asset, and her most frequent answer will likely be "our customers." This need for companies to be customer-centric is no longer questioned. Most realize that effective customer management is a key competitive advantage. Over the past decade, businesses have invested heavily in customer service systems, sales systems, and personnel. Despite these investments, most businesses are still unable to maximize the value of their customer asset.

The online revolution has brought about a fundamental shift in the way companies are thinking about customer service and support. With millions of users, the Web is changing the way that businesses interact with their customers, suppliers, and partners. The potential for improved customer communications and leveraged business offerings is enormous. It is obvious that online customer service is the "killer" application opportunity via the Web. Table 11.5 outlines some of the business reasons for customer service on the Web.

Table 11.5   Reasons Why Online Customer Service Is Hot

Lower support costs by empowering customers to solve issues independently.

Provide global access to critical customer service information and forums any time.

Improve service by focusing internal customer support resources on complex issues.

Empower business partners with hot links to related online resolution information.

Create proactive service and marketing programs.

Seamless Web/telephony integration for priority responsiveness.

The Web and Customer Service

Many companies have begun to use Web sites and e-mail systems to provide answers to frequently asked questions or to allow customers to access procedures for repairing an item or initiating a service call. Several technology companies post on electronic bulletin boards software upgrades and code patches that customers can download to upgrade or fix applications.

The Web will allow companies to achieve new heights of responsiveness. By extending service applications through a Web site, a company can provide customers with more information quickly, interactively, and eventually in real-time. A Web site can be like an ATM of customer service. Product users will get service when they want it. They can browse at their own pace, at their own level of interest. They can ask questions and get up-to-date information about parts or product availability and about service scheduling and status. And, increasingly, they will be able to receive direct service over the Web when and where they need it.

In fact, the Web represents an opportunity for companies to dramatically redefine their relationships with customers. With the many capabilities the Web offers, the nature of the relationship can change from responsiveness to involvement. Eventually, companies will be able to use Web sites not just to provide information about products and services, but to show customers new products, gather their ideas, and set up a dialog. Increasingly, when a customer says "show me," the Web will provide the way to do it. The Web's multimedia capabilities will make it possible for customers to see and hear how some products work. And customers will be able to experiment with products online, or download demonstrations and provide feedback later. By continually "listening" to customers' feedback and acknowledging or acting on it, a company will be able to build and nurture relationships with customers and thus claim their loyalty.

Information Systems Challenges   In companies committed to building world-class customer service operations, IS will be under more pressure than ever to help customer service functions operate faster, more efficiently, and cost effectively. Because the time-to-market imperatives are so strong, there is too little time for IS to design and build their own software solutions. They will need strong core applications that they can then customize to meet the organization's needs. These applications will need to be cost-effective, easy to deploy, and easy to maintain and modify.

One of the problems some companies find when they look for software solutions is that, although some applications are full of features, they may fall short in ease of use or ease of customization. Some companies report that it is too complicated and too time-consuming to make an information system fully functional and integrated with the rest of the company's operations. And with some applications, the company has had to adapt its business systems to the software, rather than the other way around. Table 11.6 summarizes the implementation challenges.

Table 11.6 Summarizing the System Challenges

Customer Support Business Problem	Training support personnel in a fast-changing area like technology is expensive.
	Need to provide customers better access to customer support information.
Solution	Internet access to product sheets, frequently asked questions, and other support information.
Requirements	Interface internal support systems with the World Wide Web.
Benefits	Expected competitive advantage via up-to-date, globally available information, reduced support overhead.

The success and effectiveness of the customer-service operation depends on the applications being able to deliver all the benefits the organization is seeking. Component-based development is becoming the enabling technology for IS staff who need to tailor the applications they use. Using prebuilt graphical business components, developers can create reusable code quickly and easily. With a minimal learning period, they can customize applications to deliver truly useful solutions, significant cost and time savings, and risk avoidance.

The Role of Technology in Customer Service

Service requests come in many ways: e-mail, Web forms, or the old-fashioned telephone call. The request could be internal—an employee with a problem that is bound to result in lost time, money, and productivity—or external—a customer with a question about your product. Whether the customer is internal or external, the support staff has one goal: Do what it takes to satisfy the customer.

To support the customer focus, companies need to change the way internal systems are being developed and deployed. Why? To date, most companies have attempted to better manage their customers by automating departmental support processes. For instance, customer support implements their own systems and database. The sales force is "automated" with laptops. Salespeople attempt to sell products to existing customers without being aware of their current service issues. Leads are not passed from service to sales because of system barriers. Product defect requests are lost in a chasm between customer support and engineering. Marketers struggle to gather customer information from various "islands" of data.

To provide superior service or become customer-centric, companies must stop automating disparate systems for sales automation, marketing, customer service, and quality assurance. Companies must implement a well-thought-out information systems strategy that treats customers as assets rather than as pests. Such a solution will provide every support person who is in contact with a customer with the information they require to sell and to serve. In short, to maximize the value of their customer asset, companies must implement customer-centric business systems.

It may sound like a tall order for customer service, an area that not long ago was considered by many a back-office necessity and a cost center. However, this view has changed enormously in the last couple of years. Consumers have become far more sophisticated and demanding, and companies are investing ever-increasing amounts of human and financial capital to be able to respond rapidly to customer questions and complaints. In fact, in many companies, customer service is now regarded as a critical front-line resource in building and maintaining profitability. But before we delve into system architecture issues we will discuss what the basic business requirements are in online customer service.

What Are the Business Requirements?

In an era when the customer is king, when the talk is of delighting and even "astonishing" customers, companies are under increasing competitive pressure not only to provide excellent service, but also to anticipate what customers will demand next by gathering intelligence for the sales function. And in many industries, it is the customer-service operation that is being tapped to carry out these dual tasks.

To remain responsive and competitive, companies need strong, well-considered customer service strategies for delivering service as well as technology resources to manage large volumes of transactions quickly, efficiently, and to the ultimate satisfaction of customers. By improving responsiveness and productivity, the well-designed customer service system can yield greater customer loyalty—and for some companies, increased opportunity for long-term service contract revenues.

Rather than treating a post-sales customer interaction as an unwanted intrusion, companies need to treat each customer interaction like a precious opportunity to:

Enhance the relationship by cross-selling additional products.

Sell new products and services.

Serve the customer better by being more proactive.

Gather feedback to improve existing products and gather input for new product development.

Hunger for Customer Feedback   Customer loyalty is earned one interaction at a time. The company must make customers feel that they are important and that what they think and say really matters. The willingness and ability to gather feedback can be a boon to virtually any company, but it is particularly important for companies that make complex products. Fast service is critical in industries that experience rapid rates of change when product lines or prices change in a competitive environment. In such industries, a company is highly vulnerable to customer defections.

Customer service function can be an information gold mine. With the right incentives, customers are willing to share information about themselves, such as income and education levels, how much they use certain products, and what kinds of products they want. Similarly, business customers are often willing to share information about how they do business and with whom, what kinds of problems they have with the company's and competitors' products, and what kinds of products and services they are looking for.

Information about customer satisfaction, product quality, and performance helps companies to reevaluate their processes, institute better controls, and operate proactively, predicting trends, opportunities, and acting on them.

Cross-selling and Upselling   Existing customers and prospects represent the best opportunity for cross-selling existing customers and upselling product lines. The concept of cross-selling is becoming increasingly prominent in the Customer Asset Management framework. Companies are focusing on converting inbound customer service calls into sales. Why? It has been proven time and again that the more products a company sells to a customer, the greater the chances are of retaining the account.

How does cross-selling work? Suppose a customer calls an insurance customer service line about an existing homeowner's insurance policy. After resolving the customer's question, the representative will attempt to sell auto insurance or sell a life, health, disability, and long-term care insurance policy to that client, since she is already familiar with the company.

Cross-selling is a key business concept. As managers develop or update the call center, they must keep in mind the critical role of technology and how it is integrated with the selling process and the knowledge level of the customer support staff. Service representatives should be trained to use technology to evaluate a customer's account profile to determine the potential for sale of additional products.

The most important requirement of technology is the ability to effectively gather information that aids in defining customer needs. For example, a customer who consistently overdraws a checking account could be sold a bank's overdraft protection product. Depending on the level of automation in the call center, one successful approach is to use a combination of expert systems, cross-sell prompts, and scripting to increase the proficiency of call center representatives in this area.

From Reactive to Proactive Service   Some call center applications now available offer "queue" systems that route a customer's problem to another "level" or department within the company, along with information about the nature of the problem, criticality for the customer, and warranty and service terms. Usually, the customer service representative who takes the call from the customer remains the contact person, tracking the customer's problems and ensuring a solution (see Fig. 11.1).

Increasingly, companies with an eye on the competitive possibilities are using the help-desk level of operations as two-way point of liaison with the customer. Typically, the contact occurs when a customer calls in with a question or complaint about the operation of an appliance. This could be a request

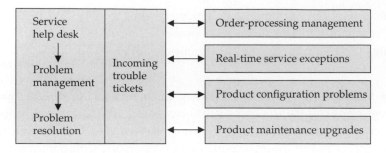

Figure 11.1   Reactive Call Center Process

for technical support under a warranty or service contract. By asking the customer certain questions and by solving the problem, the service representative can gain a significant amount of information in a short period of time. For manufacturers, the customer's call for support may constitute the first opportunity the manufacturing company has to find out what real people do with their products. Retailers do not often share that kind of information.

Companies are using technology solutions to manage more "proactive" services, like preventive and predictive maintenance. For example, customers who use sensitive or regulated equipment and items, such as a sophisticated piece of medical imaging equipment, can ensure they are not only maintaining the devices at an optimal level of operation but also that they are able to provide precise, detailed documentation of maintenance if required to do so by regulatory authorities. This kind of service attention, if it is fast, convenient, and hassle-free, tends to cement relations between customer and company.

Field Service Management   One aspect of proactive service is the ability to allocate, dispatch, and manage all of the people, tasks, and materials needed to perform services effectively and cost-efficiently. Organizations need to utilize their human and material resources wisely.

Field service software must help firms to create a work order, assign it to an appropriate technician or service provider group, request parts, track billing information, and schedule all these activities to coordinate with one another. Specifically, the software must:

Proactively evaluate and plan different services by defining the tasks to be performed, the materials needed, and the requisite skills;

Manage work orders to track all of the tasks needed to provide a service;

Assign, schedule, and dispatch services and resources using the workflow engine to automate notification; and

Log and track every aspect of a service request, including time and expenses, materials, tasks, required skills, and configuration information.

Clearly, there is market need for a software solution for managing the allocation, scheduling, and dispatching of resources, including parts and materials, to perform services or complete work orders. As an extension of Web-based support, Intranet-based field service software should take a task-oriented approach to managing the logistics process. Most typically, logistics is seen as a field dispatching service where technicians are sent to customer sites to repair or replace installed products.

Help Desk Management   Customer service can also be targeted at internal users in an organization. In today's fast-changing technology environment, the demands on the internal help desks are increasing exponentially. This increase can be attributed primarily to three factors:

> Technology is changing at an ever-increasing rate. Help desk workers are struggling to keep up with the support demands of an ever-growing variety of systems. The advent of client/server systems, GUIs, desktop software, and computer networks have expanded both the complexity and the volume of calls.

> Computing is being pushed further and further within the corporate boundaries. (Many companies, for example, are now automating areas such as sales that traditionally had little to do with computing.) The traditional help desk dealt with a small cadre of system-knowledgeable users accessing a limited set of applications with relatively simple requirements.

> Many IS groups are being downsized, with support functions often being the target for staff reductions.

Thus, help desks are receiving a growing number of calls, yet they have fewer people available to handle those calls. How are companies dealing with this paradox? Many are developing or purchasing Intranet software tools that automate their help desk support functions. Here's a sample of some key software features:

- **Easy access to customer data.** When a client calls, support people need fast access to account information. One issue to consider here is how they will access this information. For instance, will they bring up client records by entering a person's last name? Or would an interface with the phone system make more sense, in which case client records would automatically come up for the support technicians?

- **Asset and inventory tracking.** Is the ability to track serial numbers, configurations, and the whereabouts of hardware and software important? If
so, look closely at asset management and tracking features.

- **Problem hand-off and escalation capabilities.** Many support organizations today are billed as "one-stop shops," in which users can call with
almost any problem and get a resolution. But for this set-up to work,
calls typically must be routed outside the walls of the support center. In
such an environment, a system that automatically notifies management
when problems have escalated to a critical stage is a necessity.

- **A support knowledge base.** Knowledge databases, which contain solutions to common support-related problems, have become increasingly
popular. A good knowledge base can help deliver consistent problem res-
olutions. Fortunately, knowledge bases have become a key part of many
service and support automation systems.

- **Reporting capabilities.** Good reporting capabilities are essential for any
customer support system. On a basic level, managers want reports on the
number of calls taken per day, the speed with which problems are resolved, and the nature of each call received. Beyond that, managers need
to determine the information that can best assist them in managing staff
and to look for systems that readily provide that data.

Systems designed to support these environments were frequently little
more than databases of end user assets, with little or no ability to build or
retrieve a problem/solution database. These systems are not equipped to
meet today's needs for remote access by end users, multi-vendor support,
integrated network trouble ticketing, and access to both internal and external knowledge bases. For the most part, these systems are also very limited
in terms of their flexibility to adapt to changing systems and business requirements.

The Enabling Intranet Technology

Customer service representatives (CSRs) need a variety of tools to delight
customers at every interaction and build and nurture customer relationships. CSRs need access to timely, relevant, and accurate information that
portrays all aspects of the customer–company relationship. Many times this
information is specific to the CSR's area of expertise, as for example, when a
customer calls a product support group with a specific technical question.

Often, the information required to satisfy a customer resides outside the
CSR's department or area of expertise. As a result, the CSR never sees the to-

tal customer picture and lacks the essential ingredients required to meet ʟ exceed expectations. To enhance customer relationships, CSRs need access to a single enterprise Customer Asset Management solution that includes help desk, customer response, and service tracking features. Extensive customer response and service tracking systems include many capabilities, such as call management and contract administration, service delivery tracking, inventory control features, and invoicing.

Informational Needs for Effective Service   When customers call, they expect: prompt and accurate responses instead of being passed around (telephone tag); their preferences and prior history to be known; and their feedback to be responded to and incorporated in future product improvements. To be fully responsive, customer service representatives need the following:

> Information about product features and availability, problems, and upgrades, along with installation history, warranty, and contract terms.

> The capability to route and track complex queries so that each customer gets the right answer, and so no call "falls through the crack."

> The ability to gather and record valuable information relating users' experiences. This information can help other departments to make better decisions about product development, marketing, and business practices.

Accessing Service Information   By tracking such issues as installation history, warranty terms, and service contracts, companies get a better fix on costs for labor and parts used in delivering service. With information about costs and service revenues, the company can make more informed decisions about pricing of services and service contracts. Far from being a cost center, some modern customer service organizations are enabling actual profits. Why? Information about service operations can help a company not only to better manage service delivery, but also to improve existing products and develop new ones according to customers' expressed desires.

Routing and Workflow Management   To be useful, customer information must be routed to multiple sites, in various report formats, and across disparate technology platforms. It may be important to communicate product design problems to research and development, for instance, which may be

across the country and require certain parts-number codes
sort of generic names customers might use for affected
rt information dissemination, there are workflow manage-
are becoming popular.

is a series of steps that together accomplishes a certain objective. These steps, called activities, are performed either by people or programs. A workflow management system is a software function that drives
and monitors workflows by providing the responsible person with the relevant work items and the pertinent data at the right time. Additional workflow management capabilities include: who is doing what; process cycle
times; process costs; the forms, reports, and information that are required;
and the relationships of workflows in a process. In customer service, workflow management involves support for improving customer satisfaction
with timely and accurate information for the persons responding to customer inquiries, including accurate cycle time estimates (such as product
delivery schedules) and more knowledge about products and services because of global access to all information across all business systems.

Recording Customer Feedback   The contact the customer service area is
likely to have with customers is seldom lengthy, and it is important to ask
questions carefully. By asking the right questions and having the right systems in place for collecting and processing the feedback, companies can begin to harness information to build customer loyalty. Within an enterprise,
the needs for customer feedback vary from one functional department to
another. Financial and accounting areas want information presented in a
certain format; marketing requires another slice of the information with an
entirely different presentation. To maximize the value of the customer feedback, it has to be tailored for the end users.

Further challenges arise as companies' business needs change and as
technology improves—and competitive companies know that change is not
a "sometimes" thing. To compete requires continuous adaptation in the
feedback mechanism. Procedures used for collecting, analyzing, and customizing information reports should be easily and quickly adaptable to
meet the company's ever-changing needs.

11.4 Technology and Marketing Strategy

Historically, marketing managers have developed marketing strategy using
the 4Ps: product, price, promotion, and place. Strategy was developed by
focusing on individual products and their associated metrics (market share,

product performance, and penetration). Today, increasingly customized products and services, new distribution and communication channels, and multiple pricing options are making the marketing process more complex and difficult to manage. Also, the vast amounts of detailed real-time data that must be collected and analyzed to make effective decisions in this environment will require new ways of building information systems.

Firms are discovering that traditional product-oriented marketing management is not sufficient to manage the information-intensive environment. Already, traditional metrics are proving inadequate for measuring marketing activities across multiple product categories, diverse distribution channels, and constantly changing pricing schemes. New information-based metrics will enable organizations to dynamically allocate marketing resources to those activities that generate the best return. In this context several questions emerge:

How can technology help marketing to respond to challenges such as global competition, rising customer expectations, and emerging markets?

What architectures, tools, and applications will be ideal for technology-enabled marketing?

What impact will information availability have on marketing strategy and decision-making processes?

Entering new markets is time consuming, risky, and expensive. How can technology help firms expand into new markets at a low cost?

What cost-effective strategies can organizations use to market and advertise effectively?

To answer these questions, marketing organizations are increasingly looking at new applications of technology in developing marketing strategy.

Marketing Decision Support Systems

Sharper competition means that there is a business imperative for organizations to make decisions quickly. Product innovations and marketing strategies are rapidly copied, so the ability to respond quickly to a changing market becomes the crucial determinant of both profitability and survival. To do this, marketing managers need information that is timely, accurate, and relevant, and that contains the right level of detail.

Data Mining and Decision Support   The architecture that is emerging as an industry solution for marketing decision support is data mining. The most successful data mining solutions are tuned to deliver optimum performance for knowledge workers—easy data access and manipulation—enabling them to use data creatively. This is in sharp contrast to operational systems such as relational databases and online transaction processing (OLTP) systems, which are tuned for repetitive, continual updating with each task, typically using very small amounts of data.

In practice, data mining means that the data in the data warehouse exhibits characteristics that distinguish it very clearly from traditional operational systems. First of all, the data is subject-oriented—organized according to the different ways the managers view it, not for a specific function, process, or application. Second, when data resides in many separate sources, encoding is usually inconsistent, so when it is transferred to the data warehouse, it must be integrated through a consistent naming convention. Third, the data must be time-variant—collected and organized consistently over time for use in comparisons, identifying trends, and forecasting. And fourth, the data is nonvolatile. Once it is in the data warehouse, it is not updated or changed—only reloaded and accessed.

A widely cited example of an Intranet-based marketing application is Silicon Graphics, an industry-leading computer workstation vendor in Mountain View, California. Silicon Graphics has deployed Web front-ends called using a tool called BusinessObjects to more than 1,000 data warehouse users worldwide. Several hundred users access the warehouse via a corporate Intranet. Silicon Graphics is leveraging the Internet as an inexpensive communications platform behind the security of a firewall, providing employees in the United States, Europe, and Asia with direct access to the company's warehouse sales and marketing information. BusinessObjects enables Silicon Graphics to leverage current and historical corporate data stored in the data warehouse to make better business decisions across the organization, from executive management to front-line business managers. Also, by combining a comprehensive decision support solution with an Intranet approach, Silicon Graphics is able to leverage the data warehouse investment and extend the reach of this information worldwide, without making a huge networking investment.

Intranet-Based Decision Support Architecture   Figure 11.2 shows how the Intranet architecture links all the databases together with tools that summarize and aggregate data. Summarization gives tremendous speed of access to data, and information can be enhanced—for example, by adding value with data from other sources. Thus, the marketing manager can gain

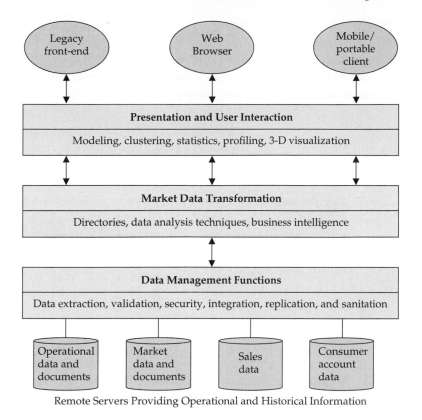

Figure 11.2   Intranet Architecture for Marketing Decision Support

a very quick overview of the situation, or can drill down to the required level of detail on a particular subject. The key in Fig. 11.2 is the use of electronic commerce technology to improve the gathering, analysis, and distribution of information among the sales, customer, and marketing functions. Linking the sales force with regional and corporate offices establishes greater access to market intelligence and competitor information that can be funneled into better customer service and service quality. Companies need to collect market intelligence quickly and analyze it more thoroughly. They also need to help their customers (relationship management) introduce their products to the market faster, giving them a competitive edge.

The architecture consists of three key components: (a) storage and loading; (b) transformation and integration of data; and (c) visualization and presentation of data. Data transformation makes the architecture efficient and effective. This dictates that the database be very flexible and dynamic—capable of supporting creative and inquisitive requests made by managers. Fully integrated directories—which are essentially data about data—are part of the architecture. These directories define how the database is structured, where the data comes from, what it represents, and how it can be used, thus providing applications with the intelligence to select and use only that information relevant to a task. Data visualization for business purposes is a major part of data mining. Managers are always looking for ways to gain new perspectives and insights.

Managers typically request information by sending queries across the network, and they access the results via desktop PCs. A query could be "drilled down" through several layers of summarized and aggregated information. For example, an inquiry into sales in the prior quarter could be extended into displays of sales by product, region, or sales representative. These reports also could be displayed graphically, with summaries of information highlighting problem areas in operations as well as text discussing numerical operating data. Interest in using data mining applications is spreading among middle management as it gives middle and lower managers access to the information with which their superiors are working, and thus allows them to work more efficiently with higher-level management.

Marketing Decision Support Applications

Decision support applications can be divided into the following categories: customer order planning, forecasting, and fulfillment; relationship management; classification trend analysis; and channel management.

Order Planning, Forecasting, and Fulfillment   Successfully meeting customer needs demands controls to ensure adequate inventory. Detailed forecasting, order fulfillment, and direct shipping capabilities guarantee that all channels can meet their obligations. The sales objective is to provide the right input to the overall plan for coordinated supply-chain management. The goal is to process entry and fulfillment of customer orders; decrease order fulfillment cycle times, reduce back orders, and provide information for production and accounting projections through automatic pricing and inventory allocation; and print customer acknowledgments and shipping documents. Most managers often do not realize that order processing and fulfillment processes may exceed 15 percent of the cost of sales.

The goal of customer order processing is to understand demand—what customers want, when they want it, and where they want it delivered. This is fundamental to managing all parts of the supply chain and is the first step under various programs like vendor managed inventory (VMI), efficient customer response (ECR), and quick response.

No matter what the industry, understanding the demand dynamics of the business by understanding customer ordering enables firms to meet customers' needs by improving in-store product availability while controlling inventory costs through improved stock control. Then, when the unexpected happens, firms are able to respond quickly and effectively. Often, the order process is initiated by marketing information systems such as point-of-sale systems in the retail environments.

Customer Relationship Management   The task of managing the relationship with the customer is often left to the marketing function. Today, consumers' wants have more impact on corporate and marketing strategies than ever before. But to what extent do consumers have well-defined wants and preferences? And, can they be trusted to provide reliable information as to what they prefer and what they would buy? If consumers do not have good insights into their own preferences, or if their preferences are unstable and easily influenced, then finding out what customers say they want and analyzing their past purchases provide only part of the needed information.

Management can use technology to globally analyze trends and understand where the sales cycle is breaking down and where resources should be applied. For example, should management concentrate resources on finding more leads, providing more targeted collateral material, streamlining the proposal process, or training the sales people on objection handling? In that case, companies must try to gain a better understanding of their customers by gathering data on the various influences on their purchase decisions and using that information to develop more effective marketing strategies.

Trend Analysis   Data mining is also used for trend analysis. Firms want to know by merchandise classification where the business was coming from. For example, retailers might have known how one particular sweater was selling, but they did not know how the whole classification was selling. With the use of data mining technology, retailers know the precise rate of sale by classification. With this kind of information available, some fast-selling items will see a quicker inventory turn, but some basic items might experience a lower turn because the company will no longer suffer stock-outs on them.

Classification trend analysis also enables sales and profit mix planning. Often, firms did not know enough about the mix of sales—whether they came from regular price, promotion, or clearance. Without this knowledge, firms were challenged to determine which type of mix was most productive for sale events from both a sales and a profit standpoint. With data mining techniques (see Fig. 11.2), firms can adjust inventories and mix plans to maximize sales and profit potential.

One of the key elements of trend analysis is gathering the sales data in real-time. For this, bar code scanning is important. In recent years, many retailers have built a strong marketing point-of-sale and inventory link when they completed the conversion of cash registers to bar code scanners. Since that time, data acquisition speed has been enhanced and the system has been providing sales information that is being translated into better merchandise procurement information. The data is often analyzed or shared with vendors as soon as it is available from the point-of-sale terminals. In this manner, suppliers know how their products are selling as soon as management does. This has led to a major decline in response time and has dramatically improved the company's ability to manage promotions.

Channel Management   While technology allows firms to target the customer directly and react to changes in demand by modifying the distribution chain, it is important for each firm to understand the impact that its marketing mix decisions have on the other members in the supply chain. For example, manufacturers' end-of-quarter promotional pricing in the grocery industry can hurt the costs of other members in the supply chain. To offer superior customer value, each firm has to design a marketing mix strategy that contributes to lower system costs or improved differentiation for the entire supply chain. The goal is to quickly disseminate information about changing operational conditions to trading partners.

Channel management also provides new impetus for integrating marketing processes, distribution, and manufacturing. Wal-Mart is a good example in retailing. Describing its advantages over competitors does not do justice to the extent that Wal-Mart's technological advantages give the company in stock positions, assortment, labor scheduling, distribution, and merchandising by store. For instance, Wal-Mart's sales and inventory planning system helps plan inventories so that markdowns could be reduced. Wal-Mart has been tracking volume by store for years, and is now analyzing the data in 15-minute increments to make advances in its labor scheduling efforts. Compare this to competitors that are still attempting to determine what their gross margin is by quarter for the company. Advances in labor scheduling allow Wal-Mart to improve service levels so that employees are behind the cash registers when they are needed and on the floor when required.

Retailers have made major strides in improving inventory management in basic merchandise lines by implementing automated replenishment systems that are designed to automatically trigger orders based on projected sales demand so that basic merchandise lines are constantly in stock. How does this work? The system analyzes each store's sales history by stock-keeping unit (SKU) against regional sales curves and upcoming promotions. It then measures the estimated sales against inventory on hand and on order, and then electronically transmits the order to the vendor. In turn, the vendor sends an advance ship notice, or electronic packing slip, back to the store for input into the system. When the shipment is ready, the vendor attaches a bar code to each box and stockrooms scan the bar code when the merchandise arrives to verify the contents against the order, which updates inventory on-hand files.

Improved logistics management allows firms to implement other sophisticated systems. For instance, Wal-Mart's logistics system interfaces with a traiting system, a merchandising system that plans SKUs by store based on the demographic and demand characteristics of each store. By using this system, Wal-Mart creates a regional flavor that makes it more attuned to local tastes than other retailers. As part of this strategy, Wal-Mart is beginning to forecast by department, creating store-unique designs by customizing products and facings by store.

11.5 Summary

This chapter discussed the Customer Asset Management functions—marketing, sales, and customer service operations—which form the front lines in the supply chain. Today, these functions are some of the least automated and represent a real opportunity in developing electronic commerce solutions.

Online sales automation systems will result in the changing sales from a science into a thoroughly engineered business process. An organization's sales process, broken into logical steps with dependent activities, can be reflected in its automation system. Automating the sales process serves two purposes. First, it helps all sales people, especially newer ones, to understand what they must accomplish to move a prospect toward a successful sale. Thus, new salespeople are brought up to speed faster and the average competency of the entire sales force is raised.

The role of customer service operations has changed greatly. In the last decade, the customer service function has grown more competitive and complex, and so has the information technology needed to support it. Companies are depending more on customer service operations, both for revenue and information. Operations that have previously gotten by with relatively simple and even homegrown databases are finding they need more robust electronic commerce applications to manage both the bulk and the complexity of their tasks.

Electronic commerce technology, in particular data mining, can have a significant role in marketing strategy. Investing in marketing systems can generate better value because wringing more cost reductions from production-related functions is becoming difficult as incremental technology investments are garnering diminishing returns. This is in sharp contrast to logistics and manufacturing functions (see Chapter 12), where over the past decade, electronic commerce in the form of EDI has been making great inroads.

Chapter 12

Intranets and Manufacturing

Chapter Outline

Today's manufacturing companies are driven by a new set of operating requirements as they face intense global competition and significant unpredictability in both customer demand and material availability. As customers insist on customized products at mass-produced prices, the pendulum has shifted in the direction of flexible, demand-driven manufacturing. In such a competitive environment, companies need to reengineer operations to produce and distribute products effectively at low cost and high quality. To cope, companies have embraced and implemented different manufacturing strategies: manufacturing resource planning (MRP 2), total quality control (TQC), just-in-time (JIT) capacity optimization techniques, and demand flow manufacturing. More recently, companies have realized that the competitive edge comes not from optimizing production or competing on price but from a holistic perspective of managing the entire supply chain, that is, their ability to deliver product faster, shortening the cycle from order to cash receipts.

The supply chain extends far beyond the traditional supplier-to-customer model. It encompasses what is becoming commonly referred to as the "virtual corporation" or extended supply chain. Almost overnight, management of the supply chain has become a critical factor in any manufacturing company's ability to compete effectively in markets at home and overseas. The gap between best-in-class and the average company is widening. Companies who cannot manage the supply chain more competitively are falling behind more rapidly. The competitive edge that can be attained from a well-managed supply chain is hardly trivial. For a computer manufacturer such as Dell Computers, the total logistics costs of managing the movement of product and raw materials can be a difference of 4 to 6 percent of revenue compared to the other performers in that industry. That is a huge margin.

However, the information systems used to implement these strategies have not evolved much and are often based on concepts developed in the sixties with mainframe computing. With the tremendous impact of the Web and Intranet technology, manufacturers are beginning to look toward applications built on these technologies to maintain their edge. For instance, in the area of procurement, manufacturers are using the Internet to be in constant contact with their suppliers and subcontractors to manage inventories and schedule shipments.

By using the Web to interact with customers, manufacturers are exploring new ways: to respond to changing customer demand; to adapt to a changing business climate; to be flexible enough to redesign their processes as control shifts in two directions: "upstream" to suppliers, and "downstream" to customers or retailers; and to operate as one integrated organization while at the same time having decentralized operations. What lies ahead? In this chapter, we examine how electronic commerce and the Web and Intranets in particular can serve as a glue to bring about a more integrated manufacturing and logistics organization. But before discussing technology, it may be helpful to describe in more detail some of the key business requirements in modern manufacturing and logistics.

12.1 Defining the Terminology

First we will define what integrated logistics and manufacturing mean in the context of supply-chain management.

Integrated Logistics

Logistics is a relatively new discipline that grew out of the integration of materials management and physical distribution. Logistics serves as a tool for identifying and effectively managing interfirm linkages in the supply

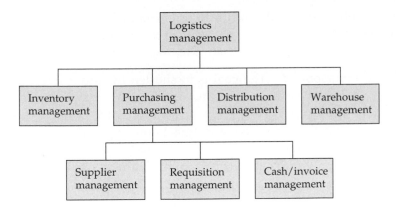

Figure 12.1 Elements of Logistics Management

chain (see Fig. 12.1). Firms that operate in isolation are placing themselves at competitive disadvantage. Not only must firms collaborate internally across business functions, but also they must establish external linkages with other firms.

Essential to optimizing the supply chain is the integration of key inbound and outbound logistics operations to reduce order cycle times, improve service levels, and reduce operating costs. Achieving these strategic goals demands efficient management of logistics operations that focus on optimum utilization of products, materials, resources, and space. The logistics function can be divided into supplier management, inventory management, distribution management, and warehouse management.

Supplier management.   With customized manufacturing there is an increasing need to integrate inventory systems with purchasing and distribution planning. The supply chain plan uses bills of distribution and sourcing rules to simultaneously plan the entire replenishment network, and then automatically release purchase orders to suppliers. The goal is to simplify routine transactions, reduce paper handling, and provide an electronic communications framework for daily procurement activities. Using online item catalogs and approved supplier lists, procurement departments can create requisitions and purchasing documents. Firms can electronically communicate purchase orders, delivery schedules, and associated invoiceless payments to their internal and external suppliers. The trend in purchasing is to reduce the number of suppliers and get them to become partners in business in a win/win relationship. The benefits are seen in reduced purchase order (PO) processing costs, increased numbers of POs processed by fewer employees, and reduced order processing cycle times.

Inventory management.   The goal is to shorten the order-ship-bill cycle. When a majority of partners are electronically linked, information that was faxed or mailed in the past can now be sent instantly. Documents can be tracked to ensure they were received, thus improving auditing capabilities. The inventory management solution should enable the reduction of inventory levels, improve inventory turns, and eliminate out-of-stock occurrences.

Distribution management.   The goal is to move documents related to shipping (bills of lading, purchase orders, advanced ship notices, and manifest claims). Paperwork that typically took days to cycle in the past can now be sent in moments and contain more accurate data, thus allowing improved resources planning. In demand chains that grow ever more complex, the logistics functionality has assumed a significant role in an enterprise's operating environment. Logistics covers these requirements with optimized purchasing operations, sophisticated warehouse management, and precise invoice auditing and materials management, as well as extensive plant management functionality.

Warehouse management.   The goal is to automate the warehouse distribution process, from receiving and put-away to picking and deployment. The goal is to optimize activity in all the functional areas: warehouse administration, receiving, product storage, picking, and shipping.

Agile Manufacturing

Manufacturers are stressing quality and speed. Increased focus on meeting specific customer requirements has led most manufacturing companies to move toward various modes of make-to-order manufacturing. One of the most influential visions of future manufacturing goes by the name of "agile manufacturing." The applicability of a manufacturing system to a variety of manufacturing modes—make-to-stock, assemble-to-order, make-to-order, engineer-to-order—involves a broad range of capabilities.

Product configurability.   With increasing make-to-order manufacturing, product configurability must be flexible and robust enough to support needed material control techniques. This includes the following functions:

Manufacturing data management, which allows the definition and use of product structure and routing information for a wide variety of components and costing needs; and

Configuration management, which automates the configuration and order-entry processes that are executed relative to a customer request for a make-to-specification product.

These specifics are influenced by the nature of the manufacturing process, associated production efficiency, product seasonality, and other variables.

Production execution systems (PES).   PES software tracks the five essential elements of the manufacturing plant floor—materials, equipment, personnel, specifications/work instructions, and facility conditions in real-time—and correlates the data for visibility and control of manufacturing operations. PES software has the following components:

- **Master production scheduling**—identifies future production and procurement actions that need to be taken in response to customer demand as well as day-to-day events, and ties overall business planning to detail operations.

- **Material requirements planning (MRP)**—identifies future production and procurement actions that are needed in response to day-to-day events, and ties overall business planning to detail operations.

- **Capacity planning (CAP)**—allows production control to identify potential capacity bottlenecks and backlog problems so that adjustments can be made.

- **Shop floor control (SFC)**—provides current status of jobs, work-in-process, and production activity to permit performance evaluation, detailed planning, and scheduling.

- **Quality management system (QMS)**—implements quality assurance and quality control functions; integrates with production, procurement, and inventory control.

Material planning, scheduling, and capacity planning must be able to support a variety of lead time, backlog, and plant layout/operational tech-

354   *Electronic Commerce: A Manager's Guide*

niques. This access to comprehensive, up-to-date information about the production process enables manufacturers to identify problems in the areas of cost, quality, service, compliance, and speed. A key component of such a systems strategy is the integration of manufacturing information systems with other supply chain solutions.

12.2 Emerging Business Requirements

Emerging requirements for manufacturing or logistics systems can be generalized into three categories: the changes created by customer behavior; the applications that reflect accepted business practices addressing current business trends and strategies; and the underlying information technology that enables the above applications.

Customer-Driven Manufacturing

Customers dictate how business is done today. Customers determine what is built, how it is built, and when it is delivered. Even the design of many products today is influenced by the customer, not the supplier. An often stated example of successful customization is Levi Strauss, which introduced "Personal Pair" jeans for women in 1994. The Personal Pair jeans, which cost $58 (compared with $48 for a normal pair), are sold through twenty Original Levi's stores in North America. How does it work? A salesperson measures the customer, who then tries on a few sample jeans in order to further narrow down the fit required. The salesperson then uses a touchscreen computer to relay information on the customer's desired size, color, and finish to a company computer that generates a digital pattern, which in turn is transmitted to a Levi's factory in Tennessee. The buyer picks up the custom-fit jeans in the store three weeks later. Since the customer can specify her waist, hip, and other measurements, there are 14,280 possible fit combinations, compared with 52 for traditional Levi's jeans. Personal Pair jeans are produced individually, but in a normal production line. And because the jeans are made to order rather than mass-produced, Levi's and its retailers have less money tied up in inventory. What is more, it is estimated that customization provides Levi's with additional business and higher profit margins [BG96].

Assemble-, make-, and configure-to-order capabilities are supplementing traditional manufacturing methods and forcing manufacturers in many industries into what is known as *product mass customization*, that is, manufacturing products to the specifications of each customer. Even in markets

with slim profit margins, manufacturers are allowing customers to configure the products they purchase. To do so, manufacturers must design products that can be readily adapted to meet the specifications of each customer.

From a business perspective, the initial focus in meeting customization
requirements was on efficiency, or gaining control over operational costs
and downsizing. This perspective has changed today. As downsizing has
reached a point of diminishing returns, the emphasis is shifting from increasing efficiency to increasing revenue and profits.

The focus on revenue growth ultimately translates into the ability to
serve, obtain, and retain customers. In order to do this effectively, companies are finding that they need to compete on their ability to build the product the way the customer wants it, when the customer wants it, and also
deliver the product where the customer wants or needs it. To compete, companies need to find new ways to take orders for products and fulfill the orders in less than a week. In some businesses, firms are offering products
that can be configured, built, and shipped to distributors or directly to the
consumer within twenty-four hours.

In order to implement this strategy, manufacturers need to develop (if
they have not already) a build-to-order or configure-to-order mindset. A
high degree of interconnectivity exists among such finance and logistics
functions as order configuration, order management, fulfillment, and manufacturing. This is a new way of thinking. The companies who recognize
trends and are the fastest to react and make the transition to customer-driven manufacturing will be the ones that prosper in an increasingly demanding and dynamic global marketplace. When flexible manufacturing
was first introduced, those companies with the vision to adopt and implement this new technology achieved an early competitive advantage. Many
of today's leading manufacturers have recognized the new trends and are
responding by making incremental improvements in their systems,
processes, and implementation of technology. The next step is full-scale implementation of new generation information systems that can complement
the new business practices.

Rapid Internal Response to Demand Changes

As stated earlier, customers expect manufacturers to respond quickly to
changing demands. This has forced many manufacturing companies into organizational and operational restructuring. In the case of organizational restructuring, many companies have benefitted from reviewing current
business processes and reorienting them from a department viewpoint to a
view across the enterprise. Eliminating redundant tasks in business processes

has become an important goal for many manufacturers. With operating margins growing ever tighter, businesses cannot afford inefficiency and must eliminate as much waste as possible.

From an operational side, techniques such as "time-fencing," used to buffer changes in demand and manage shifts in schedules, have become less effective because they focus on the supplier and not the customer. Extensive expediting (or logistics management) is becoming the norm, not the exception.

To support demand changes, manufacturers must find new ways to tailor products with the ease, speed, and cost of similar mass-produced goods. For instance, companies are demanding advanced planning and scheduling systems that enable them to perform the equivalent of the material resource planning (MRP) in minutes instead of days that traditional systems take. This allows the companies to run multiple simulations before making a critical decision or deciding on a final production plan.

However, satisfying demand changes requires tremendous management skill. For instance, the need to serve customers better often conflicts with reducing costs. This places manufacturers under pressure to balance service expectations and return on assets. Firms in fast-changing industries such as PC manufacturing are under pressure to deliver highly customized levels of service to their customers. Often, to meet the specialized needs of multiple customers, PC manufacturers must maintain a tremendous investment in assets. However, the assets a PC manufacturer has to carry in inventory in the absence of accurate planning can have a dramatic effect on the overall return on assets.

Efficiently Managing Supply Chain Complexity

Manufacturers need to efficiently manage supply chains that are more complex than ever before. With production efficiency already high in many organizations, one way to increase profits is to reduce inventory, purchasing, and distribution costs. Such pressures have spurred interest in manufacturing and logistics supply-chain management software that link design, manufacturing, and distribution processes through information systems.

Along with cost savings and efficiencies, supply-chain management tools may be able to provide managers with new insight into the production process by focusing on the coordination and fulfillment of customer orders. Why is coordination important? As suppliers upstream and customers downstream become more involved in production and distribution operations upstream, manufacturers want better internal coordination midstream to rapidly meet demand and fulfill orders.

Supply-chain management represents a departure from the way systems were structured in the past, when functional silos ruled the world. Today, companies think in terms of demand management and order fulfillment—a more holistic, interconnected process. To implement this vision, manufacturers are using technology to integrate all the steps involved in creating a product—from design through final assembly—through supply-chain management. Also, the definition of supply-chain management includes both planning and execution, and financial control. Electronic commerce is simply the glue that holds it together. Technologies such as electronic data interchange (EDI), bar-coding, interactive voice response (IVR), and electronic data collection devices enable companies to automate certain transactions and eliminate needless paper handling.

New systems required to support the above requirements are not just manufacturing, nor is it just logistics (or distribution); instead it must be both, with no distinction between the pure logistics and the manufacturing functions. This hybrid architecture would have to integrate execution systems vertically and horizontally across the enterprise, support a process rather than department orientation, and provide complete visibility. Manufacturing and logistics processes would be completely synchronized and linked. Cross-department processes would cascade and would be launched automatically and concurrently, rather than initiated through manual commands in a linear fashion.

12.3 Manufacturing Information Systems

In this section, we elaborate on information systems used in manufacturing. First we present the key differences between discrete and process manufacturing. Then, we outline the various types of manufacturing information systems.

The characteristics of the information systems depend on the type of manufacturing operations, and can be characterized as discrete, batch process, continuous process, or hybrid (combining more than one form). In discrete operations raw material is processed in distinct units. Work-in-process can be tracked by lot, work order, or batch. Typical discrete, lot-based industries include semiconductors; disk drives; and assembly operations in the auto and commercial aircraft industries.

In batch process operations, such as pharmaceutical manufacturing, material is converted from one form or state to another through various processing steps and is tracked by batch, lot, or mass quantity. Material in batch process-type operations may be spread across several conversion steps at once. Batch process manufacturers include fast-food, beverage, pharmaceutical, and chemical companies.

In continuous process operations, such as oil refining, raw material is processed without interruption in a continuous flow. Finally, some producers, such as specialty chemical companies, may require a combination of batch process and discrete operations to manufacture their products.

Discrete versus Process Manufacturing Market

Process manufacturers differ from their discrete cousins in four respects: (1) manufacturing methods, (2) packaging requirements, (3) asset allocation, and (4) product consistency. Discrete products such as automobiles, airplanes, and bicycles are produced by gathering multiple raw material and component inputs to create a single finished product. Process manufacturers, on the other hand, create finished products by heating, mixing, or separating single or multiple inputs to create multiple outputs. Take for instance, PepsiCo., which takes a single input (potatoes) and churns out multiple outputs: mashed potatoes, fries, and chips. Process companies are also distinguished by their relatively diverse packaging and regulatory requirements.

Discrete and process manufacturers differ markedly in their distribution of assets. Discrete manufacturers have a huge investment in inventory at any given moment, including raw materials, work in process, and finished goods. Process manufacturers have a much larger investment in plant and equipment. Allocating costs to finished products based on inventory is relatively straightforward in the discrete arena: the components of a specific automobile model are easily identified, sorted, and traced to the final product. A food processing plant baking saltines, cookies, and various pastries, on the other hand, faces a tougher time in allocating costs and determining profitability by product line.

What Makes Process Manufacturing Different?   Process manufacturing has to support additional requirements and has a different orientation than traditional discrete manufacturing.

> A process plant represents a considerable capital investment in instrumentation and equipment. Therefore, capacity planning is the first priority when developing a master production schedule. Production is typically accomplished via a process line wholly committed to a work order.

> Unlike discrete manufacturing, where work-in-process (WIP) inventory can act as a planning and scheduling buffer between work centers, process environments often have to complete all phases of production within tight

time tolerances. Many products have shelf-life characteristics, or can alter with time. For all these reasons, finite scheduling is often a must.

Process environments almost always have traceability requirements. Whether imposed by governmental regulation or simply a matter of good manufacturing practice, procedures for full traceability have led to a more comprehensive software solution than is typically found in the discrete manufacturing realm.

The process industries also have special requirements not easily dealt with in a bill of material structure. There is often a requirement for the manufacture of coproducts and byproducts, sometimes from several separate stages in a process. Multiple products are made concurrently, and parallel activities must be scheduled to bring intermediate products together for blending or some other process.

Units of measure have to be highly flexible to allow recipes for different batch sizes to be combined. While a bill of material's output is always a single unit, processing ingredient quantities are often expressed as "units per."

Unlike the discrete manufacturing model, quality is intimately tied into a process MRP system. For a chemical/drug manufacturer, potency, grade, acidity, and other parameters can be tied to ingredients listed on recipes and to the actual product. Procedural requirements for sampling and monitoring are also built into the recipe. Test results can be tied to specific customer orders and to product lots ready for shipment.

Process companies face unique problems in product quality and consistency. Manufacturers must ensure the correct proportion of ingredients in their finished goods. Product formulation and processing have a profound impact on a product's yield. Food, chemical, and drug producers face challenges in removing variability created by moisture, spoilage, overcooking, and other problems. Such variability increases the stakes: if a batch fails to meet specifications, it must be destroyed. In short, increased global competition spawned a new fervor among process manufacturers in the 1980s. Consolidation in fast-food, supermarket, and drug chain companies, already surviving on low margins, placed renewed pressure on manufacturers to reduce costs and improve logistics.

Process Manufacturing Industry: Key Challenges   Three key challenges that will define success or failure for process manufacturing firms in their respective industries are: (a) flexible response, (b) cost reduction and traceability; and (c) product consistency/quality.

Flexible response.   Process manufacturers must be able to respond quickly to market trends by supplying their customers with high-quality, low-cost products. Drug stores are forcing pharmaceutical firms to provide electronic communication (such as EDI) in order to integrate their production schedules tightly with their order and replenishment systems in order to avoid stock-outs and minimize lost sales. Fast food chains such as McDonald's are demanding of their suppliers more sophisticated lot tracking as a means to track down problem shipments. A week-long McDonald's promotion for a new chicken sandwich, for example, will accelerate demand for processed chicken throughout the country, leaving the few privileged processed chicken suppliers to McDonald's scurrying to meet demand. The ability to ramp up production rapidly and trace shipments promptly is essential to conducting business.

Cost reduction and traceability.   Just-in-time (JIT) inventory techniques are increasingly implemented by process manufacturers who must balance production capacity with current raw material prices in order to optimize scheduling. Process manufacturers face special inventory challenges because of the perishable nature of their raw materials, which must be properly scheduled to avoid wasting an entire batch of ingredients. Finally, food, beverage, and chemical firms want accurate costing information to make product planning decisions. Rather than accepting dated, arbitrary overhead cost allocations, manufacturers want to be able to trace energy, heating, machining, and indirect labor costs to the production of specific products. Increasingly, process manufacturers want to play what-if scenarios to determine the cost of a recipe modification for a production run of crackers or cookies, for example. Managing the inventory of flour, food coloring, and other chemical ingredients can become a nightmare for the process manufacturer who cannot adequately plan the complex factory scheduling of numerous, dissimilar products.

Product consistency/quality.   Unlike their discrete cousins, process manufacturers face unique challenges in managing and monitoring the consistency of their products. As a beer manufacturer begins to prepare a new batch of beer for production, a certain interval of time passes between the preparation of the ingredients and the time at which the yield becomes acceptable. Better control over ingredients and formula management can improve the yield and reduce the number of hours required for processing. Even a slight reduction in processing hours caused by a quicker realization of the yield, therefore, can significantly reduce costs and free up the machinery for producing the next run of product.

Today, process manufacturers are anxious for software specifically created for managing fixed costs. Discrete manufacturing systems focus on all phases of inventory management, from raw materials through the production of finished goods. Process manufacturers require a more precise allocation of staff, waste, byproducts, and plant costs because of the huge plant property and equipment costs attendant to producing their products. Using discrete automation products for process automation was like fitting a square peg into a round hole. Clearly, there is a market opportunity here.

Types of Manufacturing Information Systems

The goal of applying computer automation to the manufacturing environment is improved efficiency and lowered costs, both direct and indirect. There are several different computer software applications that are designed for various stages of the product life cycle, from computer-aided design to computer-assisted production on the plant floor.

Overview of the Market   Far from being a localized niche, the market for manufacturing software and services comprises over a $3 billion opportunity. Moreover, just 15 percent of the market is penetrated by "packaged" manufacturing software such as SAP or PeopleSoft; that is, noncustomized software supplied by software developers, as opposed to in-house, custom-written programs for mainframe or minicomputer systems.

During the 1960s and 1970s, manufacturers experimented with a variety of mainframe-based automation solutions that frequently required a team of in-house programmers and consultants to write custom programs to solve production scheduling, manufacturing and logistics, and financial cost reporting. Numerous firms began to develop generic automation tools for manufacturers, focusing on materials requirements planning (MRP-1), for the discrete environment. This allowed aerospace, automotive, machinery, and other discrete manufacturers—for the first time—to draw on a well-defined series of tools for their production and cost reporting objectives.

In the last several years, large companies have reduced their dependence on large, expensive, centrally located mainframe computing systems and information systems staffs. This movement toward downsizing or "right sizing" has resulted in the adoption of smaller, cheaper, faster departmental computer systems. The manufacturing sector has mirrored this trend. In fact, most of the major MRP systems for manufacturing run on mid-range computing systems. IBM's AS/400 line has the greatest share, and Digital's VAX computer line is second, followed by Hewlett-Packard's 3000 line. Others account for the rest of the market.

The primary software applications for planning and executing production once a product is designed include: manufacturing resource planning (MRP-2) systems, enterprise resource planning (ERP) systems, manufacturing execution systems (MES), and control systems for automated equipment. In the past, developers used a common-sense approach for identifying the business requirements. This was crucial, because an understanding of business requirements forms the basis for designing and developing manufacturing systems. The process is no different today. However, the business environment changes are much more unpredictable than they were in the past.

Manufacturing Resource Planning   Manufacturing resource planning systems contain functions for planning production and purchase orders using basic planning rules to project capacity and material requirements for a specific job. They may also be able to create dispatch lists and track work-in-process and job costs. MRP is based on the assumption that orders would be collected, grouped together for material requirements explosions, and subsequently organized into "efficient" production runs called the *weekly master production schedule* (MPS).

Traditional MRP systems are not adequate for the customer-driven model of modern business. These systems plan on a daily basis and are often oblivious to the real status of all the resources required at an operation and totally ignorant of the actual processes on the factory floor. Unfortunately, the production process is never that simple, or easy. Detailed scheduling and sequencing must be concerned with far more than available machine time. Customers' change requests or other deviations from the seasonal or production forecast, tooling, labor, engineering drawings, part programs, and other resources are factors that cause disruptions. All of these result in excessive and unnecessary manual intervention.

The realities of manufacturing are seldom reported back to the MRP system in the front office. Changes in starting and completion dates, current status of all jobs in progress, and utilization of resources are all elements that deteriorate the value of MRP. The result is a gaping canyon between the planning and the execution phases.

Enterprise Resource Planning   With the increasing push toward customized manufacturing, the need for flexibility was not addressed adequately by existing MRP systems. Thus, the desire to replace MRP with systems such as enterprise resource planning (ERP) arose. The change in nomenclature reflects the fact that system capabilities go far beyond those of core modules such as material planning, production scheduling, and bills of material.

Although ERP is sometimes thought of as the next generation of MRP systems, it is really much more. Whereas MRP schedules one plant, ERP is strong in support for multiple plants, multiple suppliers, and multiple currencies, and it will schedule an entire multisite, global organization, including such functions as plant management, inventory control, and order processing. These processes are additionally integrated with other applications such as human resources, procurement, transportation/distribution, and accounts receivable.

Enterprise resource planning systems help manufacturers translate forecasted demand or order backlog into a manufacturing plan of raw materials, gross capacity, and production orders for the plant floor. They also track the associated financial and accounting paperwork, and in fact are most commonly associated with financial transaction automation. Since ERP systems only collect historical yield and cost data and do not provide real-time information about the complete status of operations, they do not support the proactive or ongoing management of the actual production process as it occurs.

With the basic functionality needed to optimize a plant's business operations defined, ERP systems have evolved from primarily business/accounting systems into something more fully integrated with both plant-floor operations and the larger concerns of the enterprise, especially logistics management.

However, manufacturers increasingly are recognizing that these tools, while effective in the functions for which they were designed, do not have adequate capabilities to manage the critical variables of the dynamic production process on the plant floor. That is why manufacturing execution systems (MES) were developed.

Manufacturing Execution Systems (MES)   Manufacturing execution systems (MES) are factory floor performance monitoring systems that complement the planning systems. MES allows companies to track, monitor, and control the five essential elements of production: materials, equipment, personnel, work instructions, and facilities. According to Peter Drucker [HBR90], MES systems are necessary because traditional cost accounting measures only the cost of producing. They ignore the cost of not producing (often called indirect, activity-based costing), whether the result of machine downtime or quality defects that require scrapping or reworking a product.

Historically, the factory floor has been far less automated than the resource planning systems—MRP, MRP-2, and ERP. Generally, planning is accounting oriented. It can include functions such as forecasting demand, costing, sales orders management, inventory control, accounts receivable, accounts payable, purchasing, and payroll.

Across many industries, there is a growing need for MES that provide real-time visibility of production capacities, resource constraints, inventory levels, and customer orders. MES facilitates:

Utilization of available resources to be maximized.

Scheduling based on operation-level requirements rather than on time requirements.

Production monitoring via graphic display to track resources, orders, and operations.

The review of different production scenarios prior to actually performing the work.

Electronic verification of each factory order for accuracy against standards; this is increasingly important as quality standards like ISO 9000 are promulgated.

Electronic distribution of work instructions with corrective actions when necessary.

The bottom line is that MES software improves the efficiency of the manufacturing operation and, as such, speeds the time to market. These systems can help improve manufacturing performance, as cost, quality, service, and regulatory pressures on manufacturers increase.

How does MES software work? First, the factory floor receives production orders from the office; then, it must develop detailed production schedules and keep track of quantities, quality, time, and all the nuances of production. MES software monitors floor activities, manages resources, recognizes variances, and applies controls that ensure that internal supply chain objectives are executed and realized. MES software use data derived from the plant floor to provide planners and schedulers with information needed to make intelligent decisions.

Some industries, such as semiconductors, have long seen the benefit of using MES software and are considered to have fully accepted MES as a critical tool for manufacturing. Companies in other industries, such as pharmaceuticals, are not as familiar with the benefits of MES, and are therefore slower to adopt what is to them a still unproven concept. Today, MES vendors are eyeing the supply-chain arena as a logical extension to their present offerings. These vendors have previously focused on planning and real-time data analysis systems for the shop floor. Now, they are looking to link to other enterprise applications modules, both within and external to an organization.

At the same time, as system functionality is becoming more sophisticated, the kinds of computers that support the ERP, MES systems are changing as well. During the past couple of years, many new UNIX and client/server products have come on the market. The client-based decision-support tools pave the way for more extensive use of client/server platforms. Used with existing legacy systems or as part of next-generation system migration efforts, the new "software" products take advantage of the latest Intranet technologies and development tools.

The Future: Integrated Systems   The challenge for the future (and why Intranets are useful) lies in integrating the three elements in a single framework:

- **Resource planning:** the MRP, ERP, and cost accounting systems.

- **Manufacturing execution:** the factory-level coordinating and tracking systems.

- **Distributed control:** the factory floor devices and process control systems.

Why is a single framework necessary? For many years individual plants of large manufacturers or multinationals operated with a high degree of independence. Each plant might run different factory management software, employ different practices for scheduling and quality control, and even use different terminology and measurements for calculating yields, and monitoring key performance indicators, such as rework rates, customer service, unit costs, and lead times. As a result, it was difficult to benchmark or compare plants, transfer products and/or processes, or ascertain and transfer best practices.

The obvious advantage of this situation was that it encouraged each plant to innovate on its own and to make optimum use of local conditions, suppliers, employees, customers, and equipment. The disadvantage was fragmentation; innovations were rarely captured and adopted by other plants. Also, having multiple systems is expensive. A major manufacturer found that they had forty-one different plant floor management systems in place. The result: forty-one systems to maintain, enhance, document, train, provide hot-line support, integrate, and upgrade as technology changed.

To avoid duplicity of effort, many companies realized that the best practices had to be embodied within the systems that were the infrastructure of the company. Common best practices and integration then required common systems! This realization is leading firms toward Intranets, which can provide a common infrastructure to integrate the various resource planning systems and plant management systems, allowing the rapid deployment of best practices as well as the transfer of product and process between plants.

The integration of ERP, MES, and logistics functions is slowly becoming a corporate objective. However, only a handful of manufacturers and system suppliers recognize that for firms to realize greater performance levels, they will need to incorporate production processes as an integral component of their other supply-chain processes. In short, we believe that for large companies who want to share their practices, people, products, and data among plants and functions, common Intranet-based products will become a key standard method.

12.4 Intranet-Based Manufacturing

To maintain a competitive advantage in today's global marketplace, an Intranet-based software solution must take a more contemporary and innovative approach to addressing today's manufacturing issues. A new generation of manufacturing systems should embody these three critical concepts into the standard system design [PSFT96]:

Customer/demand-driven manufacturing.

Real-time decision support and advanced planning and scheduling.

Intelligent process management—proactive notification and event-driven problem solving.

Customer-Driven Manufacturing

Inevitably, information systems must address the change in focus from factory management to demand management. New systems must address changing core concepts in manufacturing, such as cycle time reductions that have been addressed by a number of methods, including JIT and flow manufacturing.

For example, demand can flow into the information system many different ways via EDI, fax, e-mail, Web pages, or a phone call. When demand is received, concurrent processing should occur: inventory reserved; drop-ship requirements placed with suppliers for nonstocked items; production allocated, adjusted, or scheduled; and resources planned. If the demand forces a change in priorities, the system should be able to reschedule resources and immediately notify the user.

Unfortunately, the solutions of today do not take advantage of the latest technology to support the new core concepts effectively. Many present systems are built on the MRP-centric model and are not designed to accommodate customer-oriented production. The overemphasis on incorporating new technology for its own sake has overshadowed the need to rethink and update the business model that traditional MRPII and some ERP implementations were designed to address.

Through creative use of Web and EDI technologies, manufacturers can now communicate directly with consumers and suppliers with little or no human intervention. Technologies like electronic forms, e-mail, and EDI can be incorporated into the system to facilitate flow-through replenishment and fulfillment; electronic commerce (for supplies, raw materials, and finished product); line sequencing and allocation; and demand-driven manufacturing (concurrent and linked processing to the automatic receipt of demand).

Fundamentally, this represents a shift from a predominantly "push" model supported by MRP to a "pull" orientation discussed in Chapter 10. Because the model also implies a closer relationship with the consumer, sales quotation and configuration systems become more important. For example, a configurator and quotation system would allow salespeople to generate a quotation and create a drawing of the product to exact specifications on a laptop in front of the prospect. When the quotation was complete, the sales representative would connect to the host system to download the quotation and receive information generated from a real-time planning and scheduling system.

Real-Time Decision Support

Traditional MRP-2/ERP systems rely on cumbersome, time-consuming batch processing. They are based on single-resource optimization (that is, material, capacity) that is performed in a linear fashion. These work in the batch mode because of the volumes of data required, and can be run during off-hours, typically weekly. However, between the last batch run and the next scheduled run, the plant is operating with outdated and, in some cases, inaccurate information.

As noted earlier, companies are beginning to replace the conventional MRP engine as the core planning mechanism with an advanced system based on real-time planning and scheduling. Advanced planning systems use technology, which allows the user to run the equivalent of an MRP in minutes.

In addition to running the MRP quickly, the planning system allows the combination of multiple resources into single planning runs such as material and capacity or material and costs. Any selection of resources can be combined. Planners can create predictive data models, which can be optimized with one another. Synchronized with the supply-chain execution processes (such as rescheduling, production order creation, purchasing, transfers, capacity leveling, and so on), advanced planning creates a system able to support "fast cycle" manufacturing.

Finally, decision support relies on the use of simulation techniques. The ability to simulate multiple schedules rapidly and review their effect on operations has become a key contributor to successful business management. There is no substitute for actually seeing the effect of changing priorities, using an alternate supply source, adding manufacturing resources, or enacting any other management change.

Intelligent Process Management

All business applications include some administrative workflow elements. Conventional manufacturing systems have typically considered administrative tasks beyond their purview and required them to be handled through manual processes. These tasks included: (a) anything that required approvals such as purchase requisitions; (b) review of exceptions on a periodic basis for lot expiration, material shortages, and cost variances; and (c) sequenced production activity that involves movement from one operation to the next, purchase requisitions to suppliers, and distribution.

Workflow technology targets these types of tasks. Applications like loan processing and human resource management applications—which have a lot of associated manual processing—have used workflow technology to achieve improvements in the quality of work and reductions in processing time and cost. Basically, workflow automates the flow of information from one person (or one company) to another. It uses intelligence to get the right work to the right person at the right time for the right action. It propels business processes through departments and out across the enterprise. By applying workflow technology, the Intranet application becomes a virtual manager, sifting through the information stream using business rules to identify aberrations or out-of-tolerance conditions, and routing work to the operations personnel who can fix the process.

In addition, workflow can also be used for proactive notification. Take the example of credit limit violations in the payment management function. Often, the customer is not aware of a credit problem until an order is placed. With workflow and agent technology, a proactive agent can be established to monitor credit conditions. When the credit limit condition is met, workflow notifies a specified account representative to take action and call the customer. The result is higher customer satisfaction and fewer payment defaults.

Why is the workflow model appropriate for manufacturing? Traditional inventory and materials management applications require each transaction to be pushed through the system. This may also require a small army of operations clerks to sift through the daily material flow reports to determine the state of the business—usually after the fact. As a result, managers know what happened yesterday, not what is occurring right now. An integrated workflow engine can automate, streamline, and control the flow of information across the enterprise, running distribution, manufacturing, and financial applications. Conventional systems do not support this type of inter- and intra-company process interaction. This can be accomplished through the use of workflow in conjunction with technologies such as the e-mail/electronic forms systems, fax recognition software, and EDI.

12.5 Logistics Management

Two terms, "logistics management" and "distribution management," are frequently applied to the processes that move goods through the supply chain. They may appear to be used synonymously, but actually, they have subtly different meanings. It is important to note the difference—because it distinguishes clearly how firms are trying to achieve a competitive edge.

Logistics management, in its widest definition, is concerned with the strategy and management of the movement and storage of materials and products from suppliers, through the firm's distribution systems, to retail outlets and customers. The scope of logistics management for the physical movement of goods starts with the sources of supply and ends at the point of consumption. In today's business environment, good logistics management often determines the success of a business. Retailers are well aware of how excess inventory, frequent stock-outs, poor item turnover, and excessive markdowns can cut into profits. Wholesale distributors have as much as 70 percent of their company's assets tied up in inventory, making timely, comprehensive forecasting a necessity. Logistics management attempts to achieve a balance between holding minimum stock while providing the best service possible to the customer.

New techniques for optimizing the movement of goods through the supply-chain system have become increasingly prevalent over the last few years. Now one regularly sees "quick response" techniques and "vendor-managed replenishment" as terms synonymous with the goals firms are seeking to achieve.

Problems with Traditional Logistics Management

The traditional logistics approach contains three major flaws:

- **Too much inventory.** Inventory buffers in the traditional supply chain drown manufacturers and retailers in inventory on many products at the same time that they are chronically stocked-out of others. The inventory problem is often amplified when firms have a lot of different storage or inventory places in the supply chain. At each stopping point in the chain, someone stores inventory. Add in the effects of error and promotions, and by the time the end of the chain is reached, inventory levels bear almost no relation to actual demand.

- **Too slow to react.** Sluggishness is endemic to traditional marketing/distribution approaches. The system may never catch up with hot product demand because of the disjointed reordering process along the supply chain.

- **One size fits all.** Traditional approaches treat all items in the same manner. Companies carry similar levels of inventory for both volatile and non-volatile items and distribute them through one type of logistics network.

In the past, the warehouse focused on storage and handling of inventory. Stock turns and cycle times were very slow. A truck delivered an inbound load of product to a distribution center. That facility received the product and put it into physical storage. Some time later, after the product was logged into the company's inventory system, it would be picked up against an outbound order and loaded onto an outbound truck. This whole turnaround may have taken several days or even weeks, during which time product sat in inventory.

Today, in logistics-savvy companies, the distribution center receives an electronic notice that product is on its way. The company knows the truck is due at the loading dock at 6:00 A.M. This allows the firm to plan an order against that truck, so when it arrives, workers can pull the product off and scan it into the system, updating the inventory records instantly. The computer tells workers to take certain product off the truck and marry it with picked product or dock product. Workers combine the products into an outbound shipment, and load it onto an outbound truck for customer delivery. Turnaround is almost immediate.

To illustrate how firms are addressing the problems associated with traditional logistics systems, let us examine how Microsoft developed an integrated supply-chain solution.

Case Study: Microsoft Corp. Integrated Logistics

In 1994, Microsoft Corp. decided it was time to rethink its entire production and distribution strategy [IWK96]. Microsoft had always manufactured in and distributed through its own plants and distribution facilities in the Seattle area. Microsoft's logistics network was sluggish and unresponsive to customers, largely because of its location in the Northwest. Most of Microsoft's customers are in the Midwest and on the East Coast, but the distribution facility was in Seattle. This meant that Microsoft had long leadtimes getting product to major markets, which created problems with inventory turns.

Microsoft decided to find a solution that would allow them to cut inventories and get product to market faster. They concluded that inventory management represents the biggest untapped piece of savings and that is where creative logistics solutions tend to offer the biggest gain. Microsoft reengineered its manufacturing approach, as well as its logistics supply chain to achieve the lowest level of investment in inventory consistent with ensuring customer service and maintaining efficient production. It improved manufacturing forecasting accuracy by installing a new demand-forecasting system that takes sales data by SKU (stock-keeping unit) from distributors and combines that with on-hand inventory. The system allows the company to keep its production schedules open until one week before product is delivered and, in so doing, make what the market will consume.

Microsoft needed a manufacturer that could accommodate such short production leadtimes, so it outsourced consumer-products production to a turnkey software producer who had excellent relationships with its raw-materials providers. As a result, the manufacturer was able to reduce cycle time for production and delivery to Microsoft's distribution center from five or six weeks to seven days.

Early in 1995 Microsoft decided to relocate its distribution facility to a high-speed flow-through distribution center in Indianapolis, and outsourced the operation of the facility. That facility handles shipping responsibilities for 70 percent of Microsoft's consumer products, which represent between 15 percent and 30 percent of the company's business, depending on the time of year. From Indianapolis, Microsoft can reach 80 percent of its market within two days, compared with former transit times of seven to ten days. To ensure that the Indianapolis facility did not get bogged down with problem shipments (returns) or slow-moving inventory, Microsoft set up the returns and overrun center in Toledo operated by a third-party warehousing firm. This facility expands and contracts in size as needed.

Microsoft's story points up the difference that state-of-the-art logistics integrated with manufacturing planning can make. As part of an integrated supply-chain management strategy, logistics is both the glue that holds the material/product pipeline together and the grease that speeds product flow along it.

Leading companies are just beginning to move in this direction. The integrated supply-chain view of business is a far cry from the way in which companies saw their world just a few years ago. In the past, companies looked at themselves and their partners functionally, spending a lot of time and effort trying to make each function world-class. The problem was that firms can have world-class functions and still not have a world-class business. Today, management of many companies is looking across horizontal business processes.

Objective of the Modern Logistics Function

The objective of the logistics function revolves around the phrase "delivering the right product to the right place at the right time" (and often added to this is "and at the right quality level"). Such an objective sets out three variables that the logistics function must manage: a predefined service (availability) level for the given range of products; cost levels, which means controlling the efficiencies of operation; and minimizing inventory levels throughout the chain.

The objectives set for a retail logistics function typically include: deliver the product ordered by the store on time, in good condition, at the correct temperature and intact, with documentation that is the minimum required for the accuracy and efficiency of operations, and all at a minimum cost. To accomplish the objectives stated above, information needs to be passed up and down the supply chain so that each function in the chain is informed of the requirements and status of the products they distribute.

High-velocity flow-through distribution systems are completely dependent on information. Unfortunately, lack of sophistication in logistics information systems is one of the biggest roadblocks to channel integration today. Most companies still focus on transactional systems that manage order processing, inventory, shop-floor production, and other discrete business functions,. These systems offer little visibility into what actually is occurring in the enterprise.

Although transaction systems are important to a company's day-to-day operations, they do not enable quick, strategic decision making that is becoming the hallmark of well-managed companies. Planning and decision-support systems need to tap into the data in the transaction systems to build a complete view of the company's manufacturing, logistics, and purchasing activities.

Logistics visibility is particularly important for large companies such as Xerox Corp. that source, manufacture, and ship globally. Unfortunately, Xerox's old proprietary system could not perform that kind of tracking; this created unnecessary problems and expenditures for Xerox. In 1993, Xerox formed a team to figure out what the ideal system would look like. Nearly a year was spent getting to understand current flows and how to reengineer them. At the end of 1994, Xerox began replacing a combination of internal tracking systems with one centralized database carrying the corporation's worldwide material flow. Xerox wanted to achieve complete worldwide material-flow visibility. This visibility allowed Xerox to see where product is in the channel and to make decisions on what is being built on the manufacturing lines, what distribution points are doing, and how to avoid using premium freight service, and more [IWK96].

The ability to pass information from the point of customer demand through to the raw-material provider has very exciting implications in terms of being able to plan and reduce the variability of forecasts. When firms eliminate demand uncertainty, they can reduce inventory, not just for one company, but for all parties in the channel.

Forecasting

Forecasting is an important part of logistics and inventory management. A good inventory management system should produce forecasts that are stable in the face of random fluctuations, but responsive to real changes in sales. Forecasts must account for sales promotions and seasonal changes. Forecasting is used to increase sales while minimizing the amount of inventory held within the business. This can be accomplished by spotting changing trends, enabling the business to react quickly.

A good forecasting system relieves the inventory analyst of juggling with many complex questions related to the restocking of inventory, and provides recommendations on when and how much to order. Forecasting employs historical sales data and uses advanced forecasting algorithms to make an accurate estimate of future demand. A good forecasting system will handle "normally behaved" items with minimal interference, allowing the inventory analyst to concentrate on the more out-of-line situations.

Forecasting is complicated by seasonality. There is a seasonality factor in all forms of retailing. For instance, in the fashion industry, each season has new styles and colors. Seasonality can also be weather-related or event-related. In food, Christmas puddings are only sold before Christmas. In sports goods, more tennis racquets are sold during or just after Wimbledon than at any other time. A seasonal profile defines the recurring peaks and troughs of demand, and it is important that retailers understand the seasonal patterns of products for accurate demand forecasts.

Purchasing

Purchasing is the act of placing an order on a supplier. This can be broken down into three major activities.

Purchase Contract Management   Contract management is in essence the long-term relationship between a buyer and a supplier. Once the decision has been taken to purchase goods from a particular supplier a contract is set up. A food retailer will set up a contract to supply beans at a certain price and call orders off as and when required. In the fashion industry the contract may only be an agreement to buy and may only contain the final agreed numbers that the retailer will take and the price at which they will buy. The decisions about which color and size and in what quantities the supplier will deliver are left to the last possible moment, so that the retailer can make the best judgment possible based on real sales trends. A retailer will often not order shipment of a large percentage of his order until after the season starts to enable him to make a final decision based on the actual performance in the stores. Contract management is therefore the management of the supply of the agreed goods.

Purchase Order Management   Purchase order management concerns reviewing required order quantities, placing an order on a supplier, and managing payment for goods received. In the last five to ten years, the placing of orders via EDI has become increasingly common. This reduces the lead time in the supply chain as suppliers receive orders quickly and can dispatch goods earlier. Typically a purchase order is directed at a single supplier and contains: supplier name and address, unique purchase order number, delivery date and time, delivery address, and description and quantity of line items required.

Receiving and Warehouse Management   Receiving, often called goods-in, is the process of accepting goods or merchandise into the warehouse. The goods are counted and checked against the purchase order that is supplied by the driver. As the goods are received, the stock position in the warehouse is updated and accounts payable is notified that the order from the supplier has been accepted. Most retailers have some form of quality control at receiving. Quality control personnel take a sample of the goods that are received and perform an audit against the quality standards of the organization.

Distribution Management

Once goods are received, they must be stored or "put away" into a warehouse. Distribution management is concerned with the movement, storage, and processing of orders for finished goods, typically once a product has entered the retailer's direct area of responsibility. As such, distribution management is about the planning, coordination, and control of the physical movement of goods once they have entered its area of control (the distribution center, supply depot, or warehouse).

The following terms define the processes within distribution management.

- **Distribution requirements planning (DRP):** the process by which the logistics system builds the relevant plans for capacity loads on warehouses, labor, transport, and fleet management. The system assesses the quantity, type, and location of distribution centers throughout the area the distribution system is required to serve.

- **Physical inventory management (PIM):** the measurement of the levels of stockholding and frequency of restocking for products. PIM will determine inventory levels, service level management for the business, allocation to stores and replenishment, inventory control at all levels, stock counting and control, and reallocation between depots and stores.

- **Warehouse management:** the processes of stock location management, product putaway and picking, receiving, and dispatch, as well as performance monitoring of these processes. The basic aim of warehouse management is to achieve a balance between the cost of the operation and the desired level of service to the stores. The associated costs are split into three categories: labor, space, and equipment. The level of service provided will be determined through effective practices and procedures to receive, store, retrieve, and dispatch the goods. This is usually measured by testing the accuracy of the pick against the desired quantity. Picking is the process of selecting products from storage and sorting them by store based on orders.

- **Transport and fleet management:** the process of selecting the modes of transport and how they are managed. This often includes fleet planning, fleet management, load planning, vehicle scheduling, route planning and scheduling, delivery scheduling, and vehicle tracking and monitoring.

- **Labor management:** the processes of labor and workload planning, labor performance monitoring, time and attendance recording, and personnel and payroll information.

In the distribution chain, the warehouse (or distribution center) plays an integral part by creating an identified break between the supply and demand aspects of any business. Historically, the physical nature of the operation has emphasized the degree of its labor intensiveness. However, the introduction of bar-coding technology, hand-held scanners, and EDI has changed the emphasis to being system driven, offering the opportunity for increased effectiveness.

12.6 Electronic Data Interchange (EDI)

Computer-to-computer exchange of business information has become an increasingly popular form of electronic commerce. EDI is important because it enables firms to exchange business information faster, more cheaply, and more accurately than is possible using paper-based systems. Take, for instance, logistics. Key areas in the logistics communication channel are likely to include: the order processing system, the demand forecasting, the sales recording system, and the stock reordering system. EDI works like a glue to support the movement of this information through the supply chain.

EDI is used in manufacturing, shipping, warehousing, utilities, pharmaceuticals, construction, petroleum, metals, banking, insurance, retailing, government, health care, and textiles, among others. EDI was first used in the transportation industry more than twenty years ago, by ocean, motor, air, and rail carriers and the associated shippers, brokers, customs, freight forwarders, and bankers.

What exactly is EDI? EDI consists of standardized electronic-message formats (transaction sets) for business documents such as requests for quotations, purchase orders, purchase change orders, bills of lading, receiving advices, and invoices. These six types of documents constitute 85 percent of the official communications associated with commercial transactions in the United States. These transaction sets allow computers in one company to talk to computers in another company without producing paper documents. To move to EDI, a company must have computerized accounting records and establish trading partners who agree to exchange EDI transactions.

A typical EDI configuration will involve translation software (to perform document conversion to a standard format) at all participating sites, with a standard communications package to shuttle the converted documents between locations. On arrival, standard documents are converted again to the internal format, a relatively straightforward business, but with compelling economies of scale.

Benefits of EDI

The benefits of EDI are cost reductions from eliminating paper document handling and faster electronic document transmission. Other benefits include:

1. Improvements in overall quality through better record keeping, fewer errors in data, reduced processing time, less reliance on human interpretation of data, and minimized unproductive time.

2. Reduced inventory. EDI permits faster and more accurate filling of orders, helps reduce inventory, and assists in JIT inventory management.

3. Better information for management decision making. EDI provides accurate information and audit trails of transactions, enabling businesses to identify areas offering the greatest potential for efficiency improvement or cost reduction.

Firms are adopting EDI as a fast, inexpensive method of sending invoices, purchase orders, customs documents, shipping notices, and other business documents. The improved ability to exchange documents quickly tends to speed up business processes. Furthermore, these processes can be closely monitored, providing the companies with the ability to trace, manage, and audit the operations. Such flexibility allows firms to adopt business techniques aimed at removing the bottlenecks and making the business processes more efficient.

EDI in Action

The idea behind EDI is very simple. EDI takes what has been a manually prepared form or a form from a business application, translates that data into a standard electronic format, and transmits it. At the receiving end, the standard format is "untranslated" into a format that can be read by the recipient's application. Hence, output from one application becomes input to another through the computer-to-computer exchange of information. The result is an elimination of the delays and the errors inherent in paper-based transactions. The benefits of EDI can be seen by comparing the flow of information between organizations before and after its implementation. For this purpose the purchasing application provides an ideal scenario. In general, EDI has been used extensively in the procurement function to streamline the interaction between the buyer and seller. Other uses for EDI are also prevalent. Universities use EDI to exchange transcripts quickly. Auto manufacturers use EDI to transmit large, complex engineering designs created on specialized computers. Large firms use EDI to send to customers online price catalogs listing products, prices, discounts, and terms.

Figure 12.2 shows the information flow when paper documents are shuffled between organizations via the mailroom. When the buyer sends a purchase order to a seller, the relevant data must be extracted from the internal database and recorded on hard copy. This hard copy is then forwarded to the seller after passing through intermediate steps. Sellers receive information in the form of letters and in some cases facsimiles. This information is manually entered into the internal information systems of the recipient by data entry operators. This process generates a considerable amount of overhead in labor costs and time delays. The reproduction of information also increases the risk of errors caused by incorrect data entries.

This pervasive practice of converting digital data into hard copy data that is reconverted into electronic information again on the receiving end generates unnecessary costs. It is quite possible to exchange the information

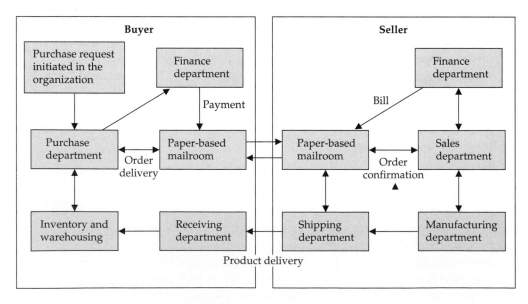

Figure 12.2   Document Flow without EDI

in its electronic format by means of other carriers. Such carriers include magnetic tapes and diskettes and, more recently, the EDI third-party services. The use of EDI carriers saves administration costs by reducing paperwork. Furthermore, the accessibility of the information is improved, which enables a more efficient audit of the operations.

EDI can substantially automate the information flow and facilitate management of the business process, as illustrated in Figure 12.3. The EDI transactions for a purchase, shipment, and corresponding payment are as follows:

Step 1. Buyer's computer sends *purchase order* to seller's computer.

Step 2. Seller's computer sends *purchase order confirmation* to buyer's computer.

Step 3. Seller's computer sends *booking request* to transport company's computer.

Step 4. Transport company's computer sends *booking confirmation* to seller's computer.

Step 5. Seller's computer sends *advance ship notice* to buyer's computer.

Step 6. Transport company's computer sends *status* to seller's computer.

Step 7. Buyer's computer sends *receipt advice* to seller's computer.

Step 8. Seller's computer sends *invoice* to buyer's computer.

Step 9. Buyer's computer sends *payment* to seller's computer.

The purchase order confirmation is the seller's acceptance of the price and terms of sale. Note that the various internal departments are aggregated and called *buyer* and *seller* to simplify the description. All the interactions occur through EDI forms and in most cases are generated automatically by the computer (see Fig. 12.3).

Why Has EDI Adoption Lagged?

Even with proven benefits, EDI has not seen widespread acceptance because of some specific limitations. These limitations are discussed next.

High costs.   EDI applications are costly to develop and operate. The high cost of development increases prices and increases the entry barrier for new entrants.

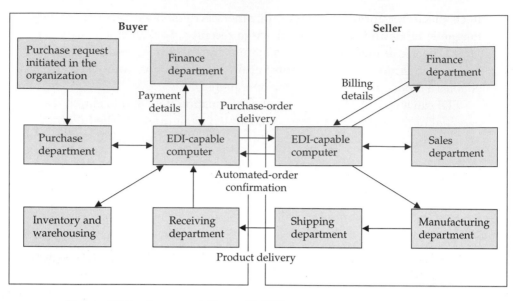

Figure 12.3 Document Flow with EDI

Limited accessibility. EDI applications do not allow consumers to communicate or transact with vendors in an easy fashion. For example, to do business with a company, a supplier must subscribe to an online service called Value-Added Network (VAN), which then provides proprietary software with which to communicate with the firm registered with that service.

Rigid requirements. EDI applications usually require highly structured protocols, previously established arrangements, and unique proprietary bilateral information exchanges. Those requirements involve dedicated connections or VANs. For example, EDI requires transacting parties to follow rigid agreements about the structure and meaning of data. These agreements are time-consuming to negotiate, inflexible, and difficult to maintain, especially in a changing environment. The resulting costs and lead times create barriers to investment in EDI applications by small companies, and inhibit its expansion beyond large companies and their trading partners.

Partial solutions. EDI applications automate only a portion of the transaction process. For example, although the ordering of a product can be nearly simultaneous, the supporting accounting and inventory information, payment, and actual funds transfer tend to lag, often by days. This time lag, and the decoupling of the accounting and payment information from the ordering and delivery of goods and services that results, increases the likelihood of discrepancies, requiring expensive and time-consuming reconciliation. Ideally, an electronic commerce application should eliminate these gaps between ordering, distribution, and payment, and enable real-time links to record keeping and accounting systems.

Closed world. EDI applications are very narrow in scope. The Web is beginning to break the "closed world" of EDI proprietary architectures. The "open world" of the Web makes it easier for suppliers to enter into market, creating a more efficient marketplace.

12.7 Summary

This chapter discussed the interplay between electronic commerce and manufacturing in order to ensure higher quality, reduced costs, and increased responsiveness. Existing supply-chain management solutions have failed to address the critical need for links between logistics activities and those in production. These management solutions addressed customer order management, procurement, logistics management, and distribution warehousing, but not production. Yet, it is often the internal production process that serves as the chain's most volatile link. For manufacturing industries, such as pharmaceuticals, chemicals, and semiconductors, the factors used by the marketplace to evaluate supply-chain performance are not limited to supply-chain activities. They also include capabilities for product traceability, strict compliance reporting, quality management, and high-capacity availability to meet demand requirements.

The chapter also discussed the logistics function as part of a cohesive supply-chain infrastructure from transportation to production management to accomplish the following objectives: reduce cycle times; gain greater efficiencies and increased productivity; reduce costs; achieve on-time and accurate deliveries; create less paperwork; and obtain online data access to inventory, capacity availability, and to order status. The conclusion reached was: To make enterprise-wide gains in cycle time, costs, and delivery performance, attention must be applied to all aspects of the supply chain simultaneously—including production—as one integrated whole. Without a unified approach, what one business process attains in performance, the others shoulder in losses, ultimately bringing down the entire organization's performance. Clearly, more thought needs to be devoted to integrated enterprise-wide business processes, supported by information systems that provide supply-chain visibility, intelligent planning, and scheduling and execution controls.

Chapter 13

Intranets and Corporate Finance

Chapter Outline

This chapter focuses on the use of Intranets for corporate real-time decision support. The true competitiveness of a firm is determined by the ability of its management to make accurate, timely decisions that improve profitability and long-term prospects. To make these decisions, an organization must possess knowledge about various customers, products, and suppliers, the availability of assets, the status of commitments, and the profitability of activities.

While most organizations have sophisticated transaction systems that collect operational data, the information that managers require for decision making and performance measurement purposes is not readily available. This is why companies are focusing increasingly on the question: How can we transform voluminous data about various supply-chain activities into useful information?

So, what is the problem? There is too much detailed data and not enough information. Firms seeking to gain a competitive advantage by making smart decisions are hampered by the inability to turn data into nuggets of information. Why? Because developing a response to an emerging business situation means sifting through large amounts of data from business units or product lines. To enable large-scale data analysis, firms are increasingly using online analytical processing (OLAP).

The problem is not just limited to tools for analyzing the data. Accuracy, timeliness, and accessibility of the data are also important. With management facing increasing pressure to make profitable decisions faster, they need to be free of the constraints of time and space to access distributed data from their office, home, or "the road," twenty-four hours a day, seven days a week. The next generation of Intranet applications will be required to provide access to the full range of corporate data needed to make strategic decisions. This might involve developing software "agents" that pull together information from a variety of relational and legacy systems at regular intervals to construct an integrated view of business activities. These "agents" then transform the data into a consistent, easily accessible format and distribute it where needed for decision making.

In this chapter, we examine the role of Intranets in financial management: How can companies deal with all that financial information? What is the role of electronic commerce and in particular, Intranets, in the financial information management process? Then, we examine the role of Intranets in the area of human resources management, especially benefits management. Finally, we examine the role of Intranets and the Web in enabling OLAP and real-time decision support. Table 13.1 summarizes the business problem and the solution requirements.

Table 13.1 Summarizing Intranet-Based Decision Support Requirements

Business Problem	Nonintegrated islands of valuable information.
	Nonintegrated financial, accounting, and human resource applications.
	Need for analysis tools and decision support function for management.
Solution	Fully integrated Web-based enterprise-wide financial, accounting, and human resource infrastructure.
Requirements	Application partitioning that allows flexible client/server design.
	Multiple servers/databases must be supported.
	Tailorable/intuitive user interface.
Benefits	Integrated information across business functions.
	Improved data analysis and decision support.
	Cost savings from increased efficiency.

13.1 Intranets and Finance

The competitive business environment is forcing firms to reengineer financial management processes. General ledger systems and spreadsheets—common tools of the traditional process—prove woefully inadequate when data is voluminous and worldwide; when corporate structures change because of mergers and acquisitions; and when timely and reliable consolidations, budgets, and forecasts are essential. In this section we provide the setting by elaborating on what financial information systems are intended to accomplish. We then explain why there is a need for functionality change and what will change in existing systems. Finally, we explain how Intranets can help.

What Exactly Are Financial Systems?

A financial system encompasses business processes, procedures, controls, and data dedicated to the operation and maintenance of corporate financial objectives. It incorporates the following tasks:

Report and analyze financial data.

Simplify the budgeting and forecasting process, enabling better planning.

Control the financial consolidation of actual results.

Answer *ad hoc* requests efficiently.

Improve cost control and performance measurement.

Financial systems are often triggered by events having financial consequences such as the receipt of appropriations or other financial resources; acquisition of goods or services; payments or collections; recognition of guarantees, benefits to be provided, or other potential liabilities; or other reportable financial activities. Technically speaking, financial systems have the following characteristics: a common database, common data element definitions, and standardized processing for similar types of transactions. A financial system includes multiple applications that are integrated through a common database or are interfaced, as necessary, to meet defined data and processing requirements.

What Do Financial Systems Do?

Just to add perspective, it might be useful to review what financial and accounting systems are supposed to do. Financial systems software developers need to understand the new business requirements that are emerging in terms of business functionality rather than emphasizing the technical architecture. Why? To be successful, the technical architecture needs to address the business issues and requirements, not vice versa.

Accounting Systems   Accounting captures a firm's financial data, records and aggregates them, and prepares statements that communicate to decision makers relevant information about business units, transactions, and events. Accounting was originally meant to keep track of what a merchant owed and what was owed to a merchant. The early accounting information systems processed transactions, stored historical information, and used that information to answer questions about the past, present, and future. Today, accounting has evolved from basic bookkeeping into a collection of methods for capturing and transforming financial data.

An important dimension of accounting is to report on the financial position of the firm and the performance of various business units to facilitate decision making. In this context, accounting is usually classified into two types: financial and management accounting. Financial accounting collects, classifies, and reports financially based transactions subject to numerous disclosure requirements. The reports provided by the financial accounting system are to be used by sources external to the organization such as shareholders, investors, creditors, financial analysts, and the IRS. Financial accounting activities include: (1) collecting, processing, maintaining, transmitting, and reporting data about financial events; (2) supporting financial planning or budgeting activities; and (3) supporting the preparation of financial statements.

Management accounting provides a financial analysis of management decisions and activities. As such, the reports generated by the management accounting system are to be used by organizations internally. In essence, management accountants prepare the report card by which operations managers are evaluated. Compared to financial accounting, management accounting is fairly new, having evolved from simple cost accounting systems. Management accounting activities include: (1) reporting historical transactions to internal and external parties; (2) accumulating and reporting cost information; (3) safeguarding the assets of a company; and (4) providing insight with respect to the value of future transactions.

Corporate Performance Measurement Systems   In recent years the discipline of accounting has come under criticism for its lack of relevance to managing in a fast-changing environment. How well are financial information systems doing their job? *The CPA Letter* [CPA96] said this about the accounting process: "The financial community is not having its information needs met by financial statements." The accounting process seems to provide too little (or too much) information, too late. There is a growing concern among executives that accounting measures that provide performance yardsticks, such as return on capital, cash flow, and net margins are inadequate tools for strategic decision making.

So, what is the solution for accounting inadequacies? Today, many executives consider performance measurement the cornerstone of their management system. Why? While accounting systems provide reams and reams of financial data, they often tell firms a lot about what had happened in the past, but do not show what levers companies needed to pull to create growth opportunities and future value. In other words, existing financial reporting systems, robust though they may be for communicating with capital markets and regulators, are ineffectual at helping managers run their businesses. Critics cite numerous problems, including a lack of predictive power and an inability to track the value of intangible corporate assets such as business processes. For operations executives, financial measures must be made meaningful to the day-to-day work of employees and their managers.

In breaking away from traditional, accounting-based performance criteria, a growing number of businesses worldwide are attempting to navigate today by a mix of "soft and hard" measures, including customer satisfaction, quality, innovation, yield, reliability, and, of course, financial soundness. The information necessary for measuring performance can be at three different levels: (1) the individual business unit performance measures; (2) the system-level performance measures—the performance measurement system as an entity; and (3) the relationship between the performance measurement system and the environment within which it operates.

At the individual business unit level, performance can be analyzed by asking questions such as: What performance measures are appropriate? What are they used for? How much do they cost? What benefit do they provide?

At the next higher level, the system can be analyzed by exploring issues such as: Have all the appropriate elements (internal, external, financial, nonfinancial) been covered? Have measures that relate to the rate of improvement been introduced? Have measures that relate to both the long- and short-term objectives of the business been introduced? Have the measures been integrated, both vertically and horizontally? Do any of the measures conflict with one another?

And at the highest level, the system can be analyzed by assessing whether the measures reinforce the firm's strategies; whether the measures match the organization's culture; whether the measures are consistent with the existing recognition and reward structure; whether some measures focus on customer satisfaction; and whether some measures focus on what the competition is doing.

A set of operating performance measurements that incorporates nonfinancial as well as traditional financial measurements is needed to measure operating performance and improvements. It is imperative that the technology support the performance yardsticks used by firms. It is also important that the measurement system be flexible, that is, continually reviewed and revised, as the environment and economy change.

So what information do managers want from the next generation of financial information systems? Basically information that reduces uncertainty. Information systems should take data from transactions and turn it into knowledge useful for managing the business process. Of course, the details that managers need differ depending on the level of the manager in the process. The CEO of a company needs to guide the overall course of the company. Mid-level managers need to monitor and control the specific functions for which they are responsible. Lower-level managers need to be sure that the day-to-day details are taken care of. Needs are different at all levels of a business and in different functions of the business. All these pieces need to fit together so that the organization as a whole is operated effectively and efficiently. The glue that holds the pieces together is going to be Intranets. Table 13.2 summarizes the business issues that need an Intranet solution.

Table 13.2 Summarizing the Performance Measurement Problem

Business Problem	Managing information about monthly progress toward annual goals of the organization.
	Providing management with many standard performance reports in a timely fashion.
	Allowing managers to spend time manipulating, not gathering, the data.
Intranet Solution	Create a central database of measurement information using the Web.
Requirements	Use the Web for end-user interface.
	Give users easy-to-use forms for querying information.
	Use a data warehouse to store information.

Financial Intranets

Finance and accounting software has typically been characterized as dull, not trendsetting. Accounting software, for instance, provided a way to enter transactions and manage those transactions in the form of an audit trail. This was the primary focus of accounting software: transaction entry and behind-the-scenes management of the audit trail, critically important but not terribly exciting stuff.

Today, there is a lot more that business managers need from the information locked inside accounting databases. In short, the information is there but it is very difficult to obtain. Intranets can play a big role in solving this problem because they will allow the integration necessary to provide accounting information that managers need, in the specific form they need, when they need it, and where they need it.

Well-managed companies watch their financial indicators carefully and set clear financial objectives for their line managers. Providing access to important financial information securely and in an easy-to-use, online manner is a top priority at many firms. By using internal Web applications, finance departments can begin to more easily disseminate this information to key managers by securely "posting" corporate finance information or by providing simple forms-based query capabilities. This will allow information to take the form of hundreds of specific views rather than one general view or report, like the typical set of financial statements.

New systems technologies offer integration and make it possible for information to be put into a system once and moved to all the different places. This frees accountants from having to spend time manually moving information from one place to another because there was no other way to accomplish the task. Accountants need to recognize the inevitable changes technology is going to bring about and must look for new ways to add value to the business. This value must be in alignment with the needs of the business process.

Finally, large financial systems developed in the era of mainframes have become too costly to maintain, troublesome to document, inefficient, ineffective, or even strategically dangerous as they are difficult to change as business conditions evolve. This viewpoint—widespread dissatisfaction with current accounting systems—is echoed by a Deloitte and Touche study of senior-level financial and accounting executives at 200 corporations. Sixty-eight percent of the respondents stated they plan to implement a new system within the next two years. From this population of respondents, 80 percent intend to purchase packaged solutions and 64 percent want client/server hardware platforms. These statistics suggest that systems based on new technology are well positioned to benefit from a major surge in demand expected to occur over the next few years.

The rapid growth of Intranet accounting applications is partly a replacement cycle phenomenon. It is estimated that the average enterprise general ledger in a "Fortune 1000" company is believed by some to be about fifteen to seventeen years old. Virtually all of these are running on mainly IBM mainframes. A significant majority are internally developed applications. Replacement of these old applications is being driven by high maintenance costs and the desire to enable accounting to provide decision support data and facilitate business process reengineering.

What Should Financial Intranets Do?   Successful Intranet implementations must help tackle four thorny problems that existing systems are not well equipped to handle:

1. Lack of insight into production control. Current systems do not produce accurate product costs for pricing, sourcing, product mix, and responses to competition.

With the increasing amount of global sourcing, financial flows related to production are getting pretty complicated. Currently, managers rely on a patchwork of systems to support financial management activities, such as accounts payable, accounts receivable, fixed-asset management, purchasing, and general ledger. These systems worked well when their primary responsibility was to collect and present historical information. Not surprisingly, most of these systems are only equipped to handle routine transactions, and little consideration is given to their connection to other business activities. For example, if the general ledger and the procurement systems were linked through an integrated information process, the financial analyst would have an accurate picture of accounts payable. Clearly, by integrating financial functions into decision making, the organization can assess the financial consequences of its strategic and operational decisions on a timely and accurate basis, regardless of the type of decision or where it is made.

2. Lack of insight into how daily operations are affecting short-term and long-term strategy. The current systems encourage managers to contract to the short-term cycle of the monthly profit-and-loss statement.

While many financial systems make the accountants happy, they often fail to give requisite operating information to line managers or provide performance information to senior management on a timely basis. To be useful, strategic information must be culled from the morass of operational data being stored; overnight batch reports are no longer sufficient. Managers need to operate in discovery mode. In the near future, the title of CFO (chief financial officer) could become CAO (chief analytical officer), with a bigger role in modeling the whole business operation. The ability to construct queries on the fly and to quickly ask follow-up questions that drill deeper into the data with each successive query is necessary to allow managers to better understand the business environment before making critical decisions.

Consider the realm of customer intelligence systems. Managers can rarely predict in advance what information they will need, other than that used to track historic performance of previous business decisions. Changing market conditions and specific business situations, such as inventory levels and detailed analysis of customers' behavior (derived by mining customer, transaction, and product data), can point analysts down potentially profitable paths that they could not have anticipated. For example, even a simple question about pricing can lead to more detailed queries about the customer base, such as: Where are we losing market share? What products are our competitors advertising? What type of customers buy on sale and when? What combinations of products are the customers buying? To accommodate such a stream of questions, the systems should be developed to help managers make better strategic decisions.

3. Lack of insight into cost control. Existing accounting information provides little help for reducing costs and improving productivity and quality. Indeed, the information might even be harmful.

New technology must be used to achieve better cost control. As businesses in the 1990s focus on downsizing and cost control as means to survive, there is a growing need for quicker, more accurate, and more useful information that allows companies to perform better financial management. Unfortunately, this is easier said than done. Many companies, especially those that are large or highly decentralized, are finding it difficult to get at the information they need to effectively manage their business. Saddled with inflexible legacy systems and a variety of different accounting methods, these companies have difficulty handling simple reorganizations, let alone using their financial information to manage strategically in a rapidly changing world.

4. Lack of control over report generation.

To illustrate the problem, imagine this recurring scene between a chief financial officer (CFO) and his finance manager (FM):

CFO: What is this?

FM: It's the report on corporate travel accounts that you asked for last month.

CFO: What took you so long? And why is it so voluminous?

FM: Well, the MIS department gave it top batch priority. However, they were busy generating numbers for the annual report.

CFO: But all I wanted to know was how much we were spending on travel. Why can't they just give me the numbers? I don't have time to digest all this data.

FM: Well, the numbers are on the first page. The rest of the report explains what they mean. You see, every department defines travel costs in a slightly different way.

CFO: Isn't travel the same everywhere?

FM: Not really. The software group includes airfare and taxis in its travel account, while sales charges airfare to a separate account and includes the costs of meals and hotels in the travel account. On the other hand, the engineering group doesn't do much travel, so it charges everything to general expense. And finally, corporate headquarters believes in tracking the costs of every hour, so it includes the labor cost of travel time.

CFO: I can't believe that something so simple can be made to be so complicated.

FM: Actually, it's worse than that. We only figured all of this out after we sorted through all of the different coding schemes that were used. Did you know that we're using five different accounting systems? And each one uses a different way of coding accounts!

CFO: Incredible! We must be spending a fortune just to get at basic management information.

FM: I can ask the MIS department if you'd like, but it might take a month for that report.

CFO: !@#$^&*... (something unprintable)

For many managers the above scenario must sound familiar. As computing has become widespread and more powerful, the balance of data processing power has shifted away from central IS staffs to individuals in functional departments. By tying together desktop computers, inexpensive Intranets enable businesses to integrate their information systems to a greater extent than was previously possible.

Clearly, the need for integration is a key driver of the financial Intranet marketplace. Many corporations are planning to integrate their accounting systems into their enterprise networks over the next several years. Financial executives desire the ease of use and timeliness that this will afford. Information systems managers, faced with scarce resources, believe this will smooth out system development and management processes, saving time and money.

13.2 Understanding the Different Software Modules

Before we get into the specifics of how electronic commerce will play a role in financial management and accounting, it may be useful to present an overview of the different elements of this marketplace. Critical areas of finance and accounting include: transaction accounting, financial planning, financial analysis, inventory accounting, payment management, and cash management.

Transaction Accounting and Electronic Commerce

This includes general ledger (G/L) accounting, consolidation, accounts payable and accounts receivable, asset accounting, and special purpose ledger. To provide some insight into the complexity of the accounting world, it may be useful to delve into the specifics of some of these modules. Table 13.3 describes some features of the standard accounting-related software modules.

Table 13.3 Generic Modules in a Financial Information System

General Ledger	Multi-ledger, automated journal entry, allocations, consolidations, and multi-currency accounting.
Accounts Payable	Streamlines vendor, invoice, and payment processing.
Accounts Receivable (AR)	Accounting and management information system to handle business requirements of AR and credit management staff.
Asset Management	Management of financial and operational assets and physical property information.
Costing	Real-time actual and committed cost tracking, user-definable project cost analysis.
Billing and Invoicing	Streamline billing processes, customize billing requirements, create enterprise-wide billing database.

General Ledger   All financial accounting transactions are posted, summarized, processed, and reported in the general ledger. This module keeps a record of financial data to provide firms with timely information about their business. It also maintains a complete audit trail of business transactions. Often general ledger modules have modules for consolidating multiple company databases. The process of consolidating data from subsidiary company databases and for reading files in multiple data formats into the parent company database are provided as standard functionality within the general ledger. With this feature, firms can consolidate company databases with both similar and differing time periods, calendar years, and account structures. For comprehensive reporting purposes, it is often necessary to retain several years of general ledger budget history.

Accounts Payable   Accounts payable involves tracking and controlling information about money firms owe, due dates, and available discounts. Often businesses can save money by carefully tracking and taking advantage of terms and discounts, predicting cash requirements, and tracking payments to make sure they are only made once.

Accounts payable databases are necessary for managerial decision making for two reasons:

1. History retention, where companies keep several periods of transaction detail and vendor balances, for comprehensive reporting, trend analysis, and reporting.

2. Period integrity, the process where firms frequently need to enter the accounts payable transactions to the next period, before they complete closing of the current period.

Accounts payable systems are being integrated with financial EDI modules to provide more complete control of cash balances. This software module automatically calculates the corresponding due dates, discount dates, and discount amounts, helping firms track potential savings on vendor payments. Firms can also set up recurring accounts payable vouchers for rent payments, leases, or other regular payments. These payments will then be generated automatically when the recurring payment is due.

How does this work? An organization's accounts payable department must match up three supporting documents: purchase order, receiving report, and vendor invoice. Because the first two documents are internally generated, they can be obtained through the internal system. Vendors transmit their invoices through the Internet or a VAN. Thus, the organization must integrate its external system with its internal system so that it can access and match the vendor invoices to purchasing orders and receiving reports.

Accounts Receivable When customers buy from firms on credit, firms need to manage that relationship effectively, identify problems in advance, and provide detailed reporting. Firms need to generate statements for receivables on a consistent basis to make sure customers receive up-to-date information about their accounts. This also incorporates credit checking features whereby a warning is displayed when a customer exceeds the credit limit by a set amount or percentage, or when a customer has invoices with due dates exceeding a specified number of days. In this system, the supplier's accounts receivable must be matched with a customer order and shipping report. The customer order is transmitted through the external network. With proper matching of the customer order to an internally generated shipping report, the supplier's accounts receivable function can produce an invoice and transmit it back through the network to the customer. With minimal human interference, an integrated system can update both customer and supplier accounts, and record necessary journal entries in real time.

Other accounts receivable functionality includes enhanced sales commission reporting for incentive management purposes. Sales commission reporting enables firms to produce reports based on all paid invoices or all issued invoices.

Intranets and Transaction Accounting Intranets offer companies new tools that harness the power of networked computers for the transaction accounting purposes. This includes:

- **Efficient transaction entry.** Financial system designs shall eliminate unnecessary duplication of transaction entry. Wherever appropriate, data needed by the systems to support financial functions shall be entered only once, and other parts of the system shall be updated through electronic means consistent with the timing requirements of normal business/transaction cycles.

- **Common transaction processing.** Common processes shall be used for processing similar kinds of transactions throughout the system to enable these transactions to be reported in a consistent manner.

- **Consistent internal controls.** Internal controls over data entry, transaction processing, and reporting shall be applied consistently throughout the system to ensure the validity of information and protection of financial resources.

- **Audit trails.** A complete, reliable audit trail of all transactions transmitted through a network is vital to accountants and auditors. This trail provides a history of record transmission, allowing the accountant to uncover any problem and, possibly, the responsible party.

Intranet technology can help integrate the various accounting modules with each other to save time and prevent errors that are caused when repetitive data entry is required. For example, when an accounts payable transaction is generated, the vendor balance that is affected by that transaction is automatically updated, and a corresponding entry for the same amount is created in the general ledger.

Financial Analysis and Management Accounting

While managing the transaction aspects of financial flows is important, there exists another facet: namely, using financial information for control purposes. This facet of financial management that is essential to support the operations and strategy of the company is called *management accounting*. Management accounting typically includes business planning and control, decision making, budgeting, and controlling, including overhead cost management, activity-based costing, product cost controlling, and sales and profit analysis.

Gathering data for management accounting is quite challenging as few companies maintain a single, integrated set of records for all of their divisions and the departments within them (marketing, human resources, manufacturing). In practice, to consolidate enterprise-wide data, companies "kludge" together data from many sources, including databases and spreadsheets. Bringing data together for periodic accounting, reporting, and budgeting has been difficult. The process adds to the time and cost required to perform consolidations at the end of a period, as well as to create and track budgets and forecasts. At the functional level, consolidation can provide the finance organization independence from the central IS organization with a set of applications that are powerful but easy to use. This includes support for management (decision-control) accounting and cost accounting.

Once the data is gathered, financial analysis tools enable authorized people in the organization to find the data they need, drill down as necessary, and see the results in seconds—without waiting for MIS or even corporate accounting's involvement. This information is meant not only for executives, but also for a broader set of people who want to make better decisions on a daily basis.

Inventory Accounting

Managing inventory can be a monumental task. Detailed management and operational reporting are required to track and control the items being assembled, stocked, and sold. Inventory accounting spans a variety of functions.

Inventory kitting   This function allows firms to combine inventory items into kits. Defining kits can save order processing and warehouse time by establishing a single kit for ordering instead of a long list of individual items. More sophisticated inventory kitting methods include subassembly or multilevel kitting, which allows a kit to be used as a subassembly component within another kit. Other variations include nonstandard component entry, which involves the ability to enter items that are not identified as standard components of the kit being assembled. This feature is valuable in operations where component substitution is common.

Pricing support and valuation methods   This feature allows price levels to be stated in terms of dollar amount or percentage—and established by customer item, unit of measure, and quantity break—for an unlimited number of pricing options per item. A variety of standard inventory valuation methods are often essential for financial reporting and stock-market valuation needs of a company's particular operational process. Inventory valuation methods include standard cost, last in first out (LIFO), first in first out (FIFO), average, and user-specific methods.

Inventory reporting   This includes quantity reporting, which helps firms monitor inventory levels by providing information for quantities on hand, quantities on back order, and quantities on sales order. Other reporting includes bill of material explosion, which assembles items into kits and calculates and specifies the kit component items that need to be reordered to achieve planned production.

Inventory accounting provides the necessary detail needed to make decisions about ordering, so firms can organize their production and track cost of goods sold. Intranets can help inventory accounting managers to obtain information for planning and control of finished goods, work-in-process, and raw material inventory; they also can provide summary and detail analysis on demand for both accounting and production control purposes.

Payment Management

Today's competitive world demands operational efficiency with strong management controls. Tight integration of purchasing, payables, and receivables is necessary to eliminate paperwork and redundant data entry, as all related data is automatically routed along the business process. The goal is to use automatic purchase order creation, automatic tax withholding, and automated invoice and payment processing to improve operational efficiency.

In this process, the company is linked with the suppliers and distributors so that payments can be sent and received electronically. This allows customer orders to be billed after shipment, with invoices printed and inventory, sales, and accounting information maintained automatically. The process increases the speed at which companies can compute invoices, reducing clerical errors and lowering transaction fees and costs while increasing the number of invoices processed (productivity).

Business-to-business payments are made using financial EDI. Financial EDI comprises the electronic transmission of payments and remittance information between a payer and payee, and their respective banks. Financial EDI allows businesses to replace the labor-intensive activities—issuing, mailing, and collecting checks with automated initiation, transmission, and processing of payment instructions. It eliminates the delays in processing checks and improves the payment flows between corporate bank accounts because the payee's bank can credit its account on the scheduled payment date and the payer's bank can debit its account on the same day.

How Financial Payments Are Made   Corporations use a variety of approaches when implementing financial EDI. The most fundamental decision a business must make is whether payment instructions and remittance data should flow together through the banking system or whether payment instructions should flow through the banking system while remittance data are transmitted over a direct data communications link with a trading partner or over a VAN. VANs facilitate the exchange of electronic data by accepting data in a variety of formats and by converting the incoming data to a format usable by the receiver of the information. VANs also manage transmission schedules and hold data until receivers are ready to accept them. The choices businesses make are based on differences in transmission costs, the extent to which the two trading partners are able to exchange business documents electronically, and the types of electronic payment services offered by their banks.

Payment and Remittance Information Flowing Together   In Fig. 13.1, the purchasing company (Company X), which is the payer, transmits remittance

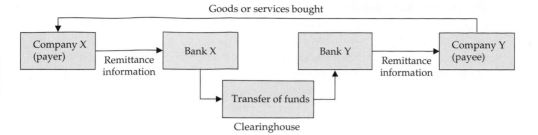

Figure 13.1 Payment and Remittance Information Flowing Together

data to instruct its bank (Bank X) to pay its supplier. Bank X creates a credit transfer instruction, indicating the specified payment date, and attaches the appropriate electronic remittance data. Bank X transmits the payment instruction with the remittance data to an automated clearinghouse (ACH) operator. After receiving the payment instructions and remittance information, the ACH operator edits the payment instructions, extracts accounting data from them, and transmits the payment instructions and remittance data to the seller's bank (Bank Y). Bank Y then transmits a payment advice and the remittance data to the selling company (Company Y), which is the payee.

When ACH credit transfers are processed by the Federal Reserve, on the scheduled payment date the reserve banks maintaining the accounts of banks X and Y debit and credit the reserve or clearing accounts of banks X and Y, respectively, for the total value of transfers sent or received. If a private sector ACH operator processed the ACH transfers, the value of all ACH transfers processed for the banks using that operator would be netted, and each participant would settle its net position through its account maintained on the books of a Federal Reserve bank.

Payment and Remittance Information Flowing Separately As shown in Fig. 13.2, the payer transmits payment instructions to its bank (Bank X) and remittance information to the payee through a VAN. The payment instructions are processed through the banking system and settled as described for funds flowing together, with the exception that remittance data are not attached.

The following example of General Motors (GM) illustrates how financial EDI payments are made using ACH credit and debit transfers. GM began using ACH debit transfers to collect payments from its dealers through their bank accounts in 1982. GM sends ACH formatted payment instructions, with information identifying the vehicles for which payment is being requested, to one of its banks. The ACH debit transfers are processed in the same way that ACH credit transfers are, except that on the settlement day

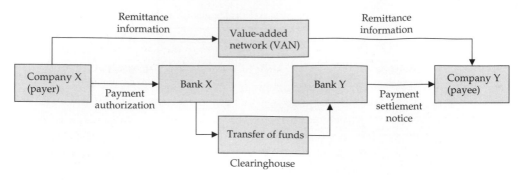

Figure 13.2   Payment and Remittance Information Flowing Separately

GM's banks credit GM's accounts and the dealers' banks debit the dealers' accounts. In 1993, using this method, GM collected 600,000 payments from its dealers, with a value of $12 billion. GM also uses ACH credit transfers to make payments to suppliers. Besides transmitting remittance information to suppliers through the banking system or a VAN, GM will mail it directly to a supplier if the supplier's bank cannot receive EDI data. In 1993, GM made 700,000 ACH credit payments valued at $38 billion to suppliers [KWY94].

To facilitate the use of financial EDI, some banks provide VAN-like services with payment services to their corporate customers. Some of these banks have developed their own networks for communicating data to their corporate customers, and some also contract with VANs to transmit remittance information to their corporate customers' trading partners.

Treasury and Cash Management

What is treasury management? The global marketplace demands support for multiple currencies, international tax methods, and other global business practices. Companies must work with financial institutions to boost their ability to deal on a global basis. The goal is to enable global companies to manage their money in various foreign exchange accounts. This includes multinational, multicurrency bank reconciliation, and cash management.

What is cash management? Large companies need prompt access to information relating to their checking accounts in order to make timely payments and reduce their exposure to check fraud. Cash management is especially crucial in retail operations where checks are used extensively. Check listings and bank reconciliation can be major problems, and relatively simple backroom applications can help.

In general, cash management requires rapid transfers of information between the bank and its customers. To accommodate customers, banks currently maintain a back-office operational staff, which manually delivers this information via phone service and faxes. This process can be costly and inefficient. To make the process more efficient, banks are looking toward Internet solutions. For instance, Banc One is using the Internet to deliver secure access to customer account information. Using Open Market's OM-Axcess software, Banc One's application gives large cash management customers the ability to access their accounts and view images of checks online, enabling them to make pay/no pay decisions instantly. Customers can review exception items online, make timely decisions to reconcile discrepancies, and return unauthorized checks from any location using the Web [OM96].

13.3 Human Resources Management Systems

It is not often realized that human resource costs represent the largest single expense an organization incurs. The human resources (HR) function within organizations has gone far beyond the roles of "personnel" management of yesterday. Today's HR departments face increasingly complex issues: fluctuating legislation; rampant changes in benefit policies and procedures; mergers, acquisitions, and downsizings; pressures to increase productivity while controlling costs; demands from a culturally diverse workforce; and the need to recruit, train, and maintain employees.

An important function of the HR department is to keep employees well informed of important company issues in addition to all the financial details pertaining to their personal health and well-being. To maintain a competitive edge, management of the workforce must be as dynamic as the world in which firms compete—a world with continuous legislative, operational, and environmental changes. To thrive in this environment, organizations need a system that helps manage change powerfully, flexibly, and with optimum accountability. In addition, the system must adapt to an organization's policies and procedures, integrate information within a department and across department lines, and allow employees at all levels to update and manage information easily.

Recently, there has been a dramatic uptick in HR systems spending. Why? One reason is HR is assuming an expanded role in the corporation. Initially, HR and payroll departments concentrated solely on paying workers, providing benefits, and tracking government regulations. Little time or effort was invested in other personnel issues, such as compensation planning, career monitoring, and job-applicant tracking. Moreover, organizations were managing their employees with outmoded, and sometimes failing mainframe and minicomputer personnel and payroll systems. Until recently, HR was the most underfunded department in the organization. Organizations did not see the benefits of investing in HR systems.

That perspective is changing, however. HR departments are finding that the Web is an effective vehicle to deliver more strategic programs and services, and to enable line managers and employees to directly access information and initiate self-service transactions. The Intranet and Web also provide a common, enterprise-wide platform to deliver solutions to support a wide range of HR functions, including recruiting and applicant tracking, organizational training and development, skills planning and performance evaluation, employee self-help, compensation and benefits administration, and HR call support. The Web also allows organizations to leverage investments in their existing HR client/server systems—such as PeopleSoft, SAP, and IBM's HR Access—as well as to implement Internet/Intranet solutions.

HRMS Functions

Human resource management systems (HRMS) essentially track all aspects of employee administration. The software modules typically include:

- Human resources—personnel, recruiting, salary administration, training/development, health, and safety.
- Payroll—time reporting, payroll calculation, and tax computation.
- Benefits administration—the management of defined benefit, defined contribution, and 401K pension programs, flexible spending account administration, and automated open enrollment.
- Health care benefits management—medical, dental, and vision insurance.

In the next section, we elaborate on the benefits administration and health care benefits management modules that we feel are in the early stages of implementation and have enormous potential for growth.

Benefits Administration   Managing benefits in today's business environment can be quite a challenge. Benefits administration typically includes a variety of benefit offerings—from cafeteria-style benefits and flexible credits to programs with limited options and no credits—and everything from initial identification of eligible employees, to flexible credit calculations, to voice response, so employees can update their own choices.

How does this work? With data drawn from personnel and payroll records, the benefits package supplies information about plan providers and employee enrollments for a wide choice of benefit plans: health, life,

AD/D, short- and long-term disability, savings, leaves, flexible spending account (FSA), retirement, pension, and vacation buy and sell. In addition to a number of online summaries employees can examine, employees need features for tracking and automatically updating leave balances—for vacation, sick time, and maternity leave. They also need to find information and calculation on before- and after-tax contribution regulations.

A major part of benefits administration is informing employees about impending changes. Many HR organizations have migrated existing employee policy or benefits manuals to the Intranet, allowing employees access to all of the company HR policies. As many companies have begun to tie Intranets into existing legacy databases, employees can conduct database lookups on their own, right from their Web browser. Employees can also look up information (such as number of vacation days outstanding, balance in 401K program) without HR intervention.

Using a browser, an employee can enter his name and company ID into a Web-based form. The Intranet server then conducts a database lookup and reports back, via HTML. Virtually all of this information resides in legacy databases within the organization, and using the Web, information can be added, updated, removed, queried, and calculated. The Intranet server simply takes the HR personnel out of the retrieval loop, reducing costs and the response time for the employee. At the same time, user IDs and passwords ensure that only appropriate personnel have access to individual resources—the employee and his or her management. These solutions meet the needs of a dynamic workforce, as they can be accessed through a variety of options including any Web browser, Lotus Notes client, or kiosk. This allows HR departments to free their staffs from answering routine questions and basic processing tasks. However, making sure all employees comply with scores of internal and external benefit plan policies can be a demanding task.

Health Care Benefits Management   As health care providers consolidate into large national and regional organizations, managing patient information at reduced cost becomes a crucial priority for organizations. To respond to these pressures, organizations are seeking to streamline patient information processes, from admissions to discharge, billing, and collections as well as medical record management. The reengineering initiative identified ways to deliver timely information on patients quickly throughout each facility. The Web is being used to develop systems that automate admissions, billing, and collections procedures and manage medical records.

The explosive growth in health care expenditures is driving two major trends, which in turn, are pressuring companies and health care providers into changing their use of information technology. Managed care, which shifts the risk for the cost of care onto the provider and away from the payor (usually an employer), is becoming an increasingly prevalent alternative to traditional fee-for-service reimbursement, radically changing the economics of health care. This, combined with increased competition, is causing an acceleration toward integrated delivery systems. Faced with this rapidly evolving environment, companies are being forced to reengineer their systems to better serve the needs of their community of patients.

The patient care process itself and the information needs of providers are increasingly recognized as functions that must be better managed. This includes development of an infrastructure capable of unifying both clinical and benefits information in order to improve the information flow as patients transition from one care area to another. It also requires that information regarding the quality and cost of care be accessible to management for objective evaluation and analysis to enable improvements in the organization's processes. Table 13.4 summarizes the key issues in health care benefits management.

Table 13.4 System Issues in Health Care Benefits Management

Business Problem	Need to improve efficiency of the process of providing and monitoring health care benefits.
	Need to help employees maximize benefits programs.
	Need to review cases more rapidly.
Solution	Establish a new electronic workflow for tracking patient services and creating a database of medical records.
	Establish an integrated infrastructure for quick access to:
	Up-to-date history on each patient and provider
	A more efficient way of handling patient information
	Quick response to inquiries.
Requirements	Automated workflow/claims management to reduce paperwork.
	Document imaging, routing, and retrieval.
Benefits	Increased customer satisfaction, which translates to fewer call-backs.
	Increased customer satisfaction from reduced workflow problems.

13.4 Size/Structure of Financials Software Market

Companies are looking for system flexibility to meet changing business requirements—corporate restructurings, new government reporting requirements, and new product lines—and the ability to link financial data throughout the enterprise. To meet the management needs of large corporations, electronic commerce solutions are being used to develop an integrated enterprise suite that enables the redesign of financial and accounting processes.

Currently, the financials software market consists of a large installed base of legacy systems. Just as companies are replacing their old manufacturing systems with new client/server-based products, they will also begin replacing their aging financial processes. Clearly, the financial software market (estimated at $3 billion) presents a substantial opportunity. However, the market for client/server-based financial management (or financials) is in its infancy and represents a tiny component of the total market. To take advantage of this market opportunity, some vendors are retrofitting existing legacy systems with graphical front-ends and back-ends, while others are writing completely new products.

Given the push to replace outdated legacy systems, it is expected that the Web portion could capture a significant part of the market. However, unlike the prior software generation, which focused disproportionately on the need to support the company's basic financial accounting requirements, the next generation of software will have to address software support for a variety of financial management activities taking place throughout the company: leasing, asset management, budget preparation, portfolio management, cash flow and revenue projections, purchasing, and other operational, analytical, and performance measurements.

Under these circumstances it is becoming increasingly unlikely that a single vendor can provide an all-encompassing solution. Fortunately, users of automation services are gravitating toward popular platforms and processing environments that facilitate the integration of software products provided by different software developers. At the same time, software developers are encouraged to produce state-of-the-art products for these popular processing environments following industry-wide programming and interoperability standards. As the prospects for technical integration among diverse product offerings improves, we are witnessing an increasing number of business combinations between product vendors.

Product Strategy

The predominant product design philosophy stresses the enterprise, rather than any functional unit. The art of linking various software products together so they can share processing resources, access and update common databases, and serve users possessing varying degrees of technical sophistication and proficiency is broadly referred to as *systems integration*. The user interface aspects of the systems integration process are often referred to as workflow redesign or reengineering activities. Increasingly, enterprise applications must be "workflow enabled"; that is, they must be able to support process redesign or simply process automation. The design philosophy also facilitates decision support. Effective dating, for example, allows corporate planners to easily analyze the impact of multiple options for a reorganization.

An important product strategy issue is system performance. Some software applications builders stress the numerical performance of their system (number of transactions handled in a unit of time). Others emphasize the accessibility of data, the flexibility of the system, and its ease of use. System performance measures can be a deciding factor for organizations that process many small transactions (such as retailers). For others it is much less important relative to the need to use applications more effectively in business decisions.

Almost all applications vendors have been struggling with making their systems easier to install and maintain. Demand for the most successful ones has challenged the vendors' ability to support them. To deal with this, vendors are developing auto-installation routines and software-assisted upgrades to lighten the burden on their consulting and support staff and lessen the potential for customer dissatisfaction. Migration from one version to the next is also being made easier.

Financial Data Warehouses

More recently, relational database vendors have also sold their databases as tools for building data warehouses. A data warehouse is defined as a store of tactical information that is used to answer "who?" and "what?" questions about past events. A typical query submitted to a data warehouse is: "What was the total revenue for the western region in the first quarter of 1996?" Companies are beginning to develop functional data warehouses—that is, build a data mart, or departmental warehouse—around a specific business need (such as consolidating worldwide financial data). Functional data warehouses are easier to implement than larger, full-blown warehouses because they do not require multiple departments within a firm to cooperate on data definitions and data ownership.

The most popular applications for building these financial data warehouses are from Hyperion, SAP, Oracle, and PeopleSoft. In general, these software products perform large-scale, network-based financial consolidation and reporting. The software collects data from multiple general ledger and planning systems and creates an enterprise-wide information base (see Fig. 13.3).

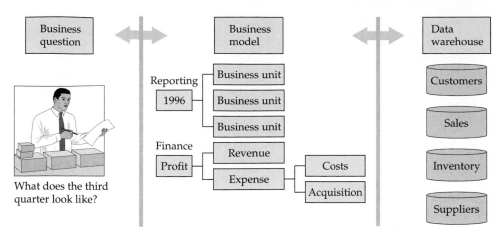

Figure 13.3 A Functional Model of a Data Warehouse [SYBS96]

Online Analytical Processing (OLAP) While a data warehouse stores and manages data, it would be useless without analytic tools, called OLAP (online analytical processing) that transform data warehouse information into strategic information. For instance, users of financial data warehouse applications want better access and analysis of the data contained in the database archives. OLAP tools range from basic data navigation and browsing (often known as "slice and dice") to multidimensional analysis of corporate data—complex "what-if" calculations, time series trend analysis, and modeling.

Who uses OLAP and why? OLAP applications span a variety of organizational functions. Finance departments use OLAP for applications such as budgeting, activity-based costing (allocations), financial performance analysis, and financial modeling. Sales analysis and forecasting are two of the OLAP applications found in sales departments. Among other applications, marketing departments use OLAP for market research analysis, sales forecasting, promotions analysis, customer analysis, and market/customer segmentation. Typical manufacturing OLAP applications include production planning and defect analysis.

What do managers do with OLAP tools? OLAP tools also enable end users to perform *ad hoc* (or just-in-time) analysis of data in multiple dimensions, thereby giving them the insight and understanding they need for better decision making. OLAP lets managers probe and access corporate data via a "slice, dice, and rotate" method that augments or replaces the more traditional relational query. This slice-and-dice method gives the user consistently fast access to a wide variety of views of data organized by criteria that match the real dimensions of the modern enterprise.

What is the difference between OLAP and a data warehouse? In contrast to a data warehouse, which is usually based on relational technology, OLAP uses a multidimensional view of aggregate data to provide quick access to strategic information for further analysis. While OLAP systems have the ability to answer "who?" and "what?" questions, it is their ability to answer "what if?" and "why?" that makes them useful for making decisions about future actions. For example, a typical OLAP query can be: "What would be the effect on pricing if raw material prices went up by $10.00 and transportation costs went down by $.05/mile?"

The key feature of OLAP systems is the ability to transform data into so-called multidimensional form. Multidimensional views are inherently representative of an actual business model. Rarely is a business model limited to fewer than three dimensions. Managers typically look at financial data by scenario (for example, actual versus budget), organization, line items, and time; and at sales data by product, geography, channel, and time. A multidimensional view of data provides more than the ability to "slice and dice"; it provides the foundation for analytical processing through flexible access to information. Database design should not prejudice which operations can be performed on a dimension or how rapidly those operations are performed. Managers must be able to analyze data across any dimension, at any level of aggregation, with equal functionality and ease. OLAP software should support these views of data in a natural and responsive fashion, insulating users of the information from complex query syntax. After all, managers should not have to understand complex table layouts, elaborate table joins, and summary tables.

How Are Firms Using the Web for OLAP?

Companies are using browsers as the front-end tool for performing query, analysis, and reporting against the data warehouse. For instance, the data warehouse enables financial analysts across different divisions to view consistent, accurate information for the first time. Using the Web, analysts can create reports and analyze information stored in the "common financial database," a central warehouse for the organization's accounting, sales, and marketing information. Table 13.5 summarizes the key reasons for using the Web for analytic processing.

Prior to the Web solution, managers based their financial analysis on data stored in mainframe-based systems specific to various divisions. This created problems because in many large firms, each division represents sales and revenues differently, making it difficult for executives of the organization to get an accurate view of the company's performance.

Table 13.5 Summarizing the Reasons for Financial Intranet Solutions

Business Problem	Enable global access to a large information warehouse.
	Incur minimal cost deploying and maintaining the solution.
Solution	Build and deploy a Web front-end to the data warehouse.
Requirements	Rapid development.
	Minimal code distribution to end users.
	Low development and maintenance cost.

With the Web browsers, managers have a powerful and easy-to-use front-end tool for delivering business analysis derived from a common data warehouse. They can choose from several predefined reports and queries created by an information technology (IT) group, or they can conduct their own *ad hoc* query, reporting, and analysis. The use of the Web page significantly extends the firm's ability to support large numbers of users. Also, putting documentation on the Web will help firms to greatly reduce costs associated with printing manuals and updates.

With the advent of browsers—which are easy to learn and to use—the analysis of data is simplified. When combined with databases restructured into multidimensional form, user interfaces for OLAP allow rapid summarizing of transactional data along a particular dimension, drilling down to more detail within a region, product, time period, or other dimension, slicing and dicing data, and pivoting tables about their axes. All this is accomplished through intuitive screens, featuring point-and-click and drag-and-drop paradigms, which are virtually foolproof and do not require users to know obscure command codes, underlying database structures, or data access languages. The advent of these interfaces greatly reduces the amount of training needed.

One of the more promising directions for the future is real-time OLAP. Since multidimensional transformation is a time-consuming process normally done overnight, the data are static and often twelve or more hours old. However, the rapid increases in the speed of computing, along with the advent of Intranet middleware, will make possible real-time OLAP. With this facility, decision makers will not only have the latest information, but will also have the analytical flexibility that OLAP offers.

Desirable Software Requirements

The critical need for companies with respect to utilizing the Web for decision support is the delivery of information and reports to a broad population of users (see Fig. 13.4). In order for executives to be truly informed, they require: (1) consistency of data; (2) completeness of data records; (3) the ability to meaningfully link and cross-reference data (also applying time-related criteria); (4) means for end users to navigate the data records; and (5) presentation that does justice to certain events or phenomena (highlighting of anomalies and depiction of trends).

Desirable features in a Web-based decision support solution include:

- **HTML queries.** Users can save queries as hypertext markup language files, so that analysts will be able to create online catalogs of reports that are easily accessible via standard Web browsers.

- **Automatic Web posting.** Analysts can use "agents" to automatically schedule and post HTML reports to the Web. For example, a user can schedule a report to run every Monday morning, and post it to the company's Web server.

- **Embedded hyperlinks.** Web software will embed hyperlinks that connect an HTML report to its associated source document. When users want to perform further analysis of the data in a given report, they can automatically download the report and its associated data to their PC for analysis, remaining connected to, or even disconnected from, the Web.

- **Access security.** The Web provides authorization capability to ensure proper security and access to underlying reports. Before downloading a report to a user, a security check is performed with user information. This facilitates enterprise deployment and administration across the Web.

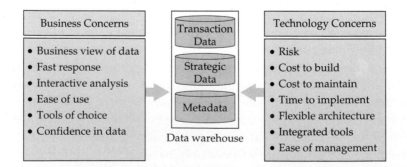

Figure 13.4   Key Requirements in Developing Data Warehouses

- **Easy access.** Web server and browser technologies offer platform independence and "thin client" front ends. Users can access Internet access providers from practically anywhere in the world for the cost of a local telephone call.

- **Easy manipulation.** The Web enables users to work with applications familiar to them (such as spreadsheets and corporate forms) to send, receive, manipulate, and analyze data. Because it is network-based, it simplifies the process of moving information around the enterprise. Modern software packages, such as Hyperion (a finance-oriented OLAP program), enable users to easily restructure departments, divisions, and whole organizations by selecting a particular unit on the screen, dragging it to another entity, and dropping it into place.

- **Data centralization.** Web-based decision support employs a central database architecture to ensure that data is consistent and up-to-date across the enterprise. The centralization of data enables security and control. For example, division managers may access and update only their own subordinates' records in a corporate-wide employee database, or enter their monthly profit/loss statement into a consolidated general ledger. However, centralization is a problem when users have different requirements for data entry, reporting, and presentation. Another business requirement that creates problems when everything is centralized is change management. Changing tax laws and other regulations force developers to incorporate frequent enhancements. Doing this in a centralized environment is both tough and costly.

In the last couple of years, there has been an explosion in product offerings with respect to Internet-oriented front-ends to OLAP systems and databases. The three leading relational database vendors—Informix, Oracle, and Sybase—interface with the Web via the Common Gateway Interface, which is the standard for linking Web browsers to executable programs on a Web server. It is purely a matter of time before every database and OLAP vendor offers Web access.

13.5 Summary

This chapter discussed the role of Intranets in supporting management needs to acquire comprehensive and timely business information. A company's accumulated data constitute a valuable resource, and in most companies, those in charge are very aware of this fact. Yet it is equally clear that the approach of simply collecting data has serious shortcomings. It neither succeeds in presenting data to corporate decision makers in a form they can understand and use, nor permits easy access to information.

Incompatible accounting and information systems are causing management tremendous problems. In the past, companies have attempted to support financial information systems by using mainframes that have been rigid in structure, expensive to maintain, and difficult to update when business requirements change. At the other end of the spectrum, firms generate business reports by assembling them manually by using spreadsheets and data from general ledgers and other operating systems. This approach would be incapable of handling large volumes of data primarily because it would require extensive data rekeying and manual consolidation. In addition, spreadsheets have limited capabilities for information sharing and lack the necessary controls to ensure corporate consistency.

As business requirements have changed, there has been an increasing push toward the ability to analyze large amounts of data in real-time. This enables management to look at different scenarios and make decisions in hours rather than in weeks. The ability to highlight unusual variances and dig deeply into the underlying causes enables managers and auditors to find the cause of aberrations while there may still be time to correct them. Inevitably, broad access to data and to the analytic tools that ease the analysis of the data will change the face of decision making. The speed and ease with which analysis can be completed and the inclusion of up-to-the-minute accurate data are powerful competitive weapons.

In conclusion, Intranet technology can aid in the collection, aggregation, and consolidation of business information from fragmented computer systems and transactional databases in a number of ways, and in many cases will replace existing systems with more efficient alternatives. However you decide to go forward, it is critical not to "miss the boat" since if the competition gets far enough ahead, it will be difficult, if not impossible, to catch up. It is clear that real-time access to data and analytical tools is coming fast, and now is the time to start the journey.

Epilogue

The primary thesis in this book has focused on the convergence of communications, computers, and business. This liaison has created a very high demand for both new types of business models and software applications linking businesses and consumers.

During the next few years, there will be two electronic commerce roads—one for consumers and one for corporations. Consumers will be driven by the desire to obtain information, to communicate with others, and, eventually, to buy and sell products or services. Consumer will experiment with innovations as rapidly as they can be offered. However, customer-driven interactivity will be the major factor in shaping demand, as consumers quickly tire of "static" content.

Corporations, on the other hand, are driven by the need to become more efficient and "do more with less." There has been a growing emphasis on developing electronic applications that streamline current business practices, in addition to developing applications that are focused on new business-to-business or business-to-consumer applications. Much of the infrastructure is in place or is being put into place. Over the next couple of years, we expect to see Intranet applications roll out in three phases—Information Sharing/Electronic Publishing, Collaborative Applications/Workgroup Computing, and Supply-Chain Management applications. These will be influenced by standards, bandwidth availability, and a trial-and-error application development process on the part of corporations.

It is conceivable that in the year 2005, many of us will look back at the last decade of this century as an era of profound change—perhaps even a historic turning point. Of course, the big question remains as to who the winners will be. We have no definitive answer to this question, as we think it is still too early to declare victory. Besides, we also believe that the anticipated "paradigm shift" will probably be more evolutionary than revolutionary, particularly for applications where consumer behavior needs to change.

References

[AB96] Brian Tracey, "Technology/Operations," *The American Banker*, March 25, 1996, p. 18.

[AJL94] Andrew Johnson-Laird, "Smoking Guns and Spinning Disks," *The Computer Lawyer*, August 1994, p. 1.

[AS95] Andrew Serwer, "The Competition Heats Up In Online Banking," *Fortune*, June 26, 1995.

[ATT96] AT&T Intranet Use, http://home.netscape.com/

[BG96] "Agility May Be Key to Firms' Keeping Balance; Manufacturing: Management," *Boston Globe*, March 7, 1996.

[BW96] Amy Cortese, "Here Comes The Intranet," *Business Week*, February 26, 1996.

[CACM94] Lance J. Hoffman, Faraz A. Ali, Steven L. Heckler, and Ann Huybrechts, "Cryptography Policy," *Communications of the ACM*, September 1994, p. 109.

[CB96] Judith Messina, "Pathfinder's Web: Time's On-Line Service Loses Money," *Crain's New York Business*, March 18, 1996.

[CC95] *Computing Canada*, January 4, 1996, p. 36.

[COPY95] Copyright Act of 1976, As Amended (1994) (including the Semiconductor Chip Protection Act of 1984 and the Audio Home Recording Act of 1992). (http://www.law.cornell.edu/usc/17/overview.html)

[CPA96] *The CPA Letter*, AICPA, January/February 1996.

[DFN88] D. Chaum, A. Fiat, and N. Naor, "Untraceable Electronic Cash," *Proceedings of Crypto '88*, 1988.

[DM92] William H. Davidow, and Michael S. Malone, *The Virtual Corporation* (New York: HarperCollins, 1992).

[DT95] Terri Dial, "Differentiate Strategies for Future Success," *Bank Management*, September/October 1995, pp. 20–22.

[EDR95] Neil G. Carn, Joseph S. Rabianski, and James D. Vernor, "Structural Trends Impacting Retail Businesses," *Economic Development Review*, Spring 1995.

[EL95] Eugene A. Ludwig, Comptroller of the Currency. Testimony before the Subcommittee on Financial Institutions of the Committee on Banking and Financial Services of the U.S. House of Representatives, October 1995.

[FD95] First Data Corporation, Annual Report to Shareholders, 1995.

[FT95] David Schmittlein, "Mastering Management," *Financial Times*, December 15, 1995.

[FT96] Jean-Pierre Jeannet, "Mastering Management," *Financial Times*, April 19, 1996.

[HBR90] Peter F. Drucker, "The Emerging Theory of Manufacturing," *Harvard Business Review*, May/June 1990, p. 94.

[HP96] Hewlett Packard Financial District Home Page. http://www.hp.com:80/fsi/index.html

[IJ96] Brill's Intranet Journal. http://www.brill.com/intranet/ijnews.html

[IMD95] Wayne Friedman and Jane Weaver, "BellSouth Calling 'Clickstreams,'" *Inside Media*, March 15, 1995.

[IW96] *Information Week*, July 4, 1996.

[IWA94] "Hackers' Break-in at General Electric Raises Questions about the Net's Security," *InformationWeek*, December 12, 1994.

[IWA95] Tom Groenfeldt, "Firewalls," *InformationWeek*, January 30, 1995.

[IWK96] Lisa Harrington, "Untapped Savings Abound," *Industry Week*, July 15, 1996, p. 53.

[JFAQ96] Java Frequently Asked Questions, http://java.sun.com/

[JM96] James S. Mahan, Chairman and Chief Executive Officer, Testimony, U.S. House of Representatives Subcommittee on Domestic and International Monetary Policy of the Committee on Banking and Financial Services, March 7, 1996.

[JPM95] Glass-Steagall Sections. Available at http://www.jpmorgan.com/

[KALA96] Ravi Kalakota and Andrew Whinston, *Frontiers of Electronic Commerce* (Reading, MA: Addison Wesley, 1996).

[KF96] Ravi Kalakota and Frances Frei, "Managing Online Financial Supply Chains," Working Paper 1996.

[KURT95] Kurt F. Viermetz, "The Strategy of an Investment Bank," Speech of Vice Chairman delivered to the Association of French Bankers. Available at http://www.jpmorgan.com/CorpInfo/Perspectives/IssuesPersp.html

[KWY94] Scott Knudson, Jack K. Walton, II, and Florence M. Young, "Business-to-Business Payments and the Role of Financial Electronic Data Interchange," *Federal Reserve Bulletin*, April 1994, p. 269.

[LOT96] Groupware White Paper, Lotus Corporation, http://www.lotus.com/info/grpware.htm

[MCN95] Edward Bennett, President of Prodigy Services, Multichannel News, July 24, 1995.

[MN93] Gennady Medvinsky and B. Clifford Neuman, "NetCash: A Design for Practical Electronic Currency on the Internet," Proceedings of the First ACM Conference on Computer and Communications Security, November, 1993. Anonymous FTP: /pub/papers/security/netcash-cccs93.ps.Z

[MW96] Cathy Taylor, "P&G Talks Tough On Web," *MediaWeek*, April 22, 1996, p. 6.

[NS94] *New Scientist*, December 17, 1994.

[NY96] Peter H. Lewis, "Free Long Distance Phone Calls!" (Computer Extra), *New York Times*, August 5, 1996.

[OCR96] Stephen Lynch, "Disney's Web Gamble," *The Orange County Register*, March 24, 1996.

[OGIL96] Monday David Ogilvy, "Ogilvy on Advertising," *Financial Times*, April 29, 1996.

[OM96] BANC ONE To Use Open Market Software for Corporate Cash Management Services over the Internet, http://www.openmarket.com/releases/bancone.htm.

[PCW96] Sean Silverthorne, "Micropayments for Applet and Game Usage," *PC Week*, March 18, 1996.

[PSFT96] PeopleSoft Manufacturing, "Reinventing Manufacturing," White Paper, May 1996.

[QRS95] Quick Response Systems, Annual Report to Shareholders, 1995.

[QVC94] Barry Diller, CEO, QVC, *Wall Street Week*, April 1994.

[RFC1510] J. Kohl and C. Neuman, "The Kerberos Network Authentication Service (V5)," *ISI* September 1993.

[SCHN96] Bruce Schneier, *Applied Cryptography*, 2nd ed. (New York: John Wiley & Sons, 1996).

[SET96] Secure Electronic Transactions (source: http://www.visa.com)

[SK95] Testimony by Sally Katzen Administrator Office of Management and Budget House Banking Domestic and International Monetary Policy, *Future of Money*, October 11, 1995.

[SYBS96] Sybase Corporation, "Customer Asset Management," White Paper, 1996.

[WALL96] *Wall Street Journal*, July 26 1996, p. A7.

[YG87] "Yankee Group Comments." *The American Banker*, February 10, 1987.

Index